PAUL CARDINAL CULLEN:

PORTRAIT OF A PRACTICAL NATIONALIST

Paul Cardinal CULLEN

PORTRAIT OF A PRACTICAL NATIONALIST

*Paul Cullen and his Relationship with the Independent Irish Party
of the 1850s and the Fenian Movement in Ireland of the 1860s*

Ciarán O'Carroll

VERITAS

First published 2008 by
Veritas Publications
7/8 Lower Abbey Street
Dublin 1
Ireland
Email publications@veritas.ie
Website www.veritas.ie

ISBN   978 1 84730 131 4 (Hardback)
         978 1 84730 162 8 (Paperback)

Designed by Lir Mac Cárthaigh
Cover photograph by John McElroy, taken from portrait hanging in Holy Cross
College, Clonliffe, Dublin.

Selection of images by kind permission of the Multitext Project in Irish History,
University College Cork, www.multitext.ucc.ie. Image of Archbishop John
MacHale courtesy of Liam and Nuala Doyle. Image of Fr Patrick Lavelle courtesy
of Gerard Moran. Image of Pope Pius IX courtesy of Mary Evans Picture
Library. Photographs of letter and Paul Cardinal Cullen crest © John McElroy.

Printed in the Republic of Ireland by Betaprint Ltd, Dublin.

To Mam and Dad, with deepest gratitude

APPRECIATION

I WISH TO EXPRESS my sincere and genuine appreciation to all those who afforded me assistance and encouragement in the compilation and writing of this book.

In particular, I thank Archbishop Diarmuid Martin for his generous support, Desmond Cardinal Connell, who contributed the foreword, and my father Tadhg O'Carroll, for his insightful counsel.

I thank Fr Giacomo Martina SJ and the staff of the Gregorian University, Rectors of the Irish and Portuguese Colleges, Rome, the students and staff of both colleges, as well as those of Holy Cross College, Clonliffe, St Patrick's College, Maynooth, the Milltown Institute, the Priory Institute and the Keough Notre Dame Centre, Dublin.

I also wish to express appreciation to all those working in the various archives and libraries that were consulted in connection with this work – most notably David Sheehy, Vera Orshel and Noelle Dowling.

The guidance of Professor Vincent McBrierty, Professor Kevin Whelan, Professor Patrick Corish, Professor Breandán Leahy, Professor Finbarr Clancy SJ, Dr Daire Keogh and Fr Sean McGraw CSC, is gratefully acknowledged.

I also wish to thank Jorge and Paulina Diaz, Ewelina Kluczniok, Caitriona Clarke and Veritas, Dr Paula Connolly and Dr Jennifer Porter. This book could not have been written without their cooperation. Finally, I wish to thank most sincerely my family for their invaluable help in writing this work.

CONTENTS

Part Two: Armed Insurrection Opposed

THE ROMAN CATHOLIC ARCHBISHOPS AND BISHOPS IN IRELAND 1850–1870

ARCHBISHOPS OF IRELAND

Armagh
Paul Cullen, 1849–52
Joseph Dixon, 1852–66
Michael Kieran, 1866–69
Daniel McGettigan, 1870–87

Dublin
Daniel Murray, 1823–52
Paul Cullen, 1852–78

Cashel
Michael Slattery, 1834–57
Patrick Leahy, 1857–75

Tuam
John MacHale, 1834–81

BISHOPS OF THE PROVINCE OF ARMAGH

Ardagh and Clonmacnois
William O'Higgins, 1829–53
John Kilduff, 1853–67
James Donnelly, 1864–93

Clogher
Charles McNally, 1843–64

Derry
John McLaughlin, 1840–64
Francis Kelly (Administrator), 1849–89

Down and Connor
Cornelius Denvir, 1835–65
Patrick Dorrian (coadjutor), 1860–85

Dromore
Michael Blake, 1833–60
John Pius Leahy OP (coadjutor), 1854–90

Kilmore
James Browne, 1827–65
Nicholas Conaty, 1865–86

Meath
John Cantwell, 1830–66
Thomas Nulty (coadjutor), 1856–70

Raphoe
Patrick McGettigan, 1820–61
Daniel McGettigan (coadjutor), 1856–70

BISHOPS OF THE PROVINCE OF DUBLIN

Ferns
Myles Murphy, 1850–56
Thomas Furlong, 1857–75

Kildare and Leighlin
Francis Haly, 1838–55
James Walshe, 1856–88
James Lynch CM (coadjutor), 1869–96

Ossory
Edward Walsh, 1846–72

BISHOPS OF THE PROVINCE OF CASHEL

Cork
William Delany, 1847–86

Cloyne
Timothy Murphy, 1849–56
William Keane, 1857–74

Kerry
Cornelius Egan, 1824–56
David Moriarty (coadjutor), 1854–77

Killaloe
Patrick Kennedy, 1835–50
Daniel Vaughan, 1851–59
Michael Flannery (coadjutor), 1858–91
Nicholas Power (coadjutor), 1865–72

Limerick
John Ryan, 1828–64
George Butler (coadjutor), 1861–86

Ross
William Keane, 1850–57
Michael O'Hea, 1858–76

Waterford
Nicholas Foran, 1837–55
Dominic O'Brien, 1855–73

BISHOPS OF THE PROVINCE OF TUAM

Achonry
Patrick MacNicholas, 1818–52
Patrick Durcan, 1852–75

Clonfert
John Derry, 1847–70

Elphin
George J.P. Browne, 1844–58
Laurence Gillooly CM (coadjutor), 1856–95

Galway
Laurence O'Donnell, 1844–55
John MacEvilly, 1856–78

Killala
Thomas Feeny, 1847–73

Kilmacduagh and Kilfenora
Edmund Ffrench OP, 1825–52
Patrick Fallon, 1852–66

PRIME MINISTERS OF THE UNITED KINGDOM 1846–1874

Lord John Russell	30 June 1846
(cr. Earl Russell, 30 July 1861)	
Edward George Geoffrey Smith Stanley,	23 Feb. 1852
14th earl of Derby	
George Hamilton-Gordon,	19 Dec. 1852
4th earl of Aberdeen	
Henry John Temple,	6 Feb. 1855
3rd Viscount Palmerston	
Earl of Derby	26 Feb. 1858
Viscount Palmerston	12 June 1859
Earl Russell	29 Oct. 1865
Earl of Derby	28 June 1866
Benjamin Disraeli	27 Feb. 1868
William Ewart Gladstone	3 Dec. 1868
Benjamin Disraeli	20 Feb. 1874
(cr. earl of Beaconsfield, 21 August 1876)	

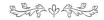

PREFACE

'THE POOREST COUNTRY that one can know,' according to a Vatican report from the mid-nineteenth century, was Ireland.[1] It was to this country, beset with a variety of problems, that Paul Cullen, having spent almost thirty years in Rome, returned in 1850. His status was that of Apostolic Delegate and he was to serve first as Archbishop of Armagh, and from 1852 as Archbishop of Dublin. For twenty-eight years this ecclesiastic, who was destined to become Ireland's first ever cardinal, was to dominate Irish ecclesiastical and religious life. The responsibility for an entire ecclesiological structure and many patterns of religious devotion as well as an impressive record of church building work, have all been laid at his feet.[2] Indeed his influence was so great that his achievements in Church affairs has been described as 'the Cullenisation of Ireland'.[3]

However, despite his formidable programme of work in Church and religious affairs, there were other matters which also commanded his attention. Here his impact was also significant, if less glorious. His motivation in involving himself in secular affairs was to improve the material conditions of the people of that 'poorest country' to which he was sent by Pope Pius IX.

The purpose of this book is to analyse and discuss two specific phases of Cullen's secular activities. It will trace his role and influence in two separate movements, one parliamentary, the other revolutionary, both of which were organised to improve the circumstances of Irish Catholics, most of whom were poor, wretched and dispirited. The first of these campaigns was the Independent Irish Parliamentary Movement of the 1850s; the other, the revolutionary Fenian movement prominent in the 1860s.

1. 'Abbiamo a trattare d'un paese il piu povero che si conosce: Irlanda – Relazione riguardo al proselitismo protestante nell'Occidente d'Irlanda. Suo successo e mezzi adoperati', n.d.: ASV, Pio IX, Oggetti Vari, no. 993.
2. E. Larkin, 'The devotional revolution in Ireland, 1850–75', American Historical Review, lxxvii (June 1972), pp. 625–52.
3. D. Bowen, Paul Cardinal Cullen and the Shaping of Modern Irish Catholicism, Dublin, 1983, p. 282.

FOREWORD

PAUL CARDINAL CULLEN was primarily a pastor. The greatness of his achievement and influence in that role can hardly be disputed. But he was soon to be drawn into the political world where he exercised an influence that was and remains controversial. The study hereupon produced by Dr Ciarán O'Carroll, by reason of its detailed research into a massive collection of sources in archives both in Ireland and abroad, will be welcomed by all who have an interest in the history of Ireland.

Cullen was not a great political leader. The tragedy of his time was the absence following the death of Daniel O'Connell of inspired lay political leadership. But a bishop fulfils his mission in the midst of his people, and their needs and concerns have a voice that appeals to his pastoral charity, especially when those concerns represent an experience of hopelessness such as the poor experienced in post-Famine Ireland. What is perceived as a need for radical change in a political system cannot be tackled by direct pastoral action. What is needed is political leadership, which may turn either to reform within the established order or to revolutionary action with a view to replacing that order. This book recounts the undistinguished efforts in the 1850s to remedy the established order, efforts in which Cullen played a part marred by a certain reticence and even ambiguity. These qualities of his leadership have brought him serious criticism, especially from those who felt they had been deceived in their expectations. The lack of success in the parliamentary forum turned attention to the alternative with the rise of the Fenians. But it was here that the voice and influence of Cullen abandoned all ambiguity. He was a patriot who abhorred the thought of revolution on the grounds that it could have no hope of success against British might and would lead to oppression. He was also unfortunately influenced in his experience of revolutionary Italy. Dr O'Carroll's account of these two movements, the parliamentary and the revolutionary, is outstanding for its scope, fairness and assiduousness.

In one hundred and fifty years, the option in favour of the use of physical force with the measure of success that it achieved has entered into the substance of our tradition. We seem to be now at the point where certain tragic consequences of that option may be about to be overcome. History has no interest in idle speculation about how Ireland would have fared in the modern world if Cullen's political philosophy of patience had been followed. History is content to leave us with our dreams. And although the tradition we have formed, not without a certain dependence on a Robespierrist conviction about *vertu*, is second nature for all who regard themselves as authentic in their Irish patriotism, there would still be some who sympathize with Cullen's option for peace and who may see in that peace the hope of the future. History has its way of passing through that which alone at the time seemed uniquely practical towards that which then seemed unrealistic and now represents the true goal for the years ahead.

Desmond Cardinal Connell
December 2008

Part One

CONSTITUTIONALISM
ENCOURAGED

Chapter One

ARRIVAL OF PAUL CULLEN
AS ARCHBISHOP

THE CATHOLIC CHURCH in Ireland to which Paul Cullen was appointed in late 1849 as Primate, Archbishop and Apostolic Delegate was, and still is, organised into four provinces: Armagh, Dublin, Cashel and Tuam. There were twenty-eight dioceses, with the Archbishop of Armagh holding the title of Primate of All Ireland, and the Archbishop of Dublin being styled, confusingly, as Primate of Ireland. The vast majority of the population were Roman Catholic. However, political power as well as most material wealth, influence and prestige resided overwhelmingly in the hands of Protestants, predominantly descendants of English and Scottish settlers. Some two centuries earlier these had been 'planted' in Ireland when colonising and 'pacifying' English rulers, lacking the funds to pay their troops and other supporters, had rewarded them instead with confiscated Catholic lands. The majority of the dispossessed Catholics then became tenants, paying rent to usurpers. These were mostly Protestants, adherents of the Established Church of Ireland. In addition to the hefty rents the tenants were obliged to pay, they were further obliged to subscribe to the upkeep of the Protestant Church in the form of 'tithes'. And many

Catholics had not merely been dispossessed, they had been banished to the poor land in the west of the country. Others were forced to leave the country. Hence, repossession of their families' land was a dominant issue for the people of rural Ireland when Paul Cullen became archbishop.

The expropriation of the land had followed a succession of penal laws which discriminated against Catholics, impoverished them and degraded them. They were harassed in the practice of their faith and their priests driven underground. There had been considerable easing of this religious discrimination in the decades preceding 1850, but the Irish Catholics now entrusted to Paul Cullen were still a people oppressed and very conscious of being oppressed. This made them anti-Protestant and anti-British, which also meant being fiercely nationalistic and strongly attached to their clergy and their Church and, by extension, to the Pope. The union with Britain, under which, since 1801, Ireland was an integral part of the United Kingdom ruled by the Parliament at Westminster, was a particular focus of nationalist discontent. The government was now head-quartered in London with a cabinet minister entitled Chief Secretary for Ireland carrying responsibility for Irish affairs from an office in Dublin Castle and a Lord Lieutenant representing the crown in the Viceregal Lodge in the Phoenix Park.

At the time of Cullen's appointment to Armagh, the minds of the people were occupied more by their own survival than possible legislative independence. The Great Famine of 1845, 1846 and 1847 resulted in the death of an estimated one million people. In addition, emigration over the following years counted for another million, out of a total population of eight million. For many years Cullen was to be confronted by the material, social, psychological and political consequences of this great catastrophe. It was to have a particularly dramatic effect on the Irish peasant class, by now mere tenants of confiscated holdings which they saw as their own. With an increasing population, the subdivision of farms into small holdings, off which large families attempted to glean a living, gave rise to major economic difficulties. Following the Famine many tenants found it impossible to pay either the high rents or the Church tithes. They were thus liable to eviction, a process which had dramatic and oftentimes tragic consequences for those who were displaced.[1] The vast majority of them were not entitled to any security of tenure under the law.[2] They could be evicted and without compensation for any improvements performed to their holdings,[3] while forcible extraction of rent, seizure of goods and eviction sometimes resulted in violence and bloodshed.[4]

In 1849 there were 90,000 evictions in Ireland and in 1850, the year Cullen arrived in Armagh, there were 104,000.[5] Most of those evicted were destitute. Some of the more able-bodied and adventurous emigrated. Those who remained had to endure the misery of mass unemployment, low wages for those who could get work, inadequate health services to deal with cholera and other diseases, and even hunger. Only a few years before Cullen's arrival, the government had extended the English poor law to Ireland and had built the 'workhouses' to house the very destitute existing in the most squalid conditions. A particular worry for Cullen was the exploitation of these conditions by proselytisers who, in the Irish phrase, 'offered the soup' to those who would embrace Protestantism.[6]

The material situation was bad enough, but the people suffered as much from the position of inferiority into which they had been thrown by these ascendancy Protestant 'usurpers'. These were now treating the native Irish as a servile class and subjecting them to derision and contempt. The English language was being pushed at the expense of the native Gaelic, notably in the government-provided national schools. Despair, depression and a feeling of hopelessness pervaded the main body of the Irish population. This condition of mind was possibly the most damaging long-term consequence of the English conquest of Ireland. The mood of the subject people was caught fairly by the Gaelic poet who had written: 'The misery we endure is bad enough, but the degradation that follows it is worse ...'[7] The situation was perceived as intolerable to the frustrated Irish mind. The overall situation was explosive, with widespread discontent leading to frequent outbreaks of agrarian violence.

Overlaying this whole scene was the confusion attaching to what historians term 'The National Question'. At one extreme there were the small but articulate Young Ireland revolutionaries who wanted an independent Ireland and complete separation from Britain. They staged a token insurrection in 1848. At the other extreme, there were those who would accept the union with Great Britain, seeking improvements for the people through Ireland's elected members of parliament at Westminster. The majority, who held the middle ground, were attracted to the idea of Repeal of the Union and a separate Irish parliament. The great national leader Daniel O'Connell had campaigned for this in the latter years of his life. Like him, they would be prepared to accept the Crown as nominal head of both states and to continue to live with the Union for the time being. It was important for them, however, to be assured of the ability of the Irish members of parliament to bring living conditions and work opportunities in Ireland nearer to British levels. They would then be happy to leave the long-term political status of Ireland to be settled later when, hopefully, the condition of the people would have improved. Paul Cullen could be said to have shared these views.

The situation would, under normal circumstances, be the responsibility of the political leadership, leaving an archbishop taking over the See of Armagh to tend to the spiritual needs of his flock and the affairs of the Church in Ireland. The sad fact about the Ireland of the time, however, was that there was really no competent political successor to O'Connell, who had died in 1847. He had dominated the political scene for two generations, championing the cause of Irish Catholics. In his campaigns he had the strong support of the Catholic clergy. By 1850 the leadership vacuum was very obvious: there were contenders but none with the stature or potential of O'Connell. So it was that Paul Cullen, as a formidable Church personality with a genuine concern for the people, found himself closer to secular affairs than he would have wished.

Paul Cullen was born in April 1803 in Ballitore in County Kildare in the rural parish of Suncroft, Prospect.[8] He was the son of Hugh Cullen and his second wife Mary Maher.[9] His father was a farmer who held a lease on some seventy-six acres of land. Paul received his early education at Shackleton's Quaker School, Ballitore, before studying for the priesthood in Saint Patrick's Seminary in Carlow town. There he showed sufficient promise to be sent to Rome.[10] He commenced his studies at Propaganda Fide on 29 November 1820[11] and distinguished himself as a student, defending his thesis on 11 September 1828 in the presence of Pope Leo XII.[12] He was ordained deacon on 22 February 1829 and priest on Easter Sunday, 19 April 1829.[13] He was retained in Propaganda as professor of Sacred Scripture and Hebrew, and held the post of Rector there for a short period during the time of the Roman Republic.[14] In 1832 he was appointed Rector of the Irish College in Rome. In this capacity he acted also as the Roman representative of many of the Irish bishops.[15] He remained as Rector until 19 December 1849 when he was selected by Pope Pius IX as Archbishop of Armagh and Primate of All Ireland.[16]

Prior to his nomination as an archbishop in Ireland, the possibility of Cullen being raised to episcopal office in the United States of America had been raised several times. In August 1834 he was actually nominated as titular bishop of Orien and coadjutor bishop of Charleston on the recommendation of the existing office holder.[17] Cullen however declined the nomination and his refusal was accepted.[18] As early as 1830 Cullen's name was mentioned in connection with a nomination as coadjutor bishop to the See of Philadelphia.[19] Cullen's name was discussed in relation to the office of coadjutor of New York in 1834 and again in 1837.[20] He was also suggested as a candidate in 1837 for a new diocese to be established in Pittsburgh.[21]

Cullen was ordained Archbishop of Armagh in Rome on 24 February 1850 and afterwards appointed Apostolic Delegate to Ireland.[22] In April 1850 he set sail for Ireland. He was confronted almost immediately with the issues already

mentioned, the land question and the National Question, and
– most sensitive for him – the implications of clerical
involvement in these issues and the disunity among the bishops.

In the wake of the Famine there were various but unsuccessful
attempts to organise protective organisations for tenants facing
eviction.[23] Success came in time to two diocesan priests in the
diocese of Ossory, Fathers Thomas O'Shea and Matthew Keefe.
On 14 October 1849, in their parish of Callan, Co. Kilkenny
they established the Callan Tenant Protection Society to protect
442 tenants from eviction.[24] This clerically inspired organisation
then provided the model for twenty similar societies that had
been founded in ten different counties by July 1850.[25] All of these
were 'checked and controlled by the supervision of the ministers
of religion', mostly Roman Catholic but some Presbyterian.[26]

A move to amalgamate these individual societies on a
common policy on tenant rights led to a conference on 6 August
1850.[27] The chief organisers were newspaper proprietors,
including Roman Catholic and former Young Irelander Charles
Gavan Duffy of the *Nation*, Protestant Sir John Gray of the
Freeman's Journal, and Frederick Lucas of the *Tablet*, a convert to
Roman Catholicism. One third of the attendants were clerics
– either Roman Catholic or Presbyterian.[28] The conference
resulted in the merger of the existing societies into the Irish
Tenant Rights League, popularly called the Tenant League,
which was to be a nationwide organisation. Its immediate aims
were to campaign by parliamentary means for fixity of tenure
and lower rents. A further aim was to provide some degree of
protection for tenants threatened with eviction.[29] While the
more radical aim of repossessing the land expropriated from
their ancestors was not articulated, this was very much in the
back of many League members' minds.

The new organisation's decision to proceed by parliamentary
means represented a significant act of faith in the parliamentarians
at the time, and the League leaders immediately recognised that
it would require important changes in the Party structures
and allegiances. The 105 Irish members of parliament in
Westminster constituting about one-sixth of the total member-

ship of the House of Commons were individually affiliated to the established English parliamentary parties, Liberals, Conservatives or Peelites. This resulted in their influence being dispersed and lacking in effectiveness.[30]

Reacting to this the Tenant League leaders called for the establishment of a new parliamentary group to be composed of those Irish members who were prepared to fight for the rights of the tenant. These would be independent of, and not aligned to, any other party in the House of Commons.[31] This call for an independent group of Irish members of parliament was a significant development. A question now was how the Irish hierarchy, and Cullen in particular, would react to this situation, remembering the strong clerical support there had been for O'Connell's great political campaigns, notably Catholic Emancipation in the 1820s and Repeal of the Union in the early 1840s.

The Irish bishops were very much alive to the plight of the poorer people, especially those working the land and those being maintained in the government-provided workhouses.[32] Cullen himself had chaired the National Synod of Thurles shortly after his arrival in 1850. He had there joined his colleagues in a strong expression of sympathy with the plight of the poor people of Ireland, to which social category most tenant farmers belonged. There is further evidence of his concern in his personal correspondence and his public pastorals. He was, even prior to his appointment as archbishop, well informed of conditions in Ireland from his visits home, his correspondence with his family, with Irish bishops and with well-placed people, including Daniel O'Connell himself.

In his very first pastoral, written from Rome before he ever took up his See, he told of how: 'I know, my dear children, that your sufferings are exceedingly great, and I cannot but weep over your privations and afflictions.'[33] Shortly after taking up his episcopal appointment, and despite the fact that he was ill, he embarked on a visitation of his archdiocese of Armagh.[34] He was shocked at the misery in which the people found themselves.[35] From then on he was to lament repeatedly the state of the mass of the people. His writings for the period 1850 to 1853 in particular record how the mass of the people were forced to endure what he describes variously as bad harvests, famine, persecution, poverty, oppression, distress, misery and disease.[36] He also wrote lamenting the high rate of emigration.[37] He reported to Rome of the destruction of whole villages as a result of mass evictions.[38]

Cullen was clearly alive therefore to the plight of the tenant farmers. It was soon evident, however, that his compassion for them was not reflected in his attitude to the Tenant League which was campaigning to alleviate their lot. When it came to supporting the League, Cullen cautiously, studiously and diplomatically refused to give direct endorsement to it as an organisation. Invitations to attend League meetings were politely refused, but in a manner which suggested support for the ideals of the League without endorsing the organisation by name.[39]

Although he declined to attend meetings he did send letters which asserted how, as was the case in February 1851, he felt most intensely for the sufferings of the agricultural population: 'No one can doubt that it is most desirable that some arrangement may be made to protect their just rights and to better their unhappy condition.'[40] Such phrasing ensured that Cullen's letters, when read out at a meeting, were greeted with loud acclaim.[41] In October 1851 he went so far as to write to a prominent League supporter and parish priest of Clonmellon, Father Dowling, sending a financial contribution towards the cause of 'obtaining legal relief for the suffering agricultural population of Ireland'.[42] His letter went on to observe: 'Their case is sad indeed: every man endowed with Christian charity must feel a deep interest in it. It is now most desirable to have the matter adopted by which the rights and interests of both proprietors and occupiers of the soil may be regulated and protected.'[43]

Understandably, tenant right campaigners interpreted such words as reflecting Cullen's support for both their cause and their organisation. In fact, this particular experience represented an early example of the enigmatic behaviour which Cullen demonstrated repeatedly in later years. On the ground however, the priests in rural Ireland did not appreciate the subtlety of Cullen's statements like that quoted, which, it should be noted, recognised proprietors' as well as occupiers' rights. The priests remembered the great O'Connell campaigns that had been strongly supported by the clergy. They were now more than receptive to approaches from the leaders of the League, and they were not at all moved by the landlords' interests.

Since many clerics, including Cullen himself, came from the class for which the League was agitating, it was not altogether surprising that many priests turned to such a task with a will.[44] The cool caution of the Primate of All Ireland was more than counterbalanced by the heated enthusiasm for the League by many clerics in the country. Indeed, so enthusiastic did some priests become that they found it difficult to restrain their language when speaking in public.[45] Dramatic and vivid pictures of the plight of the people were painted by men of the cloth.[46] Landlords were publicly condemned, pamphlets were composed and 'Professions of political faith' extolled by some priests.[47]

Such words and actions placed Cullen in a difficult situation. He sympathised with the tenant farmers but he did not feel justified in supporting the extreme language employed, or the robust ideas advocated by some of those, including priests, heavily involved in the Tenant League. Cullen appealed and prayed that a spirit of prudence, moderation and justice would guide those who organised tenant right meetings.[48] He insisted that rectification of tenant grievances should be sought by peaceful and not by violent means. Indeed, Cullen's pastorals resorted to calling on the poor, including the tenant farmers, to be patient in their sufferings, and to accept them with courage. He assured them that, for their troubles in this life they would be recompensed with the eternal crown of glory.[49]

He balanced such statements by attacking those who were depriving the poor of the comforts of this world, warning them that they would have to render account for their lack of action before God on the last day. Overall, however, his message appeared to be more of an appeal for compassion from the oppressors of the poor than a call for justice for them.[50] He appealed to the rich, the influential and the powerful for alms and charity in order to preserve the poor from 'total extermination'.[51] At the same time the poor were told to turn to God. Above all they were not to rebel by joining secret societies, a drum which Cullen was to beat many times in later years.[52] On the contrary they were forcefully called on by Cullen and his suffragan bishops to be 'always good and faithful subjects of the realm'.[53] This message of resignation to one's unhappy lot was to prove an inadequate response to the desperate situation of the Irish peasant in the mid-nineteenth century.

A variety of reasons lay behind Cullen's failure to support the League especially when its activities were being backed by other clerics and when he himself sympathised with its aims. Primarily these were his own individual priorities, which would have the land problem behind education and the disestablishment of the Church of Ireland. Further explanations derive from what he had learnt and experienced in his three decades in Rome. There was his respect for private property and for the established order, together with his opposition to Communist influences. These influences he tended to see lurking in many of the political and revolutionary activists he encountered in Ireland.[54] Allied to these was his determination to regulate the involvement of priests in politics. A particular bearing on Cullen's attitude to the Tenant League was, surprisingly, the Ecclesiastical Titles Act, 1851.

꧁꧂ Chapter Two ꧁꧂

RELIGION AND POLITICS:
AN UNEASY MIX

O N 29 SEPTEMBER 1850 Pope Pius IX restored
the English Catholic hierarchy. The British
government reacted strongly to this move. In
Protestant Britain the restoration was strongly
denounced as yet another encroachment on the
rights of both the Established Church and the civil authority by
the Roman Catholic Church. The result was that 'furious no
popery agitation' erupted.[1] So strong was the reaction that the
Liberal Prime Minister Lord John Russell himself denounced
the Papal decision to restore the Roman Catholic hierarchy. The
prime minister's anti-Roman Catholic tendencies were already
known.[2] Now he decided to respond to the Papal action by
introducing the Ecclesiastical Titles Bill. This bill would make
illegal the assumption by Catholic prelates of titles taken from
any place in the United Kingdom, which of course included
Ireland, and make them liable to heavy fines for any act
performed in virtue of territorial jurisdiction. It would also
prohibit, as Cullen was aware, every rescript, bull or pontifical
brief in the United Kingdom.[3]

Sectarian strife in England and government threats of penal
legislation initially constituted for Cullen no more than a mere

33

tempest that would soon pass.[4] It was his belief that the object of any threatened legislative action was merely to frighten the Pope.[5] Any penal enactments that the British parliament might pass held no fear for him.[6] Indeed in many respects, Cullen appears to have welcomed the prospect of some measure of penal legislation being placed on the statute books.[7] It was his belief that such legislation would do neither great harm nor any evil to the Catholic religion as it would be impossible to implement.[8] Cullen maintained that it would have the contrary effect and that the Catholic religion would benefit greatly from 'a little persecution'.[9]

The manner in which the restoration of the hierarchy in England and the subsequent furore might be beneficial to the Roman Catholic religion was varied according to Cullen. The most important benefit for him was to be seen in the numbers of people who converted to the Roman Catholic religion every week during this period.[10] Cullen grew so enthusiastic about this unexpected increase in converts that he began to believe that the passing of penal legislation would eventually lead to the total collapse of British Protestant educational structures and even to the destruction in Ireland of Protestantism itself![11]

As regards Catholics, Cullen expressed his hopes to Rome that any proposed penal legislation would act as a cohesive factor in bringing to an end the divisions that existed among them in general, and the Irish clergy and hierarchy in particular.[12] A little persecution, he believed, was necessary to end any Irish episcopal support that existed for Protestant government policies in Ireland.[13] It would also lead to the extinction of the Young Ireland movement with its revolutionary tendencies, and thereby herald the end of the nationalistic rivalries that existed between English and Irish Catholics in a common experience of sharing one persecuted religion.[14]

Cullen was perceptive enough to see that the Ecclesiastical Titles Bill would not, or could not, be implemented in Ireland.[15] He pointed out how some of the restrictions that legally existed regarding the Catholic Church, such as the prohibition on Cullen referring to himself as 'Archbishop of Armagh', were practically ignored.[16] He was nervous, however, that the authorities in Rome would not appreciate this. He foresaw the possibility whereby the Vatican might enter into negotiations with the British government, which might result in Prime Minister Russell agreeing to lift the threat of penal sanctions in return for being granted some measure of control over the affairs of the Catholic Church in Ireland.[17] Neither British government promises nor their threats of religious persecution were to be believed, Cullen insisted.[18] When rumours circulated to the effect that the British were considering sending a diplomat, Richard Lalor Sheil, to Rome, Cullen's anxiety grew, and he warned the Rector of the Irish College, Tobias Kirby, to monitor closely any such eventuality.[19] The possibility of any deal being struck with the British government was totally unacceptable, Cullen stressed, insisting that 'any concession to the Government would put us back half a century'.[20]

The restoration of the Catholic hierarchy in England led to a wave of sectarian strife in Britain. Cullen initially viewed such anti-Catholic activity in England as some form of Divine retribution against the Catholics of England for their failure to support the Catholics of Ireland in the past. Nonetheless he promised to console, defend and support his English co-religionists in every manner possible.[21] With signs of anti-Catholic bigotry beginning to manifest themselves in Ireland, Cullen promised to hold a meeting of the clergy of the Archdiocese of Armagh.[22] The aim of the meeting was twofold: to compliment Nicholas Patrick Wiseman on the red hat, and to provide a platform whereby Cullen and his clergy could speak out against both state interference in religious affairs and the threatened penal legislation.[23] This meeting was attended by some one hundred clergy who heard Cullen deliver a 'beautiful and eloquent' speech.[24] Those attending passed various solemn resolutions to defend and to maintain, with all the means that were legitimate, the religious rights of the English Catholics. Cullen immediately had the resolutions printed.[25]

While Cullen's strong attack on the British government was greeted with enthusiasm in ecclesiastical circles, it was met with disdain in London.[26] There, Prime Minister Russell denounced Cullen in the House of Commons, portraying the Archbishop as 'a true Roman monk and ... no longer Irish'.[27]

To Cullen's great satisfaction, the first reading of the Ecclesiastical Titles Bill in February 1851 was followed by a unanimous campaign of protest by the oftentimes divided members of the Irish hierarchy. In various pastorals they condemned both the bill and the government who sponsored it. Even Archbishop Murray of Dublin, a prelate who was often denounced by and to Cullen as being pro-government, publicly attacked the proposed legislation.[28] As well as individual pastorals, private meetings were held among the bishops themselves in order to determine the most advisable manner to petition against it.[29] These resulted in a decision to seek professional legal advice and to convene a meeting of the entire Irish episcopal bench, with Cullen in the chair, on 25 February 1851 in an effort to present a united front.[30] The outwardly impressive unity of resolve that manifested itself at this meeting was more apparent than real, however. It did not escape the attention of Cullen that the unity expressed was confined to opposition to the Ecclesiastical Titles Bill.[31] Divisions on other important issues, such as education, still existed.[32]

At the meeting, the bishops unanimously agreed to send two supplications, both subsequently published, protesting against the bill.[33] One they addressed to parliament, the other to 'our dear Queen', which, despite the fact that Queen Victoria was reported to be 'most angry against the Catholics', the bishops reckoned a viable exercise to try to win her over.[34]

A 'Pastoral Address of the Archbishops and Bishops of Ireland on the Penal Enactment regarding Ecclesiastical Titles', drafted by Cullen and appealing to the Catholic people of Ireland for their support, was also issued following the meeting.[35] In the course of this unusually strong address, bearing in mind Cullen's belief that any penal legislation envisaged under the terms of the Act would not be applied, the bishops took a definite stance. They urged their flocks as regards the proposed bill 'to adopt the best and surest means of defeating it, namely – the fulfilment of all your duties, loyalty to the crown, obedience to the constituted authorities, moderation, patience. Based upon the eternal principles of truth and equity, the cause with which you are identified cannot fail to succeed, when advocated by means which are consonant to its justice and holiness and such, dearly beloved brethren, are the only means which we feel convinced you are disposed to employ'.[36]

This notion that if something was intrinsically right it would of necessity win out was extremely naive to say the least. Noticeably, in calling on the people to obey the law, the bishops defiantly used their episcopal titles. This was an action that would itself be in breach of the Ecclesiastical Titles Bill, once enacted into law. In a wider sense however, the request for loyalty to the Crown and obedience to authority was in line with Cullen's general approach and was to be a cause of conflict with impatient nationalists throughout his career.

To become law, the Ecclesiastical Titles Bill had to gain the approval of both Houses of Parliament. More than sixty of the 105 Irish members of parliament were classed as Liberal and therefore could have been expected to support any proposed legislation sponsored by the Russell government. On the Ecclesiastical Titles Bill, twenty-four of these, not all of them Catholic, along with some English Protestant parliamentary members, decided to vote against the government, not only on the issue of the Bill but on policies generally.[37] These Irish members of parliament were given the popular title of 'the Irish Brigade'. This name was associated in the Irish mind with those Irish exiles who over the previous two centuries had distinguished themselves on the battlefields of Europe. Sometimes they had done so in wars against England, having been driven out of Ireland by British domination. The members involved were later to attract the less flattering title of 'the Pope's brass band'.[38]

In 1851 the government suffered a parliamentary defeat and Russell tendered his resignation. It was an action for which the members of the Irish Brigade were quick to claim credit.[39] As no viable alternative government could be formed, the most likely realistic political development at that time was for the Queen to call on Russell to return to office. Cullen held no sympathy for Russell, and distrusted the Earl of Clarendon, the Queen's viceroy in Ireland, but he refused to be frightened by the prospect of a Russell administration returning to office and persecuting the Catholic Church.[40] Characteristically he was content to put his faith in God, reporting to Rome how 'if Russell regains the position again it is said that he will be fiercer than before. But, if God is for us who can be against us?'[41]

Cullen did briefly hope however that the crisis would result in the withdrawal or defeat of the Ecclesiastical Titles Bill.[42] But his hopes were not realised. In fact, following the brief crisis Russell returned quickly to office and set about having the Ecclesiastical Titles Bill pass all of its stages in parliament. Russell failed however to gain the parliamentary support of the members of the Irish Brigade, who continued to meet separately and sit apart from their former Liberal colleagues in the House.[43] These Irish Brigade members voted consistently against the government, vowing to do so until the Ecclesiastical Titles Bill was withdrawn or defeated.[44] They even staged a walk-out from the chamber[45] and their persistence, if not their methods, won them the praise of Cullen.[46] The Irish Apostolic Delegate took comfort in the belief that, even if the Ecclesiastical Titles Bill became law, it would be unenforceable. In the long term, according to Cullen, the Bill could effectively be beneficial for the Catholic Church.[47]

Stimulated by the bishops' joint appeal urging non-violent resistance to the Ecclesiastical Titles Bill, a series of mass public protests, modelled on O'Connell's 'monster meetings' of earlier decades, began to take place all over Ireland. The outcome was overwhelming. The government felt that there was little credible action they could take to prevent such meetings occurring. By March 1851, the widespread extent of the meetings was such as to cause concern to the British authorities in Ireland. The Chief Secretary for Ireland, William Somerville, wrote in alarm to the Prime Minister of the manifest strength and size of the groundswell of opinion against the Ecclesiastical Titles Bill, warning how 'accounts from Ireland lead me to believe that the agitation against the bill in its present form is only commencing'.[48]

Subsequent events were to prove the Chief Secretary right. Peaceful protest meetings went on through the spring of 1851.[49] This mass agitation reached its climax on 11 May 1851 when protest meetings were held in all the parishes of Ireland.[50] At these meetings public prayers for the Church were offered, demands that English officials in Ireland should resign were made and petitions condemning the proposed legislation signed, while the members of parliament who opposed it were praised.[51] In fact, reacting to the strength of criticism for his failure to oppose the bill, William Fagan, member of parliament for Cork, resigned his seat.[52] The petitions were then forwarded, mostly by members of the clergy, to local parliamentary representatives and were so numerous that it took the Irish members nearly two hours to present them.[53]

As regards the effectiveness of publicly protesting in this manner, Cullen was initially convinced that, even if such action would not actually prevent any anti-Catholic bill from being passed into law, at least it would have the effect of slowing things up.[54] As time went on however and the strength of opposition feeling clearly manifested itself, Cullen began to entertain the hope that the Ecclesiastical Titles Bill might be somehow defeated.[55]

Meanwhile, the authorities in the Vatican appear to have responded with concern to reports from the United Kingdom of religious agitation. They decided in May to send the Nuncio in Madrid, on a private basis, on a secret 'fact finding' mission to Ireland and England to report on the situation.[56] In the event the Nuncio never arrived in Ireland and reported to Rome that, among other things, he was unwell and that it would be impossible to hide the true nature of his visit. [57]

The Ecclesiastical Titles Bill, despite the determined opposition of the Irish Brigade and other members, was duly passed by the House of Commons.[58] Nonetheless Cullen still, very unrealistically, held out hope of its rejection by the House of Lords.[59] It was not to be, and on 1 August 1851 the Bill received the necessary signature of Queen Victoria and became law. This whole interlude was an illustration of the priority accorded by Cullen to an issue with implications for the Catholic Church compared, for example, to the attention he would give to a secular issue such as tenants' rights. Indeed he was already preparing to mobilise Catholic opinion to defend Catholic interests generally, as the following months proved.

Several months before the Ecclesiastical Titles Bill was enacted, plans were made to organise a new society which would defend the rights of Catholics, both Irish and British, in anticipation of the renewed discriminatory legislation.[60] The new body, called the Catholic Defence Association of Great Britain and Ireland, was formally established at a meeting in the Dublin Rotunda on 19 August 1851, three weeks after the Bill was passed into law.[61]

This meeting was attended by Catholics from both islands, including thirty-five bishops between Irish, English and Scottish prelates.[62] It was chaired by Cullen. He was later to claim that the reason for his attendance was to unite Catholics in their reaction to the Ecclesiastical Titles Act.[63] In the enigmatic fashion that was already becoming characteristic of him, Cullen insisted that his presence did not mean that he was in any sense 'intruding into the domain of politics or travelling beyond the sphere of ecclesiastical duty'.[64] He did not flinch, in the course of a speech later to be studied in detail by Propaganda and by Pope Pius IX himself, from praising the Irish Brigade members of parliament for their stance in opposing the Ecclesiastical Titles Act.[65] At the same time, he openly condemned the government, asserting that 'the course of events has taught us to put no trust in them, but to rely on Heaven and ourselves'.[66]

The assembled delegates went on to approve unanimously thirteen resolutions, drafted by a committee of Irish members of parliament, condemning the Ecclesiastical Titles Act and the government.[67] One of these stated: 'That as one of the great constitutional and practical means of carrying out the objects of this meeting, we pledge ourselves to make every effort to strengthen the hands and increase the power of those faithful representatives, who, in the last session of parliament, so energetically devoted themselves to the formation of an Independent Party in the legislature, having for its object the maintenance of civil and religious liberty in the British Empire.'[68]

A significant convergence of parliamentary interests was now emerging. As already described, the conference which established the Tenant League in August 1850 had called for a separate group of Irish members of parliament to fight for tenant rights in parliament. Only a few months later, the Irish Brigade group of members of parliament had detached themselves from the main parties in the House. Now, a few months later still, a third body, the Catholic Defence Association, was calling for an independent party in Westminster. Direct support for an independent parliamentary party, coupled with the political tone of the speeches at the first meeting of the Catholic Defence Association meant that it must have been difficult to sustain Cullen's claim that the meeting was not political, but rather a mere 'manifestation of Catholic feeling in favour of the liberty of our holy Church'.[69] Unhappily, while the three separate groups, the Tenant League, the Irish Brigade and the Catholic Defence Association, had overlapping memberships, they had different priorities and this was to prove to be a recipe for misunderstanding and confusion. In particular, the United Kingdom dimension of the Catholic Defence Association would prove to be difficult to relate to the purely Irish concerns of the Tenant League and the Irish Brigade.

While Cullen had reservations about the tone of the addresses made at the first meeting of the Catholic Defence Association, he was afterwards to express satisfaction with the religious spirit that had prevailed at it.[70] He was however fully aware that his actions in chairing and addressing the meeting could be interpreted as being political, despite his assertions to the contrary.[71] After all, the method advocated for defending the liberty of the Church, namely through support for an Independent Party, was itself a political one. Therefore, three days after the inaugural meeting he wrote to the Rector of the Irish College in Rome, Tobias Kirby, who was in Ireland and who had attended the meeting, and requested him to write to Rome and explain the object of the association. He feared that Archbishop Daniel Murray of Dublin might have had time to write and possibly misrepresent the situation.[72] Cullen himself, in his anxiety to be seen as detached from political affairs, wrote also to the Vice Rector of the Irish College in Rome, Bernard Smith, stressing his belief that the association would be wholly directed to religious matters and defending the liberty of the Church.[73]

Both Kirby and Smith acted quickly on Cullen's letters and it was soon reported, much to the Irish Apostolic Delegate's relief, that both the Pope and Propaganda Fide were well satisfied with the news of the meeting.[74] Indeed Cullen's 'moderation and prudence' was reportedly 'praised by all'.[75] In fact, Alessandro Barnabò, the Secretary of Propaganda Fide, was reportedly so impressed that he predicted that Cullen would end up a cardinal.[76]

Based on the fact that both groups were advocating an independent parliamentary party, tentative proposals had been put forward for some form of cooperation between the Tenant League and the Irish Brigade members of parliament, even prior to the establishment of the Catholic Defence Association.[77] There were preliminary negotiations in London and a further meeting took place in Dublin on 20 August 1851. This meeting happened the day following the inaugural one of the Association, between the Irish Brigade parliamentarians and the Tenant League.[78] These negotiations led to an agreement for the Irish Brigade members to agitate in parliament for the cause of tenant reform. However, a reciprocal promise to commit the Tenant League to fight against religious discrimination was never made.[79] The practical political effect of this alliance between the Brigade and the Tenant League was that now, in the case of a general election, both parties would sponsor the same electoral candidate in most constituencies. This candidate would then hopefully receive the votes of both Irish Brigade and Tenant League supporters.

The prominent position of Irish Brigade members in the Catholic Defence Association caused Cullen some disquiet. This meant that, even though neither the Irish hierarchy nor the Catholic Defence Association were party to any electoral pact, they were indirectly linked with the ideals of both the Irish Brigade and of the Tenant League. In reality there were significant differences between the Tenant League and the Catholic Defence Association. Both shared the common objective of establishing an independent party at Westmininster, but one was a national Irish non-sectarian organisation with secular goals; the other was a Catholic, United Kingdom-wide association with religious goals related to the status of the Church and its members, regardless of whether they were in Ireland or in Great Britain.

The possible significance of these developments, and the likely consequences for the Church and for the Catholic Defence Association, were not underestimated in Rome. The advisability of a religiously orientated association getting involved in the issue of tenant right agitation was regarded there as highly questionable. On any such move caution was urged, as Smith from Rome advised Kirby writing: 'I think ... Dr C. [sic] might not mix the relation between landlord and tenant, for the present, with the religious question ... Please let him hear this remark.'[80]

In fact Cullen followed Smith's advice and made no public statement on the Irish Brigade-Tenant League alliance. Instead he preferred to stress the limited political dimension of the Catholic Defence Association in his correspondence with Smith. The foundation of the organisation he described as being 'altogether for religious purposes, and especially for the defence of the liberty of the Church. The only point in which it will touch anything political will be the election of members of parliament. We cannot get on without some good representatives, and exertions must be made to find them and return them. This is scarcely a political business – yet it will be misrepresented as such'.[81]

To suggest that involvement in elections for parliament was 'scarcely a political business' was bound to cause confusion, as

43

indeed it did. Cullen appears to have realised this, and following the electoral pact between the Irish Brigade and the Tenant League his scepticism about the success of the Catholic Defence Association grew. However, he continued to admit that there was a need, indeed a duty, for some effort to protect the Church because her rights were being threatened.[82] At the same time however, he was concerned about the Association's lack of any reliable lay leader who might be trusted to organise affairs.[83] He was concerned also at the continued opposition of a minority of bishops to the Association, most notably that of Archbishop Murray of Dublin.[84] Nonetheless, despite these reservations Cullen continued to participate fully in the Association. He was hoping that it might promote the spiritual as well as the temporal welfare of the people, especially as regards the fight against proselytism and non-Catholic schools.[85] He believed that something had to be done to prevent religion falling totally into ruin in a few parts of the kingdom.[86]

On this basis then Cullen justified his continued participation in the Catholic Defence Association. He was one of three prelates, along with one peer and eight Irish Brigade members of parliament, who sat on the Catholic Defence Association's steering committee.[87] They met on 26 September 1851 and drew up an address simply entitled 'To the Catholics of the United Kingdom', which listed the objectives and rules of the new association.[88] Considerable confusion surrounded the production of these rules. Indeed several modifications were made to them even between the time they were approved by the committee and the general membership on the one hand, and their publication on 18 October 1851 on the other.[89]

At all stages in the document listing the objectives and rules of the association the question of the Ecclesiastical Titles Act, and the demand for absolute freedom for the Roman Catholic Church to profess her doctrine and exercise her rights, featured. As to the manner in which such goals were to be achieved the address clearly stated that: 'All our hopes of redress, under Divine Providence, are centred in the creation and sustainment [sic] of a parliamentary party, ready to defend at all hazards, with an independent spirit, our civil and religious liberties.'[90]

To promote this, the address attributed a political, as well as spiritual, role to bishops and priests. They, through prayer and while 'without travelling out of their own avocations [sic] ...in fulfilment of their important duties will inculcate the strict and religious obligation of selecting, as representatives of the people, those men who are best fitted from integrity, ability and zeal, to support in the Imperial Parliament our religious rights, and to remove the many grievances under which Catholics of the United Kingdom will continue to labour and to carry out the objects of this Association'.[91] Meanwhile, the people were told that: 'It will become an imperative duty ... to organize and marshall the elective power of each constituent body so as to ensure a right direction being given to every available vote ...'[92]

All the while, remarkably, full adherence both to the Pope and the law of the land was emphasised in the strongest terms. The address went so far as to state that the Association would 'inculcate strict allegiance to the throne and ... be ever ready to assist in protecting the just rights of others'.[93] Any implied contradiction in this statement seems to have been ignored by its authors. After all, was it not the occupant of the Throne, to whom allegiance was advocated by the members of the Association, who had recently signed the act that the Association was attempting to get repealed? Besides, wasn't there the Coronation Oath which required her to uphold the Protestant religion?

As regards strategy, an important difference now emerged between the Tenant League and the Catholic Defence Association. The League, being the more forceful grouping, wanted absolute withdrawal of support from any government that did not adopt their demands. The Catholic Defence Association, on the other hand, wished to be open to parliamentary compromises or coalitions.

Ironically, just at the time when Cullen was stressing the importance of Catholics uniting themselves behind public representatives who would defend the rights of the Church, there occurred a controversy that would split the Catholic Defence Association. The cause lay not in any matter of principle, but in the choice for a permanent and paid post of secretary of the Association, for which applications had been invited.[94] The post had been temporarily filled by William Keogh, a member of parliament for Athlone, who was subsequently joined from October 1851 by John Sadlier and John Reynolds, the parliamentary representatives for Carlow and Dublin respectively.[95] When in December 1851, the voting took place for the permanent position between a Galway man George Burke and one of the English Oxford converts, Henry Wilberforce, it was won by the latter.[96] As the vast majority of the members of the Association were Irish, this appointment was bound to meet with a cool reception from Irish members. This would have been the case even if the election had been run on democratic grounds.[97] Opposition to Wilberforce was voiced by various members of the Irish Brigade, led by the original acting secretary, William Keogh. Keogh succeeded, despite attempts to thwart him, in voicing his objection to the election of Wilberforce publicly.[98]

Keogh's objection to Wilberforce took the form of a public appeal signed by several Irish members of parliament, some of whom it was later alleged had actually voted for Wilberforce![99] This appeal to the people against the election of Wilberforce is of interest because, in objecting to Wilberforce on the grounds of his nationality, it could be seen as identifying Roman Catholicism with Irish nationalism. The appeal went so far as to maintain that intrinsic to being Irish was to be a Catholic, and furthermore that the Irish actually drew an identity from their adherence to the Roman Catholic faith. It further claimed that 'the defence of the Catholic people of Ireland and of their national character and position, was a primary object in the foundation of the Catholic Defence Association'.[100]

In response to this in December 1851 a very ill Cullen intervened by writing an open letter conveying his 'deep disappointment' that the members of parliament had protested using a separatist Irish nationalist argument.[101] Cullen stressed the fact that: 'From the first formation of the society ... I understood the feeling to be universally entertained that all Catholics of the United Kingdom were to constitute one body, and to be in all respects upon a perfect equality, without distinction of province or country. This as far as I could judge was deemed a vital principle ... If an association were established for purely political purposes, I would earnestly desire for it the fullest measure of success in pursuit of every legitimate and patriotic object, but my peculiar sphere and spiritual associations would not allow me time to take any active part in it.'[102] By now confusion was complete!

This open letter is of special interest as it expresses Cullen's detachment from an over-identification of the Catholic religion with Irish nationalism. The protestors failed to get support from the bishops or, with the exception of the *Nation*, of the press. They therefore decided to make no public response to Cullen's letter.[103] His handling of this situation resulted in Cullen's stance over the split in the Association being received with 'universal admiration' in Rome, while at the same time his nationalistic image at home remained intact. That did not remain the case twelve months later.[104]

Local interest in the office of secretary of the Catholic Defence Association was overshadowed for a while by the coup d'état of Louis Napoleon in Paris and the dismissal of the British Foreign Secretary Palmerston by Russell. However, in Ireland, the issues raised during the Irish Brigade/Tenant League/Catholic Defence Association affair were destined not only to recur but to become complicated by personality and political differences.

The internal divisions among the leaders of the Catholic Defence Association itself were to be heightened by an incredible series of personality and political differences involving the leaders, including Cullen. For example, Wilberforce, the newly elected secretary of the Association, wrote disparagingly to Cullen not only of two of the founders of the Tenant League, Frederick Lucas and Charles Gavan Duffy, but also of one of the more prominent Irish Brigade members of parliament, George Henry Moore.[105] For his part, Lucas felt bitter at Irish Brigade member John Sadlier financially backing a new newspaper, the *Catholic Telegraph*. This was undercutting Lucas' own *Tablet* and was accusing the Irish Brigade of hypocrisy.[106] He was also alleging that the Irish Brigade had deliberately excluded him from holding office in the Catholic Defence Association.[107]

For his part Charles Gavan Duffy, one of the co-founders of the Tenant League, was publicly criticising the members of the Irish Brigade and expressing doubts about their trustworthiness.[108] The same Duffy, on whom Lucas felt he could rely to carry out a policy of independence in parliament, was a survivor of the revolutionary Young Ireland movement of 1848, and Cullen consequently held the strongest reservations about him.[109]

Throughout his career, Cullen maintained an almost fanatical hatred of people who had been associated with Young Ireland and the abortive rising of 1848. Having lived in Rome during the 1848 revolution there, Cullen had no time for anyone associated with armed revolutionary movements, especially someone he suspected of contact with Young Italy. Duffy, as far as Cullen was concerned, had been a leader of such a movement in Ireland. No matter how ineffective that movement was, Duffy was 'a wicked man, to act with whom, after his conduct in 1848, was impossible until he had fasted fifty years on bread and water'.[110] In Cullen's mind, Young Ireland was equated with Young Italy, and Gavan Duffy with Mazzini, the Young Italy leader.[111] Cullen's comparison was a grotesque exaggeration, as Lucas unsuccessfully tried to point out to him repeatedly, but it was nevertheless real for him.[112] This unrelenting attitude of Cullen was certainly a factor in shaping his attitude to both the Tenant League and later to the Independent Party, of which the League was, in effect, to become a part. He was not going to support a party in which Duffy played a leading role.

Cullen's unshakeable, if not entirely reliable, views about the associations of Irish nationalist figures with European revolutionary leaders were to continue to be significant in forming his attitudes in later years as well, notably with regard to the Fenians over the following decade.

Chapter Three

UNITED WE STAND ...

THE DAWN OF 1852 witnessed episcopal disunity in Ireland, causing increasing concern both in Armagh and Rome.[1] Cullen was now physically ill. His hopes that the row concerning the appointment of a secretary to the Catholic Defence Association had been resolved were in vain.[2] Although they had not replied to Cullen's open letter, Archbishop MacHale of Tuam and a number of the members of parliament who had been prominent in the Association absented themselves from a meeting called for 29 January 1852.[3]

This meeting, chaired by Cullen, went ahead nonetheless. The main topic was the necessity for the Catholic Defence Association to organise itself at constituency level. This would enable them to sponsor candidates in elections.[4] The importance of this move was stressed by Cullen who, in a lengthy address, publicly emphasised the need for the Catholic people of Ireland to strengthen the ranks of 'worthy' members of parliament at future elections.[5] In focusing on the personality, and possibly also the religion, of individual candidates, Cullen displayed an amazing political naivety. His search was for good men who would advance Catholic interests when elected. He appeared to be unaware of any form of whips system which bound the member to support his party in parliamentary votes.

The meeting of 29 January 1852 approved a petition cautioning the British government against any attempt to implement the Ecclesiastical Titles Act.[6] Cullen subscribed to this despite his personal belief that the act would not be enforced in Ireland. The petition closed with the warning that 'We ask that our religion be left alone – that it may be ... neither established nor proscribed by the laws of the British Empire, and if you refuse us this common justice, upon you be the blame, that one third of your fellow subjects are compelled to spend in pursuit of justice ... those energies which they would gladly devote undivided to the service of our common country'.[7] The employment of the term 'our common country' implied acceptance of Ireland's status as part of the United Kingdom. There were inconsistencies between this position and that put forward the previous month by some members who, in defiance of its constitution, attempted to portray the Association as purely Irish, Catholic and separatist. The clash between these two schools of thought as regards Irish nationalism was to intensify following the transfer of Cullen to Dublin, the very heart of British administration in Ireland.

After a sudden illness, the death of Archbishop Murray of Dublin took place on 26 February 1852.[8] Following his funeral, great interest developed regarding his successor.[9] Speculation was rife that Cullen would be the right man for this crucially important position.[10] When the Dublin clergy were consulted, he proved to be their most popular candidate.[11]

The prospect of Cullen being transferred to the Irish capital was not welcomed by all, even if enthusiastically received by some.[12] There were complaints about his Romanising influence, his political stance and his severe disciplinary approach in Church affairs.[13] While some supporters believed that his translation to Dublin would help to strengthen the common bond between the Catholics of Ireland and England and thereby reinforce the Union, the British government thought otherwise.[14] It was speculated that the government, whose partisans Cullen believed hated him without exception, would seek to impede the transfer.[15] British objections centred on his alleged approval of the Tenant League and on anti-government writings by his friend of the time, Frederick Lucas.[16] At the time, Kirby, the Rector of the Irish College in Rome, and later Cullen himself strenuously denied all such allegations.[17] As well as urging the Roman authorities to pay no heed to possible British objections, repeated calls were made for the early ratification of Cullen's nomination.[18]

In the event Cullen was translated to Dublin and reconfirmed as Apostolic delegate.[19] He received the brief on 2 June 1852. The appointment was enthusiastically greeted by many bishops in Ireland and elsewhere who saw the move as advantageous for the Irish Church.[20] However Cullen, who had earlier expressed his lack of interest in Dublin, viewed the transfer as augmenting his difficulties.[21] He quickly realised the truth of the warning of Bishop of Ross, William Keane, that Cullen would soon find himself in direct 'opposition to the insidious attacks of a powerful government'.[22]

The week before the See of Dublin became vacant there was a political crisis which led to the fall of the government. On 20 February 1852 Lord John Russell's Liberal government was defeated on a Militia Bill and he resigned, a move which, if viewed by Cullen as 'extraordinary', was also very much welcomed by him.[23]

A minority Conservative administration assumed office under the Earl of Derby as Prime Minister, with Benjamin Disraeli as leader in the House of Commons. It was expected that their tenure in power would be short.[24] Cullen's reaction to the change was mixed. On the one hand, referring in particular to the fall of foreign secretary Palmerston, he thought that: 'The change of things that happened amongst us is to our advantage. The fall of Palmerston is good for the Catholics of every country in the world.'[25] At the same time, according to Cullen, all the leading ministries had been assigned to men whom he viewed as the Catholic Church's 'most furious enemies'.[26] On such grounds he asserted that 'Catholics would lose more than they gain in the change of government'.[27] Like many Irishmen in the nineteenth century, Cullen showed that he too could be always against the government – no matter who the government were!

Cullen's vision at this time was for a United Kingdom-wide Catholic group in Westminster which would not be attached to any political party and whose members would agitate for the rights of Catholics and of the Church.[28] As he put it: 'We could need here a party who would look after religious affairs and the independence of the Church without involving themselves in fights and looking after other affairs, and without selling themselves to the ministry so as to obtain a few miserable temporal advantages. Disgracefully however our rich Catholics have nothing of the Catholic spirit.'[29]

Having expressed his disillusionment with Catholic politicians, Cullen went on to express his opposition both to those who adopted a policy of total opposition to the government and also to those who actively participated in government. He wrote: 'I believe that those Catholics who set out to openly attack the government are acting wrongly, but yet I believe that those who make themselves instruments and agents of our ministers are even worse.'[30] He was later to modify this latter view with respect to Irish people, notably Catholics serving the administration in Ireland. In effect, what he was at this time contemplating was what might be called a Roman Catholic lobby in parliament, which would hold itself aloof from the main political parties.

Cullen estimated that, as the Derby government could be voted out of office if all the Catholic members joined the ranks of the opposition and voted against them, the Conservatives would not make any moves against the Church.[31] Such reckoning led him rather naively to conclude that the outcome of any government's anti-Catholic stance would lead to the alienation of all Catholic members of parliament. As he saw it, that would bring about the collapse of the government through withdrawal of support by the Catholic members. His reasoning went on to visualise the resultant general election producing a sizeable increase in the number of Catholic members who would ensure that any 'persecution' of the Catholic Church would be greatly lessened.[32]

Simply having members of parliament who professed themselves Catholics by religion was not a guarantee of concessions to Catholics. Apart from any question of party loyalty, there was at the time a requirement for all members to be men of a certain financial standing. No commoner could be elected unless he possessed property in the United Kingdom yielding a clear annual income of £300 sterling for Borough members and £600 sterling for county members. Ordinary members of parliament commanded no salary but office holders did, a situation that could provide a considerable incentive to vote for the government. Given this situation Cullen was warned that it was possible that 'rich Catholics' would be prepared to pledge support to anyone who would advance their personal careers.[33] After all, as he informed Rome: 'The whole system of government is very open to intrigues and to villainous behaviour.'[34] Future events were to show that the warnings given to Cullen were well founded. At this time also there was a strong undercurrent of anti-Catholic feeling in Britain, which would not encourage uncommitted members to support Catholic causes.

The prediction that the Conservative government would not last long was borne out.[35] On 19 March 1852, after only a few weeks, a general election was called for the coming summer.[36] Before the election, in an effort to win Protestant electoral support in England, the government revived some anti-Catholic prohibitions, which, though still on the Statute Book, were not being enforced. A government proclamation of 15 June 1852 reminded Roman Catholics that it was against the law for religious to wear habits in public, and that it was still illegal for Catholics to hold religious services in public.[37]

When Catholics in the English city of Stockport held a religious procession in defiance of this prohibition, riots broke out in which blood was spilt, chapels were burnt and the Sacred Host was reportedly desecrated.[38] This incident was viewed by

Irish Catholics as a product of the reactionary religious policy of the Conservative government, comparable to that of the rulers in Rome during the Republic, according to Cullen.[39] Irish Catholic voters were now becoming disenchanted with both Liberals and Conservatives, for each had directed campaigns against Catholics. From this disenchantment the advocates of an Independent Irish Party perceived that they stood to gain great political support.[40]

For a new political force to capture a sizeable vote in an election the differences between the Tenant League and the Catholic Defence Association would have to be resolved. A new element was the Irish Reform Act, 1850, which trebled the electorate.[41] Many of those newly enfranchised belonged to a sector in Irish society that would be open to pressure under the public voting system still in operation. The main pressurising interests were, on the one side, the landlords exerting influence in the Conservative interest, and, on the other, certain priests doing likewise for the Liberals. The case for a united front was getting stronger.

'Preliminary negotiations', aimed at arriving at an agreed electoral strategy, had commenced as early as January 1852.[42] Clerics featured prominently in these negotiations, the details of which Cullen was kept informed.[43] In addition to political necessities, there were economic incentives also. Neither the Tenant League nor the Catholic Defence Association was financially well off, and the property requirements for potential members of parliament seriously hampered attempts to field candidates. Indeed such leading personages as Lucas and Duffy had to rely on sympathetic wealthy landowners to provide them with the necessary finance.[44]

Agreement on a common electoral platform was proving difficult. Some, including a number of priest activists, stressed the importance of the tenant issue to the relegation of Catholic rights.[45] Others did the opposite, especially after the incidents at Stockport.[46] Nonetheless, common ground on the idea of an independent Irish parliamentary group existed.[47] It was on this basis that the talks to find agreement bore fruit.[48] There does not appear to have been any appreciation at this stage of the negative implications which independence in parliament, not to mention a policy of opposition, could have for a member seeking an appointment or other favours from the government.[49] The significance of this factor would later become apparent.

In the event, the Tenant League and the Catholic Defence Association, with only some local exceptions, worked together in the election of July 1852.[50] In some constituencies such as Dublin County, the Catholic Defence Association sponsored the independent Liberal Party candidate.[51] In others, such as Leitrim and New Ross, the candidates were sponsored by the Tenant League.[52]

On a national level, in an attempt to win popular public support for their political policies, the advocates of an independent group in parliament relied on liberal newspapers to publicise their cause.[53] In their efforts at local level to have independent candidates returned to parliament, the organisers turned almost inevitably to the local Catholic parish clergy.[54] They would not be disappointed.

That members of the clergy should play a prominent role in the 1852 election was not unusual given the history of Irish politics earlier in the nineteenth century. Priests had been politically active in the Catholic Emancipation campaign of the 1820s and in the Repeal movement of the early 1840s.[55] For clerics to assume a political function in society was, in mid-nineteenth century Ireland, a social fact of life.[56] Indeed it was, as Lucas put it, 'not merely in the politics of the people that the priest takes a part, but in all their temporal affairs'.[57]

The manner in which the priests played a political role was varied. During the 1852 election campaign, priests, who often dominated local political clubs, influenced the nomination of Liberal candidates interested in joining an Independent Irish Party.[58] They were known to canvass, instruct and introduce candidates to electors.[59] As such, they were responsible for resolving in some cases, or accentuating in others, divisions in electoral committees.[60] They also hosted political dinners and addressed political meetings, many of which took place in Church property.[61]

Political prominence by the clergy had been a source of complaint after every general election in Ireland from 1826, and 1852 was no exception.[62] What was remarkable, however, was the extent and gravity of the allegations following the 1852 election. They were so numerous as to provide the grounds for rumours that the government was about to legislate to curtail clerical influence in future elections.[63] A number of pamphlets appeared condemning the manner in which the clergy exercised their influence over the voters.[64]

In the election campaign of 1852, clerics were accused of intimidating many Catholic voters by using physical and spiritual methods. There were press reports of voters being detained in monasteries against their will, or being physically intimidated under alleged clerical supervision.[65] Accounts were later given of priests being present at scenes of disorder and fighting in Clare, Cork, Mayo and Sligo.[66] Priests were accused of bribery through transporting voters to polling booths and arranging for 'refreshments' and even board.[67] Allegations were also made that priests gave money to non-voters to heckle and intimidate voters.[68]

More sinister were the suggestions of priests abusing their spiritual influence to advance political ends.[69] This was despite the fact that, at the national seminary at Maynooth, the theological professors agreed that only on the rarest occasions could priests exercise spiritual rights for political motives.[70] There were reports of voters being intimidated and bribed by clerics.[71] Complaints were also made of candidates being ridiculed, denounced and subjected to various allegations from the altar.[72] Some priests were reported to have threatened voters with refusal of the Sacraments, or publication of their names on the door of the church if they voted Conservative.[73] The parish priest of Balbriggan in Cullen's own archdiocese allegedly told his congregation, in a reference to two election candidates, that 'he would neither christen, marry nor bury the children of those persons who voted for Hamilton or Taylor'.[74]

The press reported many examples of clergy using their position for political ends.[75] Today these press reports, and also some filed by the police, give the impression of being somewhat unrestrained, and the overall picture presented was probably exaggerated.[76] The exact extent and efficacy of clerical political agitation would be impossible to estimate.[77] Indeed, some of it was counter-productive, as there were voters who openly defied their priests, something that itself resulted in rioting.[78] There were also reports of clergy attempting to prevent scenes of violence, as well as intervening to secure the release of voters held against their will.[79]

Political involvement was not the exclusive preserve of local clerics in 1852. Diocesan bishops were not beyond using their political influence and frequently discussed political issues publicly and privately.[80] In this, as in many other areas of ecclesiastical life in Ireland, divisions between the bishops continued to concern Cullen and other Irish bishops as well.[81] The most politically prominent bishop through these years was John MacHale, archbishop of Tuam. By 1852 he was nominating candidates for election, encouraging clerical participation in politics and attending political dinners.[82] In his archdiocese, political ecclesiastical conferences calling for support for tenants' rights as well as ecclesiastical reforms were organised.[83] Such a prominent political profile on the part of some Irish prelates led, in early 1852, to appeals both by Pope Pius IX and Cullen for less political involvement and greater episcopal unity in Ireland.[84] These calls, however, went largely unheeded by bishops such as MacHale.[85]

It should be observed that, despite his protestations, Cullen himself was not totally aloof from politics. His opinions on various political matters were frequently sought by politicians, among others.[86] He was constantly urged to involve himself actively in the 1852 electoral campaign and his support for a variety of prospective candidates was canvassed directly or indirectly.[87] He obviously intervened in response to some of these requests.[88] On Wilberforce's suggestion, for example, he invited More O'Ferrall, who in 1851 had secured a by-election parliamentary seat for the Liberals in Longford, to stand for re-election in 1852.[89] After O'Ferrall declined to run, both the secretary of the Catholic Defence Association Wilberforce and the Carlow borough member of parliament John Sadlier urged Cullen to try to persuade the outgoing member to conduct the campaign in favour of the Independent Party candidate.[90]

Cullen was not averse therefore to exerting his influence. It is reported that he expressed to Cardinal Wiseman his view that George Bowyer would make an excellent member for Dundalk. He also favoured the nomination and return of Frederick Lucas for Meath, believing him to be 'most useful' if elected.[91] At the same time however, Cullen flatly refused to support the sitting Liberal member for Armagh borough, J.D. Rawdon, on the basis that Rawdon had voted for the Ecclesiastical Titles Bill.[92] To what extent Cullen's interventions were responsible for Lucas' success, and for Rawdon's failure, it is impossible to assess.

It should be emphasised that Cullen's involvement tended to take the form of endorsing a particular individual as a suitable candidate for election in a personal sense, and expecting him, if successful, to support the cause which Cullen espoused. Such involvement afforded scant regard for the realities of parliamentary discipline, which would of course require a member to vote for his party in parliament.

Whatever assistance he may have given privately to candidates in the general election, Cullen publicly adopted a very low profile during the 1852 campaign. He remained aloof and neither endorsed nor denounced the policy of Independent Opposition – another enigmatic performance. However, his public silence combined with his private utterances led supporters of the policy, such as Lucas, to believe that Cullen did, in fact, support the idea of an Independent Party in Westminister.[93]

As the date for polling drew near, the general election was the main talking point in the country.[94] Cullen's bland personal comment on the electoral campaign was simply: 'Bad work it is – nothing but villainy and intriguing.'[95] In an act of implicit recognition of the political role of the clergy, he postponed a diocesan retreat that had been planned for the time of the elections.[96] However, he was not prepared to tolerate priests preaching political homilies from the pulpit. In the early stages of the election campaign, a curate in Kilsaran, Father Campbell, speaking during Sunday Mass, denounced Captain T.A. Bellew, an election candidate who was unpopular with the Catholic Defence Association.[97] Cullen reacted immediately and removed the offending priest from the parish the following day, even before the Bellew family had time to complain.[98] Cullen 'laundered' his report of this incident to Rome by discreetly omitting any reference to his own political interventions in the campaign.[99] He did complain, however, that 'all the world is fighting about the elections ... In Meath the priests are going mad preaching furiously on politics. It is a bad business. I have written to Dr Cantwell to try and stop this by them'.[100] To this complaint Cantwell, the bishop of Meath, replied that he was dealing with any 'political exhibitions from the altar' which may have occurred, later claiming that such incidents were fewer than he had himself expected.[101]

Before the general election of 1852, Cullen wrote a pastoral letter on the elections, a copy of which he sent to Rome.[102] In this pastoral, which the Pope had translated into Italian by Irish papal chamberlain George Talbot, Cullen prayed that men who were resolved to justly defend Catholic religious liberty might be returned to Westminster.[103] At the same time he stressed the necessity for the just laws of the country to be respected. Catholics could have been forgiven for being confused with this approach seeing as Cullen himself was defying the Ecclesiastical Titles Act every time he signed his name as archbishop. Presumably he did so on the grounds that it was not a 'just' law. The pastoral went on to exhort Cullen's flock who were suffering injustice or violence to endure all with Christian patience and not to take the law into their own hands.[104]

Accounts of the political activities of Irish priests reached the British attaché, William Petre, who was living in Rome. There were no diplomatic relations between London and Rome but the British government did have in Petre, from 1844 until 1853, an unofficial paid attaché, to the legation in Florence with residence in Rome. As early as May 1852, Petre was proposing to his chief, Sir William Henry Lytton Earle Bulwer, envoy to Tuscany from 1852 until 1855, that representations should be made 'in a friendly spirit to his Holiness's Govt. [sic] of the hostility and violence of the Irish clergy, and of their coarse, wicked, and exciting language, accompanied by extracts from recent speeches, letters, addresses from the altar and pulpit'.[105]

It was not until after the strong reaction of many Irish Catholic clergy to the government's anti-Catholic proclamation of 15 June 1852 and the Stockport riots, that Petre's suggestion was taken up by the British government.[106] Petre was then instructed to seek a meeting with Vatican Cardinal Secretary of State, Giacomo Antonelli. In this interview on 20 July 1852, Petre conveyed the British government's strong objections to what he termed the abuse of 'spiritual influence over a most ignorant people to effect purely political objects'. He called for public reprobation by the Holy See. Antonelli, who Petre reckoned later did not know much about the real state of Ireland, promised to raise the issues with the Pope.[107]

Three days later, on 23 July 1852, Petre had another interview with Antonelli.[108] Petre reiterated Prime Minister Lord Derby's complaint 'against the priesthood using its spiritual influence to obtain objects subversive of society'. He went on to request that the Holy See 'control and discountenance proceedings, so inconsistent with a sacred profession'.[109]

Remarkably Petre was granted a private audience with Pope Pius IX on 26 July 1852. By this stage Petre was convinced that the authorities in Propaganda were 'greatly alarmed at affairs in Ireland'.[110] He maintained that during the audience he had to correct many 'strange and erroneous notions' that the Pope held. Among these was the feeling that the Tenant League was composed wholly of the poorer classes, and that only a few priests forgot the duties of their office and joined in the most unpardonable excesses. Petre also challenged the Pope's contention that the Irish hierarchy had endeavoured to inculcate obedience and moderation in the clergy.

The Pope substantiated his 'notions' by reading out to Petre extracts from the pastoral letter written by Cullen on the eve of the election. Petre compared the Pope's defence of the Irish to 'a monk defending, as best he could, acknowledged disorders and irregularities in his order, or to an Irish priest bewailing the miseries of oppressed Ireland, perfectly ignorant of the causes'.[111] Petre 'corrected' the Pope by showing him extracts from speeches and letters written by Cullen which demonstrated the Archbishop's support for the Tenant League on the one hand and his disloyalty to the Crown on the other.[112] The Pope apparently refused, much to Cullen's relief, to believe such accusations of disloyalty.[113] Pius IX did however promise Petre to write to the archbishops of Ireland and call again on the Irish bishops to 'exert themselves in defence of the laws, and to restrain the violence of those under them'.[114]

Three days after his meeting with Petre, Pope Pius IX wrote to Cullen on 29 July 1852, the day before the final electoral results in Ireland were returned. In his letter the Pontiff deplored the conduct of some priests while at the same time being careful to praise the conduct of Cullen himself during the election.[115]

Cullen's reaction to the letter was, by all accounts, mixed. While expressing relief to Smith that his 'friends' in Rome had not made much progress, he nonetheless requested that the Vice Rector of the Irish College would continue monitoring British activity in Rome.[116] He also made an effort to explain to Rome the reasons for electoral violence, which in one incident, at Sixmilebridge in County Clare, led to the death of six people.[117] He did not deny that some priests and bishops had gone to 'great extremes of violence at the elections'.[118] This he regretted especially because he firmly believed that they could have exercised 'the same influence quietly and without appearing before the public'.[119] While sympathising with the objectives of the priests in question, Cullen did not identify with these methods. However, priests were not responsible for all the electoral violence, the reports of which, Cullen asserted, had been greatly exaggerated by the press.[120] The system of public voting was a contributory factor in inciting violence, he claimed, and he pointed out that extreme Protestant and Orange elements had also been active in provoking Catholics.[121]

In fact Cullen's last point was valid, for some landlords were very active in the Conservative interest.[122] Obviously they were able to exert their influence over their tenants.[123] There were some 'pocket boroughs' where the landlords' influence was total.[124] Accusations were made that landlords were intimidating,[125] victimising,[126] persecuting,[127] bribing[128] and even kidnapping voters.[129]

The result of the July 1852 General Election was seen as a triumph for the supporters of an Independent Party. The new parliament was due to sit on 4 November 1852. Cullen's prediction that the actual number of Catholics returned would be increased proved to be accurate.[130] Irish constituencies returned forty-two Catholic members, some of whom Cullen viewed as religious and brave men.[131] Not only were many members of the Irish Brigade returned, but many Tenant League leaders were elected as well. In all, between Catholic and Protestant, some forty-eight Irish members out of a total of 105 had pledged themselves to remaining independent of the government unless substantial legislative reforms were guaranteed. It now seemed that a strong united Independent Irish Party, ready to achieve all kinds of improvements for the Irish people, had become a reality.

Meanwhile, in order, first, to reinforce the British government claims concerning the unacceptability of clerical political activity in Ireland, and second, to promote the possibility of a concordat between the Vatican and the British Crown, Envoy Bulwer travelled to Rome on an apparently unauthorised visit on 1 September 1852 that lasted until 25 October 1852.[132] Armed with various documents that aimed at blackening the Irish clergy, he also was received in audience by the Pope. This was despite the lack of full diplomatic relation between the Court of St James and the Holy See. Bulwer later met the

Vatican Secretary of State, Antonelli and the Secretary of Propaganda Fide, Barnabò.[133]

Cullen interpreted the mission of Bulwer as a manifestation of the British government's fears of the growing political strength of the Catholic Irish not only at home but also in the United States of America. There, Catholic Irish emigrants hostile to Britain were now becoming politically active.[134] It also demonstrated Derby's determination with respect to the new Irish party to 'break them up or gain them over'.[135] Cullen wrote to Rome warning against giving in to British pressure or accepting the British version of events in Ireland.[136]

Cullen now set out to justify the strong action taken by some of the clergy during the election. He reported on how he had seen for himself scenes of great poverty and distress among the people and how 'entire villages have been destroyed, the tenants have been driven out like animals from many districts'.[137] Then having quoted from official statistics showing the devastating effects of government policy on the Irish people, Cullen asserted that the conditions he was describing 'will suffice to explain the reason why some priests speak with violence against the government of this country. They see their parishes reduced to deserts, their people, their friends and their flocks exterminated, and therefore they cannot sometimes contain their indignation. The great landlords and the agents of the government would like it if nobody would say anything and that they could perpetuate their deeds without any opposition. It is however to be deplored that some ecclesiastics do not talk and act with more decorum'.[138] Cullen went on to warn the Prefect of Propaganda, Fransoni, against accepting as true whatever clerical political writings the British might present to him. Indeed he went on to imply that the British even encouraged such writings so as to provide them with justification for attacks on the Irish clergy.[139]

In fact, as the British envoy reported back to his foreign secretary, no direct concessions were made by the Vatican. His mission had only therefore very limited success. A revealing feature of Bulwer's report was Antonelli's hope that the Catholic clergy in Ireland would not assist in promoting the Tenant Right Bill that the new Irish party were expected to introduce into parliament, on the grounds that it would interfere with the rights of property.[140] Another surprise was the disclosure by Bulwer two years later that at the interview Antonelli had suggested that, in the absence of diplomatic relations between the Vatican and London, Cullen should be the recommended medium between Her Majesty's government and the Holy See. The Archbishop of Dublin he described as a man who 'will be disposed to lend the British government every assistance which he thinks not incompatible with his duties to the Church'.[141] Unsurprisingly, this suggestion never materialised.

Meanwhile, following the general election of July 1852, two conferences were convened in Dublin. The first, organised by the Tenant League, opened on 8 September 1852 to discuss the practicalities of independence in parliament.[142] The conference was also aimed at attracting uncommitted new members to the policy.[143] Forty-one out of the forty-eight members elected on an independence ticket attended, as well as many clerics, both Catholic and Presbyterian.[144] Approval was given for a motion, proposed by Keogh, that the elected members who had been returned on tenant right principles should hold themselves 'independent of and in opposition to' all governments which did not fully meet the demands of the Tenant League.[145] This decision was in line with the policy of the Tenant League from the beginning.

A second conference, with twenty-six Irish members in attendance, took place on 28 October 1852 and it dealt with religious issues.[146] It was held under the auspices not of the Catholic Defence Association but of a new organisation, entitled The Friends of Religious Freedom and Equality. This had been founded in early September under the supervision of an independent member for Mayo, George Henry Moore, but, unlike the Catholic Defence Association, it lacked a national framework.[147] At this second conference it was also decided that the elected members of parliament attending should be

asked to remain 'independent of and in opposition to' all
governments which did not proceed to repeal the Ecclesiastical
Titles Act and disestablish the Church of Ireland.[148] Thus these
twenty-six public representatives, many of whom had also
attended the September conference, were now also mandated,
on religion-related grounds, to follow a policy of Independent
Opposition in parliament. This decision went beyond the
original declarations of the Catholic Defence Association and
appeared to contemplate parliamentary deals to advance the
Association's interests on behalf of the Catholic religion and of
Catholics generally.

There emerged therefore two parallel sets of instructions to
members elected on the independent ticket. It should be noted
that these instructions not only bound the members to
parliamentary independence – to which they had already
committed themselves during the general election in any case
– but required them also to vote against the government in
certain situations. A policy of abstention in a House of
Commons vote was not deemed sufficient in such situations.
The policy, which came to be known as Independent
Opposition, had been advocated for some time by the Tenant
League, but it was only now being adopted by the Catholic
Defence Association as far as the opposition element was
concerned.

When the new parliament met on 4 November 1852, it
included forty-eight members who had, in one way or another,
pledged themselves to a policy of Independent Opposition until
the separate grievances of Irish tenants and of Roman Catholics
were redressed, or at least addressed. Forty-one of the
remaining fifty-seven Irish seats were Conservative, with fifteen
Liberal and one Peelite. The Conservatives had failed to obtain
an overall majority in the general election and this left the Irish
members holding the balance of power.[149] Temporary support
by them for the Derby Conservative administration was
maintained after difficult discussions where personal and well
as political differences came to the fore.[150] Such agonising was
predictable given the context of the obligations of Independent

Opposition on the one hand, and on the other the pressure to avoid the odium that could attach to taking a parliamentary stance, which might make government of the whole realm impossible.

Cullen apparently agreed with this strategy, even though his opinions as to which administration would be the more favourable to Catholic interests had oscillated considerably in the months following the general election. In October he came out against the Conservatives, fearing that they would introduce new anti-Catholic penal legislation.[151] By mid-November, however, he was writing to Rome cautiously noting the possible advisability of having the same Conservatives in government following party denials that any such legislation was contemplated.[152] This was a remarkable turn of events given the previous Irish Catholic attachment to the Liberal Party. From the perspective of the Catholic Church, the Conservatives represented the lesser of two evils. As Cullen affirmed: 'Probably it is well that the Tories are likely to remain in a little longer – the Whigs wd [sic] do us more harm.'[153] In retrospect, this was an example of unintentional irony as Cullen was accused several times of being a Whig bishop in subsequent months.

The question arises as to why members, who had bound themselves to a policy of Independent Opposition, decided to continue supporting the Derby administration. The immediate reason was their hope for Conservative support for a Land Bill they were proposing. When, however, the Conservative government failed to support the Land Bill, they decided to vote against the government's budget proposals.[154] With the defeat of the Finance Bill on 17 December 1852 by 305 votes to 286, Derby's Conservative government was forced to resign.[155]

Irish members had effectively flexed their political muscle.[156] Not only had they contributed to turning a government out but, in pursuance of the policy of Independent Opposition, they had signalled that no alternative government could be formed without concessions to them. Privately Cullen expressed strong approval for the action of the Irish members. He reported how they were 'doing their duty well', singling out for special praise Sergeant Shee, who had introduced the Party's Land Bill, and Frederick Lucas.[157] As negotiations concerning the formation of a new government commenced, public expectations ran high that Irish Catholic and tenant grievances would soon be rectified through parliamentary means. However, these expectations were not shared by Cullen. Either relying on intuition or knowledge, he predicted that the unanimity which had put the Conservatives out would be followed by the new party splitting into 'a thousand fractions' over whether to support the Liberals or give the Conservatives another chance.[158] Cruelly, time was to prove Cullen right.

Chapter Four

... DIVIDED WE FALL

ONTRARY TO CULLEN'S expectations, the new
government that was eventually formed was
neither Liberal nor Conservative, but a coalition.
It was led by the leader of the minority Peelites
group, Lord Aberdeen, with the participation of
the Liberals. The Peelites had in fact opposed the Ecclesiastical
Titles Bill and this was a factor that weighed with Irish
members. However, the new coalition would give no com-
mitment to either tenant legislation or to change any existing
religious legislation.[1] For the members of the Independent
Party, therefore, this meant that they were mandated to oppose
the new government.

As Independent Party members prepared to vote against the
proposed government, the cabinet offices were announced.
Many of the positions were filled by Peelites but former Liberal
Prime Minister Lord John Russell was given the post of Foreign
Secretary and Palmerston that of Home Secretary. To the horror
of many Independent Party members, and especially of their
supporters in Ireland, the list of junior positions included two
members of the Independent Party. William Keogh, member for
Athlone, was designated Solicitor General for Ireland, and John

Sadlier, who represented Carlow, was to be Lord of the Treasury. Public shock was widespread when it was learned that these two had reneged on their promises, accepting office without obtaining any guarantees of either land or religious reform.[2] A loud outcry ensued.[3] Lucas maintained afterwards that neither himself nor Cullen was really surprised at the defections.[4] This was a revealing commentary on political standards of the time and on informed attitudes to them. The defections certainly demonstrated how difficult it would prove to keep ambitious men from furthering their own personal careers in an age of extensive patronage. This was especially true given the fact that, while office holders were paid salaries, ordinary members of parliament were not.

At this stage, the disastrous consequences of the lack of political leadership in the years following the death of Daniel O'Connell were clearly evident. The defection of Sadlier and Keogh, and of a number of others who followed them later, would have far-reaching effects in later years. It showed up the weakness of a political grouping without firm rules of procedure, discipline, and a strong elected leader who would ensure that party rules were enforced. By early 1853, only twenty-six of the 'pledged' members could be held, with any degree of certainty, to be committed to the Independent Irish Party. The defection of Sadlier and Keogh was seen by many at the time, and since, as the reason for the eventual defeat of the party.[5] The episode remains in Irish folk memory as an example of perfidy and betrayal. It was evidence to nationalistically minded activists and to the people generally of the hollowness of the promises of parliamentarians. It was also a factor in the people's disillusionment with politicians and in their support for the Fenians later. However the subsequent crisis that struck the party in the form of the conflict between the advocates of Independent Opposition and the Church was to prove far more important in the shorter term.

In the welter of public criticism, it was a matter of some surprise that public episcopal reaction to the defection of Sadlier and Keogh was not all condemnatory. Indeed it was very much divided. The bishops of Elphin and of Kildare and Leighlin actually supported the defectors.[6] Sadlier and Keogh's actions were however condemned by some other members of the hierarchy.[7] The majority of bishops, Cullen included, decided to make no public statement one way or the other, despite the revulsion felt throughout the country at what was generally seen as a cynical self-seeking move.[8] Privately Cullen expressed his total disillusionment with both politics and politicians and predicted the imminent collapse of the Independent Party.[9]

Division in the episcopal reaction to the defection of Sadlier and Keogh was reflected in the ranks of the clergy and among other members of the Independent Party.[10] To some priests they were traitors against whom opposition should be organised.[11] However, the Aberdeen government had its clerical proponents. Some accepted it on the basis that its Peelite members had supported pro-Catholic legislation and had opposed the Ecclesiastical Titles Bill.[12] Others backed it simply on the basis that it was, realistically, the best government that could be hoped for in the circumstances.[13] This argument was put forward by other Irish members who had been elected on the Independent ticket after some of them had quietly followed Sadlier and Keogh and transferred to the government side of the House.[14] There was even some, though limited, support for the defectors from Tenant Right circles.[15] The defectors' position was rejected however by many clerics, and priests who had supported them during the election were now publicly challenging them for an explanation of their behaviour.[16]

Irish episcopal opinion was divided as to the ecclesiastical posture that should be adopted regarding the Aberdeen administration.[17] In view of his earlier vacillations, Cullen found it difficult to decide on his stance.[18] He was sceptical of the value of advocating the return to office of either the Conservatives or the Liberals on their own, regardless of whatever promises they might make prior to assuming office. He noted this to Kirby, writing: 'They will promise much but do nothing. Let them begin with deeds and then we shall believe their sincerity.'[19] Cullen eventually came to the conclusion that the most prudent policy was simply to remain silent, as he had done regarding the question of Sadlier and Keogh, and wait to see how political developments unfolded.[20]

While silent in public, Cullen was privately of the opinion that, given the reality of the Aberdeen government, one should demonstrate a willingness at least to work with it, and even praise it.[21] He was aware of politics being the art of the possible. The policy of Independent Opposition had been devised in the context of a single party administration. It did not envisage the new coalition situation and Cullen now permitted himself to argue that support for the government could, in the long run, be more advantageous than any other option.[22] Looking first at the area of greatest concern to him, that of religious reform, he reflected that, even if the author of the Ecclesiastical Titles Act was now a minister, the cabinet was led by a man who had opposed that Bill. In the context of the new parliament the alignment that had been formed could hold out good prospects for Catholics. However, some of the proposed moves of Aberdeen, such as a Royal Commission on Maynooth Seminary, were strongly opposed by Cullen.[23]

As for the important issue of the land, Cullen could reflect that, with Russell as Prime Minister and the Liberals in office on their own, no movement had been made in the past, nor had they promised any for the future. The Conservative Party, which was the most likely alternative government, represented the landlord class and so would be unlikely to pass any legislation in favour of tenant right. Weighing up the situation, Cullen came to the conclusion that if any legislation beneficial to Irish tenants was going to be passed, the most likely government to move it would be that led by Aberdeen.

Acting on his private beliefs, Cullen set about attempting to utilise whatever influence he had in an attempt to curb the Protestant influence and to obtain some measure of relief for Catholics. In adopting this stance, the Archbishop was acting honourably and responsibly and in the interest of his flock. His was an important lobby, entitled to be heard by the elected government of the day, whoever they were. To brand him as

Whig, or Tory, or whatever, for representing Catholic interests to the properly constituted government of the day was an unwarranted reflection on his integrity. Regrettably he was destined to suffer such unfair accusations.

The subsequent course of events was to justify Cullen's stance to some extent. It was decided not to re-appoint Blackburne, a fervent Protestant, to the post of Chancellor of Ireland. This decision was arrived at apparently because it was reckoned that 'the Brigade ... consider the reapptment [sic] of Blackburne a declaration of war.'[24] A similar decision on identical religious grounds was arrived at as regards the possible appointment of Sir Thomas Redington to the position of Under Secretary for Ireland.[25]

February 1853 found Cullen writing in a cautious, though positive, mode to Propaganda about the new government's attitude to religious affairs.[26] By March 1853, using as a mediator William Monsell, a convert Catholic member for Limerick County and now an office holder in the government, but one who had not pledged himself to Independent Opposition, Cullen began to enter into negotiations with the government. This he did with a fairly modest religious goal, attempting to secure an exemption for Roman Catholic children from reading Protestant bibles and catechisms in an army regimental school in Dublin.[27]

The law at the time required that if an elected member accepted government office he had to stand for re-election to parliament. In most cases this was a mere formality, but such could not be expected in cases like Sadlier and Keogh. There was public dismay when, on running for re-election both Sadlier and Keogh had the support of their local bishops.[28] Keogh was re-elected in Athlone with a sizeable majority after having publicly secured the support of the bishop of Elphin, George Browne.[29] On the other hand Sadlier, who received support from Francis Haly, bishop of Kildare and Leighlin, although not from most of his priests, failed in Carlow by a mere eight votes.[30] He was later to be returned in a stormy by-election in Sligo.[31]

Cullen's silence on the defections, coupled with the support for Sadlier and Keogh by the other two bishops involved, was interpreted by some as indicating episcopal approval of the actions of the two junior government office holders. This greatly disturbed Lucas. He had taken over the leadership of the Independent Party after the defections. His suspicions concerning the motivations for Cullen's silence grew. After all, whatever about the practical advantages of their action, the point at issue in the public mind was that Sadlier and Keogh had blatantly broken their promises and so could no longer be counted as honourable men. In vain Lucas tried to convince Cullen of the value and viability of the Irish Independent Party.[32]

A sceptical Cullen remained unconvinced.[33] In fact he now took to criticising both the voting pattern of some of the Irish Catholic members in the House of Commons and their lack of cohesion. These members would, he maintained to Kirby, 'be able to obtain everything if they were united'.[34] Lucas attempted to answer Cullen's objections to the voting behaviour of the remaining Independent Party members, but in vain.[35] Cullen continued to criticise Lucas' speeches, claiming that 'they do not do anything good but rather excite a great chaos'.[36] Apparently he repeatedly endeavoured to convince Lucas in the spring of 1853 that the government of Aberdeen was going to last for the foreseeable future.[37] Cullen proposed abandoning the policy of total Independent Opposition and working with the Aberdeen government instead. Being associated with the government, instead of remaining always in opposition, should place one in a position of some influence. This was to be demonstrated in the summer of 1853.

During a debate on the Established Church in Ireland on 31 May 1853, Lord John Russell, ostensibly speaking for the government, implied that no subject of the Crown could be both a loyal subject of the Queen and a practising Roman Catholic.[38] There was indignation at this insinuation and some Irish members, who had been supporting the government, denounced this speech.[39] One of them, Bland, member for King's County, even crossed over to the Opposition benches.[40]

The three Irish Catholic members, Monsell, Keogh and Sadlier, who were office holders in the government, decided on 2 June 1853 to resign over the speech.[41] This in turn had the effect of pressurising Russell himself into tendering his own resignation.[42] His offer was however promptly refused.[43] Nonetheless, because their support was critical to the survival of the government, Lord Aberdeen was also forced to appeal to the Irish office holders to withdraw their resignations.[44] He wrote to them stating that Russell's views were not those of the government and they retracted their resignations.[45] The Irish office holders had effectively flexed their political muscle. The method in which they had done so, by publicly humiliating Russell, the author of the Ecclesiastical Titles Bill, could be said to have strengthened the case for good relations with the government. Lucas, however, did not agree.

The disillusionment that grew up between Cullen and Lucas was mutual. As Cullen's criticism of Lucas increased, some supporters of the Independent Party for their part set about sowing seeds for the later depiction of Cullen as a government bishop or a Whig bishop.[46] Such rumours were strengthened in the summer of 1853 when the possibility of a royal visit to Ireland presented Cullen with a dilemma as to whether the bishops should attend and address the official functions laid on for the royal couple. When his initial hopes that the royal visit would not take place proved false, Cullen decided to consult various other members of the hierarchy on the question of an address to the Queen.[47] He himself advocated an episcopal presence at the royal functions on the ground that, as he put it: 'It's better not to leave the field totally open to the Protestants.'[48] Some of his episcopal colleagues however, most notably MacHale of Tuam and Slattery of Cashel, thought otherwise.[49] While the Irish bishops as a body did not in the end address the royal couple, Cullen's stance on this issue tended to give foundation to an impression that he was disillusioned with the Independent Opposition movement.[50] It also lent credence to the rumour that Cullen was, by the autumn of 1853, in reality 'thick with the government'.[51]

Cullen was aware of this image, which he claimed was propagated by 'Young Ireland' newspapers such as the *Nation* and the *Freeman's Journal*.[52] Moreover, the image did not reflect the reality. Cullen was never 'thick' with the government. Neither was he prepared however to pursue what he viewed as a sterile or suicidal policy of totally boycotting it.[53] In fact he was willing, as the need arose, to seek rights for Catholics, especially through Irish Catholic office holders.[54] This did not imply however that he was lining himself up against the Independent Party. Indeed on occasions, for example in early 1854, he was praising the parliamentary members of the party who were, as he viewed it, 'beginning to assume gt [sic] moderation'.[55] Nonetheless such positive comments were the exception rather than the norm. This meant that the perception of Cullen as a pro-English bishop, in sharp contrast to the contrary nationalistic image of Archbishop MacHale, continued to increase.[56] This, in turn, was to contribute greatly to Cullen's growing unpopularity, especially among nationalists in Ireland.[57]

In the light of such allegations, it is ironic to find that Cullen himself was reporting to Rome how he was persisting in the policy, which he had adopted from the time of his arrival in Ireland, of not co-operating actively with the government.[58] This is especially true bearing in mind his considered policy of taking advantage of the policies and programmes of the administration in the interests of Catholics. He had therefore, for example, refused to attend a public reception in early 1853 to welcome the new viceroy to Ireland.[59] In turning down the invitation, he made sure to emphasise the fact that officially, as archbishop by virtue of a pontifical decree which the British government refused to recognise, he could not even be legally invited.[60] This line should not disqualify him, however, from complaining to the authorities about his people's grievances and seeking to have them redressed. It would appear that a distinction was being made between public and private stances. A cynical commentator might observe that in this matter Cullen wanted to have it both ways!

Cullen now decided that it was time to turn his attention to an issue that was to cause enormous problems for hierarchy, priests and faithful, namely the involvement of the clergy in politics. Experience during and after the 1852 general election convinced him that some form of ecclesiastical action was necessary to control, but not to eliminate, political activity by the clergy. In March 1853 he decided to convoke a Provincial Synod to consider measures to regulate clerical political agitation.[61] The idea received an enthusiastic response.[62] In April Cullen got Kirby to request Propaganda Fide to issue an instruction concerning what should be discussed at the Synod.[63] Such instruction would of course give the impression that Rome, and not Cullen, had set the agenda. In this way Cullen was protecting himself from further accusations that any restrictions that might be formulated at the Synod were reflecting his personal wishes, which in reality they would be. His actions demonstrated a failure of leadership and suggested a lack of confidence on the part of the Archbishop who, of course, was also the Apostolic Delegate.

The Provincial Synod agreed by Rome met in early June 1853.[64] Following a provisional meeting on 1 June the Provincial Synod itself, attended by Cullen and his suffragan bishops, met from 2–7 June 1853.[65] The purpose of the Synod was to ensure that the decrees passed at previous episcopal meetings, coupled with a limited number of extra regulations, would be more fully and more diligently observed. These included prohibitions on secular business taking place in churches as laid down in the 1831 Provincial Synod of Dublin. In 1835, this legislation was applied to the whole country.[66] Then at the Synod of Thurles in 1850 denunciations of a personal nature, although without the attendant penalty of suspension being specifically invoked, had been outlawed. Additional guidelines for the proper role of clergy in politics were now included in the form of three propositions passed at the 1853 Provincial Synod.[67]

The first of these propositions outlawed the holding of political meetings within, but not outside, Roman Catholic churches as well as prohibiting all political discussions in the same.[68]

The second forbade priests, under pain of suspension, from denouncing individuals by name from the altar.[69]

The third was an exhortation to the members of the cloth to keep their mind on higher things and so to refuse to engage in discussing topics of a purely secular nature, or attending meetings that were solely political.[70]

Cullen was delighted at how that the Provincial Synod developed and made sure to forward to Rome a copy of the pastoral which was issued in its wake.[71] In his correspondence however, Cullen stressed how the regulations that had been passed merely reiterated or expanded already existing legislation which, in the light of recent events, it had been felt was worth repeating.[72] The emphasis was different in a letter to Kirby where he advised that: 'We have prohibited the priests from meddling publicly in political affairs.'[73] In reality an exhortation in this regard – rather than a prohibition – was as far as Cullen could persuade the bishops to go.[74] The juxtaposition of these two accounts of the same occasion shows Cullen's capacity for economising on candour when the occasion required it.

The authorities in Rome had been apprehensive at some reports of considerable clerical involvement in political affairs and at the prospect of the Church in Ireland becoming the theatre of politics. They therefore wholeheartedly supported the regulations passed at the Dublin Provincial Synod.[75] It was now up to the prelates of Dublin Province to enforce these decrees.

Rome had good reason to worry. While Cullen had been active in trying to regulate affairs in his province, clerical activity in politics was continuing elsewhere in the country. Sligo Borough was a particularly notorious case. There, intimidation by Elphin priests during the 1852 general election had seen the ousting of sitting member John Patrick Somers, a Catholic, by another Catholic, Charles Townley. A parliamentary enquiry declared the election of Townley invalid. Consequently a by-election in Sligo Borough was called for in July 1853.[76]

Somers's opponent in this by-election was John Sadlier. Both of these candidates were, at least nominally, Catholics.[77] Sadlier saw this by-election as his chance not only to get re-elected but also to regain the junior ministry post that had forced him to run previously unsuccessfully, in Carlow. The clergy played a prominent, and at times violent, role.[78] The Independent Party clerical supporters, including Vicar General Feeny, opposed the election of Sadlier, whom they viewed as a traitor.[79] Much to their fury, J.P. Browne, the bishop of Elphin, and also Dr T. Phillips, a prominent priest of the diocese, supported Sadlier.[80] In the event Sadlier was elected.[81] Clerical Independent Party supporters blamed the victory on Phillips and on the bishop, whom they claimed had been bribed.[82]

Cullen was furious at the divisive role played by the clergy in Sligo Borough, particularly as both candidates were Catholics. He viewed the whole incident as scandalous, disgraceful and discrediting, the negative effects of which would last locally for at least ten years.[83] The blame was laid by some, including Cullen, at the feet of priests who were in disagreement with their bishop.[84] Indeed the extent of political agitation in the West of Ireland in general, coupled with the width of the political rift between the bishop of Elphin and members of the clergy, was so great as to lead Cullen to fear some form of schism in Elphin and in the neighbouring dioceses.[85]

In the light of such clerical political agitation, Cullen came to the conclusion that bishops such as Browne should be recommended by Rome to lessen the desire of priests to involve themselves in political affairs.[86] At the same time he advocated that direct punitive action should be taken by Rome against politically active clerics.[87] He was consulted on a proposal by Browne that the mensal parish of Sligo be substituted for that of Roscommon and that Phillips be made parish priest of Sligo.[88] Cullen was later to dismiss charges of support for violent land agitation, levelled against the proposed parish priest of Sligo, as 'foul and malignant'.[89] Nonetheless he strongly opposed Phillips' promotion. He did so on the grounds that it would be said that promotion was a mark of Rome's approval of Phillips' conduct in the recent violent election campaign, which had resulted in success for the candidate supported by Phillips.[90] His advice was heeded in Rome. Phillips' doctorate of Divinity, despite episcopal protestations of his innocence, was temporarily suspended.[91] This must be seen as harsh treatment for one who had supported his bishop and who, moreover, had been on the winning side.

In addition to the bishop of Elphin's problems surrounding the election of Sadlier in Sligo Borough were the allegations made by Independent Party member for Sligo County, Richard Swift, that he had to pay some three thousand pounds 'election expenses' to the clergy.[92] Cullen's view was that not too much weight should be given to the accusations as Swift had exaggerated his case.[93] Cullen's view was that Swift had only himself to blame if any bribery had taken place.[94] The allegations of Swift, Cullen claimed, had received support from British clergy as well as some disaffected Elphin priests who, urged on by MacHale, were playing on Bishop Browne's weakness to further their own purposes.[95] As Cullen viewed it, Swift's allegations were really aimed at blackening Browne even further. This was done in an attempt to make Browne a scapegoat for the political agitation of the clergy of his diocese.[96] The allegations then centred on a conspiracy in which Browne, whose missionary zeal Cullen praised, ought not to be sacrificed.[97] The solution to the 'great mess', in which the bishop of Elphin found himself, was difficult for Cullen to decide.[98] He favoured the idea of an examination by a nominee of the Holy See and that Browne might be given a coadjutor who could 'fix things up'.[99] The correct solution however, as the Pope saw it, was for Browne to retire.[100]

Five months after the by-election in Sligo Borough and five months also after he had sent the conclusions of his Provincial Synod to Rome, Cullen was to suffer yet another disappointment in his campaign to moderate the activities of priests in politics. First, there was the by-election in Clonmel in December 1853 caused by the death of the sitting member, D.J. Lawless. This campaign gave rise yet again to incidents of clerical political agitation, such as the attacks made on the local bishop in Clonmel by priests from the Meath diocese.[101] It also yielded evidence that Cullen had completely lost all faith in Lucas, the Irish Independent Party and the Tenant League.[102]

Lucas was now promoting clerical political agitation and this led to an appeal by Cullen for Kirby to reproach Lucas for 'driving things to extremes'.[103] Lucas' continued support for politically minded priests, and also for politicians such as Gavan Duffy, led to allegations by Cullen that Lucas had fallen into the hands of Young Ireland revolutionaries.[104] Cullen persisted in viewing this organisation as seeking the destruction of the power of the priests, comparing it to the Mazzinians in Italy.[105] He concluded therefore that 'no decent priest can join with Lucas'.[106] Several clerics however thought otherwise.[107] Cullen was so exercised by one Father John Ryan, a curate in Cashel, who had participated actively in the election campaign that, even after demanding disciplinary action from archbishop of Cashel, Slattery, and bishop of Cork, Delaney, he reported Ryan to Rome himself.[108]

The next setback for Cullen's policies was in Louth. There the acceptance of a junior ministry by former Independent Party member C.S. Fortescue, a Protestant, meant that he had to stand for re-election. Disaffected supporters of the Independent Party unsuccessfully sponsored J.M. Cantwell, one of the founders of the Tenant League and a Catholic, as a candidate.[109] This February 1854 by-election campaign degenerated into a 'terrible schism between the clergy, and the people and the clergy'.[110] The fact that, in the run-up to the election, 'the priests divided themselves into two hostile camps and insulted one another most violently' drew down the ire of Cullen.[111]

Cullen's anger was heightened when he learned that Callan curate Father Thomas O'Shea, one of the founders of the Tenant League, had actually travelled to Louth to canvass support for Catholic and independent candidate Cantwell.[112] In doing so, O'Shea was not in his own diocese, nor even his own constituency. The activities of O'Shea also antagonised Dixon, archbishop of Armagh, who complained about O'Shea to Cullen.[113] O'Shea's Ordinary Edward Walsh, bishop of Ossory, had for some time viewed O'Shea as an agitator and a dangerous subject and was determined to 'muzzle' him.[114] He recalled O'Shea to his own diocese and threatened him with suspension.[115] Walshe's action was commonly believed to have been taken at Cullen's instigation.[116] This raised the question as to what jurisdiction bishops had over their own priests. Another issue now emerging was how to distinguish between the priest as a citizen with citizen's rights, and his status as a priest. This issue was destined to cause much upheaval in the Irish Church.

Chapter Five

THE PRIESTS-IN-POLITICS ISSUE

ULLEN NOW SET out to define for himself what was the permissible role for the priest in political affairs. In doing so, he could hardly have imagined that the issue would become so divisive that it would engage the attention of Pope Pius IX himself. He did not want to be seen as opposing all clerical political activity. Indeed, while he personally believed that 'the church ought to be a sacred and neutral spot, where all worldly things are to be forgotten', he recognised the historic roots of clerical political agitation.[1] He also realised the fact that in the Ireland of the mid-nineteenth century it was impossible to withdraw the clergy entirely from politics.[2] As he put it to Propaganda: 'In this Kingdom one cannot prohibit priests totally from taking part in elections but they could exercise their influence and cast their votes without so much uproar and taking part with such violence.'[3]

Even if he himself protested never to have dictated any political line to his clergy, he was prepared to recognise the political reality of Ireland where for the present, 'the priests must have some share in political movements'.[4] But in admitting that clerical political agitation was sometimes necessary Cullen

85

warned that when applied in every case it was ruinous.[5] Taking the by-election that returned Sadlier to parliament as his example, Cullen expressed his fears that 'where things would go as they went in Sligo the priests will be totally discredited and they will lose all of their authority even in spiritual affairs'.[6]

Cullen realised that clerics who were of one mind in spiritual affairs were often divided when it came to temporal political affairs.[7] The question therefore was not whether the priests should, or should not, involve themselves in political matters, but rather to what extent and in what manner they should be permitted to do so.[8] A moderate involvement in this field he viewed not only as legitimate but as possibly far more effective in the long run.[9]

As regards established political parties or popular political movements, Cullen made himself out to be neutral, believing that: 'It is as bad for the clergy to be under mob rule as government rule.'[10] The conduct of vociferous priests, such as those in Navan who preached on tenant right nearly every Sunday, and all those who got involved in what he viewed as purely political affairs, Cullen described as 'disgusting'.[11] They were, he believed, be they pro or contra the government, disgracing themselves by 'making examples of themselves in public and doing gt [sic] evil'.[12] Such activity not only scandalised the people, it divided priests among themselves and risked giving offence to Catholics who differed politically from the priest.[13] It also provided specific excuses 'to the enemies of religion to slander all priests and also to make attempts against ecclesiastical liberty'.[14]

The same could be said of the political activity of the clergy of Tuam who, Cullen reported, appeared to be more concerned about 'dogmatic definitions' in the *Tablet* on tenant right and income tax than on matters of religion.[15] As he put it to Kirby: 'They are becoming regular fidei definitores – instead of minding their moral theology at the conferences, they are engaged in drawing up political resolutions.'[16] Irish clerics, he believed, were doomed to fight until the priests learned to mind their own business in the first instance.[17] They needed to learn how working through the confessional and the pulpit was a far more effective and acceptable way for clerics to intervene in political affairs than 'brawling at public meetings and writing in newspapers'.[18] All that political agitation on the part of the clergy effectively did, claimed Cullen, was to destroy the power of the clergy while providing an excuse for the adversaries of the Catholic religion to intervene in the affairs of the Irish Church.[19] 'If such things cd [sic] be stopped,' he wrote to Rome early in 1854, 'it wd [sic] be a blessing.'[20]

Cullen put forward various proposals as to what measures should, or could, be taken to realise this blessing. Recognising that because of the tradition that had built up since the time of Daniel O'Connell, and the widespread nature of the issue involved, Cullen was prepared to accept that any effective solution would require a considerable length of time.[21] For a start however, he went on to devise a remarkable sequence of procedures for dealing with the most serious infractions of the rules. First, Rome should be informed of every infringement of the rules concerning clerical political agitation.[22] This should be followed by the issue being taken up by the Vatican.[23] Due to the complexity of the argument however, Cullen thought that the most obvious action, that of a direct and unambiguous condemnation by Rome of the offending clerics, would, for the present, be inopportune.[24] This opinion he held on the basis that such a measure would play into the hands of Lucas and the revolutionary Young Ireland movement.[25] They, he feared, would use information about any such disciplinary action to provide an opportunity whereby they might more easily excite a 'bad feeling about the Holy See'.[26]

What Cullen recommended was that the Holy See might view the problem of clerical involvement in Irish politics from a long-term perspective. If this were done, a progressive series of steps could thereby be recommended. First, as regards specific allegations of clerical abuses in the political sphere, he suggested that the authorities delegate some bishop to enquire into each case with a definite instruction 'to stop the practice of altar discussions on politics'.[27] Next, he visualised the reiteration of the existing ecclesiastical legislation with possibly some additions to what already existed on the statute books.[28] The longer-term solution he advocated was the appointment of good and zealous bishops.[29] Such prelates being neither servants of the government nor of the mob would occupy themselves with ecclesiastical duties.[30] They would also be given a mandate to make the priests attend to their ecclesiastical duties regarding the people.[31] In this way, Cullen believed, the problem of priests in politics would be tackled not only locally but systematically, and little by little all would be right.[32]

Cullen himself did not hesitate to complain to Rome if bishops were other than 'good', or were too favourable towards the British government.[33] Even possible candidates for bishoprics were criticised by Cullen simply because they were perceived to be on friendly terms with the government.[34] He criticised them also on the basis of their nomination possibly being supported by, or even just pleasing to, the government.[35] Cullen's attitude is of interest in view of the allegations that would be made later that he himself had been appointed to Armagh at the behest of the British government.

In tune with this sentiment, Cullen, clearly disillusioned with the political overtones of the Catholic Defence Association, especially during the 1852 general election, decided in November 1853 to dissolve the organisation and replace it with a non-political one.[36] This was easily done due to the fact that, since the Ecclesiastical Titles Act was never enforced in Ireland, the Association had faded from public light after the summer of 1852.[37] So little was heard of it in fact that, on 18 October 1852, a denial had to be issued in response to the rumour that the Association had already been dissolved.[38] Not only was the Association still in existence however, but it was also proving to be financially very draining.[39] On 29 November 1853, Cullen officially announced its dissolution and the substitution for it of the Institution of Saint Laurence, a purely religious organisation under Cullen's own control.[40]

The reason given for such a move was that 'the circumstances of the Church, especially in Ireland, demand a society which shall devote its undivided energies to the maintenance and defence of the Catholic religion, to the exclusion of politics, and in this respect differing from the Catholic Defence Association'.[41] Politicians were deliberately excluded from the new organisation, Kirby was informed, because: 'It is impossible to get people to unite in politics. Politicians are oftentimes very apt to trade on religion. Those who engaged in the Catholic Defence Association were endeavouring to do so and on that account we let it die out. We are not going to publish anything about the new society but to act quietly and to engage in no agitation.'[42] For the members of the Independent Party, especially Lucas, such an approach was to prove totally unacceptable.

By January 1854, the relationship between Cullen and Lucas had totally broken down. It was Lucas' belief that Cullen's real aim was not so much to curtail the involvement of priests in politics generally but rather specifically to restrict clerical participation in the affairs of the Tenant League and of the Independent Party.[43] On this basis then he alleged that Cullen was 'complaining of every patriotic priest to the Holy See'.[44] He also asserted, apparently unaware of the case of Phillips, that disciplinary action had been taken only against priests who had been active supporters of the Independent Party.[45] He claimed that, in contrast, those bishops who were politically partial to the Aberdeen administration received Cullen's support.[46] In this line of thinking Lucas was apparently encouraged by both Cantwell of Meath and MacHale of Tuam.[47] Indeed MacHale reportedly went further, as James Ignatius Taylor, a former president of Carlow College and by 1854 secretary of the Catholic University in Dublin, advised Cullen. Taylor informed Rome of how the Archbishop of Tuam was 'evidently encouraging – if not giving rise to the belief that Dr Cullen is a "Government Bishop". Not only that but that he is using all his influence at Rome in favour of the government.'[48]

Lucas contended that the Independent Party – and also the Tenant League – depended on clerical support for their continuation. Therefore any restriction, no matter how small, on clerical involvement in the Independent Party's affairs would have a devastating effect on the very survival, not to mention the growth, of the party. Support for this view came from Cardinal Wiseman and the clergy of Westminster but not from the clergy or Archbishop of Dublin.[49] This disappointed and angered Lucas, who was apparently, by nature, intolerant of any opinions that differed from his own.[50] He therefore embarked on a press campaign attacking all clerics who failed to support his politics, especially Cullen, referring to him in public as a 'Whig-bishop'.[51]

Such attacks had the effect of further alienating Cullen from Lucas. While Lucas was contending that Cullen had come under the influence of the Whigs, Cullen was maintaining that Lucas had fallen prey to men like Duffy and the Young Irelanders who now had Lucas in their hands.[52] Cullen took to privately describing Lucas, his former friend, as 'most violent and reckless in his proceedings'.[53] He held him responsible for turning the Meath curates in his constituency away from things spiritual. Lucas, he claimed, had succeeded in winning over the support of the London clergy not out of any understanding of the issues involved but simply by insulting the Irish hierarchy.[54] Indeed he went so far as to accuse Lucas, and not Sadlier and Keogh, of completely breaking up the 'Catholic party such as it was'.[55]

Publicly Cullen was more restrained. Although he declined to attend a dinner in honour of Lucas in January 1854, Cullen did write a letter which was read out at the function.[56] In this letter, whose short-term effect was to moderate Lucas somewhat, Cullen made a strong appeal for unity and the avoidance of dissension amongst all who sought to redress Catholic grievances.[57] At the same time Cullen made sure to flatter Lucas as far as he felt he possibly could. He underlined how, as regards Lucas and his fellow parliamentary Liberal representative for Meath, the 'votes and the services rendered by them in parliament to our religion and our country give these gentlemen a claim to the esteem and gratitude of all'.[58]

In voicing his more private feelings to Rome however, Cullen began to write in a somewhat unrestrained manner of how much he regretted that Lucas should have gone 'so wrong' and could not be kept from doing mischief.[59] His regret was heightened as he believed that Lucas was a politician who was both 'good and clever'.[60] The outcome of Lucas' conversion to the Young Irelanders was, Cullen claimed, that the leader of the Independent Party and his colleagues spent their time fighting among themselves.[61] Meanwhile, those priests who actively supported Lucas spent their day, claimed Cullen, 'doing much mischief, losing their time, neglecting the churches and their duties and involving themselves in quarrels'.[62] All this, lamented Cullen, resulted in no time being given over to defending 'the cause of catholicity'.[63]

This was not in reality true. Members of the Independent Party did bring up issues of Roman Catholic interest in the House of Commons. Lucas himself won the praise of Bishop Keane of Ross and Vicar General of Westminister Whitty, to whom he was related by marriage, when he secured the appointment of paid Catholic chaplains in the prisons in 1853.[64] The following year, 1854, he pressed hard for the government to appoint permanent Catholic chaplains in the armed forces.[65] Cullen's criticisms continued unabated however, and he repeatedly expressed his belief that those prelates and priests who involved themselves in politics were totally misguided, discrediting the Catholic Church, and doing great evil.[66]

In 1854 the government itself set about curbing clerical activity in the political field. They did this by getting parliament to pass the Corrupt Practices Act, under which an election would be declared null and void on proof that clerical intimidation had taken place.[67] At the same time Cullen became more and more convinced that a reiteration of existing, as well as perhaps some innovative, ecclesiastical legislation was required. To this end he sought an occasion whereby such a move might be made.

The opportunity came in Spring 1854 when Pope Pius IX himself called on the Irish hierarchy to unite and to take steps to establish a Catholic university.[68] This was a project in which Cullen was particularly interested. On the urgings of Cullen, the Pope used the occasion to call for agreement on any other matters that would promote the glory of God, the discipline and sanctity of the clergy and increase the piety and devotion of the faithful.[69] Realising that the time was now ripe for definitive steps to be taken on the issue of clerical political agitation, Cullen, who as Apostolic Delegate was to chair the National Synod now to be arranged, prayed that: 'God grant now that we may be able to settle matters.'[70]

While Cullen was trying to have the issues discussed on a broad, long-term basis, repeated occasional incidents of clerical participation in political affairs continued to obtrude. One such incident took place only three days prior to the National Synod. In this case, on 15 May 1854, at a public meeting to protest against parliamentary proposals to investigate Catholic convents in Britain and Ireland, an English Jesuit priest serving in Dublin, Henry Marshall, publicly reproached the Prince Consort. Cullen promptly suspended Marshall from preaching in the archdiocese for six months – repeating an action he had already taken in the case of two other politically active priests, Cahill and O'Connell. Although in this case Cullen lifted the suspension order after appeals by the Jesuits and a public apology, as well as a promise by Marshall to refrain from politics in the future, such recurring incidents served to strengthen Cullen's resolve to quell clerical enthusiasm for political pronouncements.[71]

The National Synod, with some twenty-seven bishops and procurators attending, and which Cullen found strenuous, took place in Dublin from 18 May to 21 May 1854.[72] Ostensibly called to deal with education, it discussed also the issue of clerical participation in political affairs. The proposals passed in this regard, notwithstanding Cullen's claims that they were not very stringent, failed to attain the support of some of the attendant prelates, most notably MacHale.[73] Majority support was obtained however for decrees prohibiting political speeches and personal invectives inside church buildings in times of elections.[74] Also outlawed were speeches by priests against one another in the political sphere, and even written controversies between priests on political matters. These decrees prohibited, or at least they attempted to prohibit, priests from publicly engaging in political debates amongst themselves inside, but not outside, church buildings.[75]

Not wishing to destroy the influence of priests entirely, the bishops did leave room for a certain degree of tolerance to clerics on occasions where genuine guidance was being given to the faithful. This was acceptable to Cullen who communicated to Rome his belief that: 'It is a very good thing to have convinced the bishops to show their disapproval of political priests.'[76] In fact the imprecision of the Synod's conclusions accommodated both those clerics who wished to obey the existing regulations strictly, and at the same time those who aimed, in a subtle manner, to influence local political affairs. The latter interpretation of the synodal decrees was permissible, in Cullen's eyes, in very limited situations.[77] Indeed Cullen went further, pointing out that 'the recommendations made to the clergy on political affairs are not very stringent, but here in this kingdom where the constitutional system prevails, it is necessary that, when one treats of the elections of Members of Parliament ... the priests take some part so that enemies of religion or persecutors of the poor are not chosen'.[78]

The definition of the doctrine of the Immaculate Conception on 8 December 1854 provided the opportunity, as Cullen saw it, for all the archbishops of Ireland, most especially MacHale, who represented for Cullen nothing other than a true cross, to be summoned to Rome without causing a stir.[79] Cullen welcomed the prospect of going to Rome personally for the discussions concerning the definition, and wrote of his relief at having to forego a regular Irish episcopal meeting arranged for the same time.[80] After such meetings with their acrimonious disputes, he was always ill, sometimes for several days.[81] He was not to know that his stay in Rome was to last many months longer than he had originally anticipated, as was the illness that was going to follow it.

Neither the mere passing of ecclesiastical decrees at the 1854 National Synod, nor civil acts of parliament in Westminister were to settle the argument as to how clerics could, or could not, involve themselves in political affairs. Events in the autumn of 1854 were to show that the issue was very much alive. In September 1854, a member for County Kilkenny, Sergeant William Shee, received a letter from Father Matthew Keefe, a constituent and one of the founders of the original Tenant League at Callan where he was a curate. In this letter Keefe complained of Shee's decision to split from his Independent Party colleagues. Shee proceeded to publish this letter along with his reply.[82] The bishop of Ossory viewed this as a breach of the Synod decrees and so promptly forbade Keefe from taking any further part in politics.[83]

The bishop's action was objected to by the members of the Independent Party who saw the move as interference with the legitimate political rights of the priest.[84] After all, it was asserted that no law, ecclesiastical or otherwise, could prohibit clerics as citizens from carrying on private correspondence with their member of parliament.[85] Coupled with that was the fact that it was Shee, and not Keefe, who had had the letter published. When later Keefe's fellow curate, Thomas O'Shea, condemned Shee's action in publishing Keefe's letter, he too was silenced.[86]

If other bishops followed the Ossory line, there was a danger of the Independent Party losing all its clerical support, as Lucas was only too well aware. Already the previous year, a curate in New Ross, Father Doyle, had been transferred by the bishop of Ferns to a rural parish after he had publicly differed politically from his parish priest.[87] Lucas' suspicions of a conspiracy among certain bishops, led by Cullen, aimed at putting an end to the Independent Party, had been aroused at the time. He therefore wrote to Cullen questioning the advisability of the bishop of Ferns' actions while stressing to Cullen, in vain, the importance of clerical support for the Independent Party.[88] Now Lucas' suspicions were confirmed with the disciplining of Keefe, coupled with rumours of further restrictions on clerical participation in political affairs. These, he claimed, were about to be promulgated in the official publication of the National Synod decrees of the previous May and also in the statutes of two of the Provincial Synods that had taken place, those of Armagh and Dublin.[89]

Lucas decided that a stand should be taken against any such episcopal policy and came to the conclusion that the most appropriate action would be a direct appeal to the Pope himself.[90] At a dramatic meeting of the Tenant League in Callan on 29 October 1854, Lucas, supported by Moore and Duffy, announced, to the shock of many people, that this step was to be taken.[91] A three tier operation was planned. First, the two curates of Callan, Fathers Keefe and O'Shea, would themselves appeal on their own case against the action of their bishop. Next, a deputation of clergy from all over Ireland would travel to Rome to present a memorial of protest. Third, the Irish Catholic members of parliament, represented by Lucas, and perhaps one other, would present their own memorial objecting to Cullen's approach from a political point of view.[92]

Cullen, having set out on 6 October 1854 from Dublin on the two-week journey to Rome, was not in Ireland when this latest turn of events took place.[93] It was late November by the time the bishop of Ossory informed him of the events surrounding O'Shea and Keefe.[94] For his part, Cullen's secretary in Dublin delayed relaying any 'rumours' of the proposed appeal to Rome until shortly before Lucas' departure for Rome.[95]

In the meantime however, the *Times* newspaper of London had covered the events of the Callan meeting of 29 October 1854.[96] Upon reading the press report a British agent in Rome, Richard Lyons, sought an interview with Vatican Secretary of State Antonelli. This was granted on 10 November 1854. The British official informed Antonelli of Lucas' proposed memorials and stated his belief that, if the Vatican afforded any encouragement to clerics wishing to engage in political agitation, the outcome would be to 'produce a crisis, concerning not only the relations between the Courts of Great Britain and of Rome, but also the position of the Roman Catholic body in the United Kingdom'.[97] He even hinted darkly the possibility of further anti-Catholic legislation if Rome were now 'to approve and encourage agitation and disaffection in Ireland'.[98] In response Antonelli expressed his doubts that any appeal would in fact be brought before the Holy See.

Antonelli then explained how the Vatican supported the stance adopted by Cullen in relation to clerical political agitation while regretting 'the language and conduct of many of the Irish clergy'.[99] Antonelli, Lyons reported, also stressed Rome's desire that the clergy should devote themselves to their spiritual duties. As to the Holy See giving a decision in favour of the Irish priests engaging in political agitation, that, he repeated, was 'absolutely impossible'.[100]

If Antonelli in Rome was expressing the Vatican's support for Cullen's attitude as regards priests in politics, the same could not be said of all in Ireland. The widely publicised campaign for sending clerical, as well as parliamentary, deputations armed with signed memorials began to gather momentum, assuming a highly personalised tone.[101] Cullen became the main focus of the attack.[102] Clerical support for the campaign was reportedly on the basis that many clerics harboured resentment against Cullen in the belief that their political influence was being eroded and their advice was no longer being respected in the election of bishops.[103]

Public meetings to rally support for the memorials were held at which the link between the continued political involvement of the clergy and the survival of the Independent Party was stressed.[104] Such gatherings provided opportunities for Cullen and many of his episcopal colleagues, perceived as being opposed to clerical political involvement, to be strongly condemned.[105] Allegations that Cullen had 'sold the pass' and that the man whom a British Prime Minister had once denounced as an 'Italian monk' was now no more than a 'Castle hack' or a Whig, were repeatedly made.[106] Therefore, it was asserted that, far from clerics being withdrawn from politics, it was prelates such as Cullen who should be forced to do so.[107] At the same time a 'Committee for the Memorial', composed of three diocesan priests, was formed with responsibility for drafting, circulating and financing the project.[108]

Meanwhile Lucas decided to travel out to Rome, arriving there on 6 December 1854.[109] Such a trip, which was also contrary to the wishes of MacHale, Cullen deemed to be highly imprudent.[110] Even though none of the proposed memorial documents were in his possession, Lucas immediately set to his task of arranging meetings in Rome with Irish prelates understood to be sympathetic to his cause, most notably MacHale of Tuam and Derry of Clonfert, and the English Cardinal Wiseman.[111]

Initially Lucas was encouraged by what he learnt from his preliminary round of negotiations in Rome. Wiseman, for example, reportedly related how he had already spoken to the Pope and that, while the Pontiff himself was favourable to Lucas' cause, it was the influences that surrounded the Holy Father that had to be confronted.[112] Gradually however, with no sign of the memorials that he was being pressurised by MacHale in particular to produce, Lucas' enthusiasm began to wane.[113] This was more especially so following the alienation of Barnabò from MacHale. This occurred during meetings in Propaganda aimed at settling various Irish ecclesiastical issues and were attended by all six Irish hierarchy members who were in Rome at this time.[114] These were Cullen of Dublin, Dixon of Armagh, MacHale of Tuam, Murphy of Ferns, Derry of Clonfert and McNally of Clogher. During one of these meetings, which convened under the chairmanship of Barnabò on 12 December 1854, MacHale had stated his contention that 'the Church was a democracy and not a monarchy'.[115] Such an ecclesiological stance effectively estranged Barnabò from MacHale and meant, Cullen maintained, that the Archbishop of Tuam was now 'not likely to be able to throw much influence into Lucas' cause'.[116]

With confidence growing then that his side of the argument would prevail when the delicate issue of Irish clerical participation in political affairs would be discussed, Cullen set about preparing a memorandum for the Pope.[117] As he saw the situation, it was of vital importance that Lucas and his supporters should be both privately and publicly chastised by Rome, so as to avoid any possibility of press or public misinterpretation of events.[118] To ensure that this would in fact happen, Cullen decided to delay his departure from Rome until the question had been satisfactorily, and publicly, resolved.[119]

Much to Lucas' and MacHale's annoyance, none of the promised documentation, the Clerical Memorial, the Independent Parliamentary Party Memorial, or the appeal of the Callan curates had reached Rome even by mid-January 1855.[120] At the same time Cullen, although initially unsuccessful, did finally manage to receive a version of the proposed clerical memorial.[121] From this 'absurd' document which was the fruit of a 'vile conspiracy', as he was later to describe it, Cullen was able to ascertain the exact form of the charges being pressed against him.[122]

The actual allegations that were made, mostly against Cullen, in both the clerical and parliamentary memorials were numerous and repetitious. In fact, in their final form the charges made in both memorials were so similar that the papal chamberlain, Talbot, who translated them into Italian, recommended that they be treated simultaneously. Much later Talbot also advised a study of a later statement. This was written over a period of several months by Lucas himself, prior to his early death on 22 October 1855 and submitted to the Vatican posthumously.[123] All tended to be long, loosely worded documents in which the political liberty of the Irish clergy was asserted while the all-absorbing and uncontrollable power of Cullen was condemned.[124]

Having outlined the recent physical and spiritual sufferings of Irish Catholics, the documents traced the formation, the underlying principle of independence and the electoral success of the Independent Party in 1852. They then went on to describe the betrayal by Sadlier and Keogh, and alleged that such action had the approval of several members of the Irish hierarchy. The most influential and important member was Archbishop Cullen. In lengthy and repeated direct attacks on Cullen, about whom a whole section was dedicated in Lucas' statement, it was claimed the Apostolic Delegate had switched political allegiance from the Independent Party to the British government.

In striking terms, the clerical memorial asserted that this political betrayal, coupled with the sense of omnipotence that Cullen had instilled, had a devastating effect on the Irish clergy.

It had resulted in 'a sense of insecurity and terror among those ecclesiastics who question the wisdom and prudence of his political views, and is further calculated to make the firmest adherents among the clergy to the Holy See the terrified serfs of the English government'.[125] This sense of terror, it was claimed, explained why many priests who might otherwise have signed the memorial had decided not to do so. The clerical document claimed that some priests who had supported Independent Party policies had been disciplined by their bishops. They had been penalised by being transferred to poorer parishes, not on the basis of their pastoral ability but simply on the grounds of their political profession. All the documents made a strong and direct appeal for Rome to reverse the ecclesiastical policy that had been adopted under Cullen as regards clerical involvement in Irish political affairs. The documents also called for action to ensure that such a change be carried out.[126]

One of the strongest opponents of the ideas laid out in the memorials was Dixon of Armagh. Once he received a draft copy of the clerical memorial he set about refuting the allegations on New Year's day, 1855. He later submitted a memorandum to the Vatican authorities.[127] In this document, Dixon asserted that the accusations of the memorialists, whom he regarded as Young Irelanders, against Cullen as being pro-English were totally false. Dixon declared that Cullen was absolutely and totally independent of the government in London, neither fearing nor serving it.[128]

While strongly supporting his colleague, Dixon declared that the government held no fear for the Archbishop of Dublin. His memorandum went on to note how 'there is another fear which he does not know at all, and that is the fear of what lukewarm priests may say and do in opposition to his efforts to carry out the wishes of the Holy See by giving new vigour to ecclesiastical discipline in Ireland'.[129]

Clearly conscious of the dilemma whereby priests held rights not only as clerics but also as citizens, Dixon admitted that priests could get involved in political agitation without compromising their priesthood. However, the priests involved in the memorial had gone too far when they denounced, as being only self-interested and mere agents of the government, their fellow clerics and the bishops who refused to get involved in political matters. Such priests, Dixon claimed, citing O'Shea of Callan as an example, were intolerant of the views of others, be they clerical or lay, and provoked scenes of violence by their words and actions. Since Cullen opposed them, they wanted to have him removed. Likewise they would oppose any other bishops who shared Cullen's views.[130]

In a remarkable initiative, the Pope decided to get personally involved. He discussed the matter of clerical political agitation in Ireland with the protagonists personally. In the course of an audience on 9 January 1855 Lucas elaborated on the policy of Independent Opposition and on the historical role of priests in Irish politics, asserting that the parliamentary policy that he was advocating was the only option left to the Irish people. He argued that in the Irish context all political questions, with the exception of tenant right, were religious ones as well.[131]

In response, the Pontiff reportedly urged a middle-of-the-road policy, recommending that the British government be neither unduly pampered nor treated with hostility. On the topic of priests in politics, the Pope called for clerical moderation. The Pope then reportedly praised Lucas' actions as a member of parliament but was less enthusiastic concerning his role as editor of the *Tablet*.[132] Nonetheless, Lucas left the audience apparently content enough with the way that it had gone.[133]

Two days later, on 11 January 1855, the Pope interviewed Cullen and informed him of his intention to address all the Irish bishops, then in Rome, on the following week before their departure for Ireland.[134] Cullen apparently stressed to the Pope the importance of resolving once and for all the question of episcopal disunity in Ireland. He underlined the necessity of dictating the stance to be adopted as regards clerical political involvement. He reiterated the urgency of this latter point later to the Prefect of Propaganda Fide, warning Cardinal Fransoni of the consequences of not immediately tackling the question decisively. 'I have convinced myself,' Cullen wrote on 17 January 1855, 'that if our business is not settled while we are in Rome, we will have more violence, and greater dissensions, than have ever been seen in the past in Ireland.'[135]

The following day, 18 January 1855, the Pope chaired a special meeting of cardinals in Propaganda Fide.[136] Following discussion of a report on the whole memorial issue which Cullen had submitted, the cardinals decided to seek clarification of the other side of the argument from MacHale.[137] In the meantime the Irish hierarchical contingent were invited to remain on in Rome for the time being.

Chapter Six

DISUNITY PERSISTS

O
N LEARNING THAT no decisive outcome was forthcoming from the cardinals' meeting with the Pope on 18 January 1855, Cullen immediately set about preparing yet another report on 20 January 1855 concerning political affairs in Ireland.[1] In this he directly attacked both the memorialists and the individual priest who had brought the clerical document to Rome, the curate of Doon, Father O'Dwyer.[2]

Pope Pius IX did not want to deny any of Cullen's claims but was anxious that an amicable solution be found to the whole issue. To this end, he apparently suggested that Barnabò and Talbot make arrangements for a face-to-face meeting between Lucas and Cullen.[3] This meeting took place in the Irish College on 24 January 1855 with Kirby and Talbot also in attendance.[4] Just prior to this date, Lucas' spirits were lifted and his hand considerably strengthened by the arrival in Rome of the parliamentary memorial.[5] Six members of the Independent Party were found to have signed it.[6]

Armed now with documentary evidence to substantiate his argument, Lucas met with Cullen for two-and-a-half hours. At the meeting, a hostile Cullen, as the parliamentary leader of the Independent Party later put it, 'furnished proof that he wished to get rid of me personally, to break up our party, to discourage opposition to the Government, and to put down public opinion in Ireland'.[7] Cullen requested Lucas to put his grievances in writing and insisted that, failing a directive to the contrary by the Holy See, he would adhere to the political policy that he had adopted, which was based on the belief 'that the first duty of every Catholic was to support the Government unless it attacked the Church'.[8] This was a clear shift away from the 'non co-operation with the Government' stance of Cullen's first year in Armagh.

Speaking with 'passion and ... vehemence', Cullen outlined what he viewed as the duties of a priest and the limited circumstances in which a priest could involve himself in political affairs.[9] 'The business of a priest,' he is reported as stating, 'is to confine himself to his spiritual duties and in the intervals of these to confine himself to reading and meditation; that if the Church was attacked in such a way that all Catholics must agree upon it, then they should come out, but whenever two Catholics might differ then they should take no part lest by doing so they should get into collision with one part of their flock. With regard to elections they ought to tell the people their duty to avoid bribery and perjury and to vote for a candidate favourable to the Church. If a candidate avowedly hostile to the Church showed himself they might warn the people against him, though with caution; but if two candidates presented themselves, both not professing sentiments hostile to the Church, their business was not to interfere between them but to stick to general principles.'[10]

Such a stance Lucas utterly rejected on the grounds that the practical meaning of such a course, he explained to Cullen, was to hand over the constituency in a very short time to the enemies of the Church and the people.[11] In fact, Lucas' admission of this was a slight on himself as it was an admission of his own inability to organise a viable lay political alternative to the priests' electioneering role.

Before the talks concluded, Cullen launched a strong attack on the membership of the Independent Party. He claimed that enemies of the Church and of the Irish people were to be found within its ranks, most evidently in the presence of Charles Gavan Duffy, whom Cullen described as 'a wicked man'.[12] This being one of 'so many things that were untrue,' according to Lucas, that he professed to having the 'greatest possible objection' to having any further personal communication with Cullen of any kind.[13]

For all of this, Lucas drew great heart from the defensive stance that Cullen had adopted at the meeting. Writing to Duffy three days after the encounter, he optimistically stated his belief that there was 'now ... every ground for hope'.[14] Cullen, he claimed, had spoken like a man on the defensive, 'who has his back to the wall, who feels that his all is at stake'.[15] While this was certainly an exaggeration of Cullen's position, it is noteworthy that, whereas Lucas departed two days later, 29 January 1855, for a two-week holiday in the south of Italy, Cullen remained on in Rome continuing in his efforts to persuade the Vatican to accept his side of the argument.

On 27 January 1855, Fransoni, who held that simply because certain people had joined a government was no reason in itself for opposing it, wrote to MacHale looking for his version of events.[16] Two days later, MacHale replied recalling how the Irish clergy had previously engaged in political activity, but all the while obeying the Holy See. He denied that any serious dissension existed among the Irish clergy over the issue of clerical participation in politics. The clerics of his archdiocese for example, he asserted, were united in their approach to political agitation. MacHale, who also called for greater deliberation among the members of the Irish hierarchy, apparently had no difficulty in applying the various directives, including the May 1854 Synod decrees.[17] However, liberal interpretations of the rules tolerated practices which might be condemned by Cullen.

MacHale had an audience with the Pope and presented him with a copy of his reply to Fransoni. During it the Pope appeared to have granted MacHale permission to depart shortly for Tuam. Following this audience, it was recommended that if MacHale's reply was acceptable to Propaganda, it should be published and circulated in Ireland.[18]

If the reply was acceptable to Propaganda, or the Pope, it certainly was not to Cullen. The Archbishop of Dublin realised that, had the letter been published, MacHale's standing in Ireland would be strengthened as he would be popularly seen to have obtained the approval of the Holy See for his active political stance. Upon learning of the latest turn in events, and before MacHale might have a chance to leave Rome, Cullen decided to write directly to the Pope. In this letter dated 2 February 1855 Cullen launched a strong attack on MacHale.[19] He pleaded that MacHale be requested to write down his grievances and that the differences between them be resolved definitively while they were both in Rome. He pointed out that divisions still existed on the Irish ecclesiastical bench and cited examples for the Pope. This was true, he claimed, despite the desire of the majority of bishops and clergy of Ireland for unity. He went on to attack Duffy who had signed the parliament-arians' memorial, and Cullen then alleged that massive intimidation had been employed in Tuam to get priests there to sign the clerical memorial.[20]

At the Pope's request, Talbot gave a copy of Cullen's letter of 2 February 1855 to MacHale and requested a written response.[21] MacHale duly replied on 5 February 1855, dismissing Cullen's allegations as false and unfounded and claimed that they were aimed only at detaining MacHale longer in Rome. On the same day the Pope met with all the Irish bishops still in Rome.[22] At this meeting MacHale was instructed to write to his suffragan bishops directing them to publish the statutes of the May 1854 Synod as soon as they got a copy of them. Having complied with this requirement, as well as the one to attend a dinner at the Irish College that evening as a sign of reconciliation, MacHale, accompanied by Derry of Clonfert and MacNally of Clogher, left Rome on 6 February 1855.[23]

Cullen however did not return home. Instead, having been given a copy of MacHale's letter to the Pope of 5 February 1855, he set about systematically refuting the claims in it. He also reiterated his assertions concerning the political activities of the Archbishop of Tuam.[24] By 10 February 1855, when Lucas returned to Rome from his holiday, he was to discover not only that MacHale had left, but that the long awaited clerical memorial had still not arrived. Pessimism replaced the optimism Lucas had felt only a fortnight earlier. He reported to Duffy how MacHale's hasty departure from Rome had greatly annoyed Pope Pius IX and resulted in the *'gain de cause'*, according to Barnabò, being handed over to Cullen's side of the argument.[25]

Various factors had combined to account for the delay in forwarding the clerical memorial to Rome. For a start, it was badly organised. In the space of just over a week, three separate circulars were sent to various priests thought to be sympathetic to the goals of the organising committee.[26] To each prospective signatory, freedom was granted to change the wording if he wished before signing.[27] After the draft was circulated however, it came to light that although many clerics might possibly have been sympathetic to its objects, they were not prepared to sign a document attacking the Apostolic Delegate to Ireland.[28] Furthermore, many prominent clerics, despite rumours to the contrary, refused to support the memorial. Also, some Irish prelates, such as Cantwell of Meath, whose support was originally presumed, came out publicly against it.[29] The end result was that only 140 clerics, of whom fifty-eight were parish priests, from eleven dioceses, actually signed it.[30] Those who did sign it were popularly known as either supporters of Independent Opposition or clerics who feared the erosion of their accustomed liberties as a result of ecclesiastical legislation being advocated by Cullen.[31]

Not only had the memorialists difficulty in persuading priests to sign the document, but problems also presented themselves when it came to deciding who was to travel to Rome to present it. Those initially selected 'pleaded ill-health, urgent local duties, and other excuses'.[32] Finally Father Dwyer, a curate from Doon, Co. Limerick, was persuaded to take the memorial to the ecclesiastical authorities in Rome.[33] The initial refusal of

Archbishop Slattery of Cashel, later retracted following clerical protests, to allow Dwyer the necessary permission to make the journey caused further delay.[34] A similar decision by Bishop Edward Walsh to refuse Keefe permission to travel to Rome effectively delayed the Callan curate's appeal against his Ordinary.[35] Unlike Slattery, however, the bishop of Ossory did not reverse his decision despite Keefe's appeals and various protests by Lucas to Barnabò on the matter.[36]

By late January 1855 it was becoming obvious that earlier accounts reaching Rome to the effect that many priests, including some from Dublin, had signed the memorial were inaccurate.[37] Public opinion had begun to row in strongly behind Cullen as an ever-growing number of people viewed Lucas' trip to Rome as an act of sheer arrogance.[38] Now it became evident that attempts to persuade priests to sign the clerical memorial had decidedly failed. Indeed, some of those who had originally signed it reportedly regretted having done so. Many priests of Derry diocese, it was alleged, were so 'disgusted' with Lucas's trip to Rome that they were cancelling their subscriptions to the *Tablet* in protest. Prelates, such as Feeny of Killala, who had previously supported Independent Opposition, were openly critical of Lucas.[39]

These delays regarding the appeals to Rome, coupled with news of the lack of general support for the memorial campaign, served to increase confidence amongst supporters of Cullen that triumph would, in the end, be for him 'complete'.[40] Conversely they helped to demoralise Lucas who, on 13 February 1855, three days after his return to Rome from the south of Italy, had another meeting with Barnabò. During this the Secretary of Propaganda informed Lucas that the May 1854 synodal decrees, which he admitted only discouraged rather than banned clerical attendance at political meetings, had been approved. While such an assessment demonstrated that the Vatican was prepared to be more liberal in their interpretation of the decrees than Cullen, the parliamentary leader of the Independent Party refused to be appeased. Even such a definition of the decrees meant, Lucas claimed, that the Holy

See had put the interests of the Church and the poor of Ireland into the hands of the British government.[41]

Having failed to come to any compromise position on the issue of clerical participation in politics, Barnabò recommended that Lucas meet once again with Pope Pius IX. An audience was duly arranged and took place on 26 February 1855.[42] The Pontiff explained to Lucas that he was thinking about issuing a Brief on the whole state of the Church in Ireland and reportedly agreed to read personally whatever Lucas might write and send to him on the topic.[43] Armed with this promise, Lucas commenced composing a 'Statement' in which he outlined the grievances of the Independent Party and its supporters concerning the stance adopted by Cullen on clerical participation in political affairs. In the process of drafting his 'Statement,' which was to run to over 75,000 words, Lucas fell seriously ill and in May 1855 decided to return to England, hoping to finish it there.[44]

Even though he failed to have the Vatican's policy concerning clerical political agitation radically altered, the mission of Lucas was not fruitless. His intercession appears to have been influential in the alteration made in Rome to a decree passed at the Armagh Provincial Synod in 1854 and confirmed at a later meeting in Propaganda Fide on 12 March 1855. As drafted, this decree stated that priests in the Province of Armagh might only speak in public on political affairs after having first obtained permission from the parish priest of the parish in which they wanted to speak.[45] The effect of this would have been that if the parish priest opposed the policy of Independent Opposition, then he could forbid any pro-Independent Party priests from speaking in his parish on political matters. The draft decree had been endorsed by Propaganda following a strong appeal by Kirby. He, echoing Cullen's views, had stressed the importance of the Vatican approving 'the wise rulings ... adopted to impede the clergy from involving themselves with too much chaos and publicity in political matters'.[46] Lucas, however, had campaigned strongly against this decree.[47] In the end, despite its approval by Propaganda, it was omitted from the statutes when they were ratified by Pope Pius IX on 18 March 1855.[48] Whether this was in response to Lucas' appeals or not, the archives do not reveal. In the meantime, back home in Ireland, the campaign being waged by supporters of the Independent Party against Cullen continued. The result was that by April 1855 Cullen had become, as his secretary pointed out to him, nothing other than the 'origo malorum' in the eyes of all supporters of the Independent Party.[49] The publication in the Nation, on 14 April 1855, of a leaked and inaccurate copy of the May 1854 synodal decrees served only to confirm this image.[50] This suggested that a near total withdrawal of clerics from politics was about to be promulgated by Rome. The campaign against Cullen was so strong that, as his secretary warned him: 'Nothing is left untried in order to damage and injure your Grace's character, and your further stay in Rome throws a doubt upon the satisfactory outcome of your mission.'[51]

Despite the recommendations of his private secretary for him to return immediately to Dublin, Cullen decided to stay on in Rome until after the next sitting of the special Congregation of the Cardinals of Propaganda. Such a meeting was due to deal with Irish issues. In preparation for this and after having heard from all the major parties involved in the argument, Barnabò set in train the preparation of a comprehensive assessment of issues relating to the Irish Church.[52] These included ecclesiastical discipline and the conduct of the Irish clergy in political disputes.[53]

Aware that such an account was being compiled, Cullen consigned to the authorities, with characteristic thoroughness, various lengthy reports of his own. They described the situation of the Irish Church as he saw it. He also sent translations of many letters and newspaper extracts which he had received since his arrival in Rome.[54]

In these reports Cullen dealt with various issues including the dispute between the bishop of Ossory and the Callan curates, the memorials, the enlistment by clerics of lay support for their cause, the reasons why he was being attacked, and the benefits of the recent disciplinary ecclesiastical legislation. He also painted a very anti-Roman portrait of both Lucas and Duffy.

He depicted them as promoting a religious revolution in attempting to undermine the bishops' authority to discipline their priests.[55]

It was when dealing with the reasons why so many divisions existed in the body of the Irish clergy that Cullen addressed the question of what was, and what was not, the correct attitude for priests to adopt in relation to politics. In an apparent departure from an earlier doctrinal position, Cullen now maintained that there was no issue of principle at stake, but only one of the correct means to be adopted. In Cullen's view, the question was how the Irish clergy could best continue to preserve the influence and power that they possessed and to which, in a Catholic constitutional country, they were entitled. In advocating the policy that had been adopted by the Irish hierarchy in recent years, Cullen made out that he did not want to jeopardise the existing political influence of the Irish clergy. To permit the Irish clergy to join in an agitation that only had slight hope of succeeding, he saw as dangerous. It was something which could result in the deepening of already existing divisions. The majority of Irish prelates agreed with this stance, insisted Cullen, claiming that Irish bishops like MacHale who espoused a different outlook were in a minority.

'I have never dictated,' Cullen declared in a response to Lucas, 'and I do not believe it is my duty to dictate, a line in politics to the clergy. I have forcibly urged all of them to be ready to defend the faith and to promote charity, but otherwise I have never asked what they thought in purely political matters. The only thing on which I insisted was that all would fulfill their duties and would behave with that prudence and moderation which befits ecclesiastics.'[56]

By now Cullen was fully convinced of the practical futility of pursuing an uncompromising form of independent opposition in a parliament where the number of members supporting it was insignificant in relation to the support the government enjoyed in the House of Commons. Cullen answered the allegations made against him by Lucas in a systematic manner. To Lucas' accusations, for example, that Cullen had once supported the policy of Independent Opposition only to abandon it later, the Archbishop of Dublin now asserted, somewhat enigmatically, that he had been consistent at all times.[57]

Significantly, he denied that he had ever committed himself to Independent Opposition, a policy he now described as 'suicidal'.[58] It was true, Cullen admitted, that 'everyone would certainly desire that we should have in office and especially in Parliament, men of an independent spirit, who without binding themselves to any faction, would try to promote the interests of the country and of religion. But the heads of the Tenant League do not content themselves with such independence: they demand absolutely that their partisans place themselves in direct opposition to every Government that does not promise to remove all the burdens that weigh on the Catholics of Ireland; and since no Government in the present period of excitement against the Catholics, could with the least hope of a happy result, put its hand to such a work, so those gentlemen are obliged to perpetual hostility to every possible Government ... If all Catholics were to unite in adopting such principles I am persuaded that the English Government in self defence would have to expel them from parliament and begin to renew the penal laws'.[59] It is remarkable that, holding such strong views on Independent Opposition, Cullen delayed so long in expressing them. Whatever his real sentiments, the fact is that he left Lucas, and no doubt very many others, to believe that he had, in fact, agreed with the strategy of independent opposition.

Whether this was an accurate interpretation of the policy of Independent Opposition is open to question. Cullen was now, however, fairly highlighting the inherent weakness in a policy based on the presumption that either of the main English political parties would be prepared to grant the wishes of the Independent Party in order to secure or retain office. He went on to outline the possibility that, faced with a militant Irish Party in the House of Commons, the English parties might in fact unite against it, to the disadvantage of the mass of the Irish people.[60]

Cullen expanded still further on this statement two weeks later when, on 8 May 1855, he reiterated what Dixon of Armagh had written on New Year's Day. 'I held myself,' stated Cullen, 'aloof from the Government without attacking it, and have never wished to make myself the vassal of any popular party.'[61] As regards his silence towards Sadlier and Keogh at the time of the formation of the Aberdeen government he noted that: 'I did not take any part whatsoever in this controversy because I saw that, if on the one hand Mr Keogh were to be blamed for having broken his promise, on the other hand it could be claimed in his favour, that the promise was rash, and injurious, and therefore not binding.'[62] As in the case of Independent Opposition, Cullen's attitude to the defections of Sadlier and Keogh was also unclear at the critical time.

Cullen emphasised yet again how he himself saw nothing wrong in the principle of Catholics accepting political office. On the contrary in fact: 'I must say however that it seems to me an incalculable advantage to have Catholics in judicial positions in Ireland.'[63] Such was his opinion on the grounds that he expected that Catholics in influential positions would do something to protect the poor. However, Cullen saw Protestant officials often employing their influence in persecuting and perverting the Catholic poor. 'Hence,' he declared, referring to three specific Irish Catholic office holders in the government, 'I could not but feel great pleasure, when I saw promoted Messrs Monsell, Fitzgerald, Ball and some other good Catholics to important positions. These had never promised to follow the policy of continual opposition.'[64] What Cullen did not mention, however, was the fact that it was not for accepting office that Sadlier and Keogh had been so strongly criticised and vilified, but for violating their solemn promise not to do so.

The letters and newspaper articles that Cullen submitted alongside his own reports substantiated his arguments. They included a copy of correspondence with an Irish junior office holder in the Aberdeen government and member of parliament for Limerick County, William Monsell.[65] In such correspondence, which Cullen made sure to have shown to Pope Pius IX and

Cardinal Antonelli, Monsell expounded the possible advantages of Catholics assuming public offices and supporting the government.[66] At the same time he stressed the sterility of a policy of total independence, strongly criticising Lucas for attacking prelates and exciting the flock to go against their pastors. While praising Prime Minister Aberdeen, claiming that he was favourable to the Catholic Church, Monsell denounced both Lucas and Lord Derby as enemies of Catholicism.[67] These views found a ready audience in Antonelli, who was convinced that 'the system of so-called Independent Opposition would be likely to produce the evils occasioned in Italy by Mazzini's principles'.[68] It was surely remarkable to find these various insights emerging in 1855, three years after the relevant events.

Having discussed his side of the argument at length, Cullen waited in Rome until after the 14 June 1855 Congregation of Propaganda Fide meeting, which was called to discuss Irish affairs. At this session, the cardinals were asked specifically to consider: first, whether the decrees regulating the political activity of the clergy, passed at the 1854 Irish National Synod, were sufficient to eliminate the abuses that Cullen asserted had accompanied such deportment, or whether there should be some stricter recommendation made to the clergy; second, whether, given the complaints that Cullen had already made against MacHale, the observations made to MacHale about his conduct with regard to the clerical memorial were really sufficient; third, whether a reply should be given to Father Keefe concerning the action of his bishop in his regard; fourth, whether or not the Holy See should pronounce on the whole issue of the Tenant League and the policy of Independent Opposition.[69]

The meeting in fact gave its support for the opinions and stand of Cullen.[70] As regards the first issue, for example, it was decided that the decrees concerning priests in politics were sufficient for the moment. On the second issue, it was decided that a reprimanding letter should be sent to MacHale. This letter would invite him to unite with his brother bishops in implementing the various synodal decrees. It would point out that, however good his intentions, he was harming religion as a result of his actions. As regards the third issue of the Keefe case, it was decided to write a reply directly to him, instructing him to obey his bishop. Finally, with regard to the issues of tenant right and the policy of Independent Opposition it was decided that the Holy See would make no public declaration.[71]

Five days after this meeting, on 19 June 1855, Cullen had a final meeting with the Pope.[72] Two days later again he left Rome for Dublin. In total, Cullen had spent eight months away from his See of Dublin. During this time the Pope and senior cardinals had dedicated a considerable proportion of their time and energies on disputes relating to the Church in Ireland. It must be noted that the Irish bishops, with a remarkable degree of stubbornness and a regrettable lack of consideration for the Pope and his senior advisors, refused to settle the disputes among themselves. It had been a difficult time for Cullen but, although physically sick and reportedly 'in very bad spirits', the endorsement by the Holy See of his stance as regards clerical political involvement had meant that he had apparently won the day.[73] However, back in Ireland he was to discover that apparent victories in Rome did not mean that the fight was over at home.

If Cullen's position had been vindicated in Rome, the same could not be said of the situation at home. Shortly before his return, an attempt was made to blacken his image further in the eyes of nationalistically minded Irishmen. There was an attempt to imply that his original nomination to Armagh in December 1849 had been made at the behest of the British government. It was made by the Independent Party member for Sligo County, Swift, who Cullen was careful to point out was English by birth.[74] Swift tabled a parliamentary question requesting the government to make available to parliament the correspondence between the government and the Holy See over the nomination of a new archbishop of Armagh in 1849. Such correspondence, which the government immediately denied it had ever been engaged in, would have taken place, alleged Swift, in order to obtain in Rome for the vacant diocese a nominee of the English government.[75]

Cullen reported news of this latest move to Rome, having first heard of it as he journeyed back, continually ill, to Ireland.[76] His interpretation of the affair was that, although it was Swift who made the allegations, he had in reality done so on the suggestion of Lucas.[77] Popular support for Swift, with whom Lucas was sharing a house at the time, came from English Catholics. Such Catholics, Cullen bitterly remarked, were recompensing the Irish for the help given to them in 1851 by being ready to sacrifice Ireland.[78] Support also came from those in Rome such as the Papal Chamberlain Talbot who, Cullen claimed, did not know Ireland but who sought to serve it by promoting the interests of England.[79]

The wider object of Swift's allegations, as far as Cullen saw it, was to suggest that not only his but all Irish episcopal appointments lay in the hands of the English government.[80] The question had been tabled in parliament, he alleged, in the hope of discrediting both Cullen and the Roman authorities all the more.[81] It had also been made to suggest that his detractors' campaign was meeting with success.[82] There were indeed signs in Ireland of a belief in the rumour about British government influence in episcopal appointments. Cullen attributed this belief to those who were placing 'the Catholic Church under the feet of the English Parliament'.[83]

Upon his return to Dublin, Cullen received numerous sentiments of support for his stance in Rome.[84] Nonetheless a certain anti-Roman, anti-episcopal feeling in the country was also detected by him.[85] He decided that the way to counteract this was to get authority to publish the decisions taken in Rome on 14 June 1855.[86] Such a step could not be taken however until after Propaganda had officially communicated their decisions. He had waited in Rome until after this meeting but had left without obtaining the official documentation. Aware of the importance of early publication, he expressed his anxiety, even while en route home, that it should reach him as soon as possible.[87] He was obliged to repeat his appeal several times over the coming weeks.[88] Such repetition resulted in his patience wearing thin.[89] By the end of August 1855 he felt obliged to take the most unusual step of appealing directly to the Pope.[90]

This move was prompted both by the tardiness of Propaganda in complying with his request and by Lucas' insistence that his point of view had been successful in Rome.[91] Indeed, Lucas not only persisted in spreading the rumour that Cullen had been appointed to Armagh at the behest of the British government, but he also repeatedly asserted that he himself had presented a memorial to the Holy Father, despite statements to the contrary.[92] While initially such claims were treated with great scepticism by most people, their constant repetition meant that they began to 'disturb the souls of the people'.[93] With the passage of time and with no evidence to the contrary being produced, people gradually began to doubt Cullen's version of what happened in Rome.[94] After several weeks without the contra evidence from Rome, Cullen reported that the anti-episcopal agitation, directed principally against himself, was being revived.[95]

Responsibility for the revival of this agitation had to be borne partly by Lucas, Duffy and Swift and their supporters in the Independent Party.[96] However, Cullen also blamed the lack of support on some of his episcopal colleagues, notably MacHale of Tuam, Derry of Clonfert and Cantwell of Meath. Propaganda were also much at fault, he claimed, by failing to forward the necessary decrees.[97] As a result of it all, Cullen saw himself in an impossible position, like Mohammed caught between the earth and the sky without knowing to which he belonged.[98]

In this situation, depressed and dejected by the strain of events and feeling isolated and inadequately supported at home and from Rome, Cullen professed himself unprepared to continue in office.[99] Close to despair he admitted this to Kirby writing: 'I am so oppressed from work that I would truly like to leave this country. I do not know if the Holy Father would accept my resignation. I believe that it is impossible to put things in order — a lot of opposition and a lot of bitterness of every type.'[100] With the continued delay in Rome concerning the forwarding of the oft requested documentation, his depression was destined to deepen as time went on.[101]

The long awaited decrees from Rome finally arrived in Dublin on 3 September 1855.[102] This, coupled with the belief that the Independent Irish Party was disintegrating, caused Cullen's spirits to revive.[103]

The Independent Party was now suffering badly. The latter months of 1855 were to witness the loss, one through emigration and the other through death, of the party's two principal exponents, Duffy and Lucas. There were defectors, and by the time George Henry Moore took over the leadership, membership had fallen to twelve. Duffy resigned his seat in parliament, sold the *Nation*, and emigrated to Australia, where he was also to lead a political career.[104] His departure was greeted with thinly disguised enthusiasm by Cullen.[105] While Duffy gave as his reason that 'those who ought to guide and bless the people's cause have hopelessly deserted it', Cullen did not believe him.[106] He claimed that disillusionment with Irish politics and shortage of funds had more to do with it.[107] Much to Cullen's delight, a last attempt by Duffy to 'relight the fire' of Independent Opposition by launching a final attack on Cullen at a planned farewell function never came off due to lack of support.[108]

Lucas was in poor circumstances and in July 1855 was reported to be living in poverty.[109] Upon his return to England he was found to be very ill, suffering from a severe heart condition.[110] Cullen predicted that the condition would probably force Lucas to resign his parliamentary seat in preference to losing it at the next election.[111] In deference to Lucas' state of health, the bishop of Ossory decided not to publish the decision of Rome concerning 'the cause of which Lucas talks'.[112] Nonetheless, much to Cullen's annoyance, Lucas continued to maintain publicly that his mission to Rome had been successful.[113] The illness of Lucas, Cullen's former friend who had 'let himself be led so much astray', proved to be fatal.[114] He died on 22 October 1855 at the age of forty-three.[115]

The high praise Lucas won for himself in death from Cardinal Wiseman and from the press was understandably not echoed in the reflections of Cullen.[116] Lucas' 'Statement', with which he had occupied himself in the months prior to his death, was submitted posthumously to Rome. Attempts by Cullen to obtain a copy of it appear to have been futile.[117]

The New Ross seat vacated by Duffy remained unfilled until April 1856. However the Meath by-election for a successor to Lucas went ahead in December 1855. It took place against a backdrop of continuing tension between Cullen and MacHale as well as an apparent total disillusionment by Cullen with the political parties.[118] Of political movements, Cullen wrote how: 'The men at their head cd [sic] not be trusted and it is better not to encourage them. Many of the violent demagogues just make a noise to sell themselves. They are no support or credit to religion.'[119]

Cullen's view was not shared, however, by many of the clergy of Meath who, notwithstanding the various Synod regulations, continued to play a prominent part in the by-election.[120] The Liberal candidate was selected at a meeting attended solely by clerics and not, as had been the norm up to then, by a mixture of priests and people.[121] One possible explanation was that the priests were trying to avoid breaking the rules laid down at the National Synod. So what was meant by Cullen to remove priests from politics was now interpreted, rather cynically, in a manner which granted them even greater political power.

According to Cullen, clerics in Meath became so heavily involved in preaching politics during the by-election that they failed to prepare celebrations for the feast of the Immaculate Conception.[122] He graphically recounted to Rome how in some churches political homilies were repeatedly given. During these, furious invectives were thrown even at candidates whom Cullen deemed to be good Catholics.[123] Cullen wrote of how one priest got so excited in his political harangue that he omitted to recite the closing prayers of the Mass.[124] Meanwhile, in the grounds of churches political meetings took place under clerical chairmanship.[125]

In Navan, two candidates and their clerical supporters were involved in a public brawl.[126] Cullen decried the great scandal caused.[127] He denounced five priests to Rome by name for their political behaviour during the by-election: O'Reilly (PP, Navan), O'Ferrell (CC, Navan), Kearney (PP, Naughville), Mullen (PP, Sonna) and Langan (PP, Ardcath). He also complained both to and of the bishop of Meath, Cantwell, for his failure to implement the synodal decrees.[128] Cullen insisted that Rome act to ensure the implementation of the 1854 decrees for: 'It wd [sic] be better to make no regulations than to have them trampled on with impunity.'[129] He feared that the Meath example would serve as a precedent for priests in other dioceses in future elections.[130] Once again he made sure to reiterate his belief that 'priests could exercise very much more influence without scandalising the faithful on the altars'.[131] Showing that it took Cullen's complaints seriously, the Holy See responded by banning certain named priests from attending meetings of the Tenant League without the permission of the local Ordinary in whose diocese the meeting might take place.[132] Bishop of Meath Cantwell promised to ensure that any abuses would not recur.[133] The publication of the ban, however, led to renewed attacks in the *Nation* on Cullen, allegedly at the instigation of the same Meath priests.[134]

During this time, Cullen's state of health was creating cause for concern. On 26 October 1855, one of Cullen's secretaries, Murray, wrote to Kirby reporting that Cullen's health was failing and that the doctor had ordered him to take some rest.[135] His sickness, claimed a worried Cullen over a month later to Kirby, derived from a lack of sleep and palpitations of the heart.[136] In fact, Cullen himself thought at this time that he was, as he put it later to Kirby, 'near making my exit', adding: 'Had I gone I wd [sic] not have been a great loss.'[137] Still obviously very unwell in December and suffering from a trembling in his left hand, Cullen was warned by his doctor that he was likely to be struck down by paralysis if he did not rest.[138] A month's complete rest was ordered, but after only two weeks Cullen returned to work, maintaining that he was quite well again.[139]

But Cullen had not recovered, and as 1856 dawned, he found himself still sick, suffering from rheumatism, anxiety and lack of sleep.[140] He had no scruples about where blame for his condition lay. It was all caused, he said, by the 'foolish nonsense in retarding all their decisions in Rome'.[141] Be that true or not, by April 1856 Cullen's depression had deepened and his health had deteriorated to such an extent that he decided to write to Kirby how 'probably I will not stand the work and anxiety very long – but a long responsibility is not to be desired and if it were possible I wd [sic] be glad to get off the burden from my shoulders at the present moment and retire to some peaceable retreat, the world forgetting, of the world forgotten but I suppose that is all moonshine'.[142]

THE TIRING BUSINESS
OF POLITICS

THERE WERE THREE by-elections in March and April 1856, in none of which the Independent Party fielded a candidate. The vacancies were in New Ross following the departure of Duffy to Australia, in Sligo following the death by suicide of Sadlier, and in Athlone following the nomination of Keogh to the judicial bench.[1] Both Sadlier and Keogh had been members for constituencies in the diocese of Elphin. Following a special appeal by the bishop of Elphin to the clergy to desist from over-involvement in political affairs, there was no repetition of the clashes of previous elections.[2] In fact all these by-elections were noteworthy by the very absence of political manoeuvring by the clergy.[3]

During the New Ross campaign there was active debate within the clergy as to whether Tenant League supporters, in the absence of their own Independent Party nominee, should be urged to vote Conservative or Liberal. In the end it was decided, as it was in the other two by-elections, that Independent Party supporters should be urged to support the Opposition and vote Conservative.[4] To what extent this had a bearing on the defeat of all three Liberal candidates is not clear.[5] The campaign also proved that it was possible for elections to be carried out without rows among priests. A factor in this, of course, was the absence of Independent Party candidates.

The Independent Party supporters rejoiced in the three by-election victories for the Conservatives. Cullen was less joyous, however.[6] While favourably disposed to the Whigs, he had by this time become disenchanted with them due to their attitude to Italian unification. He therefore promised to 'try and rouse the Catholic feeling against them'.[7] In reality, he was now in a dilemma, seeing how staunchly Protestant the Conservatives were. As he informed Kirby: 'We are placed ... between Scylla and Charybdis. If we put out the Liberals we fall into the hands of the Orangemen equally hostile to the Pope and ready to devour us alive. It is hard to know what to do.'[8]

For Cullen it was indeed an unhappy experience to be forced so often to choose on the basis of the balance of disadvantage. Such choices always left him open to heavy criticism. Where he was attacked most severely was in the pages of what he termed the 'Young Ireland' press,[9] whose editors, Cullen claimed, were intent on stirring up agitation against both himself and the Catholic Church.[10] Other than refuse to read such newspapers as the *Tablet* and complain, there was little Cullen could do to counteract the constant printed assaults on him personally, in contrast to the repeated portrayal of MacHale as the 'real friend of Ireland's rights and people'.[11]

Cullen did act, however, when criticised publicly by members of the clergy. A case in point was exemplified by the Limerick Archdeacon and parish priest of Rathkeale, Fitzgerald. On 9 March 1856, in an after-Mass speech, Fitzgerald strongly denounced Cullen for his stance on the issue of priests in politics, calling on the people to unite in the face of all landlords by joining the Tenant League.[12] The incident was immediately reported to Rome, whereupon the authorities in Propaganda wrote a letter of complaint to the bishop of Limerick, John Ryan. This resulted in Fitzgerald issuing a full apology, which Ryan sent to Cullen and which he in turn forwarded to Rome.[13] Thus, this major infraction of the regulations governing clerical pronouncements on political affairs in 1856 was effectively quashed.

With the death of Lucas and the emigration of Duffy, Cullen reported to Rome that: 'The great party of which Lucas and Duffy were the heads has melted like snow – there is no trace of it now worth mentioning.'[14] This was not strictly correct. Throughout 1856, twelve members for Irish constituencies still professed adherence to the principle of parliamentary independence. The mantle of leadership now fell on George Henry Moore, a politician whom Cullen viewed as 'wickedly violent'.[15] Support for the party continued to come from Tenant League meetings, often attended by clerics, where Cullen came under sustained attack.[16] Moore himself continually criticised Cullen for attempting to withdraw priests from politics, especially after Rome's rejection of the appeal of Keefe against his bishop became public.[17]

Even after the Conservative victories in the 1856 by-elections, backing for the Independent Party continued to come from Irish and also from several English clerics. The possibility of the party making a recovery at the next general election was widely entertained by these clerics. This rumour led to the Autumn 1856 visit to Ireland by Vicar General of Westminster Archdiocese, Whitty, being seriously construed by Cullen as an attempt to revive the fortunes of the party.[18] The Crimean War was engaging the attention of parliament and press at this time and there was little time for Irish politics.

The December 1855 Meath by-election had disturbed not only Cullen but also the government. The latter were now rumoured to be considering further Corrupt Practices legislation.[19] Cullen's initial response to this was to inscribe the topic of clerical involvement in civil politics in the draft agenda at the next episcopal meeting, due to take place in the summer of 1856.[20]

By this time the situation had changed. Priests had assumed a low profile during the three 1856 by-elections, and Fitzgerald of Rathkeale had been effectively disciplined for his political pronouncements. Cullen therefore altered his approach. He now decided on a mere reiteration of existing decrees on clerical involvement in political affairs. He duly received authority from Rome to commence the synod and set about organising the agenda.[21] The bishops assembled on 20 June 1856 and met for five sessions, each for six hours.[22] No new legislation was put before them on the issue of priests in politics but the topic was discussed in the context of an enquiry from Propaganda as to how the statutes of Thurles 1850 and Dublin 1854 were being observed.[23] At the end Cullen expressed his satisfaction that the meeting had done a lot to unite the bishops – with the predictable exceptions of MacHale of Tuam and Derry of Clonfert.[24]

By this time, Cullen's physical and psychological condition was giving serious cause for concern. One of his secretaries, Lyons, wrote to Kirby in late June 1856 about how his arch-bishop was so ill that it was his belief that 'another week such as the past would send him to his grave ... he had no sleep for the past eight or nine nights. There was one night in which he did not literally close an eye ... we will send the Archbishop ... to the country to spend at least a week there ... He has suffered much for the good of the Church in Ireland. God spare him to do more than he has already done'.[25] By September Cullen, having taken time for a short break and retreat during the summer, professed to be 'very well' again.[26] Such assertions, however, were disputed by another of Cullen's secretaries, Murray, who wrote to Kirby to say that Cullen was working too hard and saying that he was going to oblige him 'to go off from us for some time. Some relaxation is absolutely necessary for him'.[27] Such a diagnosis was not accepted by Cullen, who refused to grant himself any extended period of rest. Instead, although prepared only to admit that he had not been 'very well', he launched into a busy pastoral schedule in his archdiocese.[28] It was to be the following year before his attention was seriously drawn once again to the thorny issue of clerical involvement in political matters. Cullen's fight to withdraw priests from involving themselves directly in the politics of political parties in general, and the Independent Party in particular, was not over yet.

If 1856 was a relatively quiet year for Cullen with respect to the issue of priests in politics, the general election of 1857 shattered that peace. Now the ghosts of both political priests and political bishops reappeared. Ecclesiastical political manoeuvring, secular and religious, was once again destined to dominate Cullen's thoughts in this year. As early as January 1857, he was reporting how one of the potential nominees for the bishopric of Cloyne, William Keane, had proclaimed at a meeting of Cloyne priests, to thunderous applause, that if he became the next bishop, 'he would not be the man to curtail the just rights of the priests; that politics and religion were synonymous in Ireland ... Such is the water in which we navigate,' commented Cullen wryly.[29] That the waters were in such a state, he decried to Rome, was due in large measure to the influence and example of the Archbishop of Tuam. MacHale's example, decried Cullen, was nothing other than 'a great stimulus to political priests to continue in their careers'.[30]

Whatever about the accuracy or otherwise of such a statement, there is no denying the prominent presence of priests in elections throughout 1857. By early February, Cullen was forced to admit that, despite the legislative measures that had been taken in Ireland, clerics were still involving themselves in political affairs. As he put it: 'It is however very true that some bishops and priests, instead of thinking of the true interests of religion, love rather to occupy themselves with some political projects which will never be realised and which serve only to give to the people vain hopes, promising them to obtain from Parliament a permanent right to the lands on which they are the tenants – something that the Parliament will never consent to.'[31] Within the space of two weeks, as if it was needed, Cullen was able to furnish further proof of the truth of this assertion to Rome.

When the Liberal John O'Connell resigned his parliamentary seat to accept the government post of clerk of the Crown and hanaper in Ireland, a by-election was called in Clonmel, a borough in County Tipperary. A storm of controversy erupted during the by-election surrounding the controversial canvassing

127

of Father Michael Burke, parish priest of Saints Peter and Paul's Church, in his attempts to secure the seat for Liberal candidate John Bagwell. This priest's action, wrote Cullen in reporting the incident to Kirby, 'shows how absurd it is for priests to dabble too much in politics. There will be another election in Tipperary where there will be also a great deal of trouble'.[32]

The other Tipperary by-election was that caused by the expulsion from the House of Commons of John Sadlier's brother James. One candidate, Waldron, whom Cullen described as 'a very good Catholic ... most religious and charitable', was strongly opposed by The O'Donoghue, 'a Young Ireland candidate'.[33] Both candidates claimed to support a policy of parliamentary independence.[34] The campaign, in which many of the younger priests reportedly involved themselves, provided what Cullen described as a 'sad illustration of the evil results of priestly interference'.[35]

While Cullen had now reverted to his anti-Conservative stance, he expressed the surprising view that it would be better to be badly represented in parliament by Tory members than to see the clergy destroy their own influence and disgrace the Church by engaging in unseemly political haranguing.[36] O'Donoghue's electoral victory, in which the influence of the younger clergy was a major factor, was for Moore, the leader of the Independent Party, 'a turning point of Irish history'.[37] For Cullen, on the other hand, it was to be the source of what he called 'a great deal of mischief'.[38]

It was during this Tipperary by-election that the government was brought down, on 3 March 1857, over the issue of foreign policy in China. This resulted in a general election. While expressing the hope that in his own archdiocese the clergy would 'act with moderation helping to have good subjects elected without however compromising the dignity of their state', he predicted that this would not be the case for the rest of the country.[39] On the basis of this belief, Cullen wrote to Rome of his belief that what he termed the 'usual turmoils' would take place and of his fears that 'some priest will take a too violent part in the general movement'.[40]

Paul Cullen during his time as Archbishop of Armagh

Dilecto Filio Nostro Paulo S. R. E.
Presbytero Cardinali Cullen nuncupato
ex concessione et dispensatione Aplica
Archiepiscopo Dublinensi. ~

PIUS PP. IX.

Dilecte Fili Noster Salutem et Apostolicam
Benedictionem. Ad personam tuam, quam
divina clementia magnis illustravit gratiarum
donis paternae dirigentes considerationis in=
tuitum, et attente prospicientes, quod Tu Ro=
manam Ecclesiam, cujus honorabile mem_
brum existis, tuorum honoras plenius magni=
tudine meritorum dignum, quin potius debi=
tum

Decree of Pope Pius IX granting special faculties to Cardinal Cullen

Propaganda Fide College, Rome

Top: The Synod of Thurles, 1850

Bottom: Reception at Clonliffe, 20 August 1866, after Cullen had returned to Ireland as Cardinal.
Left to right: Very Rev. James Maher, uncle and godfather to Paul Cardinal Cullen; Dr Michal Verdon,
nephew; Rev. P.J. Nowlan; Very Rev. Thomas Canon Power, president of Clonliffe; Monsignor Andrew
O'Connell, Dean; Cardinal Cullen; Ven. Archdeacon Laurence Dunne; Very Rev. J. Canon Redmond;
Mons P.F. Moran, nephew; Rev. Joseph McSwiggan

Pope Pius IX

THE FIERY CROSS!

TOP, LEFT TO RIGHT: Archbishop John MacHale; Father Patrick Lavelle
BOTTOM: Cartoon depiction from *Punch* magazine, 30 August 1851, of an all-conquering Cullen
bestriding Ireland from north to south; Charles Gavan Duffy in 1846

The episcopal crest of Paul Cardinal Cullen

Statue of Paul Cardinal Cullen, Pro-Cathedral, Dublin

At the time of the 1852 general election, Liberal Party candidates were selected at meetings attended by both members of the clergy and laity. However, following the 1854 Synod, some electoral candidates began to be selected at meetings attended by members of the clergy alone. As already noted, this happened in Meath in 1855.[41] The procedure was adopted in many constituencies in 1857, for example Mayo, Sligo and Westmeath.[42] In County Clare, the decision taken at a general meeting to propose a candidate was later overturned at a meeting attended only by priests.[43] In County Wexford the system was only slightly different in so far as the candidate was selected at a meeting of clergy and afterwards ratified at a wider meeting.[44]

The clergy probably adopted this approach on the basis that, as had happened at a by-election in Meath some time previously, they were trying to avoid breaking the letter of the new rules laid down at the National Synod. The clergy were now forbidden to dissent on political matters in front of members of the laity, so what was more appropriate than to exclude the laity, even if this meant more, not less, political influence for the priests?

This interpretation of the letter, rather than the spirit of the regulations, was challenged by many members of the hierarchy, some of whom tried hard to apply the regulations controlling clerical participation in politics. Other bishops however did not.[45] In Carlow for example, Bishop James Walshe instructed the priests not to get involved in the campaign.[46] This contrasted with the actions of Bishop of Elphin Browne, who personally chaired the meeting that nominated the Liberal candidates.[47] In Athlone, the bishop personally nominated Liberal candidate Ennis.[48] George Henry Moore, the leader of the Independent Party, was sponsored by Archbishop MacHale, despite the fact that Moore, a strong critic of Cullen, was none too popular with some priests.[49] In fact, it was a priest of the Archdiocese of Tuam who nominated Moore's election rival, Ouseley Higgins![50]

Not only were clerics prominent in the selection and nomination of various candidates in 1857, but the electoral campaign itself was to be marked by various political differences between bishops and priests. In County Kilkenny, for example, Sergeant Shee was supported by Bishop of Ossory Walsh, but the majority of the clergy appear to have been opposed to him.[51] In Waterford, Bishop Dominic O'Brien, a Whig supporter, issued an instruction to one of his priests who was reputedly of a different political persuasion, forbidding him from participating in the election.[52]

With the bishops thus divided, it was unrealistic to expect uniform behaviour from the priests. In Dublin, the clergy kept a low profile.[53] This did not apply in other areas of the country where clerical pronouncements in favour of various candidates were continuously made.[54] A candidate in Dungarvan, Maguire, claimed that the priests had spoken in his favour after every Mass.[55] Similar incidents were reported in Mayo.[56] However, priests were often not unanimous in their choice of candidate. Serious public divisions occurred among them in a number of areas on purely political issues. In some places such differences were resolved prior to the polling date. In Westmeath, for example, major trouble was avoided when one of the candidates, Urquhart, who had been nominated by a priest, retired from the campaign before polling day.[57] Meanwhile in Clare and Longford, conferences were held which successfully resolved clerical political differences.[58] However, where differences remained, voters were often treated to scenes of public clerical division. The most noteworthy example of this occurred in Mayo, where public differences divided both clergy and laity.[59]

Cullen was most annoyed with the high political profile assumed once again by the clergy.[60] It led him to predict that several election results would be annulled on account of clerical intimidation.[61] He was especially distressed at the fact that 'many young priests' were so 'very imprudent in their politics' in supporting a call from the Tenant League for Catholic voters to return Protestant Conservative candidates, in the hope of obtaining land reform.[62] Cullen deplored this tactic, which he professed to be unable to comprehend. This strategy was instigated by clever electioneering on behalf of Conservative candidates in promising local projects as well as land reform. This was considered to have been a significant factor in the defeat of twelve or thirteen Catholics.[63] In Cullen's mind, a return of the Conservative Party to power was something he reckoned would be no less than 'a great scourge for Ireland'.[64]

Cullen's own perspective on the election, and on the role that clerics might play, were laid out by him in a circular to the clergy of his archdiocese on 25 March 1857. He carefully differentiated between the duties of priests as priests and their rights as citizens. He reminded them: 'The Church teaches us to give to Caesar that which belongs to Ceasar and to the laity that which belongs to the laity, whilst she obliges us also to give to God and the Church that which is their right.'[65] As the election campaign, much to Cullen's regret, took place during Lent, he decided to take the opportunity to remind his priests that all their thoughts 'should be turned on Calvary, and fixed on the cross of our suffering Lord'.[66]

It was in this light that priests were urged to interpret and implement the various synodal regulations concerning clerical involvement in political affairs: 'These decrees were not made with the view of destroying the legitimate influence which the priesthood has a right to enjoy in directing and advising a faithful and a Catholic people, such as that in the midst of which we are placed; neither were they made for the purpose of encroaching on the rights of others, or dictating to them the course they should follow in temporal concerns. The object of those decrees was to uphold our influence by putting an end to abuses, and to render it more venerable and powerful by keeping it within its proper channel.'[67]

Priests as citizens, Cullen admitted, were often anxious to play their role in promoting public good at election time. Nonetheless, he stressed: 'This anxiety should never induce us to do anything that would compromise our utility with our flocks, expose our ministry to reproach, or to make us lose the peaceful characters of preachers of charity in the vortex of political strife.'[68]In specific terms this meant that, while the

Dublin clergy were urged to fight against 'bribery, perjury, drunkenness, violence and uncharitableness', they were 'to abstain from all personal denunciations and everything unworthy of the holiness of the priestly character'.[69]

If Cullen clearly outlined what was prohibited for the priests of his diocese, he also laid down what he viewed as a legitimate and acceptable manner in which clerics could involve themselves in the run-up to the election. The Dublin clergy were not only urged but positively directed to promote the election to parliament of candidates who were 'honest and upright men, men of religion and principle anxious only for the public good, not to be seduced from the path of honour by self interest or the ties of party'.[70]

As was his wont, it was within this context of the personal quality of candidates, rather than on the electoral programme of any political party, that Cullen went on to discuss the qualities of the candidate who might be worthy of the votes of Catholics. Such candidates, he declared, should aim to protect the people and defend their religion. People needing protection included those who were in the workhouses and the tenant farmers who were being evicted from their small holdings. Cullen then talked of 'the sufferings of the tenant classes in many parts of the country ... The attempts hitherto made to remedy them have been unsuccessful, yet we may confidently hope that if our representatives can be induced to take up this question cordially in the new Parliament and to pursue it with moderation, perseverance and union, they will at length obtain some enactment for the protection of the tenant which will be beneficial to the country'.[71] Given the state in which those in the workhouses as well as evicted tenants found themselves, Cullen said that: 'Our electors will be exercising a great work of charity if they send men to Parliament really and honestly determined to bring this vital question to a favourable issue, not seeking for anything exorbitant and unjust, and without violating the rights of anyone.'[72]

Not every member of his flock shared Cullen's confidence in the parliamentary system or agreed that land reform could be won by moderation and perseverance. Nonetheless, by phrasing the circular as he did, Cullen could later honestly state to Rome: 'I did not declare myself for any party but I sought to persuade the Catholics that in the choice of Members of Parliament they must think of the requirements of charity and of the preservation of religion.'[73] It can be reasonably deduced, however, that in writing in this way, Cullen effectively urged his priests to canvass for the defeat of Conservative candidates. Whether this would actually occur, Cullen could not say. All he could assert was that he would be greatly abused for writing such a circular.[74]

Although Cullen had stressed only a few months prior to the general election his 'disapproval of any manifestation by his clergy at public meetings on political subjects', once again he showed himself to be capable of using his own political influence during the campaign.[75] In 1857 he wrote to other bishops in an attempt to try to get certain men selected as candidates and then elected to parliament. Specific efforts were made by Cullen, for example, to have four candidates, Waldron in Tipperary, O'Hagan and O'Dwyer in Drogheda and Ball in Waterford, nominated and returned for their local constituencies.[76] All four were supporters of the outgoing Aberdeen government. Whatever about Cullen's interventions, it has to be said that they did not show in the results. Only one of those whom Cullen had supported, Waldron, was returned for Tipperary.[77]

The results of the general election gave the Liberals, headed by Palmerston, a resounding victory. The party returned 370 members to give him a majority of forty in the new House of Commons. This meant, as Cullen was quick to point out, that Palmerston did not have to rely on the Catholic vote.[78] In Ireland the Conservatives gained three seats. The Independent Party's total was somewhere between twelve and eighteen seats, depending on how the pre-election statements of candidates were interpreted.[79] No matter which way the results were analysed however, the 1857 general election signified a drastic fall in public support for the Independent Party as compared with 1852. It was also a result which led Cullen to declare that the Independent Party was nearly extinct and that it would soon die out.[80] The overall result signalled the end of any balance of power leverage for either Catholic or Irish interests in the new House of Commons.

As a result of clerical intimidation, Moore, the leader of the Independent Party, was unseated following a special petition hearing.[81] Cullen, who had predicted such an eventuality, was highly critical of the role of MacHale in the sponsorship and election of Moore.[82] As Cullen saw it, the conduct of MacHale and his clergy during the 1857 General Election campaign served to bring humiliation and disgrace to the clergy in general and to the Archbishop of Tuam in particular.[83]

The highly publicised political activities of the priests of Mayo served to prove only one thing for Cullen, which was that 'priests by involving themselves with too much violence in political affairs and by treating of these things from the altar, do nothing other than destroy their own influence also with Catholics and attract to themselves a world of trouble. While the objective was the emancipation of Catholics in the 1820s everyone, clergy and laity, was in agreement and if at that time some violence was committed by the clergy it was tolerated. But now when one treats of liberal questions on which the Catholics are divided as are the priests themselves, a parish priest and another priest cannot touch the topic in Church without offending many of their flock. In Mayo I am persuaded that for many years they will not forget the witnessed dissensions stirred up between the clergy and the people, and I do not know how the priests and the laity will be able to administer or receive the Sacraments after one having insulted and teared apart the other'.[84]

Such behaviour, claimed Cullen, underlined the wisdom of the legislation that had been approved restricting the political activities of clerics.[85] Cullen hoped that MacHale and his politically minded clerical supporters would come to this realisation so that some good might emerge from the whole affair. As he noted to the authorities in Rome: 'Perhaps they will learn from Parliament that which they did not want to learn from the instructions of the Holy See.'[86]

Nonetheless, Cullen still requested the Holy See to initiate disciplinary action against MacHale and his clergy for contravening the synodal regulations. He called for such a move on the basis of his belief that 'if some step is not made to moderate those violent priests who trample underfoot the regulations already made the moment will very soon come when Parliament will seek to strip the clergy of every influence and it will enact very strict laws to stop them from taking any part in an Election'.[87] The subsequent enactment of yet another Corrupt Practices Bill in 1858 justified Cullen's stance to an extent.[88]

Despite Cullen's request for censure, the Roman authorities, while regretting the conduct of some politically minded clergy, decided not to take strong action against MacHale. The failure of Propaganda, now under the guidance of Barnabò since June 1856 following the death of Fransoni, to take a firmer stance was a source of disappointment to Cullen. Undaunted however, he maintained his attacks on MacHale.[89] The Archbishop of Tuam in turn retaliated by reiterating the accusation that Cullen was a mere Castle bishop subservient to the British government.[90]

Cullen made sure to keep Rome informed of an 1858 government decision, which he deemed foolish, to prosecute two priests. These were Conway of Ballinrobe and Ryan of Kilmena, Westport, who faced charges arising out of the election of Moore.[91] While any such trial was calculated to discredit the Catholic clergy, this means of addressing the issue served only to create martyrs for the cause of continued clerical involvement in politics, as Cullen noted.[92] At the end of the day no verdict was returned; this was, in Cullen's view, the best result that the Church could have expected.[93]

Despite having won the general election of the previous year, Palmerston's Liberal government fell in February 1858, due chiefly to the attitude of Palmerston towards France. A Conservative administration, headed by Lord Derby, returned to office in February 1858 and lasted until June 1859.

The new, short-lived Conservative administration made various concessions to Catholics. In the Army, permanent rank and status equal to that of the ministers of the Established Church were granted to Roman Catholic chaplains.[94] This was important because almost 30 per cent of the members of the forces were Catholic.[95] The Home Secretary allowed chaplains to visit Catholics in prison and in workhouses.[96] Disraeli gave a friendly reception to a deputation urging the British government to grant degree-giving facilities to the Catholic University in Dublin.[97] While the Conservatives could not be termed 'friendly' to the Papal states, their government at least refrained from attacking them as the Liberals, Palmerston and Russell, had done, thereby alienating many Irish Catholics.

Yet again, there were examples of what Cullen termed 'an ugly and sad business' of priests campaigning against other priests during an 1858 by-election in Limerick.[98] This, coupled with the bribing of electors, led to the unseating of the elected candidate, Major Gavin.[99]

There were also issues for Cullen in his own archdiocese in 1858. Father Marshall once again launched a public attack on the government and Cullen immediately disciplined him by prohibiting him from preaching.[100] However, he claimed the action was taken not because of Marshall's politics but because of the violence of his speech.[101]

The question of Cullen's health was again a source of concern from the summer of 1857.[102] It continued to cause worry during the winter, and his poor physical condition evidently affected his handwriting.[103] By May 1858, he was complaining of feeling ill.[104] In June, weakened and weary of constant battles, he wrote to Kirby indicating that he was about to resign his office as Apostolic Delegate.[105] His grounds with respect to this office were that: 'It is only bringing trouble on me and causing opposition against me so that it is useless for me to keep.'[106]

Cullen's secretaries wrote to Kirby in July reporting on Cullen's poor health, news of which Kirby then passed on to Propaganda.[107] For health reasons, Cullen left Dublin early in July 1858 and went to Navan, Co. Meath.[108] However, with no significant improvement evident in his form, he wrote to Kirby over two weeks later reporting how, on grounds of health, he was to go away for a few weeks.[109] He went therefore, for a short period, to Liverpool, where members of his family were living. From there he wrote how, while in Ireland: 'The want of sleep was near destroying me. I looked upon everything in despair.'[110]

Upon his return to Ireland, still feeling unwell, Cullen went to the coastal resort of Bray in search of rest.[111] He was indicating to Kirby that he was beginning to get better while papal chamberlain George Talbot, on holiday in Ireland, was reporting to Barnabò how Cullen was very sick.[112] Barnabò himself intervened, and on 13 August 1858, Cullen received a letter ordering him to abstain from work for some time.[113] Although protesting to Barnabò that his health was good, Cullen decided to spend the following month on holidays in Rome.[114]

Over the following months the conciliatory attitude of the Conservative Derby administration towards Liberal demands finally led to the definitive split in the Independent Party. The particular issue that broke the party was whether or not a government-sponsored Reform Bill should be supported. When on 31 March 1859 the vote was taken, six members of the Party voted for the bill with five against. The split in the party soon spread to the grassroots and it divided prelates, priests and people. Cardinal Wiseman, for example, supported member for Dungarvan Maguire, who led the group voting for the bill, as did the clergy of Meath, the *Tablet* and the former member for Sligo County, Richard Swift, who had lost his seat in 1857. Those who voted against the government, including the so-called 'Young Irelander' member for Tipperary The O'Donoghue, received the support of Archbishop MacHale, the clergy of Tuam, the *Nation* and George Henry Moore.[115] As a result of this split, the Independent Party ceased to function as a political entity.

In May 1859, two months after the collapse of the Independent Party, parliament was dissolved. The general election was to see the return to office of the Liberals under Palmerston.

With the demise of the Independent Party the role of the priest in politics was now tending to be less significant, even though there were some priests who continued their interest in the general election campaign.[116] In that campaign, Cardinal Wiseman supported the Conservative party in the belief that they were less hostile than the Liberals to the idea of the Pope retaining the Papal states.[117] Here was a further illustration of the priority accorded by Church leaders to Church-related issues over more material concerns of the faithful at home.

In the 1859 election, Liberal support in Ireland fell and the Conservatives, though going into opposition in parliament, brought the number of their Irish seats up to fifty-seven.[118] Cullen, still unwell, had again left Ireland for a period.[119] While not pleased with the Conservative gains in Ireland or with Wiseman's intervention, Cullen was cautiously pleased that the Liberals had again taken over the reins of government.[120]

Cullen's welcome for the general election result, un-enthusiastic though it was, failed to find any kind of warm response among the people. Many were confused at an outcome which gave the Conservatives a majority of seats in Ireland while losing the overall contest. Then there was the evidence of Church support for the Conservatives, the party of the landlords and the Protestants, because of events as far away as Italy. People remembered how in 1857 they had been discouraged by bishops from voting Conservative at a time when that party was holding out the prospect, vague though it was, of land reform at home. Most immediate of all, the Independent Party was now seen to have been a colossal mistake.

After a decade of unsuccessful attempts to rectify the many grievances of the Irish people, disillusionment was growing at the ineptitude of parliamentarians and their failure to deliver any of the significant improvements sought by the people.

Cullen's role in public affairs in the decade now ending had been a significant if not very rewarding one. The line he was taking in national affairs did not prove popular with certain politicians and opinion formers of the decade. He had to endure frustrations and suffer much distress. The role he was destined to play in the 'Fenian fever' of the next decade would be different but nonetheless significant. More and more Irish people were now forming the view that constitutionalism had had a fair trial and was found wanting. The problems of the people were not being effectively tackled. There was a growing feeling that the time had come for more assertive methods to be tried. Indeed, plans for these were already being laid.

Part Two ✤

ARMED INSURRECTION
OPPOSED

Chapter Eight

ENTER THE FENIANS

B Y THE YEAR 1859 the failure of the parliamentarians to obtain any real alleviation of the main grievances of the vast majority of the Irish people was leading to a growing disenchantment. The people were becoming receptive to ideas for more direct action. Armed insurrection against British rule in Ireland had always attracted a degree of support. As the Independent Party was seen to be failing to deliver any improvements, interest in what was seen as the other option, armed revolt, now grew. The ineptitude of the parliamentarians was hard to explain or excuse. The electorate they represented in the House of Commons were citizens of the United Kingdom of Great Britain and Ireland, with the rights of citizens of that state. The Party's dismal performance could be explained only by their inability to press effectively in parliament for the rights to which the people of Ireland were constitutionally entitled.

The founders of the Fenians drew on the ideals of the Young Irelanders, who had 'foolishly' contemplated, but not seriously organised, a revolution in 1848.[1] These Young Irelanders had hoped to win self-determination for the Irish people by revolutionary means.[2] The so-called Rising of 1848 was confined to one limited engagement. The British authorities however, well-informed as to the Young Ireland leadership, used the episode as a pretext for rounding them up and having them sentenced to imprisonment or transportation, mainly to Australia.[3] Those who evaded capture fled the country and joined the many thousands of Irish emigrants who had left Ireland during and after the Famine.

The mass of those who left Ireland for economic reasons in the mid-nineteenth century sought refuge in the United States of America, Britain and Canada. Significantly, however, it was to France that certain Young Irelanders went following the 1848 Rising. Two of these who fled to Paris, James Stephens and John O'Mahony, were to become the founding fathers of the new revolutionary movement, the Fenian Brotherhood. Their time in Paris gave them the opportunity of meeting with underground groups, an association which Cullen was to highlight many times in his criticisms of the Fenians.

It was in the United States, however, that the first major steps were taken towards the foundation of a revolutionary secret Irish republican organisation. While some ideas might have been brought from the Continent, it was from the United States of America, and to a lesser extent Canada, that the men, the money and the arms were to come. John O'Mahony went to New York in 1854, where the Irish community then accounted for one quarter of the population. Both he and Stephens realised that it was among those Irish who were forced to leave their native land that the revolutionary ideal would hold the strongest attraction. Nowhere was this more evident than in the United States, where in 1851 some 221,000 Irish people had sought refuge. The vast majority of these originally rural people lived in the poorest part, the East Coast, in urban ghetto conditions. Most of them encountered major difficulties in adapting to their new environment, in establishing themselves and in getting work. Although many spoke Gaelic, the one advantage that many had over other immigrants was a knowledge of the English language.

O'Mahony gained support from other Young Irelanders now living in New York, such as John Mitchell, later to be described by Cullen as 'an arch Presbyterian or infidel', and set about organising an Irish revolutionary organisation in the United States.[4] The 'Irishmen's Civil and Military Republican Union' was founded in New York in April 1854 with the avowed aim of the expulsion of the British from Ireland.[5] The organisation, which later came to be known as the Fenians, and of which O'Mahony would later be described by Cullen as the Grand Master, was a legal open movement which quickly proved to be a popular one.[6] The fact that the Fenians in America operated openly, in contrast to the secret society status that the organisation in Ireland had to assume, was to become significant in later years. Even by 1855, the year following its foundation in the United States, it claimed, probably exaggeratedly, to be ready to send thirty thousand men over to Ireland for the liberation of the country.[7]

Meanwhile, having returned from France to Ireland in 1856, Stephens discovered that 'the ardour of Young Ireland had evaporated as if it had never existed' and that little of any type of national spirit existed among the people.[8] Judging the time opportune to re-establish a revolutionary movement that would learn from past mistakes, Stephens set about reviving the revolutionary ideal among the people.[9] With the support and assistance of O'Mahony, he resolved to organise anew a revolutionary force that would attempt to obtain juridical independence for Ireland by force of arms.[10] Stephens promised the Irish in the United States that, if entrusted with the leadership of any new organisation, given five hundred men from the United States and pledged one hundred pounds a month, he would enrol ten thousand men in a new revolutionary body within three months.[11]

While an initial financial appeal did not provide anything like the sum requested, Stephens, who was in Dublin on Saint Patrick's Day, 1858, along with some like-minded revolutionaries founded a new, secret, oath-bound organisation. Its aim was to make Ireland an 'Independent Democratic Republic.'[12] The very day of the foundation of the Fenians was the one on which Cullen, in a pastoral letter to the Catholics of his archdiocese, specifically denounced all secret societies, freemasonry and ribbonism.[13]

The Fenian movement was to be nationalistic and democratic, but not a communist organisation. Emphasis was placed on the single goal of attaining independence for Ireland. Remarkably, a fully developed financial policy formulation on land, social or other issues was largely postponed until independence would have been achieved. The popular name that was given to this new revolutionary body, which was variously referred to as 'Our Body', 'Our Movement', 'Our Organisation' or most commonly 'The Brotherhood', was 'The Fenians'.[14] It was only after 1873 that it became officially recognised as the Irish Republican Brotherhood (IRB). The fact that the movement could grow and develop without having a clearly defined programme or even a name demonstrates that, as Charles Townshend pointed out, from its inception 'the group occupied a more or less natural place in Irish political life'.[15]

All members of the Fenian movement in Ireland swore to do their utmost to make Ireland an 'Independent Democratic Republic', to obey 'in all things not contrary to the law of God' the commands of superior officers and to maintain secrecy regarding all the transactions of the society.[16] Stephens immediately embarked upon recruiting members from, among others, the supporters of already existing clubs and societies in Ireland.[17] Within the space of only a few months, by the autumn of 1858 a very active political national club in Skibbereen, Co. Cork, known as the Phoenix Club, which had been founded in 1856 by Jeremiah O'Donovan, had been taken over by the Fenians.[18]

This support given to the Fenians through their participation in the various societies caused concern in certain ecclesiastical circles. Father John O'Sullivan, parish priest of Kenmare, Co. Kerry, for example, passed on information to Lord Lieutenant Naas concerning the growth of the Fenian movement in his parish.[19] This led to the arrest and trial of several prominent Fenians in the Cork and Kerry area. Cullen took the opportunity to remind his flock that all those engaged in secret societies were excommunicated by the Catholic Church and could not therefore receive absolution.[20] In effect these early trials afforded the Fenians great publicity and won them popular support. Most of the defendants were in the end released, being merely bound to good behaviour.[21]

The movement directed itself towards, and was successful in attracting into its ranks, labourers, small tradesmen, small farmers, shop assistants, artisans, labourers, clerks, teachers and the sons of peasants, amongst whose classes dissatisfaction with the state of the country ran deep.[22] It was a matter of concern to the civil authorities to find members of the armed services and the police force being recruited.[23] Surprisingly, in view of the land problem, tenant farmers were not so numerous among its ranks, nor was any real effort made to attract the upper classes to join.[24] Great emphasis was placed on secrecy.[25] The steps taken to keep the organisation secret, however, were largely in vain. The movement was very quickly infiltrated by spies and informers who kept the British security officials in Dublin Castle well briefed.[26] Also, news of this new oath-bound society began to receive publicity in the press, some of it very critical.[27]

Progress with the organisation was slow and uneven. Following the initial flush of enthusiasm, Stephens was apparently in no rush to stage a revolution in 1859, living for a time back in France.[28] At the same time there was very little American money being sent.[29] This led to tensions between Stephens and O'Mahony.

Even if revolution did not immediately follow the foundation of the Fenians, discontent continued amongst the mass of the Irish people. Cullen was only too well aware of this. While totally opposed to revolutionary means to attain political goals, Cullen was forced to admit that there was little hope of any social advancement for the Irish through political means. If the Conservatives, who had been in power in 1858–9, were to return to political office, Cullen was now convinced that they would drive the Irish people to a rebellion within two or three years.[30] The result of any attempted rebellion in the meantime, Cullen felt sure, would be the confiscation of Catholic property and the reapplication of penal laws. Many of these, though not enforced, were still on the statute book.[31] At the same time however, Cullen felt that ecclesiastical support for the Liberal political alternative, which at one time he had welcomed, was now impossible. This was due to Liberal Party support for Italian nationalists.[32] On this basis then, and finding himself in a very difficult situation, Cullen, reflecting the dilemma which produced Independent Opposition in the early 1850s, decided to support neither the Liberals nor the Conservatives, repeatedly writing critically of both.[33]

With Italian nationalists threatening the territorial integrity of the Papal states, Cullen participated in the organisation of the armed Irish Brigade of Saint Patrick. This Brigade was despatched in 1860 to assist the pontifical military forces in their fight against Italian nationalists aiming at Italian unification. The organisation of this force, which was declared illegal by the British authorities, showed to the Fenians, to the British government and others that Cullen was not opposed to physical force being exercised in the cause of legitimate right.

There was an important issue in Ireland, however, as to who constituted the legitimate governing authority. In particular, did the over three-hundred-year-old British occupation of the country mean that the London government constituted the legitimate governing authority of Ireland? This question was to haunt Cullen throughout the years of the Fenian movement. In fact, the organisation of the Irish Brigade of Saint Patrick did more than provide evidence of episcopal support for military activity. It provided military experience, however limited, for over one thousand Irishmen. Indeed MacHale claimed that the cause of the Papal states and the question of the legitimate right of people to defend themselves made the Irish appreciate their own sufferings and 'reanimated them with the desire to have their grievances redressed'.[34]

There was a revealing test of Irish opinion when British ministers, who had supported plebiscites in Italy, were persuaded to explore the idea of a referendum on the issue of self-government in Ireland. The project had some, but not

148

universal, ecclesiastical support. In the event, the number of signatures in favour of a referendum, at 423,026, was so far short of the number of Catholic males over fifteen that the government, in April 1861, did not consider themselves bound to proceed further and the idea was dropped. The effect of this interlude was to disillusion people even further as regards obtaining separation from Britain through constitutional means.[35] The outcome was also interpreted, however, as a general lack of public support for the idea of an independent legislature and government in Ireland at that time.

There were confusing factors at work, at home and abroad. At home there was deepening hardship following a succession of poor harvests, and many felt that the best prospect of relief lay in remaining in the United Kingdom. The general scarcity of food was at the same time leading to an increase in the fortunes of the revolutionary nationalists, as Cullen was only all too aware.[36] Added to this hardship was the growing disappointment of the people with the performance of their parliamentarians. Then there were the external factors.

Abroad, a most important factor was the organisation of the Fenians in the United States, where they operated openly, indeed with the apparent approval of the American authorities. These were quite hostile to Britain in the climate of tension between the two countries in the early 1860s. The American Fenians were spurred on by fierce feelings of resentment against England. Some were survivors of the failed revolutionary effort of 1848 and had bitter memories of the Famine.

Another external element, and one which exercised Cullen to an inordinate degree, was the French interest. Added to possible support from underground French groups for a rising in Ireland was the poor state of Anglo-French relations in the late 1850s. In the event of armed Anglo-French conflict, there was always the possibility of the French using Ireland for a landing force. This possibility was never far from the minds of British governments, or indeed of Irish revolutionaries. Historically, it was one of the reasons for imposing the Union in 1801. As the *Nation* pointed out: 'Whenever and wherever the chances of war with England are discussed then and there the dissatisfaction of Ireland becomes an element in the calculation.'[37] This consideration now added a new significance to the presence of Fenian leaders in Paris and their involvement there, however slight, with various underground groups.

Meanwhile, at home, distress and food shortages continued. In Dublin, the situation was aggravated by an influx of impoverished people from the country. However, Cullen persisted in his belief that revolution was not the answer. As he put it to Kirby in October 1860: 'It is better to have famine than revolution.'[38] Cullen viewed the promotion of the secret societies as mistaken. This was because the end result of such a move could have been that the poor people, as he put it, would 'be pounced on bye and bye and made suffer'.[39] He was personally distressed at the wholly inadequate response of the British government to the conditions of the Irish poor, who as citizens of the United Kingdom were the responsibility of the government. He therefore decided to make out a case to a Commons Commission of Parliament on their behalf.[40]

Understandably, there was an increase in popular disillusionment with the government. By May 1861 Cullen was wondering if matters could be improved by the Westminster government putting Irishmen in charge of Irish administrative affairs. As he put it to Kirby: 'Irish affairs must be managed by Irishmen.'[41] In expressing this sentiment, which was not shared by MacHale and others, Cullen was reflecting the view of Daniel O'Connell, who visualised Irishmen occupying influential positions in the administration in Dublin Castle. Indeed, the Irish, he was later to assert, 'are in general very far superior in intelligence to Englishmen'.[42] Always unwilling to entertain the alternative to constitutional means however, and realising that the Irish 'cannot expect much' from the London government, Cullen resigned himself to the defeatist conclusion of the Irish poor being 'doomed to remain for years to come in their present deplorable state'.[43]

Inevitably, with so much distress around, popular support for the Fenians was now increasing. At the same time Cullen's persistence with his priests-in-politics campaign was reducing clerical influence in elections. The result was, as had been predicted by Lucas earlier, that the influence of landlords at the polling stations now became predominant and Catholic influence was declining.[44] Despite this however, Cullen maintained the policy of keeping the clerics out of politics and complained to Kirby of Cantwell, bishop of Meath, who publicly lamented the withdrawal of priests from 'wholesome agitation' in the political arena.[45] As Cullen put it to Kirby: 'God knows the priests cannot do half their spiritual business and if thrown into the sea of politics they must neglect their duties in a great part.'[46] He went on to point out how in the days of Dr Troy, who had been Archbishop of Dublin at the time of the Union in 1801, it had appeared that most of the priests who had joined in the rebellion of 1798 had previously been suspended for bad conduct. Cullen noted: 'It is curious also that many of our great patriot priests who made so much noise in our own days were not distinguished for their religious zeal.'[47] Feeling rather helpless and dissatisfied, between the English parliamentary parties and the Fenian organisation, Cullen wrote to Rome: 'You see what troubled waters we have to navigate in.'[48]

Not only Cullen but the Irish bishops in general were aware that the secret oath-bound Fenian organisation was growing in popularity and numbers. At the prospect of a large-scale revival of revolutionary nationalism, the Irish Hierarchy at their episcopal meeting of 25 April 1861, not attended by MacHale, decided to issue a warning against secret societies in general.[49] In a joint pastoral they stated: 'From the misfortunes now afflicting the fairest regions of Europe, let us learn the great evils of secret societies, which undoubtedly are the scourge of humanity and the bane of religion. On account of such evils all who are sworn in as Freemasons or Ribbonmen, or join in any other similar illegal combinations, have been excommunicated by the Popes, and cut off as rotten branches from the Church. If any designing men endeavour to promote such societies among you, continue as in the past to be on your guard against them, and preserve yourselves and your country from the dangers to which any participation in those designs of darkness would involve you.'[50] Such strictures were directed against secret societies generally and not just the Fenians.

Aware of the effects that episcopal condemnation would have amongst the Catholic people, the Fenian leadership, in a clever sidestep, decided to organise themselves under the banner of a political brotherhood rather than a military revolutionary organisation. This association they christened 'the Brotherhood of Saint Patrick', and it could be described as the political arm of the Fenians.[51] Under the umbrella of this brotherhood the first mass demonstration of Fenian revolutionary strength was organised in Ireland. The occasion was the funeral of Terence Bellew McManus in November 1861. This event was destined to become one of great significance in the history of Irish separatism.

Terence Bellew McManus, as Cullen reported to Rome, had been a prominent member of the Young Ireland movement, and for his part in the 'folly' of the 1848 Rising, he was initially sentenced to death, a sentence later commuted.[52] He was transported to Tasmania, from where he escaped to the United States in 1852. He settled in San Francisco. There, having received the last Sacraments of the Church, he died on 15 January 1861 and was buried.[53]

Several months after his death, what Cullen described as 'a few mad American and Irish' Fenians decided to repatriate his remains.[54] This the Fenian leadership organised in the hope that the funeral demonstration would increase sympathy both in Ireland and America for their cause as well as induce Irish Americans to contribute more to it.[55]

To this end, McManus' remains were exhumed, encased in a coffin with no cross but adorned with a sculptured Goddess of Liberty, and transported first to New York.[56] There, amid calls for the independence of Ireland, they were received in Saint Patrick's Cathedral by Dr Hughes, archbishop of New York. He delivered a rousing panegyric, pointing out how, in some cases, the Church permitted resistance to overthrow a tyrannical government.[57] Then, amid more calls for Irish independence and promises to raise the standard of revolt in Ireland, the remains were put on board ship for Cork en route to Dublin.[58]

Arrangements to receive the remains in Ireland were organised by the newly formed civilian Brotherhood of Saint Patrick.[59] Impressive ceremonials, which Cullen predicted were 'likely to excite disputes', were planned in Ireland before the funeral to Dublin's Glasnevin cemetery.[60] Reports reaching Rome stated how the funeral was being organised by rebels and revolutionaries, some spies for the British government, and others promoting Mazzinian ideas.[61] When the organising committee applied to Cullen for the Office of the Dead and a public funeral Mass to be celebrated in Dublin's Pro-Cathedral, Cullen found himself in a quandary.[62]

A physically ill Cullen, viewing the request as designed to discredit him as archbishop, was in a very embarrassing situation.[63] If he granted the request, he might be accused of supporting revolutionary violence.[64] If he refused, he might be represented as pro-British and anti-Irish.[65] Parrying the request, he questioned the organising committee as to the services performed by McManus and why the honour of a public funeral should be granted for a stranger who had never lived in, nor had any connection with, the Dublin archdiocese.[66] The answer was that the purpose was to honour the revolution of 1848.[67] Fearing that any public religious funeral would be seen by the people as some form of endorsement for revolutionary declarations, Cullen decided to deny the request. Rome was later to support Cullen's stance, and he afterwards claimed never to regret having taken it.[68] The reaction was predictable: support for the decision from many clerical colleagues but savage criticism from the Fenians and their supporters.[69]

In the meantime the remains, following an enthusiastic welcome in Cork, were transported to Dublin for what was to be the first in a sequence of mass funeral demonstrations of Fenian strength and of public sympathy for the revolutionary spirit.[70] Following Cullen's refusal to permit a lying-in-state or a High Mass in Dublin's Pro-Cathedral, the organisers decided that McManus' penultimate resting place would not be a Church at all but rather the secular Mechanics Institute.[71] From there, on 10 November 1861, the funeral proceeded along with a massive procession, mostly of artisans and mechanics, described variously by Cullen as 'stupid',[72] 'sad'[73] and 'dangerous',[74] through the streets of Dublin before McManus was finally laid to rest in Glasnevin cemetery.[75]

Cullen later claimed that no Catholic of any name or credit took part in the funeral. In accordance with the stance that he had adopted, no public funeral Mass was offered for McManus and no Dublin diocesan priest attended the funeral.[76] Four priests did however accompany the cortege; Ashe, a Dublin Capuchin, Courteney from Birmingham, Kenyon from Killaloe, and most prominently, Lavelle from Tuam.[77] It was this last, Patrick Lavelle, who recited the committal prayers before delivering an impromptu 'revolutionary' panegyric strongly critical of Cullen. This was aimed at exciting a revolutionary spirit among the people.[78] Lavelle drew the applause of the crowd as he declared: 'I am proud to see that the people of Ireland and of Dublin are not dead – that they have hope – that though the prophet be dead the spirit he evoked will outlive him, and even in the present generation raise his country from degradation to the glory of a nation.'[79]

Father Patrick Lavelle hailed from a family of moderate means in the Archdiocese of Tuam. By 1861, he had already achieved notoriety, having been involved in a major dispute in the Irish College in Paris.[80] Cullen's efforts to have Lavelle's bishop, MacHale, order his priest to abstain from involvement in any further political affairs proved fruitless.[81] Upon his return to Ireland from Paris, Lavelle had become parish priest of Partry, Co. Mayo and espoused the nationalist cause. He now took to severely criticising Cullen, having his criticisms posted up in a notice in eleven parts of Dublin on the eve of the McManus funeral.[82] With the notice was the text of a letter that he had already published in the *Freeman's Journal* of 6 November 1861.[83] Cullen viewed this letter as 'disgraceful'.[84] He also denounced it as nothing less than a 'wicked and mischievous production'.[85] Lavelle strongly objected to Cullen's refusal to grant a public funeral for McManus, whose only crime, he claimed, was to manifest his patriotism for all to see.[86]

Cullen first thought of suspending Lavelle himself, but then decided to throw the onus on the priest's own ordinary, MacHale.[87] Therefore, on 9 November 1861, he wrote to MacHale, 'the Lion of the West',[88] whom he suspected of conniving with Lavelle, requesting him to take steps against Lavelle.[89] MacHale, discourteously according to Cullen, responded two days later promising to forward Cullen's letter to Lavelle so that the priest could answer for himself.[90]

Meanwhile, Lavelle's role in the funeral, aimed, according to Cullen, at exciting the people to rebel against the ecclesiastical authorities, had further incensed the Archbishop of Dublin.[91] Lavelle horrified many other bishops, as well as priests and lay people, who joined in Cullen's call for disciplinary action.[92] Cullen now went further and urged, more than once, that some definite move be made by Rome instructing MacHale to discipline Lavelle, to forbid him from leaving the Archdiocese of Tuam and to prevent any further renewal of scandalous scenes.[93]

When Lavelle finally wrote to Cullen on 21 November 1861, he attempted to gloss over his behaviour by simply expressing his regret that the public letter published just prior to McManus' funeral had not pleased Cullen. He had no wish to offend anyone, he wrote, except the enemies of their holy religion, dear country and Holy Father.[94] As Cullen saw it, either Lavelle failed to understand the evil that he had done or he wished to excuse himself with good words. Meanwhile MacHale, according to Cullen, was also greatly to blame for letting Lavelle loose on the country.[95] These events were followed by a succession of unhappy experiences for Cullen involving Lavelle, MacHale and the authorities in Rome — experiences which were to both damage and humiliate Cullen and seriously undermine his status.

Following the impressive display of support for the Fenian cause at the McManus funeral, Cullen grew increasingly

155

concerned. He saw the revolutionary ideas now circulating widely in Ireland as originating with the Fenians who had come from the United States.[96] He consistently held that all who joined secret societies in the hope of attaining political ends by revolutionary means were 'as mad as possible'.[97] 'It still seems that it is not only foolish to talk in this country of revolution while the people are so weak and deprived of arms but also destructive of religion,' he declared in late 1861.[98]

In such circumstances, Cullen had no hesitation in describing it as true madness to excite such a people to resist the power of the British government.[99] As Cullen saw it, the government, well aware of the state of Ireland, had not prohibited the McManus funeral. The rationale was that as the people were unarmed and disorganised and the government in control of a powerful army and navy, it was impossible for any serious attempt at revolution to take place.[100]

One of the main practical reasons for discouraging armed insurrection now emerged, namely that such an insurrection could not succeed against the might of the British forces. Cullen was to grow increasingly conscious of this argument as the decade advanced, even though in public he refrained from emphasising it. The government also knew, claimed Cullen, that when the people preoccupied themselves with impractical and mad ideas, they did not think any more of such issues as Catholic education or of the condition of the poor. This left the government full freedom to do as it pleased.[101] Furthermore, Cullen believed that as the McManus funeral was organised by the Brotherhood of Saint Patrick, which he claimed, astonishingly, was affiliated with the Free Masons, the government had decided against banning the funeral demonstration as 'many ministers or great lords are heads of masonic lodges'.[102] He speculated that the government was delighted with the entire funeral episode, believing it threw ridicule on all of the Irish, as well as dividing the Catholics who were now fighting among themselves.[103]

In view of the support and sympathy induced by the McManus funeral and other demonstrations later, these reflections by Cullen must be seen as quite unsound. Yet for all of his criticisms of government neglect, and his consciousness of the distress of the people, Cullen again recorded his resigned acceptance of government mismanagement in Ireland.[104] It all had to be accepted because, as he put it: 'It is better to suffer the present ills than to plunge ourselves into the infinitely worse evils of revolution and disbelief which we have remained free of up to now.'[105]

Cullen was aware that sentiments of rebellion against both civil and Church authority were being spread by secret societies, in which bracket he insisted on including the Brotherhood of Saint Patrick.[106] While shortly after the McManus funeral he reported to Rome how public support for the movement seemed to have declined somewhat, he was clearly aware that support for the Brotherhood was growing.[107] Already by December 1861, the leaders of the 'highly dangerous' Brotherhood of Saint Patrick were claiming to have enrolled some 400,000 members, most of whom were 'tradesmen and mechanics who read newspapers'.[108] Cullen believed that all of the members of this Brotherhood bound themselves to fight for Irish independence by revolutionary means, although accounts differed as to whether or not the organisation was oathbound.[109] He maintained that the Brotherhood was led by Protestants or unbelievers, all of whom were followers of revolutionaries such as Mazzini or the leaders of previous Irish revolutionary organisations, such as the Young Ireland and the United Irishmen.[110]

Expressing a sentiment which was to be repeated in later episcopal statements and which sought to detach a scheming Fenian leadership from the ordinary well-meaning members, Cullen asserted that these organisers manipulated the volunteers so that revolutionary, anti-clerical and anti-ecclesiastical ideas soon began to filter down to the rank-and-file of the 'foolish poor Catholics'.[111] These were the people who constituted the ordinary membership of the Brotherhood.[112]

What Cullen was doing, in fact, was denouncing the Brotherhood as dangerous and detrimental to religion.[113] The leadership of the Brotherhood retaliated by staying away from Mass following the McManus funeral and refusing to contribute to the building of churches.[114] Cullen had overreacted to the shows of defiance by the Brotherhood. Indeed the hollowness of the Brotherhood's anti-Church protests was shown up when, in recruiting new members, the Brotherhood pleaded that they were opposing the enemy of the Catholic religion, the British government.[115] Although particularly strong in Irish cities such as Dublin, Cork and Limerick, branches of the Brotherhood were also founded by Irish emigrants in Great Britain and the United States.[116] For funds, the Brotherhood, in a venture deemed less than successful by Cullen, organised a special collection known as 'Patrick's pence', 'on the model of the Church's "Peter's pence"'.[117]

Chapter Nine

NEW FRUSTRATIONS FOR THE ARCHBISHOP

HAVING CONVINCED himself that the Brotherhood was nothing less than a sinister conspiracy encouraged by Protestants and preparing to 'fatten victims for the gallows and the convict ships' and destroy the people, Cullen began to wish that the leaders would be arrested and prosecuted.[1] He felt the government could do this, if only on the basis that the Brotherhood advocated the non-payment of rents to landlords.[2] Cullen claimed that its membership was infiltrated by the police. He maintained that its leadership, as had happened before in Irish history, was ready to betray the poor people to the government.[3] Indeed Cullen went so far as to imply that the leadership received government protection.[4] He also asserted that the government only permitted the continued existence of the Brotherhood because, if it were destined to do anything good, the government would have taken steps against it![5] It is extremely doubtful if Cullen could offer a reliable source for the most striking of the assertions made in this correspondence, especially those suggesting Protestant involvement. Indeed the signs are that he was giving free rein to his imagination.

In line with these beliefs then and in an effort to stem the tide of support for the Brotherhood of Saint Patrick, Cullen wrote a pastoral letter for the feast of the Immaculate Conception, 1861. In this he exhorted the clergy of Dublin to use every effort to stop the propagation of the secret society and of its revolutionary ideas.[6] This, as was the case with his other public denunciations, was apparently inspired by a genuine concern to protect the ordinary members of his flock from the influences and predations of what he viewed as evil-minded men. In this pastoral, for example, Cullen took care not to condemn the Brotherhood of Saint Patrick, the adoption of whose patronage Cullen viewed as profaning the name of Saint Patrick. Despite his earlier concentration on the leaders, he did not now condemn them by name for fear of being taken to the civil court for defamation.[7] In general terms he wrote of how: 'All Catholics enrolling themselves or entering into any society or brotherhood established for purposes detrimental to civil society or religion, and bound to secrecy by oath, fall under the severest penalties, and are, *ipso facto*, excommunicated; their lot is miserable indeed, for they are cut off like rotten branches from the Church.'[8]

Even after the furore over the McManus funeral had died down, the possibility of secret societies gaining support continued to worry Cullen.[9] The question of Lavelle's involvement was put to Rome, and the authorities there, much to Cullen's satisfaction, contacted MacHale.[10] No concrete sign of any punishment was visible in late January 1862 however. Instead, MacHale had responded to the instruction from Rome by showing a degree of support for Lavelle.[11]

Meanwhile Lavelle continued to live in Dublin for most of January 1862, promoting and collecting money for the Brotherhood of Saint Patrick.[12] Cullen, having written to MacHale but without receiving any immediate reply, appealed to Rome to order the Archbishop of Tuam to recall Lavelle. Cullen also took the opportunity to warn Rome not to be surprised if he himself took the step of excommunicating Lavelle, whom he denounced as a fool.[13] Cullen was reluctant to take such a step because of his fear of MacHale emerging as the great defender of ecclesiastical liberty. Clearly from Cullen's point of view, it was desirable that MacHale should be the prelate to discipline Lavelle. However, Cullen was insistent that, whoever admonished Lavelle, it was essential the priest be disciplined if order was to be maintained in the Irish Church.[14] Cullen believed that Rome should force MacHale's hand in the matter. If the Roman authorities failed to do so, however, he declared himself prepared 'to suspend publicly the little wolf who comes to devour my lambs'.[15]

However, the Church did not act to punish Lavelle. This demonstrated a remarkable failure of authority that was all the more serious since it involved the Apostolic Delegate. Unhappily for Cullen, the experience was to recur several times.

Cullen discovered that his informants with respect to the clerical support for the Brotherhood were unreliable. Initially in 1862, Cullen claimed that: 'All the clergy here are active in opposing the movement, so I hope it will not spread.'[16] Shortly afterwards however, he was forced to admit that this was not really the case.[17] Much to his amazement, he discovered that a number of priests were supporting the Brotherhood of Saint Patrick.[18] The most prominent of these was Lavelle, whom Cullen accused of making himself 'the Apostle of that Society', along with Fathers Keynon and Vaughan from the diocese of Killaloe.[19] Cullen was highly critical of such clerical support, viewing it as 'great folly' and responsible for deluding Catholics into supporting the Fenian movement.[20]

Notwithstanding this criticism, Lavelle continued to support the Brotherhood, even to the extent of delivering a lecture in Dublin on 11 February 1862. It was attended by some 4,000 people and was entitled 'The Catholic Doctrine of the Right of Revolution'.[21] In this lecture, Lavelle claimed that as Ireland was being so badly ruled by the British, her people had the right to revolt. This he deemed morally justified and therefore sanctioned by the ecclesiastical authorities.[22]

Following this lecture, Lavelle left for Great Britain on a fundraising tour for the Brotherhood of Saint Patrick. Cullen did not now know what to do in relation to Lavelle and appealed again for Propaganda to intervene with MacHale. Cullen stressed that MacHale's contention that Lavelle was always in his own parish in Tuam was simply untrue.[23] Along with several other Irish bishops, such as those of Clogher and Ossory, Cullen attempted to counteract the favourable publicity given by Lavelle to the Brotherhood. He strongly condemned all secret societies in his Lenten pastoral for 1862.[24] 'More knocks' were given to the Brothers by Cullen in his 1862 Saint Patrick's Day pastoral.[25] At the same time as Cullen was drafting this pastoral, Lavelle was preparing to attend a well-publicised Saint Patrick's Day Brotherhood dinner in Glasgow.[26] Lavelle's action in attending such a function, and using the occasion to make a revolutionary speech, inspired Cullen to renew his calls for MacHale, whom he now accused of sympathising with the Brotherhood, to be forcibly compelled 'to withdraw Father Lavelle from his apostolic labours in favour of the Brotherhood'.[27] Rome, he insisted, should pressurise the Archbishop of Tuam into taking action especially in light of the fact that MacHale himself was being invoked by the Brotherhood as a model prelate. Cullen described how the Brotherhood had taken to publicly displaying MacHale's portrait at their meetings alongside those of revolutionary Irish separatist figures such as Robert Emmett and Wolfe Tone.[28] Such a move led people to believe that MacHale supported the Brothers even though Cullen, contradicting an earlier assertion, now professed to be certain that the Archbishop of Tuam was not favourable to the Brotherhood.[29]

While ambiguity concerning MacHale's stance on the Brotherhood existed in the public mind, Cullen noted that it was difficult for him to continue his campaign of condemning the Brothers outright.[30] He also observed how Lavelle was not the only priest with pro-Brotherhood tendencies. Initial attempts to dissuade some like-minded clerics from openly espousing the cause of the Brotherhood failed.[31] As Cullen saw it, the price for such failure was to be extremely heavy.

Cullen was well aware of the dissatisfaction of the people arising from their impoverished condition, which in turn was leading them to support the Fenians. He repeatedly turned his mind to the government's neglect of the people's plight.[32] He reported to Rome frequently in 1862, describing the miserable condition of the people as well as the massive emigration from all parts of Ireland.[33] He criticised the government's failure to initiate any scheme to revitalise the Irish economy and improve the living standards of the people.[34] As Cullen put it to Rome: '...Things would go better were it not for the great misery. The people suffer a lot and there are no means to support them. The Government is determined to do nothing.'[35] The reason why such inactivity pervaded government policy was, Cullen believed, because the mass of the Irish people adhered to the Catholic religion.[36]

Cullen never abandoned certain suspicions that the government permitted the Fenian Brotherhood to operate, hoping in this manner to weaken the authority of the clergy and to divide Catholics.[37] In desperation, he himself took the initiative of calling a meeting of members of parliament, magistrates and other interested bodies who might have involved themselves in the defence of the poor.[38] The result of his efforts was the foundation of the Central Relief Committee on 11 November 1862.[39] The lack of financial resources, however, meant that this scheme had little overall impact. Nevertheless, the experience served to underline the neglect of Ireland by the Liberal government, whose policies for the relief of poverty were altogether unsuited to Irish conditions. This state of affairs seemed to underline the failure of the parliamentarians to secure even minimum services for the poor, services to which they were entitled under the law.

Meanwhile, contrary to Cullen's original predictions, Lavelle returned from his fundraising activities in Britain and went straight to his parish in Tuam archdiocese. He continued to support the Brotherhood of Saint Patrick and attempted to reply to Cullen's censures of the organisation.[40] Cullen was distressed by this, remarking that: 'The whole affair will do a great deal of mischief.'[41]

There followed some undignified exchanges. The Brotherhood of Saint Patrick maintained that it had the support of MacHale while Cullen continued to denounce it in his correspondence with Rome.[42] To substantiate his claims concerning the Brotherhood, and to try to persuade Rome to act against clerical supporters of the organisation such as Lavelle, Cullen began to deluge Rome with newspaper articles. In these articles the Brothers in general, and Lavelle in particular, outlined their philosophical and revolutionary beliefs.[43] The newspaper extracts, Cullen believed, served as 'very useful for one to know the mind of the Brothers'.[44] The fact that Lavelle was not disciplined by MacHale led Cullen to lament of how: 'It appears as if the words of Rome do not produce much effect.'[45]

Lavelle, seemingly emboldened by an absence of any imposed restraint, went even further and was elected a vice president of the Brotherhood and a president of one of its Dublin branches.[46] So while Cullen was denouncing the Brotherhood, Lavelle was actively encouraging it, and in Dublin too.[47] This necessitated Lavelle travelling well outside his own diocese promoting the Brothers. This he did 'with or without the encouragement of his bishop'.[48] Cullen forewarned Kirby when he learnt that Lavelle was scheduled to talk to the Brothers in Dublin after Easter 1862.[49] Yet again he urged the Roman authorities to get MacHale to discipline Lavelle, or failing that, to give Cullen himself permission to do so.[50] However, he remained convinced that the desired outcome would be for Lavelle to discontinue his defiance and recant, as opposed to being condemned by his ecclesiastical superiors.

By April 1862, following the condemnations of the Fenians by various prelates, Cullen reported that support for the Brothers of Saint Patrick was declining.[51] He was of the belief that the Brothers were 'coming out worse than I had imagined they were'.[52] 'If one cannot stop the course of this madness, religion will suffer a lot,' he wrote.[53] In the belief therefore that a joint 'knock from the bishops' would kill the Fenian spirit, he resolved on ecclesiastical moves to condemn them at the next episcopal meeting in May 1862.[54] To this end, he set about organising a joint episcopal condemnation, even though he realised that MacHale, if he were to take part, would create trouble by alleging that any such measure was really directed against certain of his clergy, notably Lavelle.[55]

Cullen was confirmed in his views on the Brotherhood when discussing the matter with some members who, fearing excommunication, came to see him.[56] What he learnt convinced him that: 'The whole business is most dangerous and detrimental to religion.'[57] He therefore took to denouncing the Brotherhood as 'a pain in the neck and wicked'.[58] In the absence of any apparent action by MacHale to discipline Lavelle, Cullen's relations with the Archbishop of Tuam deteriorated.[59] Cullen requested a directive from Rome as to what to do, repeating how the idea of suspending the Tuam priest himself continued to occur to him 'from time to time'.[60]

The Irish bishops met from 6–9 May 1862.[61] Despite the strong protests of MacHale and of Derry, it was decided that Lavelle should be directed to tender his resignation forthwith from the Brotherhood of Saint Patrick. This decision was taken despite the fact that Lavelle's own Ordinary, MacHale, strongly opposed it.[62] In their joint statement the bishops stated: 'We have heard with deep regret that in some parts of the country persons have been known to administer unlawful oaths and to entice foolish men to enter secret associations dangerous to religion and society. That we earnestly, and with all paternal affection, warn Catholics against all such combinations, whether bound by oath or otherwise, and especially against those that have for their object to spread a spirit of revolution which, in other lands, is now producing such disastrous results.'[63]

The bishops' statement included the following balancing passage: 'That while we warn our people against those unlawful associations we cannot be blind to the many injustices they suffer, and the manifest inequality before the law which inspires some individuals with a spirit of alienation from authority and of resistance to public order leading in some cases to crimes which we, and all good men, deplore.'[64]

Following the bishops' meeting, in a pastoral letter of 25 May 1862, Cullen declared membership of the Brotherhood a reserved sin in his archdiocese.[65] Cullen claimed in the same letter that any secret conspiracy against the government was deemed to be dangerous not only to religion but also to society.[66] Lavelle, on the basis that episcopal condemnations of the Brotherhood had no force because the organisation was a public organisation, ignored all episcopal declarations, remained an office holder in the Brotherhood and travelled widely throughout Britain and Ireland promoting its cause.[67]

Following the May 1862 episcopal meeting, Cullen set out for Rome for the canonisation of Japanese martyrs, returning to Dublin, again ill, in July.[68] Having been informed by his secretary while in Rome that Lavelle continued to ignore the bishops' condemnation and failed to repair any scandal, Cullen decided to discuss the affair with Pope Pius IX.[69]

Upon his return to Ireland Cullen enquired of a number of bishops about the strength of support for the Brotherhood. The replies showed that, while support for the Brotherhood in Britain was small, the same could not be said of Ireland.[70] All this time Lavelle, the most prominent clerical supporter of the Brotherhood, continued to be defended by MacHale, who contested that some of the many comments attributed to Lavelle had been inaccurately quoted in the newspapers.[71]

Reflecting the continuing failure of the people's elected representatives, Cullen found it necessary again in 1863 to assert that the government was still failing to relieve the distress of the mass of the Irish people. The reason, he alleged, was that they were Catholic.[72] He warned that, as a result of government inaction, general discontent and despair was growing, providing fertile ground for revolutionaries.[73]

Cullen's analysis proved correct. In the harsh conditions, public as well as clerical discontent grew, providing a breeding ground for the ideas and beliefs of the Fenian revolutionaries. Lavelle was aware of this and he took to emphasising that 'whilst the people are suffering so much it is not possible they cd [sic] love their rulers.'[74] By March 1863, Cullen was writing that: 'There is actually a terrible spirit of revolution in a few parts of the country. I believe that many young priests are infected not here but in the midlands in Meath etc.'[75] To this he later added his fears that 'we are doomed to have plenty of troubles here'.[76]

The situation was developing as Cullen predicted. There was rioting in Dublin, Cork and other centres at the time of the Prince of Wales' wedding on 10 March 1863.[77] The wedding also provided the occasion for a split in the Irish hierarchical bench as to whether to present an address to the Prince.[78] Cullen favoured a general message to the Prince wishing him: 'Every happiness and the grace of God to become a true believer.'[79] Some bishops, most notably MacHale, Cantwell of Meath and Kilduff of Ardagh and Clonmacnoise were opposed to any such address.[80] The issue was resolved, following consultations with Rome, with addresses being made on a provincial, and not a national, hierarchical level. Cullen for his province for example wished the Prince happiness but 'telling him to protect the poor and act justly'.[81]

The disturbances that occurred at the time provided proof of popular support for the Fenians.[82] Furthermore, individual clerics such as Vaughan from Killaloe diocese, were proclaiming that what the people needed was not more saints but bread and beef.[83] Lavelle meanwhile continued to travel in Britain promoting the Brotherhood, creating what Cullen termed 'an immensity of mischief'.[84] Lavelle's actions resulted in repeated protests to and by Cullen.[85] Meanwhile MacHale became increasingly identified as 'The Patriot Prelate of Ireland' on the basis of his popularly accepted support for the Fenians.[86] Cullen complained to MacHale concerning Lavelle but was simply advised against involving himself in the affairs of Tuam archdiocese.[87]

Cullen continued to have a rationalistic view of armed revolution. By 1863, he returned to the argument he had put forward at the time of the McManus funeral.[88] This was that the Irish people, starving, unarmed, untrained and without adequate finance, were ill-advised to contemplate revolution. It was therefore 'a thing to deplore that men such as Lavelle and the Brothers of Saint Patrick seek to push the people to revolutionary plots'.[89] As he put it to Rome: 'I do not cease to say to Catholics that it is truly madness to talk of revolutions since the people here are without guns, without money and without any means of resistance in such a way as to give to our enemies the occasion to ruin us totally. Disgracefully there are some mad people who do not wish to hear such reasonable council.'[90] In Cullen's eyes it must be the devil who was inoculating Ireland's young men, who were easily manipulated, he maintained, with revolutionary ideas.[91] In desperation, he requested the Holy See to reiterate its position as regards the inadmissibility of all secret societies for Catholics.[92]

Cullen realised that simply condemning secret societies without proposing some method of tackling Ireland's economic and social problems was unsatisfactory. He therefore once again took to advocating constitutional means to improve the manner in which Ireland was administered. This included approval for Catholics to accept office under the government. Such a strategy he defended as a means of securing influence.

As he wrote in a public letter to his solicitor Thomas O'Hagan in June 1863: 'I do not censure Catholics for seeking or taking office, and I am very far from joining in the outcry that everyone doing so must be a traitor to his religion or an enemy to his country. Catholics in my opinion have a full right to share in the government of their own country, a right which is still scandalously withheld from them ... Were men who act in a truly Catholic spirit, and do honour to our country by their lives and their virtues, raised to office, I would commend them for accepting it, and rejoice in their promotion. As to Catholics who either seek to gain office by denying the principles or practices of their religion, or who, having obtained office by denying the principles or practices of their religion, or who having obtained office through Catholic influence, betray their promises and pledges, it is not my business to throw the first stone at them. I leave them to the judgement of their country and their God.'[93] In this manner Cullen distinguished between corrupt abuse of the Catholic vote and the right of Catholics to a share in the public administration.

In defiance of an undertaking not to write to the news-papers, in June 1863 Lavelle publicly renewed his attacks on

Cullen for decreeing membership of the Brotherhood of Saint Patrick to be a reserved sin. Lavelle asserted that this decree should not stop any layman from joining the Brotherhood.[94] Cullen immediately reported this letter to Rome and again renewed his calls for Rome to force MacHale to take effective measures against Lavelle before Cullen would do so himself.[95] The lack of disciplinary action against Lavelle whose aim, claimed Cullen, was to excite the people to disobedience against their pastors, meant that priests supporting constitutional methods had to suffer many insults.[96] The Dublin priests even wanted to protest publicly against Lavelle's actions and would have done so but that Cullen forbade them.[97]

At the end of July 1863, a letter dated 18 April from Lavelle to the leader of an Irish political club in San Francisco was quoted in the press. In this letter Lavelle again denounced Cullen, accusing him of dictatorship. Then, offering advice to tenants facing eviction, the letter used language which was seen as incitement to acts of murder.[98]

Writing to the newspapers again a few weeks later, Lavelle proclaimed that the Irish people had 'the indisputable right to set aside their tyrannical rulers'.[99] He went on, however, to oppose an early uprising against the British forces on the basis that it would have no chance of success, a sentiment with which Cullen would agree, though from a different standpoint. Lavelle went on to write that: 'We have not alone the right, we are bound by the duty of making all preparations in our power against the day when our oppressor will herself be battling for her existence and when our efforts will be morally certain of success. Is this treason? I am then a traitor. Is this disloyal? So am I.'[100]

The appearance of Lavelle's letter coincided with a meeting of the Irish Episcopal Conference which had been especially arranged in August to suit MacHale.[101] During this meeting it was decided to condemn the Brotherhood of Saint Patrick by name. The Brotherhood was an open and unsworn organisation, admitted the bishops, thereby differing from Cullen's earlier assertions. The bishops' decision was justified however on the ground that it had for its object 'the support and defence by arms of what is called the oath of membership of the Irish Republic'.[102]

Cullen further reported to Rome that: 'All the bishops, except the Archbishop of Tuam and the Bishop of Clonfert, were unanimous in condemning the letters of Father Lavelle calling on him to submit to ecclesiastical and civil authority.'[103] Whether it was a reaction to Lavelle's strong advice to tenants facing eviction or a fear of imminent land trouble is not clear, but the bishops also called on the people to organise petitions in support of Tenant Right.[104] In fact, MacHale was extremely upset at the attitude of the other bishops as regards the whole issue of Lavelle and the Brotherhood.[105] Cullen was pleased, however, that the condemnations of the Brotherhood and of Lavelle had received such widespread episcopal support.[106]

Objections to the joint bishops' condemnation of the Brotherhood of Saint Patrick came from the Brotherhood itself. It maintained that it was an open, legal, political organisation. The Brotherhood also alleged that the condemnation had been pushed through by Cullen of Dublin and Moriarty of Kerry. Furthermore, it was hinted that, had the bishops' statement been signed, the Brotherhood would have seriously considered taking libel action against them.[107] Cullen noted that Lavelle continued to contend that the bishops' condemnation was not worth the paper it was written on.[108]

By August 1863, the fear of an attempted rising was growing as the number of incidents between tenants and landlords rose sharply.[109] Lavelle was credited with some responsibility for such activity as he had urged the driving out of oppressive landlords. On this basis, calls were made for Cullen to be granted the facility to discipline Lavelle without limitation. If such a facility were granted, Cullen's half nephew, the vice rector in the Irish College, Rome, and later cardinal in Australia, Patrick Francis Moran, promised that no more would be heard from Lavelle.[110]

Cullen, however, maintained the caution he had always exercised when dealing with Lavelle. He continued to insist that it was better for MacHale to be obliged to discipline Lavelle and lamented that this had not been done.[111] In the meantime, even after the summer episcopal meeting, Lavelle, having allegedly received a lot of money from the Brotherhood, continued his personal attacks.[112] He persisted in defending the Brotherhood of Saint Patrick, implying that Cullen was 'the ruin of Ireland'.[113] Such writings were viewed by prelates such as MacEvilly of Galway as a scandal that ought not to be tolerated.[114] This attitude was also shared by some other clerics, such as the parish priest of Arklow, Redmond, extracts of whose correspondence with him Cullen forwarded to Rome.[115]

In October 1863, Cullen again complained to Rome of the Brotherhood and of Fenians associated with them: 'They threaten to come from America with 200,000 men and invade Ireland ...The objective of the Brothers is to excite turbulence in Ireland and what is more to attract our poor peasants to join the American army so as to be slaughtered. Our Machievellian government, which is now very powerful, would not be completely against a rebellion in Ireland because they would be able to suppress it in a minute, and because it would give a spur to pilfer the churches and convents again, and to confiscate what Catholics have earned.'[116]

Cullen now took to describing the Brotherhood of Saint Patrick and the Fenians as 'enemies of Ireland'.[117] Nonetheless, what with general discontent growing as a result of yet another poor harvest, support for the Fenian movement and the Brotherhood increased in the autumn and winter months of 1863.[118]

Intervening personally yet again in a controversy involving Cullen, Pope Pius IX gave consideration to the Lavelle case on 6 September 1863.[119] Accepting a recommendation for a letter to be written to McHale, the Pope wrote on 24 September 1863 to the Archbishop of Tuam.[120] Lavelle was to be disciplined. He was also not to leave the precincts of his parish without first obtaining the permission of his archbishop on each occasion. Cullen was also authorised to exercise disciplinary action on Lavelle if necessary.[121]

171

Obliged to issue a retraction of his views, Lavelle then set about fulfilling the letter, rather than the spirit, of the Roman instruction. In what was taken for his retraction, dated 16 October 1863, and afterwards published in the press, Lavelle, instead of displaying any signs of apology, defended his actions and reiterated his political beliefs. While, for example, he expressed his sorrow at having played an active political role without having first obtained permission from his archbishop, he nonetheless continued to insist that the Brotherhood of Saint Patrick did not hold to immoral aims. He also claimed that it was not a secret, oath-bound organisation.[122]

Cullen described the retraction of Lavelle as 'a cunning defence of all of the most scandalous things that he had published up to now'.[123] In the light of this and the violence of his language, Cullen called on Rome to examine carefully Lavelle's retraction before approving it, if it was sent on to Rome.[124] Indeed for Cullen it was unacceptable as it showed a determination to antagonise those he had offended.[125] Kirby noted how Lavelle himself did not call it a 'retraction' but rather 'a few explanations'.[126] Meanwhile Moran reported a claim that Lavelle's letter was nothing less than 'a barefaced attempt to delude and bamboozle the Holy Father'.[127]

Public attacks by Lavelle on Cullen continued to appear in the press. In the *Irishman* newspaper on 31 October 1863, a letter dated erroneously 6 October 1863 (according to Cullen, thereby placing it before the so-called retraction and signed by Lavelle) strongly denounced the Archbishop of Dublin.[128] In this Lavelle, in a taunt about a project close to Cullen's heart, claimed that the Archbishop was taking money off the poor peasants of Ireland to found a Catholic university. This institution Lavelle termed 'West British, anti-Irish and aimed at denationalising Irish Catholic youth'.[129]

With the appearance of this letter, Cullen became convinced that Lavelle acted with the approval of his Ordinary, MacHale.[130] After all, as was pointed out in Propaganda, Lavelle at this time was not publicly suspended, he was not deprived of his appointment and was not obliged to retract what he wrote against the bishops.[131] Renewed calls for definite disciplinary action against Lavelle were now made by Cullen, supported by Moran and Kirby.[132]

In the United States, there was a certain degree of clerical support for the Fenians and this was heavily condemned by Cullen.[133] There Cullen conjectured that the Brotherhood of Saint Patrick was encouraged by the American authorities for their own ends. However, in the event of revolution, Cullen was convinced that the American administration would not do anything to help Ireland or the Irish.[134] At the same time in Ireland, MacHale was being hailed by the Fenians as worth more than all of the bishops put together, while Lavelle was viewed as a martyr.[135]

The Pope decided to intervene again in what was now referred to as 'the Lavelle case', having had some of Cullen's correspondence to Kirby read to him.[136] On 26 November 1863, Pius IX sent his observations to MacHale for comment, noting with disapproval Lavelle's continued membership of the Brotherhood, and calling on Lavelle to stop his Brotherhood activities. [137]

Meanwhile, Cullen was concerned that the failure of the ecclesiastical authorities to act against Lavelle to date had led people to believe that the Tuam diocesan priest was acting with the support of MacHale.[138] Lavelle's ideas were being propagated by the newspapers.[139] Calling yet again for action by Rome while noting that there was little he himself could do, Cullen asserted how: 'It is very much to be desired that an end is put to the career of that priest, otherwise he will weaken the faith of the people, excite new dissensions in the country and give occasion to our enemies to continue their abuses of the poor. The affair is now in the hands of Rome and I hope it will be carried to a good end without causing more evils in this Kingdom.'[140] In early December 1863 these calls for action by Rome were supported by the Canons of the Chapter of Dublin and from some members of the Irish hierarchy such as MacEvilly of Galway.[141]

When news of the latest Papal intervention in the Lavelle story reached Dublin, it was cautiously welcomed by Cullen.[142]

With the passage of time and firmly believing that Lavelle was in the pay of both the Fenians and the Brotherhood, Cullen grew more heartened by a decision of the Pope that MacHale should initiate definitive action against Lavelle.[143] For his part, Lavelle, however, continued to assert that the Brothers of Saint Patrick did not take any oath. Such claims were contradicted by Cullen who reported to Rome how he was continuously receiving requests for the faculty to absolve the Brothers from the oath.[144]

꧁ Chapter Ten ꧂

PRIESTS AND REVOLUTION

LREADY BESET WITH various personality, organisational, administrative and financial difficulties, the Fenian organisation now had to contend with the question of how best to promote its cause and counter Cullen's denunciations. Stephens, despite strong opposition from O'Mahony, decided on a special newspaper. The outcome was the *Irish People*, which was first published on 28 November 1863.[1] For two years the government made no attempt to prevent the publication of this organ of the Fenian movement. Its contributors and supporters included James Stephens, O'Dovonan Rossa, Thomas Clarke Luby, John O'Leary and Charles Kickham. All of these, according to Cullen, had 'drunk of revolutionary and anti-religious ideas'.[2] Under their influence, the *Irish People* publicised the Fenian belief that priests should confine themselves to spiritual affairs. Ironically, their position on this issue was similar to Cullen's throughout the previous decade in relation to the question of public clerical support for the Irish Independent Party. There was one significant difference however. Catholics were urged by the *Irish People* to obey their clergy in spiritual but not political matters.

As Kickham put it: 'Ireland cannot possibly be saved if the people are not taught to draw a clear line of demarcation between ecclesiastical authority in spiritual matters and ... in matters which are not spiritual. It is our wish that the people should revere the hierarchy and priesthood in their spiritual capacity; but in politics we see too many reasons to convince us that they are the worst guides possible.'[3]

The withdrawal of priests from the field of politics was a prerequisite for the success of the Fenians, according to Kickham. Church opposition to the revolutionary nationalist movement represented a serious obstacle to the successful spread of Fenian doctrine. As Kickham put it: 'Bishops and priests may be bad politicians and worse Irishmen.'[4] On this basis, the Fenians claimed: 'We saw from the start that ecclesiastical authority in temporal affairs should be shivered to atoms before we could advance a single step towards the liberation of our suffering country.'[5] Personal attacks were often made on Cullen.[6]

In April, the *Irish People* acknowledged the need for clerical involvement in political affairs in the past. By 1864 however, the paper was maintaining that times had changed, asserting: 'The people are now comparatively educated, and demand the right possessed by the people of other Catholic countries of acting according to the dictates of their judgement in all worldly concerns.'[7]

With regard to their revolutionary political philosophy, the *Irish People* argued that conspiring to overthrow tyrannical civil governments was not opposed by the teaching of the Catholic Church.[8] It recalled how Cullen had participated in the Irish Brigade of Saint Patrick, which had been organised in 1860 to help defend the Pontifical states, with 'secrecy, discipline and silent action'.[9]

Cullen was highly critical of this pro-Fenian paper.[10] He wrote: 'The articles in it, other than being revolutionary, often assault the temporal Government of the Church and praise Garibaldi, and every day they discredit the Catholic clergy and diminish their influence.'[11] Cullen claimed that Fenian newspapers wanted priests in politics only if they supported their political, revolutionary, republican line.[12] According to Cullen, the *Irish People* aimed to alienate the priests from the people and therefore adopted a strongly anti-Catholic Church policy, which was evident in every issue.[13] Cullen held a similar view of the *Connaught Patriot*, another newspaper which supported secular nationalism.[14]

Complaining of these publications, Cullen wrote to Rome in March 1864 of how: 'Many newspapers ... directly or indirectly assault the clergy and try to sow darnel in the country. The argument of the papers is that Ireland will never become that which it must be without a revolution and shaking to the roots the yoke of England ... The same newspapers write continually against me because I condemn secret societies and I try to stop revolutionary movements which could not take place without bringing ruin and extermination to this country because the people here do not have the slightest pretensions to be able to resist for a week the power of England. Because I do these things they write that I am a political priest and that I interfere in things which do not concern me.'[15]

Cullen continued to maintain that it was nothing less than stupid to talk of a revolution to a people without arms, without ammunition and without money.[16] Some priests, such as Joseph Flanagan from Cullen's own archdiocese of Dublin, openly supported Cullen's stance and provided information on Fenian suspects to the authorities.[17] Many other priests however, while objecting to the attempts of the Fenians and the *Irish People* to minimise clerical political influence, desisted from publicly denouncing parishioners for reading or selling the 'Fenian organs'.[18] MacHale in fact even went so far as to subscribe to such publications.[19]

Cullen replied to the Fenian press in a series of pastoral letters in the early months of 1864. In these Cullen argued that the Catholic Church could not in any sense support an organisation that bound its members to take an oath to obey unknown leaders. He also asserted that, despite Fenian protests to the contrary, the Fenians were in reality opposed to the

Catholic Church.[20] Issuing a public warning against secret societies in his Saint Patrick's Day message 1864, Cullen condemned by name both the Fenians and the Brothers of Saint Patrick.[21]

Meanwhile, on receipt of the letter from the Pope to MacHale, Lavelle had set out for Rome to explain his side of the argument there.[22] Doubt prevailed amongst many Irish bishops, however, that Lavelle would retract publicly.[23] Cullen immediately warned Kirby: 'Do not let him see the students or treat with them. If he gets among them he will upset everything.'[24] Cullen expressed the hope that while in Rome, Lavelle would only receive absolution after publishing a retraction of his errors. If this failed to occur, Cullen warned Kirby that worse would follow.[25]

Upon Lavelle's arrival in Rome in early January 1864, he set about doing a spiritual retreat in the retreat house of SS John and Paul.[26] Here, along with his apology, Lavelle wrote a letter addressed to the Pope which he left with the spiritual director to give to the Cardinal Prefect of Propaganda.[27] Lavelle also requested an interview with Barnabò so as to explain his stance in person.[28] In his apology, a copy of which was sent to Cullen, Lavelle accepted the condemnation of the Brotherhood of Saint Patrick. He also stated that he was repentent for attacking members of the Irish hierarchy. He then gave his word that in the future he would abstain from pursuing political matters through the press and apologised for having improperly written in defence of the Brothers of Saint Patrick.[29]

After writing this apology however, Lavelle also wrote a submission to the Pope originally dated 'January 1864' but later published bearing the date of 27 January 1864, an event which led to a certain degree of confusion.[30] This letter to the Pope in effect negated the retraction, for in it Lavelle praised the late Terence Bellew McManus, defended the Brotherhood of Saint Patrick, while renewing his attacks on the political views of Cullen, portraying him as nothing less than 'the cause of the ruin of Ireland'.[31] In a preface to this letter as it appeared in the newspapers, he denounced Cullen as 'the main cause of untold calamities that at this moment afflict my country ... I believe that if Dr Cullen, instead of running directly counter to the present national feeling of Ireland, lent his aid in giving it aim and direction, he would have consulted infinitely more for the interests of the Church and the people ... I believe that no man in Ireland has done more to foster the very thing that he is so zealous to put down as Dr Cullen himself ... He has adopted a policy which benefits the few selfish and grasping place hunters'.[32]

While Lavelle was still in Rome, Cullen urged the authorities there to compel Lavelle to publish a clear retraction of all of the things which he had done.[33] He also urged the Roman authorities to be cautious in believing Lavelle.[34] Cullen predicted that if a clear retraction was not published by Lavelle while in Rome, things would get even worse.[35] In fact, the Roman authorities did not heed Cullen's advice, and so, having written his two statements but having published nothing, Lavelle returned to Ireland on 2 February 1864. In this way Cullen's prediction that the situation would deteriorate was soon realised.[36]

On his return to Ireland, Lavelle claimed that his arguments had been welcomed and supported by Rome. On this basis, the *Connaught Patriot* of 13 February 1864, with an article entitled 'Arrival of Father Lavelle from Rome', announced that: 'Success has attended the cause of his mission both as regards himself and the interests of the national party in Ireland for whom we warmly pleaded.'[37] After resuming residence in his parish, Lavelle continued his association with the Brotherhood of Saint Patrick.[38] On 22 February 1864 for example, Lavelle attended a dinner along with MacHale and began proclaiming how in Rome he was received with kindness and consideration.[39] Then Lavelle claimed that the accusations made against him in Rome, of inciting the people to kill their landlords and of praying with heretics, had been refuted triumphantly.

Lavelle announced how, whilst in Rome, he had justified his attacks on Cullen in the form of a brochure that he had presented to the Pope.[40] In reporting this development to the authorities in Rome, Kirby noted how Lavelle attacked Cullen saying that the Dublin archbishop's politics were those sustained by Victor Emmanuel at the time of his invasion of the Papal states.[41] The fact that following his return to Ireland, Lavelle made no immediate move to publicise his apology gave rise to rumours that his argument, and not Cullen's, had won the day in Rome.[42]

As Lavelle delayed in publishing his retraction, Cullen was tempted to publish the copy that had been sent to him.[43] He had already received permission from Rome to take this step.[44] Cullen decided against this for fear of prosecution for defamation by Lavelle.[45] However, Cullen promised to send a copy of any retraction published by Lavelle to Propaganda as soon as it appeared.[46]

In fact, Lavelle only published his retraction of 25 January 1864 in the *Connaught Patriot* on 5 March 1864.[47] Alongside it he published his letter to the Pope dated in the press 27 January 1864 and which Lavelle claimed to have submitted to the Roman Pontiff before he left Rome.[48] He also claimed that he had spent his time in Rome trying to rectify the opinion that Irish Catholics were conspiring against the Roman Catholic Church or against a just government. Lavelle then asserted that it could not be proven that the Brotherhood of Saint Patrick was a secret society. The fact that it was thought to be so, according to Lavelle, was the result of misrepresentation by Cullen. Lavelle then went on to claim that it had been at the request of Cullen that he had been suspended from his priestly duties, despite the fact that his differences with Cullen were lawful political differences.[49]

Upon reading this, Cullen was very upset. While presuming that this second document referred to by Lavelle was a forgery, he prepared to discipline the Tuam priest. Before doing so however, Cullen decided to ascertain whether the document claimed by Lavelle to be in the possession of the Pope did really exist. He wrote to Rome noting how 'it would be advisable to know if he did truly present it'.[50] This turned out to be a wise move by Cullen as the letter to the Pope did exist.[51]

The reply to Cullen 10 March 1864 from Rome reported how Propaganda was about to write to Lavelle to force him to carry out the promises he had undertaken while in Rome.[52] Cullen, however, did not want Propaganda to correspond directly with Lavelle, for then Lavelle would be able to boast that he was important enough to be in direct communication with the Holy See.[53] Cullen wanted MacHale to be compelled to punish Lavelle. Such an approach would be doubly beneficial, Cullen noted, as it would not only result in Lavelle being silenced but it would also compel MacHale to distance himself from the Fenian movement.[54] However, knowing the nature of MacHale, Cullen warned Propaganda to be careful in the way in which it went about this delicate task. As Cullen put it: 'Undoubtedly this is a great scandal in Ireland where the Catholics are so well disposed to respect the Holy See. But in trying to induce MacHale to give proof of his obedience one needs to be very cautious not to push this prelate, who is not noted for the virtue of humility, to offer public resistance which could be the origin of greater evils.'[55] Lavelle, as Cullen was aware, was a popular priest among certain sectors of the clergy and a petition was organised in support of him and MacHale.[56]

Yet again, no immediate move was made by the Roman authorities against Lavelle despite the repeated complaints and calls for disciplinary action made by Cullen, Moran and Kirby.[57] This lack of action prompted Cullen to write of how in Ireland 'the good Catholics begin to ask if there is no power in the Church to call to order or to punish a priest who tramples on all of the rules'.[58] Cullen insisted that MacHale, whom he accused of direct connivance with Lavelle, should now be forced to discipline him.[59] Cullen left Rome in no doubt as to the effects of Lavelle's continued writings. Some of those who left the Fenian organisation had joined it on the basis that it was supported by Lavelle and MacHale.[60] The failure of Rome to warn MacHale and discipline Lavelle gave the Fenians the opportunity to pretend to have MacHale's support. Meantime, the Fenians were maintaining that 'the bishops who condemn them are mere slaves of the Government or fanatical and ignorant men'.[61]

Whether prompted by the behaviour of Lavelle or not, there were further examples of clerics openly supporting the Fenian movement.[62] Adopting the same attitude that he had insisted upon during the time of the Independent Party, Cullen reiterated his belief that priests should occupy themselves with spiritual affairs only. He denounced as totally unacceptable clerical involvement such as practised by Lavelle.[63]

By now Cullen was turning his attention away from the political wing of the Fenians, the Brotherhood of Saint Patrick, to concentrate on the actual Fenian organisation itself. At that time the Fenians were reputed to have widespread support with an estimated membership of 300,000 in the United States.[64] Cullen estimated membership of the Fenians in Ireland at some two or three thousand, mostly drawn from the same ranks as the Brotherhood of Saint Patrick.[65] The two organisations, the Brotherhood and the Fenians, were intimately related. This is what Cullen asserted as he often equated one organisation with the other, despite the protestations of the Brotherhood.[66] Cullen declared that the Fenians were an evil, anti-clerical, secret, oath-bound organisation, impregnated with the philosophy of Mazzini and Garibaldi and conspiring more against the Catholic religion than in favour of the political independence of Ireland by revolutionary means.[67] They were a scandalous organisation he claimed, led by Protestants and unbelievers and impregnated with tricksters and British spies.[68] The patriotism of Lavelle and the Fenians was, believed Cullen, simply an affair of money aimed at manipulating the people and exposing them to certain ruin.[69]

It was Cullen's view that the failure of the British government to tackle Ireland's continuing serious social and economic ills, along with its promotion of a mixed education system, were contributing to the rise of the Fenians.[70] He believed that the authorities were fully aware of the Fenian presence in the country. He deplored the failure of the government to take any firm measures against the Fenians or the Brotherhood. Speculating as to the reason for this, he put forward the opinion that 'in the first place they cannot do anything, there being in

Ireland neither arms nor munitions of war nor money, and in the second place because in a true spirit of Machiavellian a few Lords want this brotherhood preserved because by means of it one weakens … the poor Catholics'.[71]

Cullen went on to assert of the British government that, 'so great is their hate against the Catholic religion that they seem to rejoice in the destruction of the poor people'.[72] In the light of all of this then, as Cullen put it: 'It must be said that here one cannot say much against our people if they let themselves be attracted to secret societies, as they are pushed towards such things firstly by the bad treatment that they receive from the Government, and secondly by the example that is given by our Prime Minister and by the English people who do nothing these days other than defend Mazzini and grant celebrations for Garibaldi.'[73]

With incidents of disorder increasing throughout the country, Cullen had membership of the Fenians again listed as a reserved sin in his diocese.[74] The same penalty was imposed on Fenians in various American dioceses, most notably those of Chicago and Philadelphia by the local Ordinaries.[75] Such a move however, noted Cullen, had little obvious effect.[76] This, he claimed, was a result of the lack of a united ecclesiastical front with regard to the Fenians. Such views received considerable ecclesiastical support.[77] At the same time however, MacHale publicly supported the Fenians and called them 'a charitable Brotherhood'.[78]

For Cullen, the Fenians were anything but a charitable organisation. As he put it to Rome: '… I am convinced that the Brotherhood is not only illegal or contrary to the laws of this kingdom but that further it is yet evil in itself and worthy of condemnation, firstly, because assembling people of all religions exposes them to the danger of losing the faith; secondly, because it puts the members in hostility to the clergy; thirdly, because it tries to overthrow a recognised government, and fourthly because at least in Ireland (and perhaps also in America) the members are tied by an oath administered without any legitimate authority.'[79]

Raising an issue that was to become significant later, Cullen called for an authoritative ruling on whether the Fenians were excommunicated, claiming that: 'A decision on this point would be very desirable so as to maintain uniformity of practice among the clergy of Ireland.'[80]

Lavelle challenged the assertion that the Fenian organisation came under the terms of any pontifical condemnation. The Fenians were not condemned under his reading of the necessary conditions for an organisation to be outlawed as a secret society by the Church, seeing as the Fenians' meetings were public and their discourses published.[81] Cullen answered by noting how 'the Free Masons do the same by publicly having their meetings here and also issuing invitations to their dinners and balls but despite all this they do not cease to constitute a secret society'.[82]

Cullen's insistence that the Holy See pronounce on the subject of the Fenians arose from the fact that he found it impossible to believe that the mass of the people would support anything that was anti-clerical.[83] He continued throughout the spring of 1864 therefore to be highly critical of ecclesiastics like Lavelle who supported the Fenians.[84] Lavelle, Cullen insisted, should be disciplined on the basis that 'the movement would cease fast if it were not for the encouragement which it receives from Father Lavelle and some other ecclesiastics'.[85] Cullen's belief in this regard was confirmed when, having declared membership of the Fenians a reserved sin, he detected a noticeable drop of support for them.[86] This raised his hopes that 'in a few months all the other organisers of these societies will leave it and will begin to think about other things'.[87] This was also the view of various correspondents of Cullen. It was confirmed for them when one of the priests, Vaughan from Killaloe, who had publicly supported the Fenians up to now, decided in April 1864 to publicly renounce his own membership of the Brotherhood of Saint Patrick, following his condemnation at the bishops' meeting of August 1863.[88]

On 1 April 1864 Propaganda issued instructions to the four archbishops of Ireland that action was to be taken against Lavelle.[89] Propaganda also advised Lavelle of its decision.[90] A minor hitch threatened when it was seen that Lavelle's name was incorrectly written on the Vatican document as Francis and not Patrick, thereby leaving Patrick Lavelle to claim that the letter was not intended for him.[91]

Far from severing his connections with the Fenians however, Lavelle renewed his campaign in their favour. He asserted that the censure imposed by the Church on secret, oath-bound organisations plotting against Church or State did not apply to the Fenians, who were not opposed to the Church but only to the tyrannical civil government.[92] He aimed to publicise his case by means of a booklet.[93] Cullen responded by again appealing to the Vatican to state the official Church position.[94] It was an excruciating situation for Cullen.

On the 18 April 1864, Pope Pius IX wrote to MacHale repeating the direction to silence Lavelle. He reprimanded MacHale himself for not carrying out his duties as a bishop and once again urged that disciplinary action be taken against Lavelle.[95]

With the intervention of the Pope, Cullen and many others believed that the Lavelle affair had at last finished.[96] Cullen copied the letter of the Holy See to MacHale, which was later published, and circulated it to some United Kingdom and North American bishops.[97]

Cullen's hopes now grew that 'the party of Lavelle will be reduced to nothing'.[98] Financially Cullen reckoned that both Lavelle and the Fenian movement were encountering severe difficulties and that their leaders would soon be discredited.[99] Indeed by July, Archbishop Duggan of Chicago was convinced that he had 'crushed' the movement in his diocese.[100] Among the Irish bishops, there was concern at the continued growth of the Fenians and of their anti-clerical and anti-Cullen press campaign.[101]

Lavelle left Ireland before the disciplinary measures ordered by the Pope could be implemented. It was rumoured that MacHale had tipped him off with regard to the action ordered by the Holy See.[102] Claiming the support of MacHale, he went first to Scotland and later to England.[103] There, despite local episcopal protests, he publicly collected funds and campaigned for the Fenian cause.[104] He repeatedly insisted that the Brotherhood of Saint Patrick was not a secret society, denied any knowledge of a suspension order, and denounced those, specifically Cullen, who maintained otherwise.[105] Lavelle received widespread newspaper and clerical support, and MacHale refused to answer questions by prelates in England enquiring about the case.[106] Cullen was annoyed.[107] He decided to call for the publication of the Pope's letter to MacHale. The Archbishop of Dublin then accused the Archbishop of Tuam of protecting Lavelle in supporting the Fenian movement, from which MacHale publicly received subscriptions.[108] In response, Propaganda wrote to three bishops in Great Britain and two in America informing them of Lavelle's suspension.[109] Following further moves, in which Vatican concern was expressed, Lavelle was finally suspended.[110]

Cullen was convinced that the open support given by clerics like Lavelle to the Fenians must do evil.[111] Lavelle however, portraying himself as a martyr to the cause of truth, continued to insist that he had properly submitted his memorial to the Pope, a copy of which he published as a booklet.[112] Lavelle's story was supported by the Brotherhood of Saint Patrick, which formed a commission to defend him.[113] Upon Lavelle's return to his parish in late August 1864, the Brotherhood invited him to lecture to them in Dublin, Cullen's own See. In support of Lavelle, meetings were organised at which Cullen was publicly condemned.[114] A memorial was drawn up attacking Cullen and supporting Lavelle and MacHale.[115]

Meanwhile, following pressure from Cullen and various American bishops, a meeting was held in Propaganda on 30 May 1864 to discuss whether membership of the Fenians incurred ecclesiastical sanction or not.[116] It was decided to refer the question to the Office of Holy Roman and Universal Inquisition known as the Holy Office.[117] The Holy Office could draw on various precedents including the bulls *In Eminenti* (28 April 1738) of Clement XII, *Providas* (18 May 1751) of Benedict XIV, *Ecclesiam* (13 September 1821) of Pius VII and *Quo Graviora* (13 March

1825) of Leo XII. Under these authorities, the Fenians might be condemned not only on the grounds of constituting a secret society, but also because of being an 'occult movement', a term applied to illegal groups of private individuals aiming to attack the legitimate authority of Church or State.

The deliberations of the Holy Office, however, failed to produce a clear conclusion. On 2 June 1864 the Office decided not to reply in a direct manner.[118] Rather, referring to a previous decision concerning illegal occult movements taken on 5 August 1846 that had been ratified by Pope Pius IX, they declared that: 'By secret societies to which the Pontifical Constitutions refer, are understood those which propose something against the Church or government, requiring or not requiring for themselves an oath concerning something secret which needs to be kept.'[119]

This Holy Office 'decision' was communicated to Cullen with the comment that, should any problem arise concerning its application to the Fenians, Cullen could consult the Holy See again for specific clarification.[120] It is worthy of note that at the time of the publication of the Propaganda rescript, the *Irish Ecclesiastical Record* claimed that the Church's position in relation to Fenianism had been definitively clarified. It is clear, however, that the Roman authorities had evaded the specific issue as to whether or not Fenian membership was permissible for a Catholic.[121] The Vatican had preferred instead simply to indicate what sort of organisations were not permissible. This was of no help to Cullen.

While it could be contended that the Fenians did come under the terms of the Vatican rescript, the opposite could also be argued. In support of the latter view, the Fenians could genuinely claim that they were mostly loyal Catholics and not opposed to the Catholic Church. They insisted that this was the case despite disputes with priests or bishops. Furthermore, they could argue that, while the British government had been the de facto ruling power in Ireland for hundreds of years and was internationally accepted as such, their authority had been assumed by military conquest. As the Fenians saw it, the British government was an occupying foreign power and not the legitimate government. Certain moral backing was given to this argument by ecclesiastics such as Lavelle and Patrick Murray, a professor at the National Seminary at Maynooth.[122]

There were other elements of confusion in the discussion. One was the distinction between the militarily minded Fenians and the peaceful Brotherhood of Saint Patrick. Another point of confusion was the contrast between the illegal status of the Fenians in Ireland and the openly tolerated and sometimes officially encouraged position of the same organisation in the United States.

Incidents of aggressive anti-clerical behaviour by the Fenians began to be reported by the end of 1864. In the diocese of Ross, the bishop and the parish priest of Skibbereen were publicly insulted when they spoke in church against the Brotherhood.[123] With such incidents becoming more frequent, Cullen, again physically ill, was distressed by the difficulty of retaining the support of the faithful for the Church's line on the Fenians. This was especially the case as the Fenians were being perceived as outside of the strictly religious sphere.[124] He now feared that the Fenian controversy would become very serious.[125] His fears would subsequently be realised.

Chapter Eleven

CONSTITUTIONALISM
DISAPPOINTS AGAIN

IN IRELAND CULLEN favoured the political process as a vehicle for furthering the people's interests. Following the unsatisfactory reply from the Holy Office on the Fenian issue and with signs of growing support for revolutionary nationalism, he now considered it appropriate to revive the constitutional effort. Hence his support for the organisation to be called the National Association. In this he was supported for a time by A.M. Sullivan of the *Nation*[1] and Sir John Gray of the *Freeman's Journal*.[2] He was himself actively involved, consulting many of his fellow Irish prelates, twenty-three of whom favoured the project. The one principal prelate who did not lend his support however, despite all attempts to persuade him, was MacHale.[3] He agreed with the objectives but his hope was for a restoration of the Independent Party of the 1850s. He was therefore critical of the fact that the participating parliamentary members took no oath which might bind them to the new association.[4]

As well as MacHale there were prominent politicians, including one-time revolutionary Charles Gavan Duffy, now home from Australia, and constitutional nationalist John Martin, who failed to support the new association.[5] Also, the ex-leader

189

of the Independent Party, George Henry Moore, kept his distance from it.[6] A number of clerics had misgivings.[7] Indeed, the very fact that the association was so close to the Church operated to its disadvantage. It meant that the organisation, as the *Dublin Evening Mail* put it, 'will be generally regarded as only a fresh attempt to Ultramontanise the Irish people … It is Ireland's misfortune that she can never find leaders who are able to rise superior to sectarianism'.[8] Opposition came from Irish Protestants and Fenians. Protestants opposed it because it was proposing the disestablishment of the Church of Ireland; the Fenians saw in it a threat to their own revolutionary philosophy.[9]

Despite such lack of support, the promoters' efforts bore fruit when, on 29 December 1864, the National Association was officially founded. It was led by John Blake Dillon.[10] The very fact that Dillon was the accepted political leader of the Association represented a shift in Cullen's position. Dillon had been prominent in the Young Ireland movement of which Cullen had been so critical. In view of Cullen's nervousness about the Tenant League in the 1850s, the prominence given to land reform in the Association programme is also of interest.

The inaugural meeting of the Association was attended by seven bishops, including Cullen, who addressed the assembly.[11] At this gathering the objectives were laid down. These included a land bill to improve tenant rights; disestablishment of the Church of Ireland; free and equal education for all classes irrespective of religion. Somewhat surprisingly, the Association was not intended to be a political party in a parliamentary sense. It would seek to achieve its goals by canvassing public opinion, promoting what it termed 'a rational and intelligent patriotism … and by placing in representative positions … men from whose principles and character they may anticipate a disinterested and effective support'.[12] The constitution provided that no political support would be lent to any existing political grouping that did not support the goals of the Association.[13]

The task of winning public support for the Association, which combined both ecclesiastics and lay politicans, was not an easy one, despite the possible benefits.[14] For Cullen, the organisation was to prove a frustrating experience due to the fact that he was not in absolute control of it. Even in its very early days, he was sceptical about the viable prospects of turning it into an effective political weapon. Both of these factors were evident in his comment to Kirby early in 1865: 'The Association is going on slowly. It is hard to keep laymen right, especially on the education issue.'[15] In fact the association failed to excite much real public interest.[16] There was little support for the idea of working with Palmerston's Liberals in the interests of reform as promoted by the Association.[17]

As support for the Association was weak, Cullen, in a letter to his clergy on 23 January 1865, urged them to participate in it in their spare time. He made sure to warn them however that any such involvement was not to interfere with their spiritual activity, nor was it to result in them performing any action which could be deemed to be unbecoming of the clerical state. He also reminded them of the regulations of the 1854 Synod.[18] With the notable exceptions of MacHale of Tuam and McNulty of Meath, Cullen's example was taken up by the bishops, who in their lenten pastorals for 1865 recommended the Association for support.[19] The clergy were therefore being actively encouraged now to involve themselves and to propagate their views on such political questions as tenant rights and the ending of Church endowment.[20]

Despite the efforts of many prelates, the Association met with considerable scepticism on the part of a wary electorate mindful of the record of the Independent Party. There was also a lack of appeal in the Association's programme for an impoverished tenant people threatened with still greater misery.[21] Dissatisfaction with the lack of any party pledge, for example, quickly manifested itself. In sharp contrast to Cullen and other bishops, McNulty in Meath in his lenten pastoral attacked the policy recommended by the Association, which could involve Irish parliamentary members supporting the Whig party.[22] He endorsed the calls by some of his priests for a party pledge to bind Association members of parliament to parliamentary independence.[23]

A proposal to this effect, later leaked to the press, was subsequently passed. This happened following a great debate at a special meeting of the National Association committee on 28 April 1865, which was attended by various clerics and bishops, including Cullen and McNulty.[24] The rules would now state that: 'This Association pledges itself to the policy of complete parliamentary independence.'[25] They would go on to state that: 'The acceptance of place or the solicitation of favours from Government is incompatible with an independent attitude towards the ministry.'[26] As no mention was to be found of such a proposal in the existing regulations to become official policy, the constitution laid down a specific procedure to be followed. According to this, the matter would have to be discussed and approved at two consecutive committee meetings and then ratified by a general meeting before it could become Association policy.

Cullen, who was very much opposed to the proposal to resurrect the issue of Independent Opposition, now set about ensuring that no such alteration of the constitution would be ratified.[27] He drafted a lengthy memorandum, read at a committee meeting in May 1865, defending the rights of Catholics to take office under the government and stating his opposition to any change in the association's constitution. While not opposing the idea of 'parliamentary independence', he strongly objected to the proposal that office holding or active cooperation with a government would be forbidden. Some form of loose party discipline might be necessary, but to impose an obligation of Independent Opposition on Association members was unacceptable to Cullen, having regard to political realities. It would have the effect of preventing Catholics from broadening their influence in government. It would be a contentious issue, claimed Cullen, leading to internal disputes and discouraging and dissuading prospective supporters from joining the association.[28]

If support for the Association in 1865 was slow in developing, the same could not be said of the Fenians. Despite some reports to the contrary, the Fenians continued to grow in popularity, as Cullen was well aware.[29] He predicted that the Church would be ruined if this support was not checked, and he even took to criticising the government for failing to move against them.[30] Rumours, spread in the United States, that the Vatican was going to move against the Fenians were strongly denied by Lavelle.[31] He publicly claimed in February 1865, without any apparent foundation, that the bishop of Philadelphia, Woods, had been informed by Propaganda that membership of the Fenians was permitted to Catholics and that therefore, 'Fenians are not to be disquieted'.[32] Cullen immediately challenged Lavelle's statement, which was apparently widely believed even though no evidence to substantiate it was produced.[33] The following months were to witness a rise in clerical sympathy, evident even in seminaries, for the Fenians and also for Lavelle.[34] This occurred despite the fact that the 1865 Papal Jubilee indulgence was denied to the Fenians.[35] More and more priests began to empathise with Lavelle's claims that it was like asking grace from the devil to ask for justice from the British government, and with his assertion that many priests were opposed to British rule in Ireland.[36]

The divisions caused by the proposal to adopt a policy of Independent Opposition in the National Association threatened to split it in two. After much delay and the postponement of a meeting due to discuss the issue, a loosely worded compromise was worked out by Dillon. This reiterated the aims of the Association, and was approved at a meeting of 19 June 1865.[37] Shortly afterwards, on 22 June 1865, several bishops, including MacHale, met Dillon to discuss the situation and reportedly agreed to support the National Association.[38] Days later it became apparent, however, that MacHale's approval was conditional on the association adopting a policy of Independent Opposition. On 27 June 1865, MacHale was quoted as stating that: 'Nothing short of the pledge of Independent Opposition, in all its plenitude and vigour, can save the country, with the exercise of greater vigilance on the part of electors to see this pledge carried out by their representatives ...'[39] Cullen's absolute refusal to go along with this view led to strong criticism of him in various newspapers, including that edited by Sullivan, a one-time supporter of the Association, for what the *Nation* newspaper termed his 'disastrous mistakes' and 'fatal incapacity of judging public men'.[40]

Cullen's refusal to consider Independent Opposition and his positive attitude towards Irish parliamentary members accepting government offices did not mean that he unreservedly supported the British government. While he was unhappy with the proposed new direction of the National Association, he was also severely critical of the British government.[41] Cullen also continued his attacks on the Fenians, who were being refused the Sacraments in many dioceses in Ireland. Despite the illegal status of the Fenians and the no-hope outlook for an armed rising, it was apparent that a growing number of priests were now disagreeing with Cullen's attitude to the national question. These clerics had very little sympathy with the approach of the National Association.

Such divisions greatly hampered the National Association's prospects during the July 1865 general election. In the course of the election campaign, the high profile assumed by certain clerics again drew down criticism.[42] The election results were inconclusive but they allowed the Liberals to stay in office. They also provided tangible proof that the electoral impact of the National Association was only marginal, despite claims to the contrary.[43]

Concern over the growth of the Fenians continued to increase in ecclesiastical circles in the United States despite the June 1864 response from the Holy Office.[44] Prelates there differed in their approach and so requested a further directive from Rome.[45]

The first response from Rome was that the matter was again under consideration by the Holy Office.[46] Anxiety was growing there, however, following Lavelle's allegations that the Vatican had directed the bishop of Philadelphia not to disturb the Fenians. Pressure was applied to the Holy Office therefore to respond to such rumours.[47] On 13 July 1865 Propaganda communicated the position to be adopted in regard to the Fenians to a number of American bishops, as well as to Cullen and MacHale. While there was a straight denial of Lavelle's claims about a Vatican communication with Woods of Philadelphia, Rome would go no further than refer back to the rather Delphic reply that had already been made to their previous requests. Added to this was a refutation of many of the Fenian arguments in support of their claim that they did not incur any ecclesiastical censure. The Holy See substantiated its stand citing from the Papal allocution *Multiplices Inter* of 25 September 1865. Alongside this, theological analysis was provided of what constituted, and what did not constitute, an occult movement.[48]

No specific condemnation of Fenianism however was found in this decree from Propaganda, which included a request to most of the bishops to refrain from publicising it.[49] The ruling could be said to imply that Catholics could not become members of the Fenian organisation without incurring ecclesiastical censure. However, this was not expressly stated. The position was quite unsatisfactory. The Holy See appeared to argue against Catholics joining the Fenian organisation on theological grounds. But the Fenians, whose popular support was now increasing, were still left open to assert that they did not incur any ecclesiastical censure.[50] Numerous American prelates, aware of the ambiguity of the Vatican stance, decided accordingly against pronouncing publicly on the Fenians.[51] The situation whereby some bishops openly condemned the Fenians while others remained silent was to lead to much concern in the Holy See and later to confusion among priests.[52]

Cullen was most disappointed with the Roman response. Feeling ill and depressed and surmising that there was now nothing that he could do to change the situation, he decided to resign himself to the worst. As he afterwards wrote to Rome: 'I had resolved myself not to think any more of the affair and to leave things go from bad to worse.'[53]

Cullen's spirits were lifted however when, on 14 September 1865, the police raided the offices of the *Irish People*.[54] Those working there, including senior figures in the Fenian organisation, were arrested without resistance.[55] Later, many leading figures in the Fenian movement in Ireland and England were arrested.[56] The fact that during the raid some six thousand pounds sent from America was sequestrated proved for Cullen that the Fenians were still an active force in the United States.[57] Next, the government, proving for Cullen their determination to defeat the revolutionary movement, offered large monetary rewards for information leading to the arrest of Fenians still at large.[58] The police raid, during which a number of arms were discovered, was denounced by pro-Fenian clerics such as Lavelle. Cullen claimed that: 'All of Dublin is content with what was done by the Government and there was no citizen who moved to defend the poor Fenians who a few days previously were boasting of having hundreds of thousands of associates.'[59] In fact the offices were located within a stone's throw of Dublin Castle and were well known to the police.

Although he was often critical of the British government, Cullen regarded the fact that it had prevented an attempted revolution as fortuitous.[60] After all, Cullen pointed out, Ireland was suffering already from many evils such as cholera, potato blight and cattle diseases. While these might be successfully overcome, he was convinced that 'this poor country would be totally ruined by a Mazzinian revolution such as the Fenian leaders were preparing for'.[61] With relief then, Cullen reported to Rome: 'Thanks be to God we freed ourselves from the great danger that was threatening us.'[62] He also expressed his hope that there would not be any more talk of the Fenians in Ireland.[63] Indeed, he wrote of his belief by October 1865 that 'we are free from the snares of the Fenians'.[64] Subsequent events would prove otherwise.

As the trials of the captured Fenians commenced, Cullen began to fear that they would be treated with great harshness.[65] In communicating with Rome he wrote: 'I fear that our Government will hang many of these unfortunates.'[66] In reality his worst fears were not realised. No one was hanged, but a number received sentences of up to twenty years in prison.[67] Cullen viewed the sentences on Fenian activists as harsh but just, on the basis that: 'They were on the point of provoking a revolution which could not have terminated in other than total ruin and the massacre of our poor Catholics.'[68]

At the trials, during which many Fenians professed to have renounced their Catholic faith, proof of the strong American connection was given. It was revealed that several important figures in the movement had travelled from the United States in the hope of staging a revolution.[69] Evidence was also produced of Fenian plans not only to stage an armed revolution against the British in Ireland but also to attack and 'put ... out of the way' leading members of the Catholic Church such as Cullen and the Archbishop of Cashel.[70] From these disclosures Cullen deduced that Fenianism was a conspiracy more against religion than against the State.[71] This was never proven however, nor indeed could it be.

In the light of the extent of the Fenian movement, the support for which greatly surprised Cullen, he now hoped that the bishops would unite to condemn the Fenians.[72] For himself, he continued to issue warnings and he blamed the growth in support for the Fenians in the autumn of 1865 on clerics proclaiming 'patriotic speeches'.[73] No clerics were charged following the raid on the *Irish People* offices but it was evident that there was an element of clerical support for the Fenians.[74] Aware of this, Cullen was critical of Propaganda for being too soft on Lavelle who, following various appeals, appeared to have been restored and to have had his suspension lifted.[75]

On 10 October 1865, Cullen penned his strongest pastoral to date against Fenianism, denouncing it as a compound of 'human folly and wickedness'.[76] In this pastoral Cullen blamed the growth of the Fenian movement on the tolerance allowed to the Orange Order. As long as those who held power in the country were allowed to form secret societies, he wrote, then it was difficult to blame the poor for doing the same. But this was not a good enough excuse, Cullen pointed out, for Catholics to join the Fenians and to swear the Fenian oath. He stressed that the Fenians were a secret society with infidel leaders. While calling for the ills of the country to be righted, he emphasised that the only legitimate manner in which this could be done was by constitutional, and not revolutionary, means.[77]

Cullen's pastoral was written at a time of political change following the death of Liberal Prime Minister Palmerston. Hopes of an improvement in Church–State relations grew when Russell, who on 18 October 1865 assumed the leadership of the Liberals, initiated discussions with the Holy See on various Irish issues. These included the possible disestablishment of the Church of Ireland.[78] In a further attempt to win credibility for constitutional methods, John Blake Dillon, who had been elected to parliament for Tipperary in the summer of 1865, spearheaded a campaign to advance the fortunes of the National Association.[79] He succeeded in persuading twenty-two Irish members to agree on presenting a united front on topics regarding Irish educational and ecclesiastical reform, and also to come to a loose working agreement on supporting the English Liberal party in some areas.[80] Such moves, however, were viewed as too little, too late by the bishop and clergy of Meath. At a meeting on 6 November 1865 they demanded immediate and radical land reform measures to be implemented. Failing this they withdrew their support for the National Association in favour of a new tenant right organisation.[81]

If Cullen believed that Fenianism was now a spent force, the government obviously thought otherwise.[82] The police succeeded in arresting Stephens, the founder of the Fenians in Ireland, on 11 November 1865. In a daring plan, however, Stephens escaped from Dublin's Richmond prison and was smuggled to the United States. At the same time, as Cullen was well aware, a number of Fenian emissaries from America were travelling around Ireland.[83] The British responded by increasing their military presence in Ireland, causing Cullen to write to Rome of how 'Dublin is full of troops'.[84] Such a high military profile, at the expense of money that the Archbishop of Dublin felt would be better spent in tackling the social problems of Ireland, was, Cullen speculated, the result of government fears of a revolution.[85] Such fears however Cullen dismissed, asserting that in both Ireland and the United States: 'It seems that Fenianism will now finish in smoke. ... I am persuaded that there is not the least danger of turbulence.'[86] Nonetheless, Cullen wrote of his belief how 'all the clergy are working at keeping the people tranquil and obedient and with the help of God we will succeed'.[87]

A continuing fear of revolution in late 1865 was only one of the negative effects of the Fenians and 'their revolutionary and anti-religious writings'.[88] Cullen identified another negative effect when he wrote of how 'the Protestants take the occasion of the conspiracy to exclude the Catholics from every important or profitable post under the pretext that the Fenians and their supporters were Catholics'.[89] Cullen now detected an anti-clerical reaction throughout the country and speculated as to the cause. 'These evils one must attribute in great part to the celebrated Lavelle and his supporters,' he wrote.[90]

As 1866 dawned, a certain degree of support for the Fenians was still prevalent in Ireland and arrests of suspected activists continued to take place.[91] At the same time however, clerical condemnations of the movement continued and Cullen was continually reassured that the threat of a Fenian rising was over.[92] For a while, reports reaching the Archbishop of Dublin led him to believe that public as well as clerical support for the revolutionary movement was declining. Talk continued however in Fenian circles of armed and financial aid still coming from America.[93] Cullen summarily dismissed such talk, reporting: 'There is now scarcely a word about the Fenians here.'[94]

Attempts at arousing public support for the National Association were now renewed in an effort to redress the unhappy economic and social state of Ireland.[95] Legislative changes in the area of land reform were proposed and further efforts were made, with Cullen's encouragement, to win Church disestablishment and educational reform.[96] The various proposals came to nought however. The demands for educational reform were rejected by the government, while the land reforms proposed by the National Association resulted in major divisions among the Irish Catholic members of parliament.[97] Instead of increasing popular confidence in democratic methods, the initiatives only resulted in disillusionment while criticism of the government grew.[98]

At the same time, despite Cullen's protestations to the contrary, the Fenian spirit so evident in Ireland in 1865 had not been yet extinguished. The much publicised arrests in 1865 and early 1866 failed to destroy it. Rather they served to publicise the separatist cause and so win support for the Fenians, both in Ireland and among Irish emigrants abroad.[99] By February 1866, Cullen himself was beginning to realise that the extent of support commanded by the Fenians was much greater than he had previously imagined. The government was also aware of this. On 15 February 1866, it reacted by rushing through parliament a bill suspending Habeas Corpus in Ireland. Cullen complained that, even though he considered the Fenians were anti-Catholic, the Protestant ascendancy in Ireland continued to insist that Fenianism was a Catholic, anti-Protestant conspiracy.[100] He condemned the fact that the establishment were discriminating against Catholics on the basis of such allegations.[101] Cullen now feared a growth in anti-Catholic feeling by Protestants in Ireland and a resultant rebellious response from Catholics, provoked by discrimination.[102] Such confrontation, Cullen believed, would be welcomed by the Protestants who, being well armed, would easily defeat the Catholics and repress them.[103] Cullen's impressions in this respect do not appear to have had substance.

A new cholera outbreak struck at the end of the summer and remained into the winter months of 1866 and wrought renewed physical and social distress among Irish Catholics.[104] There were new waves of Irish emigrants to the United States of America, Canada and England. Many brought with them hostile feelings towards the British government.[105] At the same time a number of American, English and Scottish Fenians came to Ireland in early 1866 bringing money to formulate plans for a rising once again.[106] Conscious of this, Cullen reported that Fenianism was again beginning to flourish in Ireland and there were renewed warnings of a rising.[107] In response, the government continued to maintain a strong military and police presence in Ireland throughout 1866. This added to the grievances of the Catholics of Ireland who saw themselves paying for it out of their taxes.[108]

Fenian hostility towards the Catholic Church continued in the face of Cullen's repeated denunciations. He was now even receiving anonymous letters threatening his life.[109] Refusing to be intimidated however, Cullen, hoping that the rumours of a possible rising would come to nothing, promised Rome that the clergy of his diocese would continue to campaign against the Fenians.[110] He continued to view the Fenians as highly damaging to Ireland.[111] He continued his campaign against them but he was careful to balance this by criticising the government also for their half-hearted attempts to crush Fenianism in the country.[112]

All this time the government maintained a strong military profile while Fenian suspects continued to be arrested and occasional arms caches discovered. Nonetheless, in 1866, Cullen reckoned that the government was less than sincere in its efforts to eradicate Fenianism from Ireland.[113] He felt that it was prepared to tolerate the Fenian movement because it effectively divided and thereby weakened the Irish people.[114] 'These are the benefits,' claimed Cullen, 'which we receive from the patriotism of Lavelle and others who, for the past four years, encouraged a system which was not able to produce anything good and which of its nature tends to evil.'[115]

With the country reportedly quiet in March 1866, Cullen, whose health by this time was once again giving cause for concern, reported to Rome how he was persuaded that there was no danger of an immediate rising.[116] Reflecting his opinion that the Fenian threat was a short-term one, Cullen went on to assert that the possibility of an American-backed revolution had passed throughout 1866.[117] An armed Fenian rising could possibly be outruled but, an increasingly ill Cullen asserted, further trouble from the Fenians could not.[118]

The attempts by the parliamentary members of the National Association to win land reforms through constitutional means failed to win concessions for Ireland. It did, however, lead to the fall of the Liberal government and divisions within the National Association members of parliament. The National Association members split first on a land bill.[119] The crisis did not occur however until 18 June 1866, when a vote on an amendment to a Reform Bill was taken. Eight of the National Association group voted contrary to their official line. As a result the vote was lost by eleven votes by the government and Liberal Prime Minister Russell resigned office.[120] The Earl of Derby became Prime Minister of a minority Conservative government following the defeat of the Russell Administration in June 1866. Such a situation was not conducive to radical change, despite Cullen's constant attempts to have the National Association press for immediate educational reforms.[121]

In the same month as the fall of the Liberal government, Cullen, as had been expected for some months previously, was created the first ever Irish cardinal, much to the acclaim of many in Ireland and abroad.[122] While Cullen was in Rome to receive the red hat however, an ominous warning of the continued presence of the Fenians in Canada reached him. There, at the end of May, in the hope of arousing anti-English sentiment, a small Fenian outbreak took place that was quickly suppressed.[123] Despite this, the event aroused considerable excitement in Fenian circles as their confidence grew that, with the aid of some outside assistance, a rising in Ireland could be attempted after all.[124] Proof was now provided to Cullen of the unreliability of claims being made in certain ecclesiastical circles in Ireland that the Fenian movement was dead.[125] In fact the opposite was the case, and it also became evident that clerical support for the Fenians was growing.[126]

After the sudden death of Dillon on 15 September 1866 at the age of fifty-one, the National Association underwent a crisis through lack of direction.[127] Rumours of imminent revolution were increasing despite assurances given to Cullen that popular support for the Fenians was slight and waning.[128] Cullen was continuing to use his influence to encourage parliamentary methods.[129] He also continued to hope that the renewed activity of the Fenians, whose presence in Ireland he was to describe as 'a scourge that threatens to be even worse than cholera', would not lead to any great ill.[130] Once again, as the British military

202

presence in Ireland increased, Cullen expressed the hope that talk of a republican revolution would come to nought.[131]

Cullen's hope that a revolution would never occur was not because he deemed such a revolution to be morally wrong, but because of the very practical situation of the Fenians being few in number and militarily impotent.[132] In this argument, Cullen received support even from pro-Fenian clerics such as Lavelle who warned against any 'premature and therefore fruitless attempt, no matter how provoked or otherwise justified, at a violent uprising'.[133] One of Cullen's arguments against armed insurrection had always been that in military terms it had to fail. At this stage, he realised that a failed attempt would strengthen Conservative arguments for renewed anti-Catholic legislation. This would destroy the hopes of progress through any alliance with the Liberals which he had worked hard to build up.[134] In this particular effort, he took heart from Liberal successes, with ecclesiastical support, in two by-elections in Tipperary and Waterford in the closing months of 1866.[135]

In the pastoral issued 8 December 1866, Cullen repeated yet again his familiar two-pronged message that an armed revolution would be wrong, and that it could not possibly succeed. The pastoral also reiterated the argument that the grievances of the Irish people — tenant right, disendowment, education, deficiencies in the poor law, and others — could be redressed by parliamentary means. In a development of his stance at the time of the Ecclesiastical Titles issue, Cullen claimed that, by using parliament, the people of Ireland were bound to win. Not only were the people's demands just, but there was now growing sympathy towards the Irish cause in England.[136] A physically failing Cullen was pleased with the reception of his pastoral. As time passed and no revolutionary attempt was made, Cullen grew increasingly confident that support for the Fenians had collapsed and, in a despatch to Rome, stated that 'I am persuaded that there is no danger in fact of a rising or of trouble'.[137]

In reality, Cullen's hopes for constitutionalism as a vehicle for advancing the interests of the Irish people were again disappointed a mere two years after the formation of the National Association. Although he did not seem to appreciate it, a likely consequence of this would be a strengthening of support for Fenianism as 1867 dawned.

Chapter Twelve

THE FENIAN RISING
AND AFTERMATH

DESPITE RECENT EXPERIENCES with the National Association, Cullen assured himself that any revolutionary attempt could now be outruled. Determinedly maintaining his campaign for constitutionalism, he went to a meeting of the National Association on 8 January 1867. At this meeting, he recommended that a policy of political cooperation with the English Reform Party be adopted.[1] He was sceptical of the Conservative government of Lord Derby. He remained so despite the withdrawal of emergency powers, imposed to deal with an earlier threat of Fenian revolt, and a promise of land reform in the Queen's speech at the opening of Parliament.[2] His attitude was soon to be justified, for when the terms of the proposed land bill were published in February 1867, they were found to be unacceptable to both the National Association and most Irish Liberal members.[3] In the light of such opposition, the government in fact withdrew the bill.[4]

Meantime, many Fenians who had been sentenced in 1865 were released from prison in early 1867. Reporting on the premature release of these men Cullen wrote that: 'These poor people suffered a very cruel imprisonment for their madness and I hope that they will be wiser in the future.'[5] Cullen continued to report how: 'It seems that Fenianism is now completely defunct in Ireland. At least it is not spoken of any more.'[6] This, incredibly, remained Cullen's belief, despite warnings from Manning, who had been nominated Archbishop of Westminster on 30 April 1866, that the Fenians were still an active movement.[7] There was evidence that Fenianism was a potent force among Irish immigrants in the United States and also that it commanded a degree of clerical support, as the authorities in Propaganda were well aware.[8] It was clear that Cullen was grossly misinformed for, even on the day of the Fenian Rising in March 1867, he was writing to Rome of the great evil of Fenianism having ceased to exist![9]

While the government was releasing those who had supported the Fenians, the economic and social problems of Ireland were persisting.[10] In addition to the shortage of foodstuffs and a renewed threatened outbreak of cholera, very severe weather conditions resulted in many deaths from hypothermia.[11] In the light of this, Cullen appealed to the British government, of whose inactivity on behalf of their citizens in Ireland he remained highly critical.[12]

In a speech delivered in the presence of the Lord Lieutenant and the Lord Mayor of Dublin on 19 February 1867, Cullen dealt with the theme of Irish nationalism.[13] While condemning revolutionary nationalism, he had stated: 'The people of Ireland love their country. I love it myself. I love her religion, her history, her antiquity and all that that regards but I do not think that our love of country should degenerate into a false patriotism. The love of country is a noble virtue, an emanation of charity, but it can be perverted and turned right around by those who profess it as have some seducers in recent times. ... If we unite ourselves, if those who govern take the initiative with a series of measures of justice, if the others follow with a spirit of gentleness to law and order, there is no doubt that happy results will be seen in the country.'[14] What Cullen demanded of the government was that they make 'good provisions in the country. If it were to protect the people and act justly we will not ask anything else.'[15]

By the time Cullen was giving this speech the first attempts at a rising had already occurred. He was later to blame the intrigues of the American Fenians without whom the country, in his opinion, would have remained tranquil.[16] In January 1867, Thomas Kelly, accompanied by a small group of ardent supporters, travelled from America to England. The previous year Kelly, a Galway printer, had replaced Stephens as the head of the Fenians. He quickly set about organising a revolution. The date for the planned uprising in Ireland, along with a planned attack on Chester Castle in England to seize arms, was fixed for 11 February 1867. This date was postponed however at the last minute due to the fact that, as a result of informers, the British authorities had become aware of the plans.

The order postponing the rising by just under one month was not communicated to Fenians in County Kerry in time, and so they staged a small uprising there which was almost immediately suppressed.[17] As regards this Kerry insurrection, Cullen reported to Rome how 'the telegraphs carried the news at first that there were eight thousand armed men prepared to assail the Government, but in two or three days it became known that the precise number was thirty-seven; which formidable corps was resolved to overthrow the power of England! A revolution of this nature is too ridiculous to talk of it seriously.'[18]

Bishop of Kerry Moriarty reacted strongly. His ringing denunciation of the Fenian leaders, in the phrase 'eternity is not long enough, nor hell hot enough to punish such miscreants', was later inaccurately and mischievously taken to mean that he was castigating the ordinary members of the Fenians as well.[19] Cullen, along with many priests including Lavelle, was very critical of Moriarty, writing to Kirby that: 'He is very much to be blamed for so foolish an exaggeration ... I wish he could be called to an account for it.'[20]

Having referred to the abortive Kerry insurrection Cullen reported to Rome how: 'Things here are very quiet and I believe that there is no danger of any serious movement.'[21] Ironically, within twenty-four hours of his comment the delayed official

Fenian Rising took place, on the night of 5–6 March 1867. What those taking part could not have foreseen was that that night would be one of inclement weather with freezing temperatures and a heavy fall of snow, which would severely hamper their plans.[22] There were outbreaks in Dublin, Cork, Tipperary and Limerick, and to a lesser extent in Clare, Waterford and Louth. In all of these locations the insurgents were quickly surrounded and overcome by the police – most of whom were also Catholic. Surprisingly, there was no outbreak in Wexford.[23] And it was not even necessary to call on the army for assistance.[24]

This attempted rising was met with widespread clerical condemnation.[25] A week later, on 12 March 1867, Cullen, in what he professed was an attempt to put an end to incidents of turbulence in the country, penned yet another pastoral.[26] In it he emphasised the conscientious duty of Catholics to give allegiance to authority and stressed their obligation to resort only to constitutional methods in their attempts to win redress of their grievances. He then condemned the Fenian leaders for their Mazzinian affinities and he ended by praising the police and appealing to the government to act with leniency, moderation and humanity:[27] 'It is seen that the Government has reason to be grateful to all Catholics, ecclesiastics as well as the laity, for the fidelity that they displayed on this occasion. That notwithstanding, I do not hold hope that any measure will be adopted to put an end to the ills of this country which are the true cause of Fenianism.'[28] As regards these 'evils' however, Cullen stressed not the social or economic, but rather the educational aspects. He wrote how: 'It is a singular thing in relation to the disturbances that a great number of national school teachers took part in them and yet the Government still is determined to maintain the mixed system in Ireland and exclude religion from schools although it sees that such a manner of acting produces very bad fruits.'[29]

Support for the Fenian movement continued to grow even after the failed Rising.[30] There were clerics, such as Father Gerald Barry in Kilteely, Co. Limerick, who were never charged although widely suspected of active cooperation with the

Fenians.[31] Lavelle had not actually backed the rising when it occurred. He continued however to support the Fenian movement, notwithstanding his public profession not to engage in further public political discussions on the topic.[32] In reference to Lavelle, Cullen wrote: 'It is a very evil thing to publish revolutionary doctrines and incite to resistance a few poor artisans or peasants who are in this way exposed thereby to certain destruction.'[33] Cullen, with great perception, was also prepared to admit that the Fenian outbreak of violence could be used to emphasise to the government the urgency of alleviating the material lot of the Irish.[34]

Numerous arrests followed the failed Rising and many of those convicted received lengthy prison sentences.[35] Exceptionally, two activists, Burke and Doran, were sentenced to death.[36] Cullen initially held high hopes that the sentences would be commuted to life imprisonment, and in the case of Doran it was.[37] No such reprieve was announced for Burke. No Irish revolutionary had been executed since 1803 and so popular agitation grew as the date for Burke's execution drew closer.

There was a public meeting at Dublin's Mansion House to demonstrate solidarity with Burke and to appeal to the government for clemency. In a letter read at the meeting and afterwards published, Cullen made it clear that the execution of Burke would cause him the greatest pain.[38] At the meeting, a committee, which included some notable Dublin priests, organised a petition which was presented to the governing authorities on 24 May 1867.[39] This was only five days before the scheduled execution of 29 May. The response was an announcement that the government had decided not to grant any reprieve to Burke. Thereupon a deputation of over forty Irish members of parliament was organised to request an audience with the the Prime Minister, Lord Derby, on 25 May 1867.[40]

On the same day, 25 May 1867, Cullen, in an unprecedented move, went personally to the Vice Regal Lodge, the residence of the Lord Lieutenant.[41] There, Cullen stressed that he and the Irish bishops and clergy, while wholeheartedly opposed to

Fenianism, totally opposed the death sentence on Burke, and demanded a reprieve.[42] Reportedly deeply moved by the Archbishop of Dublin's personal intervention, the Lord Lieutenant promised to communicate the representations immediately to the cabinet.[43] On 27 May 1867, Burke's reprieve was announced and his sentence commuted to life imprisonment. No motive was given for the reprieve, the news of which the Lord Lieutenant immediately communicated to Cullen.[44]

If Cullen won acclaim, even in Fenian circles, for his efforts in the Burke case, this did not mean that the Fenians followed his advice and abandoned their revolutionary philosophy in favour of constitutional action. On the contrary, Fenian support swelled in the summer of 1867, a feature which was accompanied by continuous waves of police arrests.[45] At the same time, living conditions in Ireland failed to improve following a poor harvest and a renewed outbreak of cholera.[46] Cullen himself, who spent part of the summer in Rome attending the nineteenth centenary of the martyrdom of the Apostles, was all this time physically unwell.[47]

Despite his poor health, Cullen attended the Irish bishops' meeting of October 1867. In a joint statement the bishops repeated their warnings against the 'criminal folly' of secret societies.[48] At the same time they warned the government of the prerequisites for peace in Ireland as they saw them, namely the Church of Ireland to be disestablished, free education granted and land reform measures taken.[49]

The October 1867 statement of the bishops was issued just after the leader and chief organiser of the Fenian Rising, Thomas Kelly, was dramatically rescued from police custody in Manchester, England. Kelly had been arrested in September and was being escorted in a prison van when the Fenians raised a rescue attempt. They succeeded in rescuing Kelly but in the process they unintentionally shot a policeman dead.[50] Five Fenians were tried and all received the death sentence, even though no definitive evidence was provided as to which, if any, of them had fired the fatal shot.[51] One of the accused, Maguire, was given an unconditional pardon, which strengthened the case for a retrial. The sentence of another, Condon, was commuted to life imprisonment following American intervention. Various petitions appealing for the commutation of the death sentence for the three remaining accused, William Allen, Michael Larkin and Michael O'Brien, including those signed by a variety of prelates and priests, were to no avail.[52] On 23 November 1867 Allen, Larkin and O'Brien, all Catholics, were publicly hanged in Manchester.[53]

In a wave of mass protests these 'Manchester Martyrs' were established as symbols of Irish nationalism. 'God Save Ireland', the last words spoken by one of them from the dock, were used by T.D. Sullivan as the title of a stirring ballad that was to serve as the anthem of republican nationalism for fifty years. The anniversary of their execution came to be honoured in republican circles as the Feast of the Martyrs. For a time it competed with Saint Patrick's Day itself in the calendar of national commemorations.

In contrast to his action in the case of Burke a few months earlier, Cullen made no intervention on behalf of the condemned men. Privately he denounced as hypocritical the British government's decision to go ahead with the executions of Irish nationalists while supporting Italian nationalists.[54] It was apparent that, unlike the case of Burke, the prospect for success here was minimal. British public opinion was outraged at the fatal shooting of a police officer and was clamouring for the executions. As Queen Victoria put it in a speech in November 1867: 'The treasonable conspiracy, commonly known as Fenianism, baffled and repressed in Ireland, has assumed in England the form of organised violence and assassination. These outrages require to be vigorously put down, and I rely on their effectual suppression upon the firm administration of the law and the loyalty of the great masses of my subjects.'[55] Cullen, while realising the futility of any representations to save the three men, was conscious of a degree of British government inconsistency and cynicism in proceeding with the executions. The day following the executions he wrote: 'The government had three Fenians hanged yesterday, at the same time they praise the Garibaldians who have done things thousands of times more evil than the wretched Fenians.'[56] Cullen pointed out the negative effects for the British government itself, which he claimed was unwise in putting these men to death. It had in fact, he pointed out, excited in the population in general a great sympathy for the executed men and led the people to threaten reprisals on the British authorities.[57]

The sheer fact that Cullen, who was personally so opposed to the Fenian movement, should have written in such a manner against the British government is an indication of the strength of anti-British feeling that swept across the whole country at this time. A general sympathy for those Fenians who were detained in British prisons grew not only among the lay people but among members of the clergy as well.[58]

Cullen was aware of the depth of nationalistic feeling that was stirred up by the executions of Allen, Larkin and O'Brien. For fear that public religious ceremonies for the repose of the souls of the three Fenians might be construed as political demonstrations, Cullen rejected repeated calls for public High Masses.[59] Fearing moves to 'canonise' the 'martyrs', he instructed his clergy that no public High Masses for Allen, Larkin and O'Brien were to be celebrated. Priests could however pray privately for the souls of the three men.[60] Cullen's instructions in this regard were not always followed to the letter.[61]

The widespread protests following the execution of the three 'martyrs' led Cullen to fear more disturbances during the winter of 1867.[62] These failed to transpire even if, as Cullen reported to Rome in January 1868, one did not hear of other than rumours of turbulence.[63] Large public processions, numbering over fifty thousand people protesting against the government's action, took place in Dublin in December 1867.[64] A series of collections were also made for the families of the three 'martyrs' to which MacHale was a prominent contributer.[65] Pro-Fenian protests also took place among Irish communities abroad. When forty Irishmen, in Rome to enlist in the pontifical army, attempted to have a Mass celebrated for the 'Manchester martyrs', their plans were foiled and they were subsequently repatriated.[66] The government, of whom Cullen remained highly critical, remained on the alert and maintained a high military profile in Ireland through the winter of 1867.[67]

If in Ireland there was a marked growth in sympathy for the Fenians following the execution of Allen, Larkin and O'Brien, the executions had the opposite effect in England where there was the impression that Fenianism was a threat to English society.[68] There was another tragedy outside Clerkenwell jail at the close of 1867. A gunpowder explosion, aimed at blasting some Fenian prisoners to freedom, failed in its purpose but led to the deaths of several innocent people. The incident incensed British public opinion further. A Fenian, Michael Barrett, was arrested, tried and sentenced to death, his hanging being the last public execution in England. This was followed by more calls for a firm stand by the British government.

In the midst of this widespread agitation, there was a minority, led by the Liberal Opposition leader Gladstone, who saw in the support which the Fenians had aroused in Ireland a sign of the need for serious government action to rectify the grievances of the Irish people.[69]

There were differences of view among the lay people, and the clergy too, as to how solutions could be found for the problems of Ireland which even the British Opposition leader was now acknowledging. A minority of priests, among whom Lavelle was prominent, continued actively to support the Fenians, even though public sympathy for them was reported to have declined throughout 1868. The majority of the people would however support constitutionalism, that is if it genuinely promised results.[70] Reflecting this latter attitude, many Irish priests kept up their attacks on Fenianism.[71] It was necessary also, of course, for the people to be convinced that constitutional action had a real prospect of success before they could confidently be expected to abandon the Fenian option.

There were priests who were anxious to show that such opposition they might have at this stage to Fenianism did not mean support for British rule in Ireland. In January 1868, at a

213

clerical meeting in Limerick, 198 priests signed a declaration calling for Irish independence. The declaration stated that: 'We simply ask the Repeal of the Union and the restoration of an Irish Parliament; and we ask it by no other means than those consecrated by the long years of O'Connell's teaching – constitutional and legal means ... We feel certain that the restoration of Ireland's nationality will do more to conciliate the Empire than the greatest power or the greatest severity which the Government could employ.'[72] At the meeting, the assembled clerics noted that: 'A national legislature means neither revolution nor weakening of the Empire, but on the contrary its better consolidation and progress.'[73] This was a carefully balanced statement designed to show attachment to separatist aims pursued by constitutional methods and not threatening wider British interests. Whether it reflected the views of the mass of the Irish clergy, especially in rural parishes, is open to debate.

Cullen, whose health improved in January 1868, did not support the calls for repeal of the Act of Union, believing no doubt that the best hope of material improvement for the people at that time lay in the status quo. However, he did call on the British government to enact measures to improve the living conditions of the Irish.[74] In a pastoral in January 1868 he proclaimed how: 'Our poor country has been reduced to a state of the greatest misery and destitution. Our towns and cities are filled with poor men, women and children half starved, without shoes or stockings or proper clothing to preserve them from the snows and frosts of Winter. More squalid poverty of this kind is to be seen in Dublin alone than in all the great cities of France, Austria or Spain. The country has lost more than 3,000,000 of inhabitants who have been obliged to brave the dangers of the wide Atlantic in order to save themselves and their families from starvation. About 400,000 cottages of the poor have been levelled to the ground lest they should ever again afford shelter to their former inmates.'[75]

This appeal for government intervention was followed by the now familiar condemnation of Fenianism. It concluded with the equally familiar exhortation to his flock to adopt constitutional means of redressing their grievances. He called on them once again to return to parliament members who would defend the right of Catholics in such areas as the disestablishment of the Church of Ireland, freedom of education and land reform.[76]

If Cullen was critical of the government in a diplomatic manner, Lavelle's criticism was less guarded, as was his support for the Fenians.[77] Cullen reported to Rome: 'The celebrated Lavelle writes terrible letters against the Government well calculated to promote a spirit of revolution in the country.'[78] In relation to such letters Cullen was prepared to admit that: 'Without doubt one can say many true and strong things against the Government but it is truly madness and a great crime to push the poor people, divided and without arms or discipline, to assault a very powerful Government which has at its disposal ships and armies prepared for any scope.'[79]

The forum still favoured by Cullen was the National Association. This must have been seen by others as a forlorn hope, as the Association had failed to make any real impact in 1867.[80] In fact there were rumours that it would soon be wound up for lack of support, and it had to give up its rooms in October 1867.[81] Meetings were suspended for the winter of 1867–8 and when they resumed on 20 March 1868 the members limited themselves to campaigning for disestablishment of the Church of Ireland and tenant reform.[82]

On the basis of his fears of another outbreak of 'Fenian fever', Cullen availed of the opportunity of a pastoral letter for the feast of St Brigid on 1 February 1868 to repeat his warnings against the dangers of Fenianism. Again he called on the people to support constitutional means to redress grievances. In appealing once again to the people however, he had to admit that there was no sign of anything being achieved in the near future.[83] This pastoral was very heavily criticised in the British press even before it was officially delivered. It was claimed that by stressing the grievances of the Irish, Cullen was in fact encouraging the Fenians.[84] It was a criticism that was patently unfair.

꧁ Chapter Thirteen ꧂

FORWARD IN LONDON; BACKWARD IN ROME

POLITICAL INITIATIVES towards Church disestablishment were made in Westminster shortly after
Disraeli assumed office as Conservative Prime
Minister following the resignation of Lord Derby on
25 February 1868. On 23 March 1868, Gladstone,
leader of the Liberal Opposition following Russell's retirement,
and who had already shown an enlightened interest in Irish
grievances, revealed an intention to disestablish the Established
Church.[1] He had already been formulating views on various
Irish problems. In a remarkable initiative as leader of the
Opposition, he brought proposals for disestablishment to the
House of Commons and had them put to a vote. He won by a
majority of sixty.[2] His bill, which met with general episcopal
support as well as that of the National Association, was duly
voted through the House of Commons.[3] After the government
had suffered such a humiliating defeat it could only survive on
sufferance. It was also now inevitable that the question of
Church disestablishment would feature in the general election
later in the year.

Meanwhile, there was a moderation in the climate of opinion
in Ireland, as reflected in the enthusiasm with which the Prince
and Princess of Wales were received on a visit in April 1868.

Referring to the Royal couple Cullen wrote that they 'for the first time sought to treat the Catholics in the same manner as they treated the Protestants. ... If they acted always like this I am persuaded that all Catholics, rich and poor, would always be faithful subjects – but the suburbia of the English generally is discontent if it cannot mistreat and tread on the others.'[4]

Conversion of British parliamentary opinion to the idea of responding to Irish grievances was attributed in various circles to the heightened awareness of the plight of the Irish, apparently as a result of the Fenians.[5] Even Cardinal Antonelli was alleged to have said: 'Fenianism is good for something.'[6]

While Church disestablishment was seen as one Irish grievance that was being addressed, Cullen was aware that there were still others awaiting attention. Any immediate intention of supporting a constitutional campaign was frustrated however by the fact that he became seriously ill in July 1868. For a while his life was in danger and public prayers were offered in the archdiocese for his recovery.[7] Signs of recovery were reported in late July 1868 but he remained ill right through to the following year.[8] During the 1868 general election campaign, the position of the Established Church and other Church issues played a part. In the campaign, Cullen and the National Association were associated with the Liberal cause.[9] The election was marked by controversial incidents of direct political campaigning by clerics.[10] However, if the National Association and the bishops were politically active, so too were the Fenians. They were hoping for an amnesty for those who had been sentenced to long periods of imprisonment following the rising. A meeting in the Mechanics Institute in Dublin on 12 November 1868 decided to establish a committee to organise a petition for the prisoners' release.[11] The idea was promoted as an act of clemency and was not intended as endorsement of the actions of prisoners. Support was forthcoming from those who advocated a working agreement with the English Liberals and from the majority of the Irish hierarchy.[12] Cullen was ill but his half-nephew and then secretary, Moran, was reported to have informed the organisers that he would willingly sign.[13]

218

In Ireland, the election campaign, dominated as predicted by the issue of disestablishment, resulted in the Liberals capturing sixty-six Irish seats, a gain of nine, while the Conservatives won only thirty-nine. Only thirty-seven of the 105 Irish members of parliament were Catholic.[14] Gladstone became Prime Minister on 3 December 1868 with a majority of 112 in the House of Commons. With this election victory, it appeared as if a bond had been forged between constitutional-style Irish nationalism and English liberalism. Irish public support for the new administration rose considerably when on 22 February 1869 Gladstone announced an amnesty for over half the Fenian prisoners.[15] Out of eighty-one jailed civilians, some forty-nine, who were considered to have been unimportant members of the movement, were released. The other thirty-two, including the leaders, continued to be held. This disappointed many Irish people but at the same time it increased in the mind of the people the perception of those who had been released as national and patriotic heroes.[16] On their return to Ireland they were greeted with mass receptions and republican speeches, some of which were embarrassing to the government.[17]

On 1 March 1869, Gladstone introduced the Disestablishment Bill in the House of Commons. As the principle had been accepted by the previous House of Commons, the legislation was assured of success. Thus Gladstone effectively resolved one longstanding Irish grievance.[18]

In an attempt to have the remaining prisoners released, a Fenian Prisoners Committee was established to promote yet another petition. This was signed by various Catholic bishops including MacHale of Tuam, Keane of Cloyne and Conaty of Kilmore.[19] Leahy of Cashel and Cullen refused to sign. Cullen's attitude reflected the distinction that he always made between the leaders, whom he condemned for leading ordinary people astray, and the rank-and-file with whom he sympathised.[20] The amnesty campaign reawakened interest in the Fenian movement and there was a new wave of recruitment, which received occasional individual clerical support.[21] There were some acts of violence and these were denounced by various priests.[22]

There was no intervention by the government, however. The reason for the government's inaction, claimed Cullen, was because it was aware that the Fenians could be crushed at any moment and so the government did not feel threatened by them.[23]

As well as a petition, a Church collection, described as 'a national tribute to Ireland's Martyrs', was organised on 'humanitarian grounds' by the Fenians.[24] The money raised was destined to support the amnesty campaign and the plan for the collection, to commence on Saint Patrick's Day 1869, was to cause a split in the Irish episcopal bench.[25] While some of the Irish bishops such as Butler of Limerick, Keane of Cloyne and O'Hea of Ross allowed the collection, probably out of fear of the Fenians, others such as MacEvilly of Galway and Leahy of Cashel did not.[26] A few days before the collection the Fenian committee, without Cullen's permission, wrote to the Dublin priests instructing them to publicise the collection at all Masses and to name collectors. In response Cullen, on 12 March 1869, wrote a letter to the clergy of his archdiocese in which he condemned the Fenians and specifically prohibited the collection.[27] Cullen claimed that if he authorised the collection, it could very well be interpreted as approval of the Fenians and of the politics of recently released prisoners.[28] This response, although supported by some, resulted in Cullen being subjected to a barrage of abuse and threats from the Fenians.[29]

Even without collective episcopal support, the collection went ahead. In some cases, much to Cullen's annoyance, it actually took place in the churches.[30] The collection was well supported and the sums collected were published weekly in the press.[31] With the subsequent release of most of the remaining prisoners, the amnesty committee split on the issue of whether they should continue to press for the release of the small number still held.[32] Again great celebrations greeted the homecoming of released Fenians and renewed calls were made for the revolutionary struggle to continue.[33] Priests such as Lavelle supported these calls.[34] Despite the split in the amnesty committee, public meetings were still being called in support of the campaign. [35] A number of clerics joined in these appeals. [36] Lavelle continued to dispute Cullen's condemnation of the Fenians as a secret society incurring Papal censures. He argued that the Fenians did not come under this heading, which applied to Freemasons and those who plotted against Church and State. Indeed most Fenians, Lavelle claimed, were good Christians. [37] Eight days after a major demonstration, on 10 October 1869, Prime Minister Gladstone announced that for reasons of public safety he would not be releasing the remaining Fenians. It was an announcement that resulted in renewed demands by the amnesty committee. [38]

Earlier that year, on 8 February 1869, Cullen expressed his hopes that the government would act to improve the situation of the Irish. In the course of a speech delivered at the Lord Mayor of Dublin's dinner in which he praised Prime Minister Gladstone, Cullen stressed that: 'The peace we enjoyed permitted our legislators to engage in peaceful reforms and to undertake the redress of the evils brought on the country by former bad government.' [39]

While still ill, Cullen kept up his campaign to win reform by constitutional means. Lavelle, now promoted parish priest of Cong, Co. Mayo, openly maintained his 'patriotic' pro-Fenian attitude and kept up his attacks on the Cardinal throughout 1869. [40] The continued maintenance of such a stance resulted in more calls for disciplinary action against Lavelle. [41] For their part, the Fenians renewed their attacks on clerics who failed to agree with their philosophy and grew increasingly more violent. [42] Individual acts of murder were attributed to them. Reporting this to Rome, Cullen commented: 'It is a sad thing to have human blood shed and it must bring evils on the country ... I suppose the poor people act under provocation but blood ought not to be spilt.' [43] All this time the British agent in Rome, Odo Russell, was attempting to persuade Secretary of State Antonelli to take further steps against the Fenians. [44]

Cullen, who reckoned that support for Fenianism was declining throughout 1869, was eager to see the movement definitively defeated and the pro-Fenian newspapers closed down.[45] He gradually came to the belief that, as he put it, even as regards ecclesiastical disputes in Ireland: 'The Fenians and Fenianism are at the bottom of all.'[46] In a pastoral read on 30 October 1869, Cullen announced that Fenians could not avail of the special indulgence on the occasion of the forth-coming Vatican Council. Cullen also called on the people yet again to desist from supporting a conspiracy that was secret and led by those hostile to the Church.[47] In response, Lavelle defiantly published a rousing defence of Fenians and Fenianism.[48]

In their efforts to sustain public interest in the campaign for the release of the remaining prisoners, the amnesty committee meetings were becoming increasingly violent, going so far as to disrupt meetings called to discuss land reform measures being considered by Gladstone's government.[49] As a result of these tactics, Cullen feared 'our Fenians are likely to do great mischief and to prevent all useful legislation'.[50] The police responded by raiding the headquarters of the amnesty committee, breaking up fittings and assaulting committee members.[51] Further clashes with police marked the anniversary of the hanging of the Manchester Martyrs.[52] There appeared to be an increase in support for the Fenians and Cullen began to fear further violence in the coming months.[53]

As well as recourse to militant tactics to highlight their cause, the Fenians in 1869 began to involve themselves in democratic politics.[54] This culminated on 22 November 1869 with the nomination of a convicted Fenian, Jeremiah O'Donovan Rossa, serving his sentence in Millbank Jail, as a candidate in a by-election in County Tipperary. This was the first time a prisoner serving a sentence stood for election to parliament. It was somewhat unfortunate that the other candidate was a Liberal and a Catholic, Caulfield Heron, who had been invited to stand by members of the clergy in Tipperary. O'Donovan Rossa won the election, which was marked by intimidation and voter absenteeism. The by-election served to prove that Fenianism was still very much alive two years after the Rising.[55]

Conscious of a resurgence of Fenian popularity, Cullen, in a controversial move, seized the opportunity of a pastoral letter for the feast of the Immaculate Conception in 1869 to warn his flock yet again against the danger of Fenianism. In this letter, he emphasised that they were opposed to the Catholic Church.[56]

Having written this pastoral Cullen, still physically unwell, left Ireland to attend the First Vatican Council.[57] Shortly after his departure, a circular calling for the release of all remaining Fenians in prison, while not condoning the crimes for which they were imprisoned, was sent to many members of the Irish clergy by the Dean of Limerick, Richard O'Brien.[58] Some 1,400 clerics signed the circular, although the Vicars General of the Archdiocese of Dublin advised the priests there that it might be imprudent to sign it while Cullen was out of the country.[59] By 16 December 1869, only four Dublin diocesan priests had signed the declaration and two of them were to retract following the advice of the Vicars General.[60] Those Irish bishops who were in Rome also opposed the canvassing of O'Brien.[61]

The Irish bishops, in Rome for the Council, held a series of meetings in the Irish College to discuss what further measures should be taken against Lavelle. Cullen was insistent that further disciplinary measures should be taken against him but MacHale and Derry objected.[62] Lavelle circularised his views on the Fenians to some of the bishops in Rome.[63] However, Cullen's arguments won out and at a meeting, not attended by either MacHale or Derry, it was decided to petition the Pope to expressly condemn the Fenians.[64]

A request was therefore made for a definitive decision as to whether or not the Fenians were included under the terms of the censure incurred by members of secret societies.[65] It was hoped by some that a condemnation would put a definitive end to the question of the Fenians.[66] Cullen feared another attempted rising and he put a high personal store on having Lavelle disciplined and the Fenians condemned.[67] He thought that a revolutionary attempt would be made because by this time it was generally held that the Fenians in Ireland were now more revolutionary-minded than those in America, although suffering from lack of funds.[68] Correspondence from Ireland however, while noting some outrages, did not support the view that a further revolution was proposed.[69] Despite this and notwithstanding the reservations of American bishops, Cullen used the prospect of another revolution as an argument that the Fenians should be excommunicated.[70]

Now there was the remarkable spectacle of a two-pronged approach to the Holy See: one from members of the Irish Hierarchy excluding MacHale and Derry, and the other from British government representative Odo Russell. Each side was seeking condemnation of the Fenians, but of course for very different reasons. Both requests received a positive response in January 1870.

At this point, the Holy See specifically condemned the Fenians to excommunication, proclaiming that: 'The American or Irish Society known as the Fenians is included among the societies forbidden and condemned in the Papal Constitutions, and particularly in the most recent pronouncement of His Holiness, *Apostolicae Sedis* of 12 October 1869, in which under number 4, the following are declared to be subject to an excommunication *latae sententiae* reserved to the Roman Pontiff: Members of the Society of Masons, Carbonari or others of the same kind which plot against the Church or legitimate authorities, either openly or secretly: and also any who give any support to these societies, or who fail to denounce their secret leaders, as long as they shall persist in their refusal to denounce them.'[71]

This declaration produced a variety of reactions. Cullen and Moriarty welcomed it, as well of course as Odo Russell. The Fenians themselves, though familiar with Cullen's many denunciations, were nevertheless seriously taken aback by the grim finality of it all. Some of the Fenian leaders reacted with a measure of defiance against the Catholic Church, which was to last a long time. Various prelates from America, where the Fenians, under various names, had always been a legitimate organisation enjoying a respectable measure of public support, were most upset by it.[72] Some American bishops at first refused to implement the decree while others requested Rome to exempt them from promulgating it.[73]

When the condemnation was leaked to the press there was widespread outcry that Cullen had misled the Vatican as to the precise nature of the Fenian organisation.[74] The validity of the decree was questioned and, seeing that the Fenians had already achieved one by-election victory, allegations were made that the Church was interfering with the political rights of the Irish.[75] Cullen responded by denouncing the Fenians yet again as 'worthy disciples of Mazzini or Garibaldi' in his lenten pastoral for 1870, which he penned in Rome on 27 February 1870.[76] In this pastoral, he also made certain to emphasise the efforts of the government to redress some of the Irish grievances and pointed out how they were doing this by constitutional means.[77]

The strength of the Fenians was known to ecclesiastical figures and also to the Liberal government. The government were put under pressure by the Conservatives to repress possible violence in Ireland by introducing special coercive legislation. Responding to this pressure Gladstone introduced a Peace Preservation Bill on Saint Patrick's Day 1870, providing for various restrictions including one on the press to which Cullen was favourable.[78] The bill became law on 4 April 1870.[79]

The Peace Preservation Act was unpopular in Ireland and dissatisfaction with the government grew, a fact that influenced Cullen to return to Ireland for Easter.[80] He immediately set about denouncing the Fenians yet again in a pastoral letter read on 1 May 1870. The pastoral accused the Fenians of having no principles and of aiming only at 'confusion, anarchy and despotism'.[81] They were responsible, claimed Cullen, for the recently introduced coercive measures which, though unwelcome, were unfortunately necessary.[82] Referring to existing grievances, the pastoral repeated Cullen's exhortation for reliance on constitutional methods, especially as the government was now favourably disposed. Violence and disturbances, he thundered, could only have the effect of surrendering power to the 'patrons, perhaps the abettors, of Orange lodges, always the curse and bane of Ireland, men who, if in power, would think of nothing but the interests of a faction, and the most efficacious means of upholding old abuses'.[83]

Even after their condemnation however, the Fenians remained active.[84] In July 1870, while Cullen was back in Rome, there were rumours of American Fenians threatening to kick up a 'shindy'.[85] They also continued to support MacHale and enthusiastically welcomed him back from the Vatican Council where he opposed the doctrine of Papal Infallibility.[86] Cullen reported further that the Fenians had initiated a rumour that the people of Dublin had also declared against the doctrine.[87] A rumour of this kind was particularly hurtful to Cullen because he had been so closely associated with drafting the text of the doctrine during the Vatican Council. Further, Cullen suspected the Fenians of being behind a collection in aid of French Republicans wounded in the Franco-Prussian war.[88]

As late as November 1870 Cullen was reporting to Rome that: 'We still have a good deal of Fenianism in the towns. Their organ is *The Irishman* which condemns the Pope most severely.'[89] Indeed, after the fall of Rome, Cullen, in a November 1870 pastoral, was to link the plight of Pius IX with a denunciation of Fenianism, freemasonary and secret societies.[90]

In December 1870, Gladstone, following a review of the remaining Fenian prisoners, decided to release them all, on condition that they left the United Kingdom and did not return until after their sentence periods had expired.[91] At the same time, Cullen was writing to Kirby to report that by now the Fenians appeared 'almost defunct'.[92] They were not by any means 'defunct' but they were becoming less of a feature in the lives of the people and in the thoughts of Cullen. Following the failure of the rising three years before, the people were disposed to look once again at constitutional possibilities, especially as Gladstone was so favourably disposed.

The alternative of armed insurrection had failed to achieve its immediate goal in 1867. However, it had succeeded in highlighting the poor conditions of the Irish people. It had alerted the Liberal Party to the obligations of the British government in respect of the more deprived citizens of the realm. It had also proven that a secular national movement, even though opposed and condemned by the Catholic Church, could be organised countrywide and enjoy a wide measure of public support. The Fenian movement also showed the potential for support from Irish emigrants abroad.

~~~~ Chapter Fourteen ~~~~

CONCLUSION

ONE OF THE most significant figures in the
ecclesiastical history of Ireland in the nineteenth
century, the visible legacy of Paul Cullen's
episcopacy in Dublin, where he spent all but
two of his years as a prelate, is still there for all
to see. Evident yet in the rituals and rubrics of many churches,
schools, hospitals, religious houses and the impressive former
seminary of Holy Cross, where his remains lie, the religious
practices that 'Cullenisation' brought from Rome flourished for
a hundred years until the liturgical changes introduced by
Vatican Council II.

Disappointingly, the brilliance of Cullen's religious achievement was not matched by his record in the secular areas. The
Papal brief appointing Cullen made no mention of any secular
or political non-ecclesiastical duties, as would normally have
been the case. The question of why he engaged in, and
persevered in, non-episcopal work is therefore intriguing,
especially when one reflects on his many experiences of fatigue,
distress and sickness.

His spiritual and administrative responsibilities as archbishop
required considerable attention, especially as his mandate

included the Primacy of the Irish Church and the role of Apostolic Delegate. Curiously, he expressed a dislike of politics several times and even proclaimed that he was not getting involved, even when his actions and utterances clearly had political implications, as, for example, in advising on the selection of candidates for election. But he was clearly appalled at the living conditions of so many of his flock and felt strongly motivated to do what he could to improve their lot.

A conventional view as to why he was involved in the political field emerging from papers of the time is that he was conscious of the weakness of the national leadership after the death of Daniel O'Connell in 1847; that he was anxious that the politics developed by O'Connell should be carried forward; and that he was fearful of the consequences of what was perceived at the time as the alternative, namely armed insurrection. This alternative he first saw as a possibility in the climate of desperation after the Famine, and also in the spirit of revolution that had spread over Europe in 1848. His personal experience of revolution in Rome in 1848, that of the Young Italy Movement under the leadership of Giuseppe Mazzini, which he paralleled with the Young Ireland agitation of that same year, marked him greatly.

On Cullen's appointment to Ireland there were many materially pressing issues to be tackled. The two closest to Cullen's heart were the civil disabilities of Catholics and of the Catholic Church under the Penal laws, and the contrasting privileged status of the Protestant Church as the Established Church of Ireland. Next were the entirely inadequate services for providing food, basic health and medical care for the very survival of the people, especially the sick and destitute, including the victims of the Famine. Then there was his interest in equipping Catholics, through education especially, to get a share of the country's job opportunities. These included positions of influence in the administration of the poor relief, the police, the armed forces and in public life. Finally, even if it first appeared remote from Cullen the Churchman, there was the land question, an issue with which many Catholic priests were already prominently identified by 1850, when Cullen arrived from Rome.

A common feature of all these issues was that, whether there was armed rising or not, parliamentary action was needed to solve them. Armed force and constitutional agitation were not therefore real alternatives, even though seen at the time as such. Rather were they complementary. Unhappily, in the twenty-year period covered by this work, the constitutional lobby failed to mobilise the support of the militants for any programme of measures to be processed through parliament.

Not included in Cullen's agenda for action was the National Question, namely, the future constitutional status of Ireland. The reason for this omission was that Cullen believed that the best material interests of the people lay with remaining in the United Kingdom, at least until tolerable living conditions had been established and the morale of the people improved. It would then be time enough to consider constitutional change. Acting in accordance with the logic of that position, Cullen sought during the 1850s to encourage Irish parliamentary representatives to exploit their membership of the House of Commons, and there to advance the interests of the Irish people. Through the 1860s he did what he could to discourage armed insurrection and so keep attention focused on political possibilities. His instincts were based on his firm belief that what he advocated was for the long-term betterment of the Irish people. However, because the methods he was advocating were not producing the results, he came under fierce and heavy criticism.

There was another remarkable factor in Ireland at the time. In contrast to other countries in Europe where minorities were complaining of being persecuted by the majority, the situation in Ireland was that the majority population were suffering at the hands of the minority. This was a situation that, if popular democracy meant anything, should have been capable of being rectified over time by improving the educational services and by political action, notably by extension of the franchise. It was notable that O'Connell had backed up his campaigns in parliament by shows of massive public support demonstrated at his 'monster meetings', a strategy which the bishops themselves were quick to employ when organising the protest against the Ecclesiastical Titles Bill in 1851.

In the circumstances of the time of his arrival from Rome, it is then understandable how Cullen, keenly interested as he was in bettering the conditions of the people, allowed himself to be drafted into secular activity, even encroaching, albeit uncomfortably, onto politics itself, in the hope of making a contribution to the recovery of his people from the appalling conditions of the late 1840s.

Convinced of the potential of parliament as a forum for advancing various Irish causes and impressed by O'Connell's parliamentary achievements, Cullen determined on using the leverage in Westminster, initially of Irish members, later on of all Catholic members, and ultimately of non-Catholic members sympathetic to Catholic causes. The first aim would be to secure the disestablishment of the Established Church; the next would be to eliminate the disabilities attaching to individual Catholics arising from the penal laws and other enactments. Improvements for Catholics of course automatically meant improvements for the Irish. He would have hoped that this strategy could be employed later to rectify other, non-religion related grievances of the people as well – even if it sought to cut across the two-party structure of the House of Commons. It was also part of Cullen's strategy to facilitate and encourage the people to take advantage of the schemes and services provided by the government. Hence his concern to have Irish people appointed to public jobs where they would be sympathetic to the people's needs and have opportunities to have those needs met.

Central to Cullen's thinking was the fact that the people of Ireland were citizens of the United Kingdom, and had a democratic right to the conditions and opportunities of citizenship of that realm. And parliament was the forum for asserting that right. Cullen cherished initially a rather naive notion of parliament as an assembly of well-intentioned men

232

interested in righting wrongs once issues were properly presented to them. He liked to think that if a cause was a deserving one, it would be favourably heard in a fair-minded House of Commons. This notion was a monumental misconception. Ever since the Act of Union the members of parliament at Westminster, including successive ministers carrying responsibility for Irish affairs, were well aware of conditions in Ireland. If the Union was really effective, conditions in Ireland should by the 1850s have attained British levels. In fact there were wide gaps, with the Irish seriously lagging behind their fellow citizens in Britain in such areas as electoral reform, land tenure and the poor law.

Cullen's general approach of accepting the existing constitutional status for the time being was in danger of being undermined by some unforeseen developments. There was the parliamentary reaction to the restoration of the English Hierarchy in 1851 in the Ecclesiastical Titles legislation. However, these events, even if for a time they threatened possibilities of improvement in the area of religious rights, had their positive effect too. They gave the opportunity for the Irish bishops to demonstrate to the British political parties their power to mobilise massive public support for a campaign against the government. In the event, the idea of organising the Catholic Defence Association into some kind of United Kingdom-wide Catholic lobby in parliament failed to materialise.

Then there was the historically unfortunate decision to mandate the elected members of the new Independent Party in 1852 to adopt the negative policy of opposing any government that failed to concede certain demands of the party. It is remarkable that this policy of Independent Opposition was not seen to be so wrongheaded. It alienated the Irish members from all parties in the House of Commons instead of the alternative of supporting one or other party to keep it in power in return for concessions. By committing members to decline offices under the government it denied Irish members even the slightest role in the administration. Carried to its logical conclusion it could make parliamentary government unworkable.

It was shaky from the start and was in a short time seen to have much less support than its promoters claimed it would have. It also produced the unfortunate and damaging episode of Sadlier and Keogh and the others who followed.

To his credit, Cullen foresaw all this. To his discredit however, he failed to make his reservations known in time, and it was much later, when the situation was in confusion following the defections of Sadlier and Keogh, before his lack of support for the policy became known. Worse still, the members of the Independent group had been left to assume that Independent Opposition had his support. Unfortunately for his reputation, the ultimate disclosure of his views badly affected his credibility and was seen by critics as aligning him with men who had broken solemn pledges. His contention that these pledges were not binding disappointed and confused many people. His credibility suffered further when he sought to justify the defectors by pointing to the benefits in having Irishmen and Catholics in positions of influence in the community.

In his dual capacity as a prelate and as a man concerned with the living conditions of the people, Cullen had a role to play in giving advice and leadership to a community suffering serious privation and looking to their leaders for guidance. It is relevant to recall the nature of that advice. Three examples will illustrate.

First, he used his influence to seek relief from the wretched conditions suffered by many Catholics. This included pleading their case before parliamentary commissions and the Central Relief Committee initiative in 1862. He was also prominent in castigating the government for their failure to take remedial action and he took every opportunity to show them how neglect of the plight of the people could be a cause of disaffection leading to public unrest and even armed revolution. Nevertheless, at the same time he persisted in cautioning the deprived masses that they must suffer with resignation and patiently wait for improvements. That this advice met with such a high degree of acceptance from the poor of Dublin merely shows how dispirited they were. The incidence of disturbances in the streets was less than what might be expected, having regard to the

234

number of unemployed and socially deprived in the capital, and bearing in mind also the wretched conditions of the workhouses operated under the poor law.

Second, and closely allied to the first, there was his counsel to the tenant farmers to refrain from any physical action but to await the land reform legislation, which would hopefully ease their lot. He declined to support the Tenant League as an organisation while sympathising with the grievance of its members. As happened in the case of Independent Opposition, his real attitude to the Tenant League was unclear for some time, and his behaviour here, as in the case of Independent Opposition, also gave rise to suspicions as to his reliability. His inhibitions took until 1865 to moderate, when land reform was included in the programme of the National Association. In this sensitive area of land tenure the deeply felt resentments of the tenant farmers were quite resistant to this kind of advice. There was also the frustrating factor that parliament was not a promising place for seeking redress from land tenure inequalities, due to the presence of many landlords as members. This was evident in the refusal of both main parties to support land reform bills sponsored by Irish members in the 1850s and the 1860s.

Third, there was the repeated message to continue to submit to established British rule, a message that he backed up with extreme Church action against the Fenians.

It is scarcely to be wondered at that some of the obsequious postures Cullen was advocating raised questions about his status as a leader figure for a people yearning for release from so much oppression.

A feature of Cullen's career was the priority he gave to Church and religious issues. Hence the mobilisation of such massive opposition to the Ecclesiastical Titles legislation in 1851. It was a campaign puzzling in itself seeing that his personal view was that the law would never be operated in Ireland – which it was not. And it was clear that for almost the next two decades another religious issue, the disestablishment of the Church of Ireland, was also a priority target of Cullen's, until it was achieved in 1869.

Cullen was already aware upon his arrival in Ireland of the record of clerical backing for Daniel O'Connell's campaigns, first in the successful campaign for Catholic Emancipation, which was achieved in 1829, and then in the Repeal movement. This record of sustained clerical support no doubt had the effect of blurring any distinction which Cullen might have been drawing between a religion-based objective like Emancipation and the political objective of Repeal, even as a long-term aim. Indeed, in the Ireland of O'Connell very few would have made any distinction between the two campaigns, for 'Faith and Fatherland' was the contemporary slogan that expressed the popular aims of religious and political advance.

By the mid-1850s however, the scene was changing. Certain Tories of the landlord class had found ways to seduce numbers of their constituents, including some priests, with promises not only of land tenure reform but also of new roads, piers, railways and other local improvements, and were winning electoral support. Therefore, instead of the collaboration of earlier years between priests and 'friendly' Liberal politicians, or more recently the Independent Party, Cullen was now confronted with the divisiveness and the scandal of priests publicly opposing one another in political campaigns. Predictably, he reacted by seeking to control the participation of priests in politics. He relied heavily on rigidly interpreted disciplinary rules, especially decrees handed down by Irish synods under his own direction.

In restraining priests in politics Cullen found himself in most difficult situations. Opposing him were nationalist churchmen like MacHale and Lavelle, as well as elected members of the Independent Party. His 'allies' were really uncongenial company, for they included the British government and later the Fenian leadership!

A particular flaw in the strictures on priests involving themselves in politics was that the regulations were being seen by critics, including some fellow bishops like Keane of Cloyne, as curtailing the just rights of the clergy as citizens in a democracy. It is clear from subsequent history that in believing that he could by decree get the clergy to exclude themselves

236

from politics, Cullen had made a miscalculation. Clerical involvement in nationalist politics was set to continue for many years. 'Who was it that led the van? *Soggart aroon, soggart aroon,*' as a line in a popular nationalist ballad had it.

Later during the 1880s the Irish political leader, Charles Stewart Parnell, found that the impact of Vatican condemnations was actually being deflected by Archbishops Croke of Cashel and Walsh of Dublin so that the clergy could continue to co-operate with an Irish parliamentary party, and in particular, take part in the selection of candidates at conventions.

In the light of the priority given by Cullen to Church and religious matters, it is to be inferred that the influence of Rome impaired the effectiveness of his leadership in material affairs, diminishing his appeal to the people and his acceptability to politicians. The turn-the-other-cheek responses he was advocating, like resignation to harsh living conditions, acceptance of dispossession of one's land, and submission to domination by a usurping power, might indeed have been in line with the official teaching of the time. As time went on however, they were meeting with less acceptance by the people according as their patience was running out; and there was also their growing self-confidence according as educational levels were rising. The latter was thanks largely to Cullen's own great work in this field.

With all its difficulties and disappointments however, Cullen persisted in backing peaceful constitutional methods as a means of advancing the Irish people's interests within the United Kingdom. Clearly many people were dissatisfied with the lack of progress, but it would be wrong to blame Cullen for this. He was not an elected political personage and he should not have been expected to carry political responsibility. In making any judgement, regard should be had to his horror at the prospect of the reality, and the aftermath, of a failed military uprising. Rather does the explanation for failure lie in the disregard of the United Kingdom authorities for their obligations to their Irish citizens and in the ineffectiveness of the Irish members of parliament.

Account must be taken of the many strong personalities who dogged Cullen's footsteps. First, there was Archbishop MacHale who, having welcomed Cullen at the start, found in a short time that he was unable to accommodate himself to an ultramontane, non-Maynooth prelate, and who widened the area of non-cooperation down the years. Then there were the other clerics, the most notable being Lavelle, who defied his authority. Next, Lucas and the other parliamentarians who were prepared to combine with disaffected priests to challenge his orders controlling priests in politics. Then there were the British ministers of the day, no matter what their political affiliation, who could be depended on to abuse him as opportunity arose.

All the time there was the absence of a political personality with the capacity to provide the lay leadership that Daniel O'Connell previously gave and that Charles Stewart Parnell was to give in later years. And, most unkindest cut of all, there was the failure of senior Vatican figures to give Cullen the support to which he felt the Apostolic Delegate was entitled. One can only speculate about the reasons for the Vatican's failure to reciprocate his great loyalty. This is especially true seeing how interested the Pope himself was in Cullen's letters, and remembering the Pope's personal mediation in the two main controversies involving Cullen: the Lucas affair in 1854–5 and the Lavelle problem in the 1860s. These then are some of the elements that prevented Cullen from achieving the potential of the efforts he so energetically made in the material interest of the Irish people.

Because the political line he was taking meant acceptance, for the time being at least, of Ireland's status as part of the United Kingdom, Cullen found himself in conflict with the separatist nationalist movement. It also exposed him to mischievous and unfounded taunts of being pro-British. His was a difficult line to maintain, seeing that his own family had suffered tragedy at the hands of the Crown forces during the rebellion of 1798, itself one of the events that had precipitated the Union. Separatism had a growing popular appeal, among

238

priests as well as others, and there were some who saw the connection with England as the main source of Ireland's ills.

It is appropriate to examine the factors which determined Cullen's attitude to the Fenians, for his record in relation to them has ever since been used to overshadow much else in his career. It was typical of him that, when confronted with the problem, his first reaction was to look to Rome for guidance. How would Rome approach the Fenian movement? Without waiting for an authoritative answer – which in fact didn't come until 1870 – he decided that they were to be regarded as a secret society plotting against the Church and State and should be treated as such. There were also unproven suggestions of association with Young Italy and other subversive interests who were seen as a threat to the established order and to private property.

Cullen was not deterred by the cloudy interpretation originally issued from the Holy Office. He proceeded to condemn and ostracise the Fenians, invoking all the powers of the Church, up to the refusal of the Sacraments, to deal with them. Indeed, in his anti-Fenian enthusiasm he came to criticise the British authorities for the inadequacy of their repressive measures against them. This in itself added to his separation from the Fenians and their growing number of supporters.

Cullen did not appear to appreciate fully the powerful emotions which produced revolutionary nationalism, and Fenianism in particular, and which ensured so much support for the separatist idea. The grievances of the Irish Catholic people were deeply felt. There was especially the fierce anti-British resentment of post-Famine emigrants who, by the early 1860s, felt motivated to do something to right the wrongs of their people at home in Ireland. The most telling point of all was the fact that the constitutional methods were still failing to produce the solutions.

As far as Cullen's own relations with the Fenians were concerned, his animosity manifested itself as early as the McManus funeral in November 1861. His refusal to admit the remains to his Pro-Cathedral or allow a requiem High Mass and funeral service was a decision that enraged Irish opinion. Resentment was heightened by the fact that the remains had been venerated in Saint Patrick's Cathedral in New York. The massive turnout of the people of Dublin for the funeral suggested that Cullen was perhaps mistaken. He stubbornly refused to admit to any such possibility however.

In his long public campaign against the Fenians, Cullen did not obscure the most powerful practical reason of all for condemning them and for discouraging members of his flock from joining them. This was that, in any encounter with Crown forces, they had no chance whatever of military success, as was indeed proved in 1867; and further, armed insurrection could be followed by heavy repressive measures by the government.

In contrast to the British authorities, Cullen's information about the Fenians was notoriously unreliable. He ought to have known that links with European subversives were minimal and irrelevant, at times more imagined than real. The Fenians could be described as quite impractical. Their aim was to establish an independent Irish republic by physical force and members were to defend the independence and integrity of the republic. However, they had not comprehensively developed any policies, even for the land, which was the source of greatest discontent with them, and unhappily were shown to be most ineffectual. As regards military action, it turned out that their supplies of firearms were meagre in the extreme, and when they attacked their targeted police barracks in March 1867 they were repulsed without any unit of the RIC having to call on the army for support. Despite all this, the Fenians continue to enjoy an honoured place in Irish history for their steadfast pursuit of the aim of national independence.

British worries at the time of the Fenian rising were not of course centred in isolated police barracks in Ireland. They were concerned with their relations with the United States and Canada, where anti-British feelings were being stirred up by Irish emigrants now making themselves felt politically. In a military sense, they were also keeping an eye on French intentions with a view to being prepared for a possible landing of troops in some disaffected part of the United Kingdom, especially Ireland.

Another misjudgement of Cullen in relation to the Fenians was that they were in some way a threat to the Catholic Church. It is true that a number of prominent Fenians turned against the Church. At no time however did the Fenians threaten to kidnap priests, burn churches or confiscate Church property. On the contrary, they would make common cause with a Church which was itself at loggerheads with the British government. Witness the Irish Brigade who fought for the Pope against British-backed Italian nationalist forces in 1860, in a campaign that incidentally served to undermine Cullen's anti-Fenian stance later, notably in the columns of the *Irish People*.

It was remarkable how Cullen allowed himself to become obsessed by Fenianism. Even while he was reporting to Rome on what he took to be declining support for the movement, he was preparing yet another pastoral condemning Fenianism and calling all kinds of punishments on its members. This obsession led to the requests in Rome, one by some, but not all, of the Irish bishops led by Cullen, the other by the British government, to have the Fenians excommunicated. Siding with Irish constitutionalists against the Fenians might be tolerated, even excused. To join with the British government against them, even though the motivation was not the same, proved to be unacceptable to popular Irish public opinion at the time, and indeed for generations after. And then there was the final tragic denouement: the Pope acceded to those requests, and in the year of Infallibility too!

The era covered by this work was indeed a dismal one in Irish history. A time of missed opportunities, the most fateful of these the failure to have in place the politicians and the organisations that would build on the successes of Daniel O'Connell in constitutional politics. Specifically, there was the failure to exploit 'people power' as developed by O'Connell through the widely reported monster meetings.

For underprivileged people seeking redress, constitutionalism, whatever its merits, did not depend solely on ordered debates in the rarefied air of a parliamentary assembly. Governments, and Oppositions too, had to be made forcibly aware of the strength of feeling among the people represented by their elected members, and of the possible consequences of refusal to deliver overdue reforms whether in the form of rejection by the electorate, or more seriously in the form of civil unrest. And indeed Cullen played his part in this.

The constitutionalists of the time were at fault in refusing to recognise militants like the Fenians as potential allies, not enemies, of the parliamentary process. It was left to English Liberal leader Gladstone to recognise the change in public opinion and respond to it as he started to do in the late 1860s.

Attitudes were changing however, and during the period there was indeed a growing recognition that parliamentary action was a necessary pre-requisite for any improvements to be secured. The fact that, in time, the Fenians could persuade the electorate in Tipperary to return O'Donovan Rossa to parliament would suggest that the Fenians themselves, despite their early stance, were becoming amenable to the constitutional process, if the parliamentarians cultivated their friendship and welcomed them into the fold. Remarkably, the country had not long to wait, for the efforts of such as Isaac Butt, Michael Davitt and John Devoy were about to lead to a formidable combination of constitutional, militant and land reform forces under the leadership of Charles Stewart Parnell.

As a Catholic and an Irishman Cullen had the task of accommodating his secular as well as his religious policies for Ireland to the principles he was taught in Rome. It is observable in other occupations that the skills and attitudes developed in the sheltered atmosphere of the general headquarters do not always prepare one for conditions experienced later. An introspective personality like Cullen would scarcely have the flexibility and the openness called for in such situations; and conflicts of priority and of loyalty were bound to arise. In such conflicts Cullen, no doubt conscious of his episcopal role, was inclined to lean towards Rome, heightening rather than lowering the tension of the situation.

Cullen's preferences undoubtedly antagonised those who did not share them. His loyalty to the Holy See, though not fully reciprocated, also had the unfortunate consequence of giving credence to the 'Home Rule is Rome Rule' slogan of those Tory-led Protestants who opposed self-government for Ireland in later decades.

Lacking training or experience in politics, Cullen did not possess the armoury which would have enabled him to project his image, defend himself from attack, and adapt to the many changing situations. Nor was there any newspaper or journal to espouse his cause or explain his message. The *Irish Catholic*, which sought to fulfil this role in later times, did not start until ten years after his death.

The anxiety of Cullen to refer so many issues to Rome, including matters which appeared to be within his own competence, would suggest some lack of confidence in his own abilities. So often on the defensive, so much misrepresented and misunderstood, Cullen was seriously handicapped in his efforts to contribute to the process of promoting the interests of the people within the existing structures. Nor did his secretive and somewhat enigmatic personality enable him to cultivate the friendships which would have helped him in his many agonising dilemmas. His very many attacks of sickness and depression must have seriously impaired him. Thus, disappointingly for him and for the people, so many of the grievances of 1850 were still there at the end of his episcopacy over two decades later. The exception, appropriately enough in view of his priorities, was the legal status of the Catholic Church and the Catholic religion.

By the 1916–22 period when the next armed rising took place, both Church and Nationalism had learned from Cullen's experience with the Fenians. A generation of bishops, themselves imbued with the distinctive Irish cultural ethos of the early twentieth century, found it possible to accommodate the struggle for self-determination to the declarations of the

Vatican. The record is not 100 per cent clear, but confrontation and condemnation were largely avoided, despite the participation of secret oath-bound groups, and the Catholic Church and the revolutionary movement, though dominated by the lineal descendants of the Fenian Brotherhood, found in time that they could work together. One party which could be said not to have learned a lesson, however, was the British government. By dismissing the considerations which spared the lives of the Fenian leadership half a century earlier and by executing the leaders of what was initially an unpopular uprising in 1916, they helped to cause public opinion to sympathise with republican nationalists and turn violently against the government.

Cullen was dedicated to his faith. A practical nationalist, he applied his considerable talents to both the church and to what he was convinced were the best material interests of the people he was sent to serve. When it comes to the National Question, a degree of puzzlement survives about a patriotic Irish churchman who somehow was involved in moves that had the effect of alienating significant elements of Irish separatism from the Catholic Church. It is safe to say that, as regards the topics addressed in this work, Cullen's various other controversial actions, such as his tolerance of the defection of Sadlier and Keogh, his ambivalence in regard to the Tenant League and his support for certain election candidates while ordering his priests to keep out of politics, are long forgotten. A personality of history in the sacred affairs of religion and the Catholic Church, Cullen is still the towering figure who made Catholic Ireland what it remained for over one hundred years. Credit must be afforded for his work in the area of civil rights for Catholics, for education, for public health, and for the relief of poverty. Today his statue occupies a prominent place outside Holy Cross College, Clonliffe. His commanding presence is also remembered in Dublin's Pro-Cathedral. He is not represented so far, however, in the capital's monuments to her patriot sons and daughters.

244

ABBREVIATIONS

Abp.	Archbishop
ACPF	Archives of the Congregation of Propaganda Fide
Acta	*Acta Sacrae Congregationis*
Ad.	Adminstrator
Anon	Anonymous
Apos.	Apostolic
Apr.	April
ASS	*Acta Sanctae Sedis*
Assess.	Assessor
Assoc.	Association
ASV.	*Archivio Segreto Vaticano*
Aug.	August
BAR	Benedictine Archives Rome
BM. Add. MS	British Museum Additional Manuscript
BN	*Belfast Newsletter*
Bp.	Bishop
Brit. Dip.	British Diplomat
BT	*Belfast Telegraph*

Cath.	Catholic
CC	Catholic Curate
CE	*Cork Examiner*
CJ	*Clare Journal*
Co.	county
Coadj.	Coadjutor
Coll.	College
Committ.	Committee
Cong.	Congregation
Conn. Pat.	*Connaught Patriot*
corr.	Correspondant
CP	*Congregazioni Particolari*
cr.	created
CSO	Central Statistics Office
CT	*Catholic Telegraph*
DA	*Drogheda Argus*
DDA	Dublin Diocesan Archives
DE	*Daily Express*
Dec.	December
Def.	Defence
DEH	*Dublin Evening Herald*
DEM	*Dublin Evening Mail*
DEP	*Dublin Evening Post*
Digest	Digest of the report of the Devon commission, ie. [J.P. Kennedy], Digest of evidence taken before Her Majesty's commissioners of inquiry into the state of the law and practice in respect to the occupation of land in Ireland.
dist.	District
DT	*Dublin Telegraph*
Duffy, League	C.G. Duffy, 'The League of North and South'
DUM	*Dublin University Magazine*
Ecc.	Ecclesiastical
ed.	Editor
edit.	edition

248

Elec.	Elect
Elect. Comm.	Report on Election Commission
Elect. Pet.	Report of the Trial of Election Committee
EM	*Evening Mail*
f.	foglio
Feb.	February
Fen.	Fenian
ff.	foglie
FJ	*Freeman's Journal*
FO	Foreign Office
Gen.	General
GFP	*Glasgow Free Press*
HA	*Hull Advertiser*
H.C.	House of Commons
Hon.	Honorary
ibid.	ibidem
ICAR	Irish College Archives, Rome
ICD	*Irish Catholic Directory*
IER	Irish Ecclesiastical Record
IHS	Irish Historical Studies
IP	*Irish People*
Ire.	Ireland
IT	*Irish Times*
Jan.	January
Journ., WR	Journalist Weekly Register
KDA	Kerry Diocesan Archives
lay corr.	lay correspondent
LDB	*Lettere e Decreti della Sacra Congregazione e Biglietti di Monsignor Segretario*
Lieut.	Lieutenant

Lucas, *Life*	E. Lucas, *Life of Frederick Lucas*
LR	*Limerick Reporter*
Mar.	March
memo	memorandum
MH	*Morning Herald*
MN	*Munster News*
MP	Member of Parliament
MS	Manuscript
Nat.	National
NC	New Collection
n.d.	no date
NE	*Newry Examiner*
NG	*Nenagh Guardian*
NLI	National Library, Ireland
no.	number
nos	numbers
Nov.	November
nrth.	north
NT	*Newry Telegraph*
Oct.	October
op. cit.	opere citato
OR	Outrage Papers
org.	organiser
p.	page
Parl. Deb.	Parliamentary Debate
PM.	Prime Minister
pp.	pages
PP	Parish Priest
Pres.	President
Prop.	Propaganda Fide
Prot.	Protestant

Rec.	Rector
Reg.	Regional
Rel.	Relation
Relg.	Religious
Rep. Novum	*Reportorium Novum*
S.Br.	*Secretaria Brevium*
SC	*Scritture riferite nei Congressi*
Sec.	Secretary
Sept.	September
ser.	series
sess.	session
SOCG	*Scritture Originali riferite nelle Congregazioni Generali*
SPO, CSO, RP	State Paper Office, Chief Secetary's Office, Registered Papers
SS	Saints
TC	*Tralee Chronicle*
TFP	*Tipperary Free Press*
Univ.	University
v	verso
VECAR	Venerable English College Archives Rome
Vic. Gen.	Vicar General
Vice Rec.	Vice Rector
Vict.	Victoria
vol.	volume
vols.	volumes
WDA	Westminster Diocesan Archives
WFJ	*Weekly Freemans Journal*
WG	*Westmeath Guardian*
WI	*Wexford Independent*
WRJ	*Weekly Register Journal*
wst.	west

NOTES

Chapter One

1. S.G. Osborne, *Gleanings in the West of Ireland*, London, 1850, pp. 107–8; *WFJ*, 29 April 1848.

2. *Digest* of the Devon Report, vol. 1, pp. 156–7.

3. *Parl. Deb.* ser. 3, cxxiii, 1545–57.

4. *Nation*, 15 Sept. 1849.

5. *Return ... of Cases of Evictions which have come to the Knowledge of the Constabulary in each of the years from 1849 to 1880*, H.C. 1881 (185) lxxvii.

6. 'Irlanda — Relazione riguardo al proselitismo protestante nell'Occidente d'Irlanda. Suo successo e mezzi adoperati', n.d.: ASV, *Pio IX, Oggetti Vari*, no. 993.

7. 'Ní ins an ainnise is meas a linn bheith síos go deo ach an tarcuisne do leanas sin', Eoghan Rua O Suilleabhain in T.F. O'Rathaille (ed.), *Burdúin Beaga*, Dublin, 1950, p. 12.

8. In Cullen's academic records the date given is 27 April 1803. See ACPF, *SC, Collegio Urbano*, vol. 15, f. 56 (*v*); P. MacSuibhne, *Paul Cullen and his Contemporaries*, vol. 1, Naas, 1961, p. 2 and Bowen, op. cit., p. 2, both give the date as 29 Apr. 1803. However Cullen himself was later to maintain that he was born sometime in 1804. See Cullen to Kirby, (*Rec. Irish Coll. Rome*), 29 Dec. 1876: ICAR, *NC, III*, 3, 5, no. 64.

9. P. MacSuibhne, 'The Early Cullen Family', *Rep. Novum*, vol. 2, no. 1, 1955, p. 191.

10. Troy (*Abp., Dublin*) to Prop., 3 Oct. 1820: ACPF, *SC, Collegio Urbano*, vol. 13, f. 264 (*269*).

11. ACPF, *SC, Collegio Urbano*, vol. 13, f. 280 (*285*); Bowen, op. cit., p. 5, maintains that Cullen came to Rome in 1821.

12. ACPF, *SC, Collegio Urbano*, vol. 15, ff. 56 (*v*), 101–22.

13. AVR, *Liber Ordinationum*, vol. 43, ff. 153, 163.

14. Cullen to Maher (*PP, Carlow Graigue, Rel. Cullen*) 30 Apr. 1831, as quoted in Mac Suibhne, op. cit., vol. 1, Naas, 1962, p. 182; see also MacSuibhne, ibid., vol. 2, p. 327.

15. MacSuibhne, ibid, vol. 1, p. 11.

16. Fransoni (*Prefect, Prop.*) to Barnabò (*Sec., Prop.*), 20 Dec. 1849: ACPF, *SC, Irlanda*, vol. 30, f. 286; see also ASV, S. Br. 5166, f. 19.

17. England (*Bp., Charleston*) to Cullen, 1/2 Aug. 1834: ICAR, *American Papers, 1828–49*, no. 28; O'Connor (*Vice Rec. Irish Coll., Rome*) to Cullen, 2 Aug. 1834: ICAR, *O'Connor Papers, 1834–47*, no. 4; Memo. n.d. (Aug. 1834): ACPF, Congressi, *America–Antille*, vol. 5, ff. 836–41; Sec. of Cong. of Extraordinary Ecc. Affairs to Prop., 22 Aug. 1834: ACPF, *SC, America–Antille*, vol. 5, f. 834; Prop. Fide to Sec of Briefs, 22 Aug. 1834: ACPF, LDB, vol. 315, f. 469; O'Connor to Cullen, 2 Sept. 1834: ICAR, *O'Connor Papers, 1834–47*, no. 5.

18. Cullen to O'Connor, n.d. (*Aug. 1834*): ACPF, *SC, Irlanda*, vol 25, ff. 808–9; Cullen to Mai (Sec. Prop.), 4 Sept. 1834: ACPF, *SC, Irlanda*, vol. 25, ff. 820–21; Cullen to Prop., 4 Sept. 1834: ACPF, *SC, Irlanda*, vol. 25, f. 822; O'Connor to Cullen, 10 Sept. 1834: ICAR, O'Connor, Papers 1834–47, no. 7; Prop. to Cullen, 11 Sept. 1834: ACPF, *LDB*, vol. 315, ff. 505 (*v*), 506 (*v*); Prop. to England, 11 Sept. 1834: SCPF, *LDB*, vol. 315, f. 506; England to Prop., 24 Sept. 1834: ACPF, *SC, America Centrale*, vol. 11, ff. 370–71; O'Connor to Cullen, 1 Oct. 1834: ICAR, *O'Connor Papers*, 1834–47, no. 9.

19. Kenrick (*Bp., elect. Arathia & Coadj. Bp., Philadelphia*) to Prop., 5 May 1830: ACPF, *SC, America Centrale*, vol. 10, f. 369 (*v*); Kenrick to Prop., 11 June 1830: ACPF, *SC, America Centrale*, vol. 10, f. 388 (*v*); Prop. to Kenrick, 27 July 1830: ACPF, *LDB*, vol. 311, ff. 644–5.

20. England to Cullen, 13–15 May 1834: ICAR, *American Papers*, 1828–49, no. 22; Kenrick to Prop., 6 February 1837: ACPF, *SC, America Centrale*, vol. 12, f. 30

21. Kenrick to Prop., 12 Sept. 1837: ACPF, *SC, America Centrale*, vol. 12, f. 189.

22. ASV, S. Br. 5172, f. 59.

23. *Parl. Deb.*, ser. 3, xciii, 645; *FJ*, 31 Jan. 1847 for Cork; *FJ*, 1 Dec. 1847 for Mayo; *FJ*, 31 Dec. 1847 for Waterford, Wexford and Tipperary; B. Kennedy (ed.), 'Sharman Crawford on Ulster Tenant Right, 1846', *IHS*, Mar. 1963, vol. 8, pp. 246–53 for Ulster.

24. *Nation*, 20 Oct. 1849; *TFP*, 20 Oct. 1849; E. Lucas, *Life of Frederick Lucas*, London, 1886, vol. 2, pp. 217–8.

25. J.H. Whyte, *The Independent Irish Party 1850–9*, Oxford, 1958, p. 6.

26. *Tablet*, 1 Mar. 1851.

27. *Nation*, 27 Apr., 11 May 1850; *FJ*, 7, 8, 9 Aug. 1850.

28. *LDB*, 15 Aug. 1850; *Nation*, 10 Aug. 1850; *CE*, 12 Aug. 1850.

29. *FJ*, 10 Aug. 1850.

30. J.H. Whyte reckons that in 1850 there were sixty–four Irish Liberal MPs, thirty–seven Irish Conservative MPs and four Irish Peelites. All the Peelites belonged to the Established Church as did all of the Conservatives with the exception of a solitary Presbyterian. Meanwhile the Liberals included thirty members of the Established Church and thirty–four Catholics. See, Whyte, op. cit., p. 14.

31. Sir C.G. Duffy, *My Life In Two Hemispheres*, London, 1898, vol. 1, p. 249.

32. 'The Synodical Address of the Fathers of the National Council of Thurles 1850', P.F. Moran, *The Pastoral Letters and Other Writings of Cardinal Cullen*, Dublin, 1882, vol. 1, p. 44.

33. 'Pastoral letter … on the occasion of the Archbishop's consecration 24 February 1850', Moran, op. cit., p. 13.

34. Kirby (*Rec. Irish Coll., Rome*) to Prop., 8 May 1850: ACPF, *SC, Irlanda*, vol. 30, f. 293; Cullen to Kirby, 11 May 1850: ICAR, *NC, III*, 1, 2, no. 17; Cullen to Prop., 16 May 1850: ACPF, *SC, Irlanda*, vol. 30, f. 419; Cullen to Kirby, 16 May 1850: ICAR, *NC, III*, 1, 2, no. 18; Cullen to Prop., 7 June 1850: ACPF, *SC, Irlanda*, vol. 30, f. 430; Cullen to Kirby, 12 June 1850: ICAR, *NC, III*, 1, 2, no. 26.

35. Cullen to Prop., 16 May 1850: ACPF, *SC, Irlanda*, vol. 30, f. 419; Cullen to Prop., 7 June 1850: ACPF, *SC, Irlanda*, vol. 30, f. 430.

36. Cullen to Kirby, 1 Oct. 1853: ICAR *NC, III*, 1, 3, no. 98; Cullen to Smith (*Vice Rec. Irish Coll., Rome*), 7 Oct. 1851: BAR, *Smith Papers*. Cullen to Kirby, 18 Nov. 1853: ICAR, *NC, III*, 1, 3, no. 109; Cullen to Kirby, 20 Jan. 1851: ICAR, *NC, III*, 1, 2, no. 68; Cullen to Kirby, 8 Feb. 1851: ICAR, *NC, III*, 1, 2, no. 72; Cullen to Prop., 11 Oct. 1851: ACPF, *SC, Irlanda*, vol. 30, f. 725 (*v*); Cullen to Prop., 16 May 1850: ACPF, *SC, Irlanda*, vol. 30, f. 419 (*v*); Cullen to Prop., 20 Sept. 1851: ACPF, *SC, Irlanda*, vol. 30, f. 706; Cullen to Prop., 24 Apr. 1851: ACPF, *SC, Irlanda*, vol. 30, f. 603 (*v*); Cullen to Prop., 31 Jan. 1852: ACPF, *SC, Irlanda*, vol. 31, f. 76; Cullen to Prop., 7 June 1850: ACPF, *SC, Irlanda*, vol. 30, f. 430. Cullen to Prop., 8 May 1852: ACPF, *SC, Irlanda*, vol. 31, f. 157 (*v*). Cullen to Smith, 1 June 1851: BAR, *Smith Papers*; Cullen to Smith, 12 July 1851: BAR, *Smith Papers*; Cullen to Smith, 12 May 1851: BAR, *Smith Papers*; see also Kirby to Prop., n.d. (*Feb. 1851*): ACPF, *SC, Irlanda*, vol. 30, f. 556 (*v*); Kirby to Prop., n.d. (*Nov. 1853*): ACPF, *SC, Irlanda*, vol. 31, f. 665 (*v*).

37. Cullen to Prop., 16 May 1850: ACPF, SC, Irlanda, vol. 30, f. 419 (v); Cullen to Kirby, 25 Oct. 1850: ICAR, NC, III, 1, 2, no. 53; Cullen to Kirby, 8 Feb. 1851: ICAR, NC, III, 1, 2, no. 72; Cullen to Prop., 24 Apr. 1851: ACPF, SC, Irlanda, vol. 30, f. 603 (v); Cullen to Smith, 12 July 1851: BAR, Smith Papers; Cullen to Smith, 7 Oct. 1851: BAR, Smith Papers; Cullen to Prop., 10 Oct. 1851: ACPF, SC, Irlanda, vol. 30, f. 726; Cullen to Prop., 8 May 1852: ACPF, SC, Irlanda, vol. 31, f. 157 (v); Cullen to Prop., 22 Sept. 1852: ACPF, SC, Irlanda, vol. 31, f. 249; see also Kirby to Prop., n.d. (Feb. 1852): ACPF, SC, Irlanda, vol. 30, f. 556 (v).

38. Cullen to Kirby, 8 Feb. 1851: ICAR, NC, III, 1, 2, no. 72; Cullen to Prop., 24 Apr. 1852: ACPF, SC, Irlanda, vol. 31, f. 166; Cullen to Prop., 22 Sept. 1852: ACPF, SC, Irlanda, vol. 31, f. 248; see also Kirby to Prop., n.d. (Feb. 1851): ACPF, SC, Irlanda, vol. 30, f. 556 (v).

39. Cullen to Girdwood (Tenant League org.), 24 Jan. 1851: Tablet, 1 Feb. 1851; Cullen to Keappock (Tenant League org.), 11 July 1851: Tablet, 19 July 1851.

40. Cullen to Girdwood, 24 Jan. 1851: Tablet, 1 Feb. 1851.

41. Tablet, 1 Feb. 1851.

42. Cullen to Dowling, (PP, Clonmellon) 27 Oct. 1850: FJ, 28 Oct. 1851.

43. ibid.

44. Tablet 23 Mar. 1850; LM, 19 Mar. 1850, 21 Mar. 1851.

45. TFP, 1 June 1850 for views of Fr William Heffernan (PP, Clerihan) who had a drastic solution for the so–called land grabber: 'Let no father give him his daughter in marriage, let no one attend his funeral or say the Lord have mercy on his soul'; see letter in the Tablet, 18 May 1850, of Fr James Redmond (PP, Arklow) who claimed that he would use the confessional to question a landlord on his valuation during the famine and if it had been unfair would call him a murderer; see also LR, 23 Mar. 1850; Tablet 30 Nov. 1850.

46. TFP, 27 Feb. 1850; Tablet, 2, 23 Mar., 19 Oct. 1850; Pobal Ailbe 36, 88, 90.

47. Tablet 2, 23 Mar. 1850; 23 Mar. 1850; 2 Dec. 1851; CE, 26 Feb., 19 Mar. 1851; W. Meagher, The Roman Law of Landlord and Tenant with Suggestions for Its Application to Irish Tenure, Dublin, 1854.

48. Cullen to Girdwood, 24 Jan. 1851: Tablet, 1 Feb. 1851.

49. 'Pastoral letter … on the occasion of the Archbishop's consecration, 24 Feb. 1850': Moran, op. cit., vol. 1, p. 13; 'Pastoral Letter for the Feast of the Assumption 28 July 1852': Moran, op. cit., vol. 1, p. 200; 'Pastoral Letter on the festival of Saint Patrick, 1 March 1853': Moran, op. cit., vol. 1, p. 224.

50. 'Pastoral Letter for Lent, 1852': Moran, op. cit., vol. 1, p. 188; 'Pastoral letter on the fast of Lent, 1853': Moran, op. cit., vol. 1, p. 217.

51. 'Pastoral Letter for Lent 1852': Moran, op. cit., vol. 1, p. 187. See also 'Pastoral letter … on the occasion of the Archbishop's consecration, 24 Feb. 1850': Moran, op. cit., vol. 1, p. 12; 'Discourse at the General meeting of the Catholic Association 29 January 1852': Moran, op. cit., vol. 1, p. 182.

52. 'Pastoral letter … on the occasion of the Archbishop's consecration, 24 February 1850': Moran, op. cit., vol. 1, p. 13; 'Discourse addressed to the Catholic Association, 29 January 1852': Moran, op. cit., vol. 1, p. 182; 'Pastoral Letter for Lent 1852': Moran, op. cit., vol. 1, p. 188.

53. 'Synodal address of the Bishops of the Province of Dublin 1853': Moran, op. cit., vol. 1, p. 270.

54. 'Pastoral letter … on the occasion of the Archbishop's consecration, 24 February 1850': Moran, op. cit., vol. 1, p. 16.

Chapter Two

1. Cullen to Kirby (Rec. Irish Coll., Rome), 3 Dec. 1850: ICAR, NC, III, 1, 2, no. 60.

2. In 'Relazione sullo stato generale della Religione Cattolica in Inghilterra ed Irlanda', 15 Feb. 1848, Russell is described as 'un nemico manifesto della nostra Santa Religione': ASV, Pio IX, Oggetti Vari, no. 440.

3. Cullen to Prop., 4 July 1851: ACPF, SC, Irlanda, vol. 30, f. 678 (v).

4. Cullen to Kirby, 25 Nov. 1850: ICAR, NC, III, 1, 2, no. 57.

5. Cullen to Kirby, 25 Oct. 1850: ICAR, NC, III, 1, 2, no. 53.

6. Cullen to Smith (Vice Rec. Irish Coll., Rome), 11 Sept. 1851: BAR, Smith Papers; Cullen to Smith, 17 Nov. 1851: BAR, Smith Papers.

7. Cullen to Kirby, 25 Oct. 1850: ICAR, NC, III, 1, 2, no. 53.

8. Cullen to Kirby, 3 Dec. 1850: ICAR, *NC, III,* 1, 2, no. 60; Cullen to Prop., 5 Apr. 1851: ACPF, *SC, Irlanda,* vol. 30, f. 597; Cullen to Prop., 25 Apr. 1851: ACPF, *SC, Irlanda,* vol. 30, f. 605 (*v*); Cullen to Smith, 1 June 1851: BAR, *Smith Papers;* Cullen to Prop., 7 June 1851: ACPF, *SC, Irlanda,* vol. 30, f. 644 (*v*); Cullen to Smith, 28 June 1851: BAR, *Smith Papers;* Cullen to Prop., 4 July 1851: ACPF, *SC, Irlanda,* vol. 30, f. 678 (*v*); Cullen to Smith, 7 July 1851: BAR, *Smith Papers;* Cullen to Prop., 20 Sept. 1851: ACPF, *SC, Irlanda,* vol. 30, f. 707.

9. 'Un poco di persecuzione ci farà molto bene', Cullen to Kirby, 8 Feb. 1851: ICAR, *NC, III,* 1, 2, no. 72; see also Cullen to Smith, 24 Dec. 1850: BAR, *Smith Papers;* Kirby to Prop., n.d. (*Feb. 1851*): ACPF, *SC, Irlanda,* vol. 30, f. 556; Cullen to Prop., 25 Apr. 1851: ACPF, *SC, Irlanda,* vol. 30, f. 605 (*v*); Cullen to Smith, 28 June 1851: BAR, *Smith Papers;* Cullen to Smith, 30 July 1851: BAR, *Smith Papers.* This was a position that he was to maintain. Cullen to Kirby, 24 Dec. n.d. (*1850*): ACPF, *SC, Irlanda,* vol. 30, f. 534; Cullen to Kirby, 5 Mar. 1851: ICAR, *NC, III,* 1, 2, no. 81; Cullen to Kirby, 1 Mar. 1851: ICAR, *NC, III,* 1, 2, no. 78; Cullen to Prop., 7 June 1851: ACPF, *SC, Irlanda,* vol. 30, f. 644 (*v*).

10. Cullen to Kirby, 3 Dec. 1850: ICAR, *NC, III,* 1, 2, no. 60; Cullen to Smith, 24 Dec. 1850: BAR, *Smith Papers;* Cullen to Kirby, 13 Feb. 1851: ICAR, *NC, III,* 1, 2, no. 74; Cullen to Prop., 5 Apr. 1851: ACPF, SC, Irlanda, vol. 30, f. 597; Cullen to Smith, 1 June 1851: BAR, *Smith Papers;* Cullen to Prop., 4 July 1851: ACPF, SC, Irlanda, vol. 30, f. 678 (*v*).

11. Cullen to Kirby, 8 Feb. 1851: ICAR, *NC, III,* 1, 2, no. 72; Cullen to Kirby, 1 Mar. 1851: ICAR, *NC, III,* 1, 2, no. 78; see also Kirby to Prop., n.d. (*Feb. 1851*): ACPF, *SC, Irlanda,* vol. 30, f. 556.

12. Cullen to Kirby, 13 Feb. 1851: ICAR, *NC, III,* 1, 2, no. 74; Cullen to Kirby, 18 Mar. 1851: BAR, *Smith Papers;* Cullen to Prop., 25 Apr. 1851: ACPF, *SC, Irlanda,* vol. 30, f. 605; Cullen to Smith, 12 May 1851: BAR, *Smith Papers;* Cullen to Kirby, n.d. (*June 1851*): BAR, *Smith Papers.*

13. Cullen to Kirby, 1 Mar. 1851: ICAR, *NC, III,* 1, 2, no. 78; Cullen to Kirby, 5 Mar. 1851: ICAR, *NC, III,* 1, 2, no. 81.

14. Cullen to Kirby, 13 Feb. 1851: ICAR, *NC, III,* 1, 2, no. 74; Cullen to Prop., 28 Sept. 1851: ACPF, *SC, Irlanda,* vol. 30, f. 712.

15. Cullen to Kirby, 13 Feb. 1851: ICAR, *NC, III,* 1, 2, no. 74; Cullen to Smith, 18 Mar. 1851: BAR, *Smith Papers;* Cullen to Prop., 4 July 1851: ACPF, *SC, Irlanda,* vol. 30, f. 678 (*v*); Cullen to Prop., 20 Sept. 1851: ACPF, *SC, Irlanda,* vol. 30, f. 707.

16. Cullen to Kirby, 8 Feb. 1851: ICAR, *NC, III,* 1, 2, no. 72; see also Kirby to Prop., n.d. (*Feb. 1851*): ACPF, *SC, Irlanda,* vol. 30, f. 556.

17. Cullen to Smith, 3 Feb. 1851: BAR, *Smith Papers.*

18. Cullen to Kirby, 11 July 1850: ICAR, *NC, III,* 1, 2, no. 31; Cullen to Kirby, 8 Feb. 1851: ICAR, *NC, III,* 1, 2, no. 72; Cullen to Prop., 5 Apr. 1851: ACPF, *SC, Irlanda,* vol. 30, f. 597; see also Kirby to Prop., n.d. (*Feb. 1851*): ACPF, *SC, Irlanda,* vol. 30, f. 556.

19. Cullen to Kirby, 24 Dec. (*1850*): ACPF, *SC, Irlanda,* vol. 30, f. 534.

20. Cullen to Kirby, 13 Feb. 1851: ICAR, *NC, III,* 1, 2, no. 74; see also Cullen to Kirby, 12 Mar. 1851: ICAR, *NC, III,* 1, 2, no. 83; Cullen to Prop., 31 Jan. 1852: ACPF, *SC, Irlanda,* vol. 31, f. 80.

21. Cullen to Kirby, 25 Nov. 1850: ICAR, *NC, III,* 1, 2, no. 57.

22. Cullen to Kirby, 10 Jan. 1851: ICAR, *NC, III,* 1, 2, no. 66; Cullen to Smith, 23 Jan. 1851: BAR, *Smith Papers.*

23. Cullen to Kirby, 10 Jan. 1851: ICAR, *NC, III,* 1, 2, no. 67.

24. Kirby to Prop., 16 Feb. 1851: ACPF, *SC, Irlanda,* vol. 30, f. 563 (*v*); see also Cullen to Kirby, 31 Jan. 1851: ICAR, *NC, III,* 1, 2, no. 69; Kirby to Prop., 9 Feb. 1851: ACPF, *SC, Irlanda,* vol. 30, f. 558.

25. Cullen to Kirby, n.d. (*Jan. 1851*): ICAR, *NC, III,* 1, 2, no. 70; Cullen to Kirby, 8 Feb. 1851: ICAR, *NC, III,* 1, 2, no. 72; Kirby to Prop., 16 Feb. 1851: ACPF, *SC, Irlanda,* vol. 30, f. 563.

26. Brown (*Bp., Shrewsbury*) to Cullen, 18 Feb. 1851: ICAR, *NC, III,* 1, 2, no. 71.

27. Cullen to Kirby, 20 Mar. 1851: ICAR, *NC, III,* 1, 2, no. 85; see also *Parl. Deb.* ser. 3, cxiv, 189.

28. *FJ*, 21 Feb. 1851; Cullen to Kirby, n.d. (*Feb. 1851*): ICAR, *NC, III,* 1, 2, no. 76; Cullen to Kirby, 15 Mar. 1851: ICAR, *NC, III,* 1, 2,

no. 84; Cullen to Kirby, 21 July 1851: ICAR, *NC, III*, 1, 2, no. 98; Cullen to Smith, 30 July 1851: BAR, *Smith Papers*; McNally (*Bp., Clogher*) to Cullen, 25 Mar. 1852: DDA, 325\1, no. 45.

29. Cullen to Kirby, 20 Feb. 1851: ICAR, *NC, III*, 1, 2, no. 75.

30. Cullen to Kirby, 1 Mar. 1851: ICAR *NC, III*, 1, 2, no. 78; see also Moran, op. cit., vol. 1, pp. 129–37.

31. Cullen to Kirby, 1 Mar. 1851: ICAR, *NC, III*, 1, 2, no. 78; Cullen to Kirby, 1 and 5 Mar. 1851: ICAR, *NC, III*, 1, 2, no. 80.

32. Cullen to Kirby, 5 Mar. 1851: ICAR, *NC, III*, 1, 2, no. 81.

33. Cullen to Kirby, 12 Mar. 1851: ICAR, *NC, III*, 1, 2, no. 83.

34. Cullen to Kirby, 1 Mar. 1851: ICAR, *NC, III*, 1, 2, no. 78; see also Cullen to Kirby, 1 and 5 Mar. 1851: ICAR, *NC, III*, 1, 2, no. 80.

35. Cullen to Kirby, 1 and 5 Mar. 1851: ICAR, *NC, III*, 1, 2, no. 80.

36. 'Pastoral Address ... on the Penal Enactment regarding Ecclesiastical Titles', Moran, op. cit., vol. 1, p. 127; see also: *The Address of the Catholic Archbishops and Bishops of Ireland to their beloved flocks on the Penal Enactment with which the Catholics of England and Ireland are threatened*, Dublin, 1851: ACPF, *SC, Irlanda*, vol. 30, ff. 784–91; Cullen to Prop., 4 July 1851: ACPF, *SC, Irlanda*, vol. 30, f. 678 *(v)*; Cullen to Prop., 20 Sept. 1851: ACPF, *SC, Irlanda*, vol. 30, f. 707.

37. *FJ*, 17 Feb. 1851; Cullen to Prop., 7 June 1851: ACPF, *SC, Irlanda*, vol. 30, f. 644.

38. *Tablet*, 1 Mar. 1851; M.G. Moore, *An Irish Gentleman – George Henry Moore*, London, 1913, p. 183.

39. *FJ*, 24 Feb. 1851.

40. Cullen to Kirby, 1 Mar. 1851: ICAR, *NC, III*, 1, 2, no. 78; Cullen to Kirby, 5 Mar. 1851: ICAR, *NC, III*, 1, 2, no. 81; Cullen to Kirby, 8 May 1851: ICAR, *NC, III*, 1, 2, no. 92.

41. '... si Deus pro nobis, quis contra nos', Cullen to Kirby, 1 Mar. 1851: ICAR, *NC, III*, 1, 2, no. 78.

42. Cullen to Kirby, 12 Mar. 1851: ICAR, *NC, III*, 1, 2, no. 83; Cullen to Kirby, 8 May 1851: ICAR, *NC, III*, 1, 2, no. 92.

43. Moore, op. cit., p. 183; *Parl. Deb.* ser. 3, cxv, 1193; cxvi, 1444.

44. Whyte, op. cit., pp. 22–3.

45. *FJ*, 1 July 1851.

46. Cullen to Smith, 18 Mar. 1851: BAR, *Smith Papers*; Cullen to Smith, 1 June 1851: BAR, *Smith Papers*; Cullen to Prop., 7 June 1851: ACPF, *SC, Irlanda*, vol. 30, f. 644.

47. Cullen to Prop., 7 June 1851: ACPF, *SC, Irlanda*, vol. 30, f. 644 *(v)*; Cullen to Prop., 4 July 1851: ACPF, *SC, Irlanda*, vol. 30, f. 678 *(v)*; Cullen to Prop., 20 Sept. 1851: ACPF, *SC, Irlanda*, vol. 30, f. 706.

48. Somerville (*Chief Sec. Ireland*) to Russell (*PM*), 4 Mar. 1851: PRO, 30\22, no. 9.

49. Swanbull (*Tenant League org.*) to Moore (*MP, Mayo co.*), 22 Mar. 1851: NLI, MS. 819, no. 292; Cullen to Prop., 5 Apr. 1851: ACPF, *SC, Irlanda*, vol. 30, f. 597; Cullen to Prop., 25 Apr. 1851: ACPF, *SC, Irlanda*, vol. 30, f. 605 *(v)*.

50. *FJ*, 30 Apr. 1851.

51. Cullen to Kirby, 1 Mar. 1851: ICAR, *NC, III*, 1, 2, no. 78; Somerville to Russell, 4 Mar. 1851: PRO, 30\22, no. 9; Cullen to Kirby, 1 Mar. 1851: ICAR, *NC, III*, 1, 2, no. 78.

52. CE, 14 Apr. 1851.

53. MacHale (*Abp. Tuam*) to Moore, 12 Feb. 1851: NLI, MS. 891, no. 252; MacHugh (*PP, Kilmainmore*) to Moore, 15 Feb. 1851: NLI, MS. 891, no. 253; Roynane (*CC, Aghabologue*) to Moore, 15 Feb. 1851: NLI, MS. 891, no. 254; Browne (*PP, Balla, Roslee, & Minola*) to Moore, 17 Feb. 1851: NLI, MS. 891, no. 255; Molone (*PP, Kilmoremoy*) to Moore, 17 Feb. 1851: NLI, MS. 891, no. 258; Curran (*CC, Donoghpatrick, & Kilcoony*) to Moore, 17 Feb. 1851: NLI, MS. 891, no. 256; Hughes (*CC, Abbeyknockmoy*) to Moore, 17 Feb. 1851: NLI, MS. 891, no. 257; Toomey (*CC, Athlone*) to Moore, 18 Feb. 1851: NLI, MS. 891, no. 261; Greene (*CC, Kilcommon, & Robeen*) to Moore, 24 Feb. 1851: NLI, MS. 891, no. 266; Henry (*CC, Crossboyne & Tagheen*) to Moore, 26 Feb. 1851: NLI, MS. 891, no. 271; MacHale (*PP, Eglish, Ballyhane, Breaghfy*) to Moore, 12 May 1851: NLI, MS. 891, no. 309; Flannelly (*PP, Burrishoole*) to Moore, 13 May 1851: NLI, MS. 891, no. 312; *FJ*, 17 May 1851.

54. Cullen to Prop., 25 Apr. 1851: ACPF, *SC, Irlanda*, vol. 30, f. 605 *(v)*.

55. Cullen to Kirby, 8 May 1851: ICAR, *NC, III*, 1, 2, no. 92.

56. ASV, *Pio IX, Oggetti Vari*, no. 677.

57. ibid.

58. On the first reading thirty–nine Irish Liberals opposed the bill, *Parl. Deb.* ser. 3, cxiv, 699. On the second reading, forty–eight Irish Liberals, including seventeen Protestants, joined by two Irish Peelites and one Conservative, voted against it, *Parl. Deb.* ser. 3, cxv, 618. However a combination of Conservatives and English Liberals ensured that the bill received significant majorities at every stage.

59. Cullen to Prop., 4 July 1851: ACPF, *SC, Irlanda*, vol. 30, f. 678 *(v)*.

60. *FJ*, 19 May 1851; Irish Cath. Assoc. Committt. to Moore, 20 May 1851: NLI, MS. 891, no. 324; *Tablet*, 31 May 1851; Moore to Lucas *(Founder of* Tablet*)*, 22 June 1851: NLI, MS. 892, no. 332.

61. *FJ*, 20 Aug. 1851.

62. *The Memorial of ... Irish Members of Parliament to Pius IX*: NLI, MS. 1587; ibid, ASV, *Pio IX, Oggetti Vari*, no. 1212.

63. Cullen to Smith, 15 Sept. 1851: BAR, *Smith Papers*.

64. *FJ*, 20 Aug. 1851.

65. *FJ*, 20 Aug. 1851; Anon. *(Smith)* to Kirby, 4 Sept. 1851: ICAR, *Kirby Papers*, no. 927; Anon. *(Smith)* to Kirby, 8 Sept. 1851: ICAR, *Kirby Papers*, no. 928; Anon. *(Smith)* to Kirby, 23 Sept. 1851: ICAR, *Kirby Papers*, no. 932.

66. *FJ*, 20 Aug. 1851.

67. *FJ*, 11, 14 Aug. 1851. The members of parliament were Keogh *(MP, Athlone)*, Reynolds *(MP, Dublin city)*, Sadlier *(MP, Carlow borough)*, Moore *(MP, Mayo co.)*, O'Flaherty *(MP, Galway borough)*, Higgins *(MP, Mayo)* and Meagher *(MP, Waterford city)*.

68. *FJ*, 20 Aug. 1851; ICD, 1852, pp. 132–33.

69. *FJ*, 20 Aug. 1851.

70. Cullen to Prop., 3 Sept. 1851: ACPF, *SC, Irlanda*, vol. 30, f. 701; Cullen to Prop., 28 Sept. 1851: ACPF, *SC, Irlanda*, vol. 30, f. 712; Cullen to Smith, n.d. *(Sept. 1851)*: BAR, *Smith Papers*.

71. Cullen to Smith, 22 Aug. 1851: BAR, *Smith Papers*; Cullen to Smith, 15 Sept. 1851: BAR, *Smith Papers*.

72. Cullen to Kirby, 22 Aug. 1851: ICAR, *NC, III*, 1, 2, no. 103.

73. Cullen to Smith, 22 Aug. 1851: BAR, *Smith Papers*.

74. Cullen to Smith, 15 Sept. 1851: BAR, *Smith Papers*.

75. Anon. *(Smith)* to Kirby, 4 Sept. 1851: ICAR, *Kirby Papers*, no. 927; Anon. *(Smith)* to Kirby, 23 Sept. 1851: ICAR, *Kirby Papers*, no. 932.

76. Anon. *(Smith)* to Kirby, 23 Sept. 1851: ICAR, *Kirby Papers*, no. 932.

77. Moore to Lucas 22 June 1851: NLI, MS. 892, no. 332.

78. *FJ*, 21 Aug. 1851; Duffy, op. cit., p. 158.

79. *The Irish Tenant League*, Dec. 1851.

80. Anon. *(Smith)* to Kirby, 8 Sept. 1851: ICAR, *Kirby Papers*, no. 928.

81. Cullen to Smith, 15 Sept. 1851: BAR, *Smith Papers*.

82. Cullen to Prop., 28 Sept. 1851: ACPF, *SC, Irlanda*, vol. 30, f. 712; Cullen to Smith, n.d. *(Sept. 1851)*: BAR, *Smith Papers*.

83. Cullen to Smith, n.d. *(Sept. 1851)*: BAR, *Smith Papers*; Cullen to Smith, 7 Oct. 1851: BAR, *Smith Papers*.

84. Cullen to Smith, n.d. *(Sept. 1851)*: BAR, *Smith Papers*; Cullen to Prop., 28 Sept. 1851: ACPF, *SC, Irlanda*, vol. 30, f. 712.

85. Cullen to Smith, 7 Oct. 1851: BAR, *Smith Papers*; Cullen to Ed., 19 Dec 1851: *FJ*, 20 Dec 1851.

86. Cullen to Prop., 10 Oct. 1851: ACPF, *SC, Irlanda*, vol. 30, f. 725 *(v)*.

87. The members were Cullen, MacHale, Cantwell *(Bp., Meath)*, Gormanstown *(Lord)*, Keogh, Reynolds, Sadlier, Moore, O'Flaherty, Higgins, Scully *(MP, Tipperary)* and Blake *(MP, Galway borough)*: *FJ*, 26 Sept. 1851.

88. ICD, 1852, pp. 135–8; *FJ*, 27 Sept. 1851.

89. *FJ*, 18 Oct. 1851; ICD, 1852, p. 139.

90. *FJ*, 27 Sept. 1851.

91. ibid.

92. ibid.

93. *FJ*, 18 Oct. 1851; ICD, 1852, p. 139.

94. *FJ*, 14 Nov. 1851.

95. Reynolds, Sadlier and Keogh to Moore, n.d.: NLI, MS. 892, no. 333.

96. *FJ*, 18, 22 Dec. 1851.

97. James Maher *(PP, Carlow–Graigue, Rel. Cullen)* to Keogh: *FJ*, 23 Dec 1851.

98. *FJ*, 19 Dec. 1851.

99. *FJ*, 19, 22 Dec. 1851; *Tablet*, 20, 27 Dec. 1851; they were Keogh, Moore, O'Flaherty, Scully, Meagher and O'Brien *(MP, Cashel)*.

100. *FJ*, 19 Dec. 1851.

101. Cullen to Ed., 19 Dec. 1851: *FJ*, 20 Dec. 1851; see also Cullen to Smith, 13 Dec 1851: BAR, *Smith Papers*.

102. ibid.

103. Moore, op. cit., p. 194; *FJ*, 27 Dec. 1851.

104. Anon. *(Smith)* to Kirby, 10 Jan. 1852: ICAR, *Kirby Papers*, no. 970.

105. Wilberforce *(Sec. Cath. Def. Assoc.)* to Cullen, 25 Mar. 1852: DDA, 325\2, no. 117. Some illustrations from Wilberforce's character sketches were: 'Mr Moore seems to me a clever, brilliant ... goose. Mr Duffy – an able, simple–minded honest man, imperfectly educated, but if he fell into good hands, capable of much good. Mr Lucas – less clear–headed and less considerate of the views of others than Mr Duffy.'

106. *Tablet*, 20, 27 Dec. 1851; B. O'Reilly, *John MacHale, Archbishop of Tuam, his Life, Times and Correspondence*, New York & Cincinnati, 1890, vol. 2, pp. 305–8.

107. *Tablet*, 25 Oct. 1851; *FJ*, 22 Dec. 1851.

108. *Nation*, 1, 8 Mar. 1851; Duffy, op. cit., pp. 153–4.

109. Lucas *(Founder of* Tablet) to Cullen, 6 Apr. 1852: DDA, 325\2, no. 40.

110. Lucas, op. cit., vol 2, pp. 123–4; see also Cullen to Moriarty *(Coadj. Bp., Kerry)*, 20 Jan. 1855: NLI, MS. 8319; Cullen to Pius IX, 2 Feb. 1855: ACPF, *SC, Irlanda*, vol. 32, ff. 402–3; ibid, *CP*, vol. 158, ff. 87–8; ibid., O'Reilly, op. cit., vol. 2, pp. 368–71; Cullen to Prop., 1855: ACPF, *CP*, vol. 158, ff. 345–60.

111. Duffy, op. cit., p. 174; F. McGrath, *Newman's University: Idea and Reality*, Dublin, 1951, p. 362.

112. Lucas to Cullen, 6 Apr. 1852: DDA, 325\2, no. 40; Cullen to Moriarty, 20 Jan. 1855: NLI, MS. 8319; Lucas, op. cit., vol. 2, p. 124.

Chapter Three

1. Anon. *(Smith, Vice Rec. Irish Coll., Rome)* to Kirby *(Rec. Irish Coll., Rome)*, 10 Jan. 1852: ICAR, *Kirby Papers*, no. 970; Cullen to Prop., 31 Jan. 1852: ACPF, *SC, Irlanda*, vol. 31, f. 76.

2. Cullen to Prop., 9 Jan. 1852: ACPF, *SC, Irlanda*, vol. 31, f. 53; Cullen to Smith *(Vice Rec. Irish Coll., Rome)* 15 Jan. 1852: BAR, *Smith Papers*; Cullen to Smith, 24 Jan. 1852:

BAR, *Smith Papers*; Cullen to Prop., 31 Jan. 1852: ACPF, *SC, Irlanda*, vol. 31, f. 76.

3. *FJ*, 30 Jan. 1852.

4. DT, 28 Jan. 1852 has a leaked version of the proposal; see also *FJ*, 29 Jan. 1851.

5. 'Discourse at the General Meeting of the Cath. Assoc. in Dublin', 29 Jan. 1852, in Moran, op. cit., vol. 1, pp. 163–82.

6. *Circular of Cath. Def. Assoc.*, 5 Feb. 1852: DDA, 325\2, no. 7.

7. *FJ*, 30 Jan. 1852.

8. MacNally *(Bp., Clogher)* to Cullen, 25 Feb. 1852: DDA, 325\1, no. 35; Cullen to Kirby, 26 Feb. 1852: ICAR, *NC, III*, 1, 3, no. 18; Cullen to Prop., 26 Feb. 1852: ACPF, *Acta*, vol. 214 *(1852)*, f. 282 *(v)*; Skelly *(lay corr.)* to Cullen, Feb. 1852: DDA, 325\2, no. 111; Kirby to Prop., 3 Mar. 1852: ACPF, *SC, Irlanda*, vol. 31, f. 111.

9. Derry *(Bp., Clonfert)* to Cullen, n.d. *(Mar. 1852)*: DDA, 325\1, no. 37.

10. Forde *(CC, Booterstown, Blackrock, Dundrum)* to Smith, 25 Feb. 1852: BAR, *Smith Papers*; Cullen to Prop., 8 Mar. 1852: ACPF, *SC, Irlanda*, vol. 31, f. 156*(v)*; Kirby to Smith, 9 Mar. 1852: BAR, *Smith Papers*; Anon. *(Smith)* to Kirby, 11 Mar. 1852: ICAR, *Kirby Papers*, no. 985; Cullen to Smith, 13 Mar. 1852: BAR, *Smith Papers*; Anon. *(Smith)* to Kirby, 20 Mar. 1852: ICAR, *Kirby Papers*, no. 989; Cooper *(CC, Marlborough St.)* to Kirby, 28 Mar. 1852: ICAR, *Kirby Papers*, no. 991.

11. *Postulation for election of Dr Cullen as Archbishop of Dublin*, 2 Apr. 1852: DDA, 325\1, no. 127; *Minutes of meeting ... for successor to Murray*: DDA, 325\2, no. 33; Memo. 10 Apr. 1852: ACPF, *SC, Irlanda* vol. 31, f. 181.

12. Miley *(ex Rec. Irish Coll., Paris)* to Smith, 20 Mar. 1852: ACPF, *Acta*, vol. 214 *(1852)*, ff. 284 *(v)* –5; Yore *(PP, Arran Quay)* to Smith, 23 Mar. 1852: ACPF, *Acta*, vol. 214 *(1852)*, f. 285; Doyle *(ex Student, Prop.)* to Prop., 29 Mar. 1852: ACPF, *Acta*, vol. 214 *(1852)*, f. 285; Lucas *(Founder of* Tablet) to Cullen, 6 Apr. 1852: DDA, 325\2, no. 40; Cooper to Smith, 2 Apr. 1852: *Smith Papers*; Miley to Smith, 2 Apr. 1852: BAR, *Smith Papers*.

13. Miley to Smith, 20 Mar. 1852: BAR *Smith Papers*; Miley to Smith, 20 Mar. 1852: ACPF, *Acta*, vol. 214 *(1852)*, f. 285; Yore to Smith, 23 Mar. 1852: ACPF, *Acta*, vol. 214 *(1852)*, f. 285; Anon. *(Smith)* to Kirby, 4 Apr. 1852:

ICAR, *Kirby Papers*, no. 996; Cooper to Cullen, 1 May 1852: DDA, 325\2, no. 59.

14. Miley to Smith, 20 Mar. 1852: ACPF, *Acta*, vol. 214 (*1852*), f. 285; Kirby to Smith, 4 Apr. 1852: ACPF, *Acta*, vol. 214 (*1852*), f. 288; Briggs (*Bp., Beverley*) to Kelly (*lay corr.*), 5 Apr. 1852: DDA, 325\1, no. 154; Kirby to Prop., 6 Apr. 1852: ACPF, *Acta*, vol. 214 (*1852*), f. 289 (*v*); see also Cullen to Smith, 6 Apr. 1852: ACPF, *Acta*, vol. 214 (*1852*), f. 288 (*v*).

15. Miley to Smith, 20 Mar. 1852: ACPF, *Acta*, vol. 214 (*1852*), ff. 284 (*v*)−5; Cullen to Smith, 6 Apr. 1852: ACPF, *Acta*, vol. 214 (*1852*), f. 288 (*v*); McGinity (*lay corr.*) to Cullen, 3 May 1852: DDA, 325\2, no. 61; see also Cullen to Prop., 8 Mar. 1852: ACPF, *SC, Irlanda*, vol. 31, f. 156 (*v*); Diary of Bernard Smith, 7 Aug. 1852: BAR, *Smith Papers*.

16. Anon. (*Smith*) to Kirby, 4 Apr. 1852: *Kirby Papers*, no. 996.

17. Kirby to Smith, n.d. (*Apr. 1852*): BAR, *Smith Papers*; Cullen to Kirby, 9 Dec. 1853: ICAR, *NC, III*, 1, 3, no. 114.

18. Kirby to Smith, n.d. (*Apr. 1852*): BAR, *Smith Papers*; Cullen to Kirby, 9 Dec. 1853: ICAR, *NC, III*, 1, 3, no. 114.

19. ACPF, *Brevi*, vol. 5, f. 426; ASV, S. Br. 5211, ff. 233, 237.

20. Cullen to Kirby, 2 June 1852: ACPF, *SC, Irlanda*, vol. 31, f. 42; Slattery (*Abp., Cashel*) to Cullen, 4 June 1852: DDA, 325\1, no. 112; O'Brien (*PP,Waterford City*) to Cullen, 7 June 1852: DDA, 325\1, no. 75; Keane (*Bp., Ross*) to Cullen, 16 June 1852: DDA, 325\1, no. 77; Wiseman (*Abp.,Westminster*) to Cullen, 17 June 1852: DDA, 325\1, no. 176; Ullathorne (*Bp., Birmingham*) to Cullen, 21 June 1852: DDA, 325\1, no. 177; Walsh (*Bp., Ossory*) to Cullen, 29 June 1852: DDA, 325\1, no. 143.

21. Cullen to Smith, 6 Apr. 1852: ACPF, *Acta*, vol. 214 (*1852*), f. 288 (*v*); Cullen to Prop., 13 Apr. 1852: ACPF, *Acta*, vol. 214 (*1852*), f. 290; Cullen to Prop., 11 June 1852: ACPF, *SC, Irlanda*, vol. 31, f. 183.

22. Keane to Cullen, 16 June 1852: DDA, 325\1, no. 77.

23. Cullen to Kirby, 24 Feb. 1852: ICAR, *NC, III*, 1, 3, no. 16; Cullen to Prop., 8 Mar. 1852: ACPF, *SC, Irlanda*, vol. 31, f. 155.

24. Cullen to Smith, 13 Mar. 1852: BAR, *Smith Papers*; see also Kirby to Prop., 3 Mar. 1852: ACPF, *SC, Irlanda*, vol. 31, f. 112.

25. 'Il cambiamento di cose che è succeduto fra di noi è tutto a nostro vantaggio. La caduta di Palmerston è buona per li cattolici d'ogni paese del mondo', Cullen to Prop., 8 Mar. 1852: ACPF, *SC, Irlanda*, vol. 31, f. 155; see also Cullen to Prop., 26 Mar. 1852: ACPF, *SC, Irlanda*, vol. 31, f. 125 (*v*).

26. '… più furiosi nemici', Cullen to Prop., 26 Mar. 1852: ACPF, *SC, Irlanda*, vol. 31, f. 125 (*v*).

27. 'I Cattolici però perderanno più che guadagneranno in questo cambimento', Cullen to Prop., 8 Mar. 1852: ACPF, *SC, Irlanda*, vol. 31, f. 156; see also Cullen to Prop., 24 Apr. 1852: ACPF, *SC, Irlanda*, vol. 31, f. 166.

28. Cullen to Prop., 8 Mar. 1852: ACPF, *SC, Irlanda*, vol. 31, f. 156 (*v*); Cullen to Smith, 13 Mar. 1852: BAR, *Smith Papers*; 'Circular to the Clergy of Dublin City', 25 Mar. 1857: DDA, 43\3; ibid, ACPF, *SC, Irlanda*, vol. 33, f. 233.

29. 'Avressimo qui bisogna d'un partito che badasse alle cose religiose e all'indipendenza della chiesa senza mettersi in lotta ed ministero per altre cose, e senza vendersi al ministero per ottenere alcuni meschini vantaggi temporali. Disgraziatamente però i nostri ricchi Cattolici non hanno niente di spirito Cattolico', Cullen to Prop., 8 Mar. 1852: ACPF, *SC, Irlanda*, vol. 31, f. 156 (*v*); see also Cullen to Smith, 13 Mar. 1852: BAR, *Smith Papers*; 'Circular to the Clergy of Dublin City', 25 Mar. 1857: DDA, 43\3; ibid, ACPF, *SC, Irlanda*, vol. 33, f. 233.

30. 'Io credo che quei cattolici che si mettono ad assaltare pubblicamente il governo, fanno male, ma credo ancora che quei che si fanno agenti ed istrumenti de'nostri ministri fanno ancora peggio', Cullen to Prop., 8 Mar. 1852: ACPF, *SC, Irlanda*, vol. 31, f. 156 (*v*); see also Cullen to Prop., 25 Apr. 1855: ACPF, *CP*, vol. 158, f. 161 (*v*).

31. Cullen to Prop., 26 Mar. 1852: ACPF, *SC, Irlanda*, vol. 31, f. 124 (*v*); see also Cullen to Prop., 8 Mar. 1852: ACPF, *SC, Irlanda*, vol. 31, f. 156; Cullen to Prop., 24 Apr. 1852: ACPF, *SC, Irlanda*, vol. 31, f. 166.

32. Cullen to Prop., 24 Apr. 1852: ACPF, *SC, Irlanda*, vol. 31, f. 166 (*v*).

33. Cullen to Smith, 8 Mar. 1852: BAR, *Smith Papers*; see also Cullen to Prop., 8 Mar. 1852: ACPF, *SC, Irlanda*, vol. 31, f. 156 (*v*);

Wilberforce (*Sec. Cath. Def. Assoc.*) to Cullen, 15 Mar. 1852: DDA, 325\2, no. 16.

34. 'Tutto il sistema di governo è assai favorevole agli intrighi e alle birberie', Cullen to Prop., 24 Apr. 1852: ACPF, *SC, Irlanda*, vol. 31, f. 166 (v).

35. Kirby to Prop., 3 Mar. 1852: ACPF, *SC, Irlanda*, vol. 31, f. 112.

36. *Parl. Deb.*, ser. 3, cxix, 1301.

37. *London Gazette*, 15 June 1852.

38. *FJ*, 2 July 1852; DE, 2 July 1852.

39. Cullen to Prop., 12 July 1852: ACPF, *SC, Irlanda*, vol. 31, f. 201 (v); see also *Tablet*, 3 July 1852.

40. *Telegraph*, 16, 19 July 1852; *FJ*, 21 July 1852.

41. 'The Representation of People (Ireland) Act', 1850, (*13 and 14 Vict. c.69*). Those entitled to vote rose from 31,832 in 1849–50 to 135,245 in 1851. The borough electorate on the other hand declined from 40,234 to 28,301. See 'Return of no. of Parliamentary electors ... 1848–9 and 1849–50', H.C. 1850 [345], xlvi, pp. 200–3; 'Registered Electors (Ireland)', H.C. 1851 [383], l, p. 879.

42. *TFP*, 28 Jan. 1852.

43. Wilberforce to Cullen, 25 Mar. 1852: DDA, 325\2, no. 117; TFP, 28 Jan. 20 Mar. 7 Apr. 1852, 14 Apr. 1852; NG, 17 Apr. 1852.

44. For Lucas see under list of election petitions in *Telegraph*, 1 Dec. 1852; for Duffy see Duffy, *League*, p. 255.

45. Preston (*lay corr.*) to Cullen, 22 Apr. 1852: DDA, 325\2, no. 53; *Tablet*, 24 Apr. 1852.

46. *TFP*, 14 Apr., 26, 30 June 1852; Election Papers, NLI, MS. 11037; see also Septon (*lay corr.*) to Police Commissioners, 10 July 1852: SPO, OR, Tipperary.

47. 'The Address of the Council of the Tenant League to the Irish People', *FJ*, 7 Feb. 1852; 'The Address of the Cath. Def. Assoc. to the Irish People', *FJ*, 12 June 1852.

48. *FJ*, 12 June 1852.

49. Moore received a letter from a constituent in Galway, Rev. O'Kane, who, having congratulated Moore on his opposition to Russell, went on to enquire of him the possibility of obtaining a position by means of patronage from the government of Russell. See Kane (*CC, Galway*) to Moore, 6 Mar. 1851: NLI, MS. 891, no. 276.

50. *FJ*, 26, 27 Apr. 1852; *Tablet*, 12 June 1852.

51. *FJ*, 1 Apr. 1852.

52. *FJ*, 23 June 1852; Duffy, op. cit., *League*, p. 193.

53. *FJ*, 30 July, 4 Aug. 1852.

54. *FJ*, 23 June 1852.

55. Cullen to Prop., n.d. (*1854*): ACPF, *SC, Irlanda*, vol. 32, f. 67 (v).

56. Cullen to Prop., n.d. (*1854*): ACPF, *SC, Irlanda*, vol. 32, ff. 64–9; Scally (*Relg. Kilkenny*) to Prop., 14 May 1854: ACPF, *SC, Irlanda*, vol. 32, ff. 173–7 (v).

57. Lucas, op. cit., vol. 2, p. 174; ASV, *Pio IX, Oggetti Vari*, no. 1212.

58. McCullagh (*Prot. businessman*) to McGinity, 6 May 1852: DDA, 325\2, no. 66; McGinity to Cullen, 7 May 1852: DDA, 325\2, no. 67; *Tablet*, 5, 10 Apr., 8, 22 May, 10 July 1852; *FJ*, 4, 7 May, 25 June 1852; NE, 10, 14 July 1852; *Mayo elect. pet.*, H.C. 1852–3, vol. 16, p. 297.

59. *Tablet*, 24 Apr., 8 May, 10 July 1852; *FJ*, 4 May 1852; *Telegraph*, 4, 11 June 1852; NT, 13 July 1852; DEM, 28 July 1852 *Clare elect. pet.*, H.C. 1852–3, vol. 9, p. 754, New Ross elect. pet., H.C. 1852–3, vol. 16, p. 355; *Mayo elect. pet.*, H.C. 1852–3, vol. 16, pp. 240, 262; see also McGinity to Cullen, 1 May 1852: DDA, 325\2, no. 60.

60. WI, 14, 17 July 1852; see also Duffy, op. cit., p. 196; Lucas, op. cit., vol 2, pp. 190–1; ASV, *Pio IX, Oggetti Vari*, no. 1212.

61. *Tablet*, 12 June 1852. *FJ*, 4 May 1852, 13, 19 July 1852; Telegraph, 28 June 1852; ASV, *Pio IX, Oggetti Vari*, no. 1125; *Cork elect. pet.*, H.C. 1852–3, vol. 11, pp. 388–96; *Mayo elect. pet.*, H.C. 1852–3, vol. 16, p. 263; *Sligo elect. pet.*, 1852–3, H.C. vol. 18, p. 628.

62. J. Whyte, 'The Influence of the Catholic Clergy on Elections in Nineteenth-Century Ireland' in *English Historical Review*, no. 75, pp. 239–59 (*Apr. 1960*); Cullen to Prop., n.d. (*1854*): ACPF, *SC, Irlanda*, vol. 32, f. 66 (v).

63. *FJ*, 19 Nov. 1852.

64. A. Barrister, *Observations on Intimidation at Elections in Ireland*, Dublin, 1854; Eladrius, *Thoughts on the Late General Election in Ireland*, Dublin, 1853; F. Head, *A Fortnight in Ireland*, London, 1852, J. Lord, *Popery at the Hustings*, London, 1852.

65. *DE*, 2, 4 Aug. 1852; *Clare elect. pet.*, H.C. 1852–3, vol. 9, pp. 572, 710, *Mayo elect. pet.*, H.C. 1852–3, vol. 16, pp. 249–54; *Sligo*

elect. pet., H.C. 1852–3, vol. 18, pp. 642–8, 676–7; *Cork elect. pet.*, H.C. 1852–3, vol. 11, p. 3.

66. *FJ*, 26 July 1852; McGinity to Cullen, 21 Aug. 1852: DDA, 325\2, no. 85; *Clare elect. pet.*, H.C. 1852–3, vol. 9, pp. 537, 573, 599; *Cork elect. pet.*, H.C. 1852–3, vol. 11, pp. 104, 114, 139, 177, 182, 207, 217, 310, 324; *Mayo elect. pet.*, H.C. 1852–3, vol. 16, pp. 234, 243, 259, 262; *Sligo elect. pet.*, H.C. 1852–3, vol. 18, pp. 629, 657, 677.

67. *Tablet*, 10 July 1852; DEM, 22 July 1852. see also *Sligo elect. pet.*, H.C. 1852–3, vol. 18, p. 630; *Cork elect. pet.*, H.C. 1852–3, vol. 11, p. 3; *Mayo elect pet.*, H.C. 1852–3, vol. 16, p. 236. Cullen to Kirby, 16 Jan. 1854: ICAR, *NC, III*, 2, 1, no. 4.

68. Cullen to Kirby, 28 Jan. 1854: ICAR *NC, III*, 2, 1, no. 7; *Sligo elect. pet.*, H.C. 1852–3, vol. 18, p. 629.

69. Cantwell (*Bp., Meath*) to Cullen, 18 June 1852: DDA, 325\1, no. 79; Dawson (*PP, Kiltoghert*) to Cullen, 16 Oct. 1852: DDA, 325\1, no. 97; Bulwer (*Brit. Dip., Tuscany*) to Malmesbury (*Foreign Sec.*), 23 Oct. 1852: FO, 79\160; Bulwer to Malmesbury, 31 Oct. 1852: FO, 79\160; *Mayo elect. pet.*, H.C. 1852–3, vol. 16, p. 211; *Sligo elect. pet.*, H.C. 1852–3, vol. 18, pp. 624–5.

70. 'Report of the Royal Commission on Maynooth', ii, H.C. 1854–5, (1896–I), xxii, pp. 379, 402, 423, 432, 452, 467, 532.

71. *Sligo elect. pet.*, H.C. 1852–3, vol. 18, pp. 708–9; Towneley (*lay corr.*) to Clarendon (*ex Lord Lieut., Ire.*), 9 Aug. 1852: PRO, 30\22, 10 (*d*); Police Reports 18, 24 July 1852: NLI, MSS., Mayo Papers; *Times*, 13 July 1852; BN, 17 July 1852; Warder, 24 July 1852; DEH, 26 July 1852; DE, 9 Aug. 1852; *Mayo elect. pet.*, H.C. 1852–3, vol. 16, pp. 270–1.

72. Bellew (*lay corr.*) to Cullen, 4 May 1852: DDA, 325\2, no. 62; Bellew to Cullen, 9 May 1852: DDA, 325\2, no. 69; Dawson to Cullen, 16 Oct. 1852: DDA, 325\1, no. 97; *Sligo elect. pet.*, H.C. 1852–3, vol. 18, pp. 624–5; *Times*, 13 July 1852; Warder, 17 July 1852; EM, 17 July 1852; NT, 22 July 1852; BT, 26 July 1852; DE, 17 Aug. 1852.

73. *Cork Constitution*, 15 July 1852; DE, 24 July 1852; BN, 26 July 1852; Police reports, 18 July 1852: NLI, MSS., Mayo Papers.

74. Police reports, 24 July 1852: NLI, MSS., Mayo Papers; DEM, 30 Aug. 1852.

75. NT, 13 July 1852; *Times*, 13 July 1852; *FJ*, 30 July, 4 Aug. 1852; *Tablet*, 31 July, 21 Aug. 1852; MH, 31 July 1852; *DEM*, 30 Aug. 1852.

76. Cullen to Smith, 21 Aug. 1852: BAR, *Smith Papers*; O'Connor (*ex Student, Prop.*) to Prop., 30 Nov. 1852: ACPF, *SC, Irlanda*, vol. 31, ff. 299–300.

77. *Tablet*, 26 Mar. 1853.

78. *Times*, 13 July 1852; *FJ*, 6 July 1852; DE, 26 July 1852; DEM, 26 July 1852; *Cork elect. pet.*, H.C. 1852–3, vol. 11, pp. 129, 133; *Mayo elect. pet.*, H.C. 1852–3, vol. 16, p. 270.

79. *Clare elect. pet.*, H.C. 1852–3, vol. 9, pp. 624–5. *FJ*, 13 July, 14 Aug. 1852; *Cork elect. pet.*, H.C. 1852–3, vol. 11, pp. 139, 207.

80. Cantwell to Cullen, 3 Apr. 1852: DDA, 325\1, no. 50; Cantwell to Cullen, 14 Apr. 1852: DDA, 325\1, no. 51; when the election committee failed to agree as to who should be the candidate in Waterford it was the bishop himself who solved the impasse with his intervention: *Times*, 28 June 1852, *Telegraph*, 2 July 1852; following his electoral victory in County Kilkenny, Sergeant Shee thanked in the first place the bishop of Ossory without whose support his electoral victory would have been 'impossible': *Tablet*, 31 July 1852.

81. Cullen to Prop., 9 Jan. 1852: ACPF, *SC, Irlanda*, vol. 31, f. 76; Cullen to Prop., 31 Jan. 1852: ACPF, *SC, Irlanda*, vol. 31, f. 79; ASV, *Pio IX, Oggetti Vari*, no. 1125; see also Murphy to Cullen, 10 May 1852: DDA, 325\1, no. 68; O'Donnell (*Bp., Galway*) to Cullen, 11 May 1852: DDA, 325\1, no. 70; Haly (*Bp., Kildare & Leighlin*) to Cullen, 27 May 1852: DDA, 325\1, no. 64.

82. ASV, *Pio IX, Oggetti Vari*, no. 1125; Cullen to Prop., n.d. (*1854*): ACPF, *SC, Irlanda*, vol. 32, f. 66 (*v*); O'Reilly, op. cit., vol. 2, pp. 301–2; *Telegraph*, 21 July 1852.

83. Cullen to Prop., n.d. (*1854*): ACPF, *SC, Irlanda*, vol. 32, f. 66 (*v*); *Tablet*, 13 Mar. 1851.

84. Pius IX to the Irish bishops, 25 Mar. 1852: ACPF, *SC, Irlanda*, vol. 31, ff. 132–9; Cullen to Prop., 9 Jan. 1852: *SC, Irlanda*, vol. 31, f. 76; Cullen to Prop., 31 Jan. 1852: *SC, Irlanda*, vol. 31, f. 79; ASV, *Pio IX, Oggetti Vari*, no. 1125.

85. ASV, *Pio IX, Oggetti Vari*, no. 1125.

86. Wilberforce to Cullen, 26 Feb. 1852: DDA,

325\1, no. 10; McCullagh to Cullen, 28 Feb. 1852: DDA, 325\2, no. 13; Wilberforce to Cullen, 5 Apr. 1852: DDA, 325\2, no. 38; Wilberforce to Cullen, 11 Apr. 1852: DDA, 325\2, no. 37; McGinity to Cullen, 15 Apr. 1852: DDA, 325\2, no. 48.

87. Wilberforce to Cullen, 11 Mar. 1852: DDA, 325\2, no. 15; Wilberforce to Cullen, 15 Mar. 1852: DDA, 325\2, no. 16; Bowyer (*MP, Dundalk*) to Wilberforce, 18 Mar. 1852: DDA, 325\2, no. 20; Brodigan (*lay corr.*) to Cullen, 19 Mar. 1852: DDA, 325\2, no. 22; Bowyer to Wilberforce, 23 Mar. 1852: DDA, 325\2, no. 26; Wilberforce to Cullen, 24 Mar. 1852: DDA, 325\2, no. 21; Brodigan to Cullen, 25 Mar. 1852, no. 27; O'Dwyer to Cullen, 11 Apr. 1852: DDA, 325\2, no. 41; Wilberforce to Cullen, 14 Apr. 1852: DDA, 325\2, no. 45; Caulfield Heron (*lay corr.*) to Cullen, 20 Apr. 1852: DDA, 325\2, no. 50; Bowyer to Wilberforce, 22 Apr. 1852: DDA, 325\2, no. 54; Wilberforce to Cullen, 23 Apr. 1852: DDA, 325\2, no. 55; Wilberforce to Cullen, 24 Apr. 1852: DDA, 325\2, no. 57; Bagot (*lay corr.*) to Cullen, 22 July 1852: DDA, 325\3, no. 61; Wilberforce to Cullen, n.d. (*1852*): DDA, 325\2, no. 114.

88. Wiseman to Cullen, 12 Apr. 1852: DDA, 325\1, no. 160.

89. Wilberforce to Cullen, 10 Apr. 1852: DDA, 325\2, no. 36; O'Ferrall (*lay corr.*) to Cullen, 12 Apr. 1852: DDA, 325\2, no. 42.

90. O'Ferrall to Cullen, 12 Apr. 1852: DDA, 325\2, no. 42; Wilberforce to Cullen, 14 Apr. 1852: DDA, 325\2, no. 45; Sadlier (*MP, Galway borough*) to Cullen, 14 Apr. 1852: DDA, 325\2, no. 46; Wilberforce to Cullen, n.d. (*1852*); DDA, 325\2, no. 115.

91. Cullen to Kirby, 9 July 1852: ICAR, *NC, III*, 1, 3, no. 36; see also Lucas (*Founder of Tablet*) to Cullen, 6 Apr. 1852: DDA, 325\2, no. 40; Lucas to Cullen, 10 May 1852: DDA, 325\2, no. 71; 'Address of Frederick Lucas', 13 May 1852: DDA, 325\2, no. 73; Cullen to Kirby, 9 July 1852: ICAR, *NC, III*, 1, 3, no. 36.

92. Cullen to Smith, 26 Mar. 1852: BAR, *Smith Papers*.

93. Lucas, op. cit., vol. 2, p. 361; ASV, *Pio IX, Oggetti Vari*, no. 1212.

94. Kirby to Prop., 13 June 1852: ACPF, *SC, Irlanda*, vol. 31, f. 188.

95. Cullen to Smith, 28 Apr. 1852: BAR, *Smith Papers*.

96. Cullen to Kirby, 9 July 1852: ICAR, *NC, III*, 1, 3, no. 36.

97. Wilberforce to Cullen, 24 Apr. 1852: DDA, 325\2, no. 57; Wilberforce to Cullen, n.d. (*1852*): DDA, 325\2, no. 114.

98. Cullen to Kirby, 13 June 1852: ICAR, *NC, III*, 1, 3, no. 31; Bellew (*MP, Louth*) to Cullen, 4 May 1852: DDA, 325\2, no. 62.

99. Cullen to Kirby, 13 June 1852: ICAR, *NC, III*, 1, 3, no. 31.

100. ibid.

101. Cantwell to Cullen, 18 June 1852: DDA, 325\1, no. 79; Kirby to Prop., n.d. (*1852*): ACPF, *SC, Irlanda*, vol. 31, f. 277.

102. 'Dublino – Circolare di Mgr. Arcivescovo al Clero nell'occasione delle elezioni', 6 July 1852: ASV, *Pio IX, Oggetti Vari*, no. 943; Diary of George Talbot (*Papal Chamberlain*) (D), 3 Aug. 1852: VECAR, *Talbot Papers*; see also Cullen to Kirby, 9 July 1852: ICAR, *NC, III*, 1, 3, no. 36; Cullen to Smith, 21 Aug. 1852: BAR, *Smith Papers*.

103. ibid.

104. ibid.

105. Petre (*Brit. Dip., Tuscany, Resident in Rome*) to Bulwer, 30 May 1852: FO, 170\57.

106. Petre to Bulwer, 24 July 1852: FO, 170\57; Diary of George Talbot (D), 11 Aug. 1852: VECAR, *Talbot Papers*.

107. Petre to Bulwer 24 July 1852: FO, 170\57; Petre to Bulwer, 27 July 1852: FO, 170\57; see also Diary of George Talbot (D) 11 August 1852: VECAR, *Talbot Papers*.

108. ibid.

109. ibid.

110. Petre to Bulwer, 27 July 1852: FO, 170/57; Diary of Bernard Smith, 7 August 1852, BAR, *Smith Papers*; Diary of George Talbot (D), 11 August 1852: VECAR, *Talbot Papers*.

111. ibid.

112. ibid.

113. Diary of Bernard Smith, 7 August 1852: BAR, *Smith Papers*; Cullen to Smith, 21 August 1852: BAR, *Smith Papers*.

114. Petre to Bulwer, 27 July 1852: FO, 170/57.

115. Pius IX to Cullen, 29 July 1852: ASV, *Pio IX, Oggetti Vari*, no. 1125.

116. Cullen to Smith, 21 August 1852: BAR, *Smith Papers*.

117. FJ, 24, 26 July, 19 August 1852; Clare elect. pet., H.C. 1852–3, vol. 9, p. 537.

118. Cullen to Smith, 21 August 1852: BAR, Smith Papers.

119. ibid.

120. Cullen to Smith, 21 August 1852: BAR, Smith Papers.

121. Cullen to Prop., 21 August 1852: ACPF, SC, Irlanda, vol. 31, f. 235; Cullen to Smith, 21 August 1852: BAR, Smith Papers.

122. McCabe (CC, Phibsboro, Circular Rd) to Cullen, 26 May 1852: DDA, 325\3, no. 50; Moore, op. cit., p. 207.

123. DE, 11 June 1852.

124. NW, 6 January 1852; FJ, 27 April 1852; Parl. Deb., ser. 3, cxxii, 597–602; C.R. Dod, Electoral Facts, London, 1853 (2nd edit.) pp. 91, 100, 110, 190, 253.

125. DE, 11 June 1852, 19 August 1852; Telegraph, 26 July 1852; FJ, 29 July, 6 August 1852; Telegraph, 29 September, 6 October 1852; Clare elect pet., H.C. 1852–3, vol. 9, p. 633, Mayo elect. pet., H.C. 1852–3, vol. 16, p. 274.

126. Anon. (tenants) to Palmer (landlord), n.d.: NLI, MS. 892, no. 398; Palmer to tenants, n.d.: NLI, MS. 892, no. 399; Moore (MP, Mayo co.) to Palmer, 23 February 1853: NLI, MS. 892, no. 414; Palmer to Moore, 26 February 1853: NLI, MS. 892, no. 421.

127. Clare elect. pet., H.C. 1852–3, vol. 9, p. 675; Mayo elect. pet., H.C. 1852–3, vol. 16, p. 252.

128. FJ, 6 Nov. 31 Dec. 1852.

129. Telegraph, 19 July 1852.

130. Cullen to Kirby, 9 July 1852: ICAR, NC, III, 1, 3, no. 36; Cullen to Smith, 21 Aug. 1852: BAR, Smith Papers.

131. Cullen to Prop., 21 August 1852: ACPF, SC, Irlanda, vol. 31, f. 235 (v); Cullen to Smith, 4 October 1852: BAR, Smith Papers.

132. Diary of Bernard Smith, 10 Sept. 1852: BAR, Smith Papers.

133. Diary of George Talbot (D), 6, 19 Sept., 1, 2 Oct. 1852: VECAR, Talbot Papers; Diary of Bernard Smith, 10 Sept. 1852: BAR, Smith Papers; see also Bulwer to Malmesbury, 23, 31 Oct. 1852: FO, 79\160; Bulwer to Malmesbury, 3, 16 Nov., 7 Dec. 1852: FO, 79\161; Bulwer to Clarendon (ex Lord Lieut. Ire.), 6 Nov. 1854: FO, 79\179; Wiseman to Talbot, 10 Nov. 1852: VECAR, Talbot Papers, no. 1144; FJ, 24 Sept., 25 Oct. 1852.

134. Cullen to Smith, 22 Sept. 1852: BAR, Smith Papers; Cullen to Smith, 4 Oct. 1852: BAR, Smith Papers.

135. Cullen to Smith, 22 Sept. 1852: BAR, Smith Papers.

136. Cullen to Prop., 22 Sept. 1852: ACPF, SC, Irlanda, vol. 31, f. 249 (v); Cullen to Smith, 22 Sept. 1852: BAR, Smith Papers.

137. 'Interi villaggi sono stati distrutti, li contadini sono stati cacciati come belve da molti distretti', Cullen to Prop., 22 Sept. 1852: ACPF, SC, Irlanda, vol. 31, f. 248 (v); see also Cullen to Smith, 22 Sept. 1852: BAR, Smith Papers.

138. '... (I fatti che ho menzionati) basteranno a spiegare la ragione perch, alcuni preti parlano con violenza contro il governo di questo paese. Essi vedono le loro parrochie ridotte a deserti, i loro parenti, i loro amici e le loro gregge 'sterminate, e perciò non possono qualche volta contenere la loro indignazione. I grandi Signori e gli agenti del governo vorrebbero che tutti tacessero e che potessero perpetrarsi le loro scelleratagini senza alcune opposizioni. E però da deplorarsi che alcuni ecclesiastici non parlino ed agiscano con più decoro'; Cullen to Prop., 22 Sept. 1852: ACPF, SC, Irlanda, vol. 31, f. 249.

139. Cullen to Prop., 22 Sept. 1852: ACPF, SC, Irlanda, vol. 31, f. 249 (v); Cullen to Smith, 22 Sept. 1852: BAR, Smith Papers.

140. Bulwer to Malmesbury, 31 Oct. 1852: FO, 79\160; Bulwer to Malmesbury, 16 Nov., 7 Dec. 1852: FO, 79\161.

141. Bulwer to Clarendon, 6 Nov. 1854: FO, 79\179.

142. FJ, 9, 10 Sept. 1852.

143. Lucas to Moore, 3 Aug. 1852: NLI, MS. 892, no. 373.

144. FJ, 28 Aug., 9 Sept., 5 Oct. 1852.

145. FJ, 9 Sept. 1852.

146. FJ, 29 Oct. 1852.

147. Duffy, op. cit., p. 220, n. 2; Tablet, 30 Oct. 1852; FJ, 20 Oct. 1852.

148. FJ, 29 Oct. 1852.

149. Clarendon (ex Lord Lieut.) to Russell (PM), 8 Aug. 1852: PRO, 30\22, 10 (D).

150. Cullen to Kirby, 6 Nov. 1852: ICAR, NC, III, 1, 3, no. 43.

151. Cullen to Smith, 4 Oct. 1852: BAR, Smith Papers; Cullen to Smith, 9 Oct. 1852: BAR, Smith Papers; Cullen to Smith, 18 Oct. 1852: BAR, Smith Papers.

152. Cullen to Kirby, 16 Nov. 1852: ACPF, *SC, Irlanda*, vol. 31, f. 291.

153. Cullen to Kirby, 30 Nov. 1852: ICAR, *NC, III*, 1, 3, no. 50; see also Cullen to Kirby, 9 Dec. 1852: ICAR, *NC, III*, 1, 3, no. 53.

154. Parl. Deb., ser. 3, cxxiii, 1207–10; *Telegraph*, 15 Dec. 1852.

155. *FJ*, 18 Dec. 1852.

156. Duffy, op. cit., pp. 232–5.

157. Cullen to Kirby, n.d. (*Dec. 1852*): ICAR, *NC, III*, 1, 3, no. 54.

158. ibid.

Chapter Four

1. *FJ*, 4 Jan. 1853.

2. Other Irish members of parliament also received offices in the new administation such as William Monsell (*MP, Limerick co.*) who became Clerk of the Ordinance, and Sir John Young (*MP, Cavan co.*) who became the Chief Secretary for Ireland.

3. *FJ*, 30 Dec. 1852, 3, 12, 13 Jan. 1853; *Tablet*, 1 Jan. 1853; *Nation*, 1 Jan. 1853.

4. Lucas, op. cit., vol. 2, p. 362.

5. Some nineteenth century writers who claimed that the defection was the main reason of the party's failure included T.P. O'Connor, *The Parnell Movement*, London, 1887, p. 129; A.M. Sullivan, *New Ireland*, Glasgow & London, 1882, p. 168; A.M. Sullivan, *A Record of Traitorism or the Political Life and Adventures of Mr Justice Keogh*, n.d., p. 5.

6. *FJ*, 20 Jan., 21 Apr. 1853; see also Cullen to Prop., 8 May 1855: ACPF, CP, vol. 158, f. 81 (*v*).

7. MacHale (*Apb., Tuam*) to Moore (*MP, Mayo*) 15 Jan. 1853 in *FJ*, 18 Jan. 1853; O'Reilly, op. cit., vol. 2, pp. 340–1; *FJ*, 2 Feb., 12 Apr. 1853; see also Cullen to Prop., 8 May 1855: ACPF, CP, vol. 158, f. 81 (*v*).

8. Cullen to Kirby (*Rec. Irish Coll., Rome*), n.d. (*Jan. 1853*): ICAR, *NC, III*, 1, 3, no. 57; see also Cullen to Prop., 8 May 1855: ACPF, CP, vol. 158, ff. 81 (*v*) –2.

9. Cullen to Kirby, 3 Jan. 1853: ICAR, *NC, III*, 1, 3, no. 56; see also Cullen to Kirby, 24 Mar. 1853: ICAR, *NC, III*, 1, 3, no. 66.

10. Bowyer (*MP, Dundalk*) to Cullen, 23 Apr. 1853: DDA, 325\6, no. 16; *FJ*, 5, 7, 12 July 1853.

11. *Tablet*, 8, 15 Jan., 5 Feb. 1853; *FJ*, 12 Jan. 1853.

12. See *TFP*, 24 Mar. 1853.

13. *LR*, 18 Jan. 1853.

14. *Tablet*, 24 Mar. 1853.

15. *TFP*, 4 May 1853.

16. *FJ*, 12 Apr. 1853; *Tablet*, 16 Apr., 14, 21 May 1853.

17. *FJ*, 12 Apr. 1853.

18. Cullen to Kirby, 16 Apr. 1853: ICAR, *NC, III*, 1, 3, no. 70.

19. Cullen to Kirby, 24 Mar. 1853: ICAR, *NC, III*, 1, 3, no. 66.

20. Cullen to Kirby, n.d. (*Jan. 1853*): ICAR, *NC, III*, 1, 3, no. 57; see also Cullen to Prop., 8 May 1855: ACPF, CP, vol. 158, ff. 81 (*v*) –2.

21. Cullen to Prop., 18 Apr. 1853, (*undelivered*): ICAR, *NC, III*, 1, 3, no. 71; Cullen to Kirby, 18 June 1853: ICAR, *NC, III*, 1, 3, no. 79; Cullen to Prop., 8 May 1855: ACPF, CP, vol. 158, ff. 81 (*v*) –2; see also Cullen to Prop., 25 Apr. 1855: ACPF, CP, vol. 158, f. 63 (*v*).

22. Cullen to Kirby, 24 Mar. 1853: ICAR, *NC, III*, 1, 3, no. 66; Cullen to Kirby, 16 Apr. 1853: ICAR, *NC, III*, 1, 3, no. 70.

23. Cullen to Kirby, 3 Jan. 1853: ICAR, *NC, III*, 1, 3, no. 56; Cullen to Kirby, 24 Mar. 1853: ICAR, *NC, III*, 1, 3, no. 66; Cullen to Prop., 18 Apr. 1853, (*undelivered*): ICAR, *NC, III*, 1, 3, no. 71.

24. Clarendon (*ex Lord Liut., Ire*) to Aberdeen (*PM*), 23 Dec. 1852: BM.Add. MS. 43188, f. 1 (*v*).

25. Aberdeen to Russell (*Foreign Sec.*), 29 Dec. 1852: BM.Add. MS. 43066, f. 169; Russell to Aberdeen, 18 Jan. 1853: BM.Add. MS. 43066, ff. 218–19; Aberdeen to Russell, 18 Jan. 1853: BM.Add. MS. 43066, f. 220.

26. Cullen to Prop., 21 Feb. 1853: ACPF, *SC, Irlanda*, vol. 31, f. 395.

27. Cullen to Kirby, 16 Apr. 1853: ICAR, *NC, III*, 1, 3, no. 70; Cullen to Kirby, n.d. (*Apr. 1853*): ICAR, *NC, III*, 1, 3, no. 73.

28. *FJ*, 20 Jan., 21, Apr. 1853; see also Cullen to Prop., 8 May 1855: ACPF, CP, vol. 158, f. 81 (*v*).

29. *FJ*, 21, 23 Apr., 1853; see also Cullen to Prop., 8 May 1855: ACPF, CP, vol. 158, f. 81 (*v*).

30. *FJ*, 20, 21 Jan. 1853.

31. *FJ*, 8 July 1853.

32. Lucas (*MP, Meath, Founder of* Tablet) to Cullen, 1 Mar. 1855: DDA, 325\6, no. 59.

33. Cullen to Kirby, 24 Mar. 1853: ICAR, *NC, III*, 1, 3, no. 66.

34. Cullen to Kirby, n.d. (*Apr. 1853*): ICAR, *NC, III*, 1, 3, no. 73; see also Cullen to Kirby, 16 Apr. 1853: ICAR, *NC, III*, 1, 3, no. 70; Bowyer to Cullen, 23 Apr. 1853: DDA, 325\6, no. 16.

35. Lucas to Cullen, 8 and 16 Apr. 1853: DDA, 325\6, no. 60.

36. Cullen to Kirby, 30 July 1853: ICAR, *NC, III*, 1, 3, no. 85.

37. Lucas to Cullen, 1 Mar. 1853: DDA, 325\6, no. 59; Lucas to Cullen 8/16 Apr. 1853: DDA, 325\6, no. 60; Lucas to Cullen, n.d. (*1853*): DDA, 325\6, no. 61; Lucas to Cullen, n.d. (1853): DDA, 325\6, no. 62.

38. Parl. Deb., ser. 3, cxxvii, 945.

39. ibid.

40. *FJ*, 6 June 1853.

41. Monsell to Aberdeen, 2 June 1853: BM.Add. MS. 43250, ff. 131–3; Keogh (*MP, Athlone*) to Aberdeen, 2 June 1853: BM.Add. MS. 43250, ff. 135–7; Sadlier (*MP, Sligo borough*) to Aberdeen, 2 June 1853: BM.Add. MS. 43250, ff. 139–40.

42. Russell to Aberdeen, 2 June 1853: BM.Add. MS. 43067, ff. 36–8.

43. Aberdeen to Russell, 2 June 1853: BM.Add. MS. 43067, f. 38.

44. Aberdeen to Monsell, 3 June 1853: BM.Add. MS. 43250, f. 141; Aberdeen to Sadlier, 3 June 1853: BM.Add. MS. 43250, f. 146; Aberdeen to Keogh, 3 June 1853: BM.Add. MS. 43250, f. 146; see also Aberdeen to Russell, 2 June 1853: BM.Add. MS. 43067, f. 38.

45. Aberdeen to Monsell, 3 June 1853: BM.Add. MS. 43250, f. 141; Monsell to Aberdeen, 4 June 1853: BM.Add. MS. 43250, ff. 147–9; Keogh to Aberdeen, 4 June 1853: BM.Add. MS. 43250, ff. 151–3.

46. St John (*CC, East Farleigh, Rec. Walmer*) to Newman (*Rec. Cath. Univ. Ire.*), 19 Sept. 1853: McGrath, op. cit., p. 209; see also Taylor (*PP, Kilbritain*) to Kirby, 5 Jan. 1854: ICAR, *Kirby Papers*, no. 1344; Cullen to Kirby, 30 May 1854: ICAR, *NC, III*, 2, 1, no. 20; MacNeave (*lay corr.*) to O'Donnell (*Bp., Galway*), 20 Dec. 1854: ICAR, *NC, III*, 2, 1, no. 36; Dixon (*Abp., Armagh*) to Prop., 1 Jan. 1855: ACPF, CP, vol. 158, f. 332 (v); Cullen to Prop., 20 Mar. 1858: ACPF, SC, *Irlanda*, vol. 33, f. 635; Cullen to Kirby, 28 Mar. 1858: ICAR, *NC, III*, 2, 2, no. 67.

47. Cullen to Kirby, 14 July 1853: ICAR, *NC,*

III, 1, 3, no. 84; Cullen to Kirby, 19 Aug. 1853: ICAR, *NC, III*, 1, 3, no. 87; St John to Newman, 19 Sept. 1853: McGrath, op. cit., p. 209.

48. Cullen to Kirby, 19 Aug. 1853: ICAR, *NC, III*, 1, 3, no. 87.

49. MacHale to Cullen, 18 Aug. 1853: DDA, 325\5, no. 68; Cullen to Kirby, 19 Aug. 1853: ICAR, *NC, III*, 1, 3, no. 87; Slattery (*Abp., Cashel*) to Cullen, 21 Aug. 1853: DDA, 325\5, no. 37.

50. *FJ*, 9 Sept. 1853.

51. St John to Newman, 19 Sept. 1853: McGrath op. cit., p. 209.

52. Cullen to Kirby, 21 Dec. 1853: ICAR, *NC, III*, 1, 3, no. 116; Cullen to Kirby, 28 Jan. 1854: ICAR, *NC, III*, 2, 1, no. 7; see also Cullen to Smith (*Vice Rec. Irish Coll., Rome*), 18 Dec. 1853: BAR, *Smith Papers*.

53. Cullen to Prop., 25 Apr. 1855: ACPF, CP, vol. 158, f. 161 (v).

54. Sadlier to Cullen, 23 Nov. 1853: DDA, 325\6, no. 46.

55. Cullen to Kirby, 16 Jan. 1854: ICAR, *NC, III*, 2, 1, no. 4.

56. Taylor to Kirby, 5 Jan. 1854: ICAR, *Kirby Papers*, no. 1344.

57. St John to Newman, 19 Sept. 1853: McGrath, op. cit., p. 209.

58. Cullen to Kirby, 11 July 1850: ICAR, *NC, III*, 1, 2, no. 31; Cullen to Kirby, 12 July 1850: ICAR, *NC, III*, 1, 2, no. 32; Cullen to Kirby, 13 Feb. 1851: ICAR, *NC, III*, 1, 2, no. 74; Cullen to Kirby, 5 Mar. 1851: ICAR, *NC, III*, 1, 2, no. 81.

59. Cullen to Kirby, n.d. (*Jan. 1853*): ICAR, *NC, III*, 1, 3, no. 119.

60. ibid.

61. Cullen to Kirby, 9 Mar. 1853: ICAR, *NC, III*, 1, 3, no. 64.

62. Murphy (*Bp., Ferns*) to Cullen, 10 Mar. 1853: DDA, 325\5, no. 21; Cullen to Kirby, 18 Apr. 1853: ICAR, *NC, III*, 1, 3, no. 71; see also Murphy to Cullen, 24 Apr. 1853: DDA, 325\5, no. 22; Walsh (*Bp., Ossory*) to Cullen, 24 Apr. 1853: DDA, 325\5, no. 50.

63. Kirby to Prop., n.d. (*Apr. 1853*): ACPF, SC, *Irlanda*, vol. 31, f. 437.

64. Cullen to Kirby, 11 May 1853: ICAR, *NC, III*, 1, 2, no. 75; see also Cullen to Kirby, 9 Mar. 1853: ICAR, *NC, III*, 1, 3, no. 64; ACPF, *Acta*, vol. 215 (1853), ff. 270–5; Epistola S.Cong. de Prop. Fide ad

Metropolitanos Hiberniae, 3 May 1853: ICAR NC, III, 1, 3, no. 74; ibid.: ACPF, SC, Irlanda, vol. 31, f. 453.

65. ACPF, Acta, vol. 215 (1853), ff. 270–5.

66. Cullen to Kirby, 11 May 1853: ICAR, NC, III, 1, 3, no. 75; J.F. Broderick, The Holy See and the Irish Movement for the Repeal of the Union with England 1829–1847, Rome, 1951, pp. 58–9.

67. ACPF, Acta, vol. 215 (1853), ff. 273 (v) –4.

68. 'Omnibus hujus provinciae sacerdotibus in memoriam revocamus obligationem qua mysteria fidei, sacramenta, Dei praecepta, et alia ad religionem spectantia fideli populo diebus festivis exponere tenentur. Cum vero periculum sit ne haec negligantur, si de alienis ac profanis negotiis in Ecclesiis agatur, districte prohibemus ne inter Missarum solemnia, quod omnino indecens esset, aut omnino in Ecclesiis de rebus mere saecularibus, ut de politicis electionibus, aut aliis ejusmodi rebus agatur, quae facile dissidia inter pastorem et populum promovere valeant, et magnam, animorum commotionem excitare': ACPF, Acta, vol. 215 (1853), ff. 273 (v) –4.

69. 'Quod si quis de hujusmodi rebus agat, aut spreto synodi Thurlesiae praecepto, nominatim in aliquem in Ecclesiis invehatur, eum poena suspensionis aut alia pro nostro arbitrio plectemur': ACPF, Acta, vol. 215 (1853), f. 274.

70. 'Hortamur vero omnes sacerdotes ut a conventibus mere politicis et a discussionibus de rebus saecularibus, quae magna quandoque vehementia in hisce regionibus habentur, se abstineant, ne propria dignitas in iis aliquid detrimenti capiat, et ne rixis et contentionibus cum aliis implicentur. Si vero a parochianis sacerdotis sententia exquiratur, eos privatim et cum omni charitate instruere poterit, nemini dans ullam offensionem ne vituperetur ministerium nostrum': ACPF, Acta, vol. 215 (1853), f. 274.

71. Moran (Vice Rec. Irish Coll., Rome) to Kirby, 7 June 1853: ICAR, NC, III, 1, 3, no. 77; Cullen to Kirby, 18 June 1853: ICAR, NC, III, 1, 3, no. 79; Cullen to Kirby, 20 June 1853: ICAR, NC, III, 1, 3, no. 80; See 'Pastoral Address ... to the Catholic Clergy and Laity of the Province'; Moran, op. cit., vol. 1, pp. 256–73.

72. Cullen to Kirby, 18 June 1853: ICAR, NC, III, 1, 3, no. 79; Cullen to Kirby, 20 June 1853: ICAR, NC, III, 1, 3, no. 80; see also ibid.: Acta, vol. 215 (1853), f. 277; Kirby to Prop., 9 July 1853: ACPF, Acta, vol. 215 (1853), ff. 275 (v) –6.

73. 'Abbiamo proibito ai preti d'impicciarsi pubblicamente nelle cose politiche', Cullen to Kirby, 20 June 1853: ICAR, NC, III, 1, 3, no. 80; see also ibid: Acta, vol. 215 (1853), f. 277.

74. ACPF, Acta, vol. 215 (1853), f. 274.

75. ACPF, Acta, vol. 215 (1853), f. 263.

76. Sligo elect. pet., H.C. 1852–3, vol. 18, pp. 624–5.

77. Cullen to Prop., 9 July 1853: ACPF, SC, Irlanda, vol. 31, f. 509 (v).

78. Cullen to Prop., 9 July 1853: ACPF, SC, Irlanda, vol. 31, ff. 509–10.

79. FJ, 12 July 1853; see also Cullen to Prop., 9 July 1853: ACPF, SC, Irlanda, vol. 31, ff. 509 (v) –10.

80. FJ, 12 July 1853; see also Cullen to Prop., 9 July 1853: ACPF, SC, Irlanda, vol. 31, ff. 509 (v) –10; Cullen to Kirby, 20 Oct. 1853: ICAR, NC, III, 1, 3, no. 103; Diary of Bernard Smith, 13 Jan. 1854: BAR, Smith Papers.

81. FJ, 8 July 1853.

82. Anon. (Cullen) to Kirby, 24 Dec. 1853: ICAR, NC, III, 1, 3, no. 117.

83. Cullen to Prop., 9 July 1853: ACPF, SC, Irlanda, vol. 31, f. 510; Cullen to Kirby, 12 July 1853: ICAR, NC, III, 1, 3, no. 82; Cullen to Prop., 12 July 1853: SC, Irlanda, vol. 31, f. 511 (v); Cullen to Kirby, 14 July 1853: ICAR, NC, III, 1, 3, no. 84.

84. Cullen to Kirby, 20 Oct. 1853: ICAR, NC, III, 1, 3, no. 103; Cullen to Kirby, 24 Oct. 1853: ICAR, NC, III, 1, 3, no. 104.

85. Cullen to Kirby, 20 Oct. 1853: ICAR, NC, III, 1, 3, no. 103; Cullen to Kirby, 24 Oct. 1853: ICAR, NC, III, 1, 3, no. 104; Cullen to Kirby, 21 Mar. 1854: ICAR, NC, III, 1, 3, no. 13.

86. Cullen to Prop., 12 July 1853: ACPF, SC, Irlanda, vol. 31, f. 511.

87. Cullen to Kirby, 14 July 1853: ICAR, NC, III, 1, 3, no. 84; see also Cullen to Kirby, 12 July 1853: ICAR, NC, III, 1, 3, no. 82.

88. Anon. (Kirby) to Prop., n.d. (June 1853): ACPF, SC, Irlanda, vol. 31, f. 503.

89. Cullen to Kirby, 16 Jan. 1854: ICAR, NC, III, 2, 1, no. 4.

90. Cullen to Prop., 9 July 1853: ACPF, *SC, Irlanda*, vol. 31, f. 510; see also Cullen to Kirby, 12 July 1853: ICAR, *NC, III*, 1, 3, no. 82.

91. Kirby to Browne (*Bp. Elphin*), 24 July 1853: ACPF, *SC, Irlanda* vol. 31, f. 522 *(v)*; Browne to Kirby, 14 Aug. 1853: ICAR, *Kirby Papers*, no. 1259; MacHale to Prop., 29 July 1853: ACPF, *SC, Irlanda*, vol. 31, ff. 524–5; Cullen to Kirby, 19 Aug. 1853: ICAR, *NC, III*, 1, 3, no. 87; Browne to Prop., 14 Sept. 1853: ACPF, *SC, Irlanda*, vol. 31, f. 580 *(v)*.

92. Cullen to Kirby, 20 Oct. 1853: ICAR, *NC, III*, 1, 3, no. 103; see also Anon. (*Cullen*) to Kirby, 24 Dec. 1853: ICAR, *NC, III*, 1, 3, no. 117; Slattery to Ryan (*Bp., Limerick*) 19 Dec. 1853; ICAR, *NC, III*, 2, 1, no. 4; Cullen to Kirby, 28 Jan. 1854: ICAR, *NC, III*, 2, 1, no. 7; Cullen to Kirby, 21 Mar. 1854: ICAR, *NC, III*, 2, 1, no. 13.

93. Cullen to Kirby, 16 Jan. 1854: ICAR, *NC, III*, 2, 1, no. 4; Cullen to Kirby, 21 Mar. 1854: ICAR, *NC, III*, 2, 1, no. 13; see also *Tablet*, 12 June 1852; DE, 4 Aug. 1852.

94. Cullen to Kirby, 20 Oct. 1853: ICAR, *NC, III*, 1, 3, no. 103.

95. Cullen to Kirby, 14 Feb. 1854: ICAR, *NC, III*, 2, 1, no. 7; Cullen to Kirby, 17 Mar. 1854: ICAR, *NC, III*, 2, 1, no. 12; Cullen to Kirby, 21 Mar. 1854: ICAR, *NC, III*, 2, 1, no. 13.

96. Anon. (*Cullen*) to Kirby, 24 Dec. 1853: ICAR, *NC, III*, 1, 3, no. 117; see also Cullen to Kirby, 16 Jan. 1854: ICAR, *NC, III*, 2, 1, no. 4; Cullen to Kirby, 21 Mar. 1854: ICAR, *NC, III*, 2, 1, no. 13.

97. Cullen to Kirby, 16 Jan. 1854: ICAR, *NC, III*, 2, 1, no. 4; Cullen to Kirby, 26 May 1854: ICAR, *NC, III*, 2, 1, no. 18.

98. Cullen to Kirby, 21 Mar. 1854: ICAR, *NC, III*, 2, 1, no. 13.

99. Cullen to Kirby, 24 Feb. 1854: ICAR, *NC, III*, 2, 1, no. 9; see also Cullen to Kirby, 17 Mar. 1854: ICAR, *NC, III*, 2, 1, no. 12; Cullen to Kirby, 21 Mar. 1854: ICAR, *NC, III*, 2, 1, no. 13.

100. Kirby to Prop., 11 Feb. 1854: ACPF, *SC, Irlanda*, vol. 32, f. 110.

101. Cullen to Kirby, 9 Dec. 1853: ICAR, *NC, III*, 1, 3, no. 114.

102. ibid.

103. Cullen to Kirby, 9 Dec. 1853: ICAR, *NC, III*, 1, 3, no. 114; see also Cullen to Kirby, 19 Dec. 1853: ICAR, *NC, III*, 1, 3, no. 115.

104. Cullen to Kirby, 9 Dec. 1853: ICAR, *NC, III*, 1, 3, no. 114; see also Cullen to Smith, 17 Dec. 1853: BAR, *Smith Papers*.

105. Cullen to Smith, 17 Dec. 1853: BAR, *Smith Papers*.

106. Cullen to Kirby, 9 Dec. 1853: ICAR, *NC, III*, 1, 3, no. 114.

107. Anon. (*Cullen*) to Kirby, 24 Dec. 1853: ICAR, *NC, III*, 1, 3, no 117.

108. Anon. (*Cullen*) to Kirby, 24 Dec. 1853: ICAR, *NC, III*, 1, 3, no. 117; Delaney (*Bp., Cork*) to Cullen, 19 Dec. 1853: DDA, 325\5, no. 41.

109. *FJ*, 23 Feb. 1854.

110. Cullen to Kirby, 24 Feb. 1854: ICAR, *NC, III*, 2, 1, no. 9.

111. Cullen to Kirby, 17 Mar. 1854: ICAR, *NC, III*, 2, 1, no. 12; see also Dixon to Cullen, 17 Feb. 1854: DDA, 332\1, no. 103; Dixon to Cullen, 21 Feb. 1854: DDA, 332\1, no. 104; Cullen to Kirby, 24 Feb. 1854: ICAR, *NC, III*, 2, 1, no. 9; Dixon to Smith, 1 Jan. 1855: BAR, *Smith Papers*; Dixon to Prop., 1 Jan. 1855: ACPF, CP, vol. 158, f. 331.

112. Cullen to Prop., 25 Apr. 1855: ACPF, CP, vol. 158, f. 56; see also Dixon to Prop., 1 Jan. 1855: ACPF, CP, vol. 158, f. 331.

113. Dixon to Cullen, 17 Feb. 1854: DDA, 332\1, no. 103.

114. Walsh to Cullen, 16 Feb. 1854: DDA, 332\1, no. 102; see also Walsh to Cullen, 5 Oct. 1853: DDA, 325\5, no. 63.

115. Dixon to Cullen, 21 Feb. 1854: DDA, 332\1, no. 104; Duffy, *League*, p. 287; see also Cullen to Prop., 26 May 1854: ACPF, *Acta*, vol. 218 (1854), f. 338.

116. Duffy, *League*, p. 287.

Chapter Five

1. Cullen to Kirby (*Rec. Irish Coll., Rome*), 12 Jan. 1854: ICAR, *NC, III*, 2, 1, no. 3; see also Cullen to Prop., n.d. (*1854*): ACPF, *SC, Irlanda*, vol. 32, f. 67 *(v)*; Kirby to Prop., n.d. (*Jan. 1854*): ACPF, *SC, Irlanda*, vol. 32, f. 107 *(v)*.

2. Cullen to Prop., 12 July 1853: ACPF, *SC, Irlanda*, vol. 31, f. 511.

3. 'In questo regno non si può proibire totalmente ai sacerdoti di prendere parte nelle elezioni, ma potrebbero esercitare la loro influenza e dare i loro voti senza fare tanto chiasso, e prendere parte con tanta violenza', Cullen to Prop., 12 July 1853:

ACPF, *SC, Irlanda*, vol. 31, f. 511; see also Cullen to Monsell, (*MP, Limerick co.; Clerk of the Ordnance*) 10 Mar. 1855: NLI, MS. 8317; Kirby to Prop., 25 Nov. 1854: ACPF, *Acta*, vol. 219 (*1855*), f. 189.

4. Cullen to Kirby, 12 Jan. 1854: ICAR, *NC, III*, 2, 1, no. 3; see also Kirby to Prop., n.d. (*Jan. 1854*): ACPF, *SC, Irlanda* vol. 32, f. 107; Cullen to Kirby, n.d. (*1854*): ACPF, *Acta*, vol. 218 (*1854*), f. 341 (*v*); Cullen to Prop., 25 Apr. 1855: ACPF, CP, vol. 158, f. 63 (*v*).

5. Cullen to Kirby, 17 Mar. 1854: ICAR, *NC, III*, 2, 1, no. 12; see also Cullen to Prop., 26 May 1854: *Acta*, vol. 218 (*1854*), ff. 337 (*v*) −8 (*v*).

6. 'E da temersi che ove le cose vanno come sono andate in Sligo, i preti saranno totalmente screditati, e perderanno tutta la loro autorità anche nelle cose spirituali', Cullen to Prop., 12 July 1853: *SC, Irlanda*, vol. 31 f. 511 (*v*); see also Cullen to Kirby, 17 Mar. 1854: ICAR, *NC, III*, 2, 1, no. 12; Cullen to Kirby, 21 Mar. 1854: ICAR, *NC, III*, 2, 1, no. 13; Cullen to Prop., 26 May 1854: ACPF, *Acta*. vol. 218 (*1854*) f. 337 (*v*) 8; Cullen to Kirby, 16 Mar. 1857: ICAR, *NC, III*, 2, 2, no. 12.

7. Cullen to Prop., n.d. (*1854*): ACPF, *SC, Irlanda*, vol. 32, f. 68; Cullen to Prop., 26 May 1854: ACPF, *Acta*. vol. 218 (*1854*), f. 337 (*v*).

8. Cullen to Prop., 12 July 1853: ACPF, *SC, Irlanda*, vol. 31, f. 511; see also Murray (*Sec. Cullen*) to Cullen, 17 Apr. 1855: ICAR, *NC, III*, 2, 1, no. 46.

9. Cullen to Prop., 12 July 1853: ACPF, *SC, Irlanda*, vol. 31, f. 511.

10. Cullen to Kirby, 7 Jan. 1854: ICAR, *NC, III*, 2, 1, no. 1.

11. Cullen to Kirby, 9 Dec. 1853: ICAR, *NC, III*, 1, 3, no. 114; see also Cullen to Kirby, 12 Jan. 1854: ICAR, *NC, III*, 2, 1, no. 3; Cullen to Prop., n.d. (*1854*): ACPF, *SC, Irlanda*, vol. 32, f. 66 (*v*); Kirby to Prop., n.d.: ACPF, *SC, Irlanda*, vol. 32, f. 107.

12. Cullen to Smith (*Vice Rec. Irish Coll., Rome*), 10 Jan. 1854: BAR, *Smith Papers*; see also Cullen to Kirby, 7 Jan. 1854: ICAR, *NC, III*, 2, 1, no. 1; Cullen to Kirby, 12 Jan. 1854: ICAR, *NC, III*, 2, 1, no. 3; Kirby to Prop., n.d. (*1854*): ACPF, *SC, Irlanda*, vol. 32, f. 107; Cullen to Prop., n.d. (*1854*): ACPF, *SC, Irlanda*, vol. 32, f. 66; Cullen to Kirby, 16 Mar. 1857: ICAR, *NC, III*, 2, 2, no. 12.

13. Cullen to Prop., 26 May 1854: *Acta*, vol. 218 (*1854*), f. 337 (*v*); Kirby to Prop. n.d. (*Feb. 1854*): ACPF, *SC, Irlanda*, vol. 32, f. 107 (*v*); Cullen to Kirby, 2 Dec. 1855: ICAR, *NC, III*, 2, 1, no. 87; Cullen to Kirby, 8 July 1857: ICAR, *NC, III*, 2, 2, no. 32.

14. 'possono ... dare dei pretesti troppo speciosi ai nemici della religione di calunniare tutt'il ceto sacerdotale, o anche di fare degli attentati contro la libertà ecclesiastica', Cullen to Prop., n.d. (*1854*): ACPF, *SC, Irlanda*, vol. 32, f. 66.

15. Cullen to Kirby, 19 Dec. 1853: ICAR, *NC, III*, 1, 3, no. 115; see also Cullen to Smith, 18 Dec. 1853: BAR, *Smith Papers*; *Tablet*, 17 Dec. 1853.

16. Cullen to Kirby, 19 Dec. 1853: ICAR, *NC, III*, 1, 3, no. 115.

17. Cullen to Kirby, 9 Dec. 1853: ICAR, *NC, III*, 1, 3, no. 114.

18. Anon. (*Cullen*) to Kirby, 24 Dec. 1853: ICAR, *NC, III*, 1, 3, no. 117; see also Cullen to Kirby, 28 Jan. 1854: ICAR, *NC, III*, 2, 1, no. 7; Cullen to Kirby, 2 Dec. 1855: ICAR, *NC, III*, 2, 1, no. 87; see also Cullen to Prop., 24 Feb. 1856: ACPF, *SC, Irlanda*, vol. 32, ff. 726 (*v*) −7.

19. Cullen to Prop., n.d. (*1854*): ACPF, *SC, Irlanda*, vol. 32, f. 66; Cullen to Kirby, 16 Mar. 1857: ICAR, *NC, III*, 2, 2, no. 12.

20. Cullen to Kirby, 12 Jan. 1854: ICAR, *NC, III*, 2, 1, no. 3; see also Anon. (*Kirby*) to Prop., n.d. (*Feb. 1854*): ACPF, *SC, Irlanda*, vol. 32, f. 107.

21. Cullen to Kirby, 21 Jan. 1854: ICAR, *NC, III*, 2, 1, no 5; Cullen to Prop., n.d. (*1854*): ACPF, *SC, Irlanda*, vol. 32, f. 67 (*v*); see also Kirby to Prop., n.d. (*Feb. 1854*): ACPF, *SC, Irlanda*, vol. 32, f. 112.

22. Cullen to Kirby, 19 Dec. 1853: ICAR, *NC, III*, 1, 3, no. 115.

23. Cullen to Kirby, 14 July 1853: ICAR, *NC, III*, 1, 3, no. 84; Cullen to Kirby, 12 July 1853: ICAR, *NC, III*, 1, 3, no. 82.

24. Cullen to Kirby, 20 Oct. 1853: ICAR, *NC, III*, 1, 3, no. 103; see also Cullen to Kirby, 18 Feb. 1854: ICAR, *NC, III*, 2, 1, no. 8; Kirby to Prop., n.d. (*Feb. 1854*): ACPF, *SC, Irlanda*, vol. 32, f. 112.

25. Cullen to Smith, 10 Jan. 1854: BAR, *Smith Papers*; Cullen to Kirby, 12 Jan. 1854: ICAR, *NC, III*, 2, 1, no. 3; Taylor (*Sec. Cath. Univ., Ireland, ex Pres. Carlow Coll.*) to Kirby, 5 Jan. 1854: ICAR, *Kirby Papers*, no. 1344.

26. Cullen to Kirby, 21 Mar. 1854: ICAR, NC, III, 2, 1, no. 13; see also Cullen to Kirby, 21 Jan. 1854: ICAR, NC, III, 2, 1, no. 5.

27. Cullen to Kirby, 12 Jan. 1854: ICAR, NC, III, 2, 1, no. 3; see also Kirby to Prop., n.d. (1854): ACPF, SC, Irlanda, vol. 32, f. 107.

28. Cullen to Prop., 26 May 1854: Acta, vol. 218 (1854), ff. 337 (v) –8.

29. Cullen to Kirby, 25 Nov. 1850: ICAR, NC, III, 1, 2, no. 57; Cullen to Kirby, 21 Jan. 1854: ICAR, NC, III, 2, 1, no. 5; Cullen to Kirby, 18 Feb. 1854: ICAR, NC, III, 2, 1, no. 8; Kirby to Prop., n.d. (Feb. 1854): ACPF, SC, Irlanda, vol. 32, f. 112.

30. Cullen to Kirby, 21 Jan. 1854: ICAR, NC, III, 2, 1, no. 5; see also Kirby to Prop., n.d. (Feb. 1854): ACPF, SC, Irlanda, vol. 32, f. 112 (v).

31. Cullen to Kirby, 18 Feb. 1854: ICAR, NC, III, 2, 1, no. 8.

32. Cullen to Kirby, 21 Jan. 1854: ICAR, NC, III, 2, 1, no. 5.

33. Cullen to Kirby, 15 Mar. 1851: ICAR, NC, III, 1, 2, no. 84; Cullen to Kirby, 21 July 1851: ICAR, NC, III, 1, 2, no. 98. Cullen to Prop., 31 Aug. 1850: ICAR, NC, III, 1, 2, no. 39.

34. Cullen to Prop., 16 Feb. 1854: ACPF, Acta, vol. 218 (1854), f. 167 (v); see also Cullen to Kirby, 16 Jan. 1854: ICAR, NC, III, 2, 1, no. 4; Kirby to Prop., n.d. (Feb. 1854): ACPF, SC, Irlanda, vol. 32, f. 112 (v).

35. Cullen to Prop., 13 July 1849: ACPF, Acta, vol. 214 (1852), f. 493; Cullen to Kirby, 9 Aug. 1852: ICAR, NC, III, 1, 3, no. 39; ibid: ACPF, Acta, vol. 214 (1852), ff. 490 (v) –1.

36. Wilberforce (Sec. Cath. Def. Assoc.) to Cullen, 9 June 1852: DDA, 325\2, no. 77; McGinity (lay corr.) to Cullen, 21 Aug. 1852: DDA, 325\2, no. 85; 'Circular to the Clergy on the Institution of Saint Laurence', 29 Nov. 1853: Moran, op. cit., vol. 1, pp. 280–2.

37. Enquiries were made about the possible execution of the Act in Donegal and Galway. However, due to the opposition of the local clergy and the difficulty of securing a successful prosecution the Attorney General decided against any prosecution. See SPO, CSO, RP, 1859\ 2632. See also Parl. Deb. ser. 3, cxxxvi, 944–6; cxxxvii, pp. 169–74.

38. FJ, 18 Oct. 1852.

39. Wilberforce to Cullen, 24 Nov. 1852: DDA, 325\3, no. 97.

40. 'Circular to the Clergy on the Institution of Saint Laurence', 29 Nov. 1853: Moran, op. cit., vol. 1, pp. 280–82; Anon. (Cullen) to Kirby, 24 Dec. 1853: ICAR, NC, III, 1, 2, no. 117.

41. 'Circular to the Clergy on the Institution of Saint Laurence', 29 Nov. 1853: Moran, op. cit., vol. 1, p. 280.

42. Anon. (Cullen) to Kirby, 24 Dec. 1853: ICAR, NC, III, 1, 3, no. 117.

43. Lucas (MP, Meath, Founder of Tablet) to Newman (Rec. Cath. Univ. Ire.), 1 Jan. 1854: McGrath, op. cit., p. 231.

44. Taylor to Kirby, 5 Jan. 1854: ICAR, Kirby Papers, no. 1344.

45. Lucas, op. cit., vol. 2, pp. 200–2; ASV, Pio IX, Oggetti Vari, no. 1212; Diary of Bernard Smith, 14 Jan. 1854: BAR, Smith Papers.

46. Lucas to Newman, 1 Jan. 1854: McGrath, op. cit., p. 231; see also Lucas, op. cit., vol. 2, pp. 192–7; ASV, Pio IX, Oggetti Vari, no. 1212.

47. Cullen to Smith, 10 Jan. 1854: BAR, Smith Papers.

48. Taylor to Kirby, 5 Jan. 1854: ICAR, Kirby Papers, no. 1344.

49. Cullen to Kirby, 27 June 1854: ICAR, NC, III, 2, 1, no. 25.

50. Taylor to Kirby, 5 Jan. 1854: ICAR, Kirby Papers, no. 1344. Cullen to Kirby, 28 Jan. 1854: ICAR, NC, III, 2, 1, no. 7.

51. Cullen to Kirby, 30 May 1854: ICAR, NC, III, 2, 1, no. 20; see also Lucas, op. cit., vol. 2, pp. 192–7; Pio IX, Oggetti Vari, no. 1212; Lucas to Newman (Rec. Cath. Univ., Dublin), 1 Jan. 1854: McGrath, op. cit., p. 231; Cullen to Kirby, 16 Jan. 1854: ICAR, NC, III, 2, 1, no. 4; Cullen to Kirby, 7 Jan. 1854: ICAR, NC, III, 2, 1, no. 1.

52. Cullen to Kirby, 21 Jan. 1854: ICAR, NC, III, 2, 1, no. 5; Cullen to Prop., n.d. (1855): ACPF, CP, vol. 158, f. 346 (v).

53. Cullen to Kirby, 21 Mar. 1854: ICAR, NC, III, 2, 1, no. 13.

54. Cullen to Kirby, 27 June 1854: ICAR, NC, III, 2, 1, no. 25.

55. Cullen to Kirby, 21 Mar. 1854: ICAR, NC, III, 2, 1, no. 13.

56. Cullen to Kirby, 16 Jan. 1854: ICAR, NC, III, 2, 1, no. 4; see also FJ, 18 Jan. 1854.

57. Cullen to Kirby, 16 Jan. 1854: ICAR, NC, III, 2, 1, no. 4; see also Cullen to Kirby,

18 Feb. 1854: ICAR, *NC, III*, 2, 1, no. 8; *FJ*, 18 Jan. 1854.

58. *FJ*, 18 Jan. 1854; see also Cullen to Kirby, 21 Jan. 1854: ICAR, *NC, III*, 2, 1, no. 5.

59. Cullen to Kirby, 15 June 1854: ICAR, *NC, III*, 2, 1, no. 23; see also Cullen to Kirby 3 Sept. 1855: ICAR, *NC, III*, 2, 1, no. 68

60. Cullen to Kirby, 21 Jan. 1854: ICAR, *NC, III*, 2, 1, no. 5.

61. Cullen to Kirby, 4 Mar. 1854: ICAR, *NC, III*, 2, 1, no. 10.

62. Cullen to Kirby, 21 Jan. 1854: ICAR, *NC, III*, 2, 1, no. 5.

63. Cullen to Kirby, 4 Mar. 1854: ICAR, *NC, III*, 2, 1, no. 10.

64. Keane (*Bp., Ross*) to Cullen, 15 Aug. 1853: DDA, 325\5, no. 67; Lucas to Cullen, n.d. (*1853*): DAA, 325\6, no. 61; Whitty (*Vic. Gen., Westminster*) to Cullen, 15 Aug. 1853: DDA, 325\5, no. 153; see also Parl. Deb., ser. 3, cxxix, 1568–70. This concession was later rescinded. Parl. Deb., ser. 3, cxxxiii, 1419.

65. *Parl. Deb.* ser. 3, cxxxi. 314–27.

66. Cullen to Kirby, 4 Mar. 1854: ICAR, *NC, III*, 2, 1, no. 10; Cullen to Kirby, 15 June 1854: ICAR, *NC, III*, 2, 1, no. 23; Cullen to Prop., n.d. (*1854*): ACPF, *SC, Irlanda*, vol. 32, f. 66.

67. See the Corrupt Practices Act 1854 (*17 and 18 Vict., c. 102*).

68. Pius IX to Cullen, 20 Mar. 1854: ACPF, *SC, Irlanda*, vol. 32, ff. 140–1; Pius IX to the Archbishops and Bishops of Ireland, 20 Mar. 1854: ACPF, *SC, Irlanda*, vol. 32, ff. 142–3.

69. Pius IX to Cullen, 20 Mar. 1854: ACPF, *SC, Irlanda*, vol. 32, ff. 140–1; Pius IX to the Archbishops and Bishops of Ireland, 20 Mar. 1854: ACPF, *SC, Irlanda*, vol. 32, ff. 142–3; 'Prossimo Sinodo dei Vescovi Irlandesi. Alcune Avvertenze', n.d. (*1854*): ACPF, *SC, Irlanda*, vol. 32, f. 7; see also Anon. (*Kirby*) to Prop., n.d. (*Mar. 1854*): ACPF, *SC, Irlanda*, vol. 32, f. 40.

70. Cullen to Kirby, 11 Apr. 1854: ICAR, *NC, III*, 2, 1, no. 14; see also 'Prossimo Sinodo dei Vescovi Irlandesi. Alcune Avvertenze', n.d. (*1854*): ACPF, *SC, Irlanda*, vol. 32, f. 7 (*v*).

71. Cullen to Kirby, 30 May 1854: ICAR, *NC, III*, 2, 1, no. 20; see also Cullen to Kirby n.d. (*June 1854*): ICAR, *NC, III*, 2, 1, no. 21;

Anon. (*Kirby*) to Prop., n.d. (*June 1854*): ACPF, *SC, Irlanda*, vol. 32, f. 217.

72. ACPF, *Acta*, 218 (*1854*), ff. 320–42; see also Minutes n.d. (*May, 1854*): DDA, 332\1, no. 152; *Acta e decreta conventus Archiepiscoporum et episcoporum Hiberniae... cum duabus litteris encyclicis D.N. Pii Papae IX*, Rome, 1855: Cullen to Kirby, 21 May 1854: ICAR, *NC, III*, 2, 1, no. 17.

73. Cullen to Kirby, 21 May 1854: ICAR, *NC, III*, 2, 1, no. 17; Cullen to Prop., 26 May 1854: ACPF, *Acta*, vol. 218 (*1854*), f. 337; Kirby to Prop., 4 June 1854: ACPF, *Acta*, vol. 218 (*1854*), f. 340 (*v*); see also Cullen to Kirby, 17 June 1854: ACPF, *SC, Irlanda*, vol. 32, f. 238; Cullen to Kirby, 5 July 1854: ICAR, *NC, III*, 2, 1, no. 26; Cullen to Kirby, n.d. (*1854*): ACPF, *Acta*, vol. 218 (*1854*), f. 341 (*v*).

74. Cullen to Prop., 26 May 1854: ACPF, *Acta*, vol. 218 (*1854*), f. 338.

75. 'Omnibus hujus regionis sacerdotibus in memoriam revocamus obligationem, qua mysteria Fidei, Sacramenta, Dei praecepta, et alia ad Religionem spectantia fideli populo diebus festivis exponere tenentur. Cum vero periculum sit ne haec negligantur, si de alienis ac profanis negotiis in Ecclesiis agatur, districte prohibemus ne inter Missarum solemnia, quod plane indecens esset, aut omnino in Ecclesia de rebus mere saecularibus, ut de politicis electionibus, aut aliis ejusmodi rebus agatur, quae facile dissidia inter pastorem et populum promovere valeant, et magnam animorum commotionem excitare, quae tamen ita interpretanda non sunt, quasi de largitionibus non ricipiendis, de perjurio evitando, de juribus Ecclesiae, et de charitate et cura erga pauperes saerdotibus [sic] non esset agendnm [sic].

'Quod si quis sacerdos saecularis aut regularis de hujusmodi rebus agat, aut spreto Synodi Thurlesiae praecepto, nominatim in aliquem in Ecclesiis invehatur, is poena suspensionis aut alia pro arbitrio ordinarii plectatur.

'Hortamur vero ut lites et jurgia inter se de rebus politicis in conventibus publicis, et magis adhuc in foliis seu ephemeridibus publicis, non ineant sacerdotes, ne dignitas sacerdotalis aliquid detrimenti capiat, ne charitas illa, quae robur Ecclesiae est, violetur, et ne rixis et contentionibus cum aliis implicentur.

'Haec vero dum statuimus Religionis bonum et Ecclesiae libertatem exigere putamus, ut quotiescumque de curatoribus pauperum, et Parliamenti membris eligendis agatur, a quorum agendi ratione pauperum catholicorum fides incolumitas, et Ecclesiae jura et libertas detrimenta pati possunt, soliciti esse debent, ut hominibus probis et Religionis catholicae minime hostibus munera haec conferantur: attamen extra ecclesias, sine tumultu, absque charitatis violatione, et cum debita subjectione proprio Episcopo, ne dissensiones in clero oriantur, et cum ea moderatione, quae statui clericali omnino convenit, relicta unicuique in dubiis libere pro se sentiendi facultate, de omnibus hujusmodi rebus agendum esse arbitramur'; Cullen to Prop., 26 May 1854: ACPF, *Acta*, vol. 218 (*1854*), f. 330.

76. 'E un gran bene d'avere indotti i Vescovi a manifestare la loro disapprovazione de' preti politici', Cullen to Prop., 26 May 1854: ACPF, *Acta*, vol. 218 (*1854*), f. 338.

77. Cullen to Kirby, n.d. (*1854*): ACPF, *Acta*, vol. 218 (*1854*), f. 341 (*v*).

78. 'Le racomandazioni fatte al clero sulle cose politiche non sono molto stringenti, ma qui in questo regno ove prevale il sistema costituzionale, è necessario che quando si tratta dell'elezioni di membri del Parlamento ... i preti vi prendano qualche parte affinchè non vengano scelti nemici della Religione o persecutori de' poveri', Cullen to Kirby, n.d. (*1854*): ACPF, *Acta*, vol. 218 (*1854*), f. 341 (*v*).

79. Cullen to Kirby, 5 July 1854: ICAR, *NC, III*, 2, 1, no. 26; see also Cullen to Kirby, 17 June 1854: ACPF, *SC, Irlanda*, vol. 32, f. 238.

80. Cullen to Kirby, 5 July 1854: ICAR, *NC, III*, 2, 1, no. 26.

81. ibid.

82. *FJ*, 23 Oct. 1854.

83. *FJ*, 31 Oct 1854; see also Walsh (*Bp., Ossory*) to Cullen, 20 Nov. 1854: DDA, 332\1, no. 207; Cullen to Prop., 25 Apr. 1855: ACPF, CP, vol. 158, f. 56 (*v*).

84. Lucas, op. cit., vol. 2, pp. 207–10; ASV, *Pio IX, Oggetti Vari*, nos. 1212, 1125; see also MacNeave (*lay corr.*) to O'Donnell (*Bp., Galway*), 20 Dec. 1854: ICAR, *NC, III*, 2, 1,

no. 36; Cullen to Prop., 25 Apr. 1855: ACPF, *CP*, vol. 158, f. 56 (*v*).

85. Lucas, op. cit., vol. 2, p. 209; ASV, *Pio IX, Oggetti Vari*, nos. 1212, 1125; Walsh to Cullen, 20 Nov. 1854: DDA, 332\1, no. 207.

86. Walsh to Cullen, 20 Nov. 1854: DDA, 332\1, no. 207; see also Cullen to Prop., 25 Apr. 1855: ACPF, CP, vol. 158, f. 56 (*v*).

87. *Nation*, 5 Feb. 1853; see also Cullen to Kirby, 20 Oct. 1853: ICAR, *NC, III*, 1, 3, no. 103.

88. Lucas to Cullen, n.d. (*1853*): DDA, 325\6, no. 62; Cullen to Kirby, 1 Apr. 1853: ICAR, *NC, III*, 1, 3, no. 68.

89. *Tablet*, 21 Oct., 11 Nov. 1854.

90. *Tablet*, 4 Nov. 1854; see also Lyons (*Sec. Cullen*) to Cullen, 23 Nov. 1854: DDA, 332\1, no. 8.

91. *FJ*, 31 Oct. 1854: Lucas, op. cit., vol. 2, p. 98; MacNeave to O'Donnell, 20 Dec. 1854: ICAR, *NC, III*, 2, 1, no. 36; Monsell to Cullen, 18 Feb. 1855: ASV, *Pio IX, Oggetti Vari*, no. 1125; Cullen to Prop., 25 Apr. 1855: ACPF, *CP*, vol. 158, f. 56 (*v*).

92. Duffy, op. cit., p. 331.

93. Cullen to Kirby, 27 Oct. 1854: ICAR, *NC, III*, 2, 1, no. 35; Lyons to Bulwer (*Brit. Dip., Tuscany*), 25 Oct. 1854: FO, 170\65; see also *ICD*, (*1855*), p. 213.

94. Walsh to Cullen, 20 Nov. 1854: DDA, 332\1, no. 207; Walsh to Cullen, 18 Dec. 1854: DDA, 332\1, no. 210; Walsh to Cullen, 26 Dec. 1854: DDA, 332\1, no. 211.

95. Lyons to Cullen, 23 Nov. 1854: DDA, 332\1, no. 8; Lyons to Cullen, 27 Nov. 1854: DDA, 332\1, no. 10.

96. *Times*, 1 Nov. 1854.

97. Lyons to Bulwer, 10 Nov. 1854: FO, 43\58.

98. ibid.

99. ibid.

100. ibid.

101. Dowley (*Relg., Pres. Castleknock Coll.*) to Cullen, 29 Dec. 1854: ACPF, *CP*, vol. 158, ff. 339–40; see also Lyons to Cullen, 30 Nov. 1854: DDA, 332\1, no. 11.

102. McNamara (*Relg. Phibsboro*) to Cullen, 26 Dec. 1854: DDA, 332\2, no. 62; Cullen to Haly (*Bp., Kildare & Leighlin*), 21 Dec. 1854: ICAR, *NC, III*, 2, 1, no. 37; Dowley to Cullen, 29 Dec. 1854: ACPF, *CP*, vol. 158, f. 339.

103. Dowley to Cullen, 29 Dec. 1854: ACPF, CP, vol. 158, f. 339.

104. Lyons to Cullen, 27 Nov. 1854: DDA, 332\1, no. 10; Lyons to Cullen, 30 Nov. 1854: DDA, 332\1, no. 11.

105. MacNeave to O'Donnell, 20 Dec. 1854: ICAR, NC, III, 2, 1, no. 36.

106. MacNeave to O'Donnell, 20 Dec. 1854: ICAR, NC, III, 2, 1, no. 36; See Dixon (Abp., Armagh) to Prop., 1 Jan. 1855: ACPF, CP, vol. 158, f. 332(v).

107. MacNeave to O'Donnell, 20 Dec. 1854: ICAR, NC, III, 2, 1, no. 36.

108. Mullally (PP, Anascarty) Cahill (CC, Mullinahone) O'Dwyer (CC, Doon) to clergy, 4 Dec. 1854: ACPF, CP, vol. 158, f. 79 (v); O'Dwyer to clergy, 6 Dec. 1854: DDA, 332\2, no. 217; ibid., ACPF, CP, vol. 158, ff. 79 (v); O'Dwyer to clergy, 12 Dec. 1854: DDA, 332\2, no. 220; ibid., ACPF, CP, vol. 158, f. 80; Lucas, op. cit., vol. 2, p. 110. See also Cullen to Prop., 20 Jan. 1855: ACPF, SC, Irlanda, vol. 32, ff. 393–4.

109. Lyons to Cullen, 27 Nov. 1854: DDA, 332\1, no. 10; Lyons to Bulwer, 12 Dec. 1854, FO, 170\67.

110. Cullen to Haly, 21 Dec. 1854: ICAR, NC, III, 2, 1, no. 37; see also Lucas, op. cit., vol. 2, p. 110.

111. Cullen to Haly, 21 Dec. 1854: ICAR, NC, III, 2, 1, no. 37; Meagher (PP, Rathmines) to Cullen, 27 Dec. 1854: DDA, 332\1, no. 21; Lucas, op. cit., vol. 2, p. 110; O'Reilly, op. cit., vol, 2, p. 366; MacGrath, op. cit., pp. 235, 392.

112. Lucas, op. cit., vol. 2, p. 110.

113. Lucas to Duffy, 23 Dec. 1854: NLI, MS. 3738; Anon. (Lucas), 7 Jan. 1855: NLI, MS. 3787; Lucas, op. cit., vol. 2, pp. 111–3.

114. Diary of Bernard Smith, 12, 14, 16, 17 Dec. 1854: BAR, Smith Papers; see also Lucas, op. cit., vol. 2, p. 111.

115. Anon. (Lucas), 7 Jan. 1855: NLI, MS. 3738; see also Lucas, op. cit., vol. 2, p. 114; Diary of Bernard Smith, 16 Dec. 1854: BAR, Smith Papers.

116. Cullen to Haly, 21 Dec. 1854: ICAR, NC, III, 2, 1, no. 37.

117. Cullen to Prop., 16 Dec. 1854: ACPF, SC, Irlanda, vol. 32, f. 342; see also Cullen to Haly, 21 Dec. 1854: ICAR, NC, III, 2, 1, no. 37.

118. Cullen to Haly, 21 Dec. 1854: ICAR, NC, III, 2, 1, no. 37: MacNeave to O'Donnell, 20 Dec. 1854: ICAR, NC, III, 2, 1, no. 36; Dowley to Cullen, 29 Dec. 1854: ACPF, CP, vol. 158, ff. 339–40; ASV, Pio IX, Oggetti Vari, no. 1125.

119. Cullen to Haly, 21 Dec. 1854: ICAR, NC, III, 2, 1, no. 37.

120. Lucas to Duffy (MP, New Ross), n.d. (Dec. 1854): NLI, MS. 3738; Lucas to Anon. (Lucas), 7 Jan. 1855: NLI, MS. 3738; Lucas, op. cit., vol. 2, pp. 111–13.

121. Cullen to Haly, 21 Dec. 1854: ICAR, NC, III, 2, 1, no. 37; O'Ferrall (lay corr.) to Cullen, 23 Dec. 1854: DDA, 332\2, no. 223; Walsh to Cullen, 26 Dec. 1854: DDA, 332\1, no. 211; n.d. (Feb. 1855): NLI, MS. 3738; Lucas, op. cit., vol. 2, p. 132. See also copy of the priest's Memorial: DDA, 332\2, no. 225.

122. Walsh to Cullen, 26 Dec. 1854: DDA, 332\1, no. 211.

123. See ASV Pio IX, Oggetti Vari, no. 1212; see also Lucas to Anon. (Lucas), n.d. (Feb. 1855): NLI, MS. 3738; Lucas, op. cit., vol. 2, p. 132.

124. 'To His Holiness Pope Pius IX. The Memorial of the undersigned Catholic priests of Ireland': NLI, MS. 1587; ibid: DDA, 332\2, no. 225; ibid: ASV, Pio IX, Oggetti Vari, no. 1212; ibid: ACPF, CP, vol. 158, ff. 365–7; 'The Memorial of the Undermentioned Irish Members of Parliament': NLI, MS. 1587; ASV, Pio IX, Oggetti Vari, no. 1212; 'Statement of Frederick Lucas'; Lucas, op. cit, vol. 2, pp. 139–442; ASV Pio IX, Oggetti Vari, no. 1212; see also Rush (PP, Ballinasloe) to Cullen, 30 Nov. 1854: DDA, 332\2, no. 213; O'Brien (PP, Waterford) to Kirby, 16 Dec. 1854: ICAR, Kirby Papers, no. 1513; Haly to Kirby, 6 Jan. 1855: ICAR, Kirby Papers, no. 1526.

125. 'To His Holiness Pope Pius IX. The Memorial of the undersigned Catholic priests of Ireland': NLI, MS. 1587; ibid: DDA, 332\2, no. 225; ibid: ASV, Pio IX, Oggetti Vari, no. 1212; ibid: ACPF, CP, vol. 158, ff. 365–7.

126. ibid.

127. Dixon to Prop., 1 Jan. 1855: ACPF, CP, vol., 158, ff. 330–4; see also Dixon to Smith: 1 Jan. 1855: BAR, Smith Papers.

128. ibid.

129. 'Vi è un altro timore, che egli non conosce punto, è questo e il timore di cio che i preti

tiepidi possono dire e fare in opposizione ai suoi sforzi per compiere i desideri della Santa Sede col dare nuovo vigore alla disciplina ecclesiastica nell'Irlanda'; Dixon to Prop., 1 Jan. 1855: ACPF, CP, vol. 158, f. 333; see also Dixon to Smith, 1 Jan. 1855: BAR, *Smith Papers*.

130. Dixon to Prop., 1 Jan. 1855: ACPF, CP, vol. 158, ff. 330–4; see also Dixon to Smith, 1 Jan. 1855: BAR, *Smith Papers*.

131. Lucas to Anon. (*Lucas*), 9 Jan. 1855: NLI, MS. 3738; Lucas, op. cit., vol. 2, p. 118; see also Diary of Bernard Smith, 11 Jan. 1855: BAR, *Smith Papers*.

132. Lucas, op. cit., vol. 2, p. 118.

133. ibid.

134. Diary of Bernard Smith, 11 Jan. 1855: BAR, *Smith Papers*.

135. 'Io mi sono persuaso che se non si accomodano le cose nostre mentre stiamo in Roma avremo più violenza, e maggiori dissensioni, che si sono mai vedute per lo passato in Irlanda', Cullen to Prop., 17 Jan. 1855: ACPF, CP, vol. 158, f. 364.

136. ACPF, CP, vol. 158, f. 84 *(v)*; Diary of Bernard Smith, 18 Jan. 1855: BAR, *Smith Papers*.

137. ACPF, CP, vol. 158, ff. 345–60; see also Diary of Bernard Smith, 18 Jan. 1855: BAR, *Smith Papers*.

Chapter Six

1. Cullen to Prop., 20 Jan. 1855: ACPF, SC, *Irlanda*, vol. 32, f. 393.

2. ibid.

3. Talbot (*Papal Chamberlain*) to Cullen, 22 Jan. 1855: ICAR, NC, III, 2, 1, no. 44; Lucas, op. cit., vol. 2, pp. 119–20.

4. Diary of Bernard Smith, 24 Jan. 1855: BAR, *Smith Papers*.

5. Lucas, op. cit., vol. 2, p. 119.

6. 'The Memorial of the Undermentioned Irish Members of Parliament', NLI, MS. 1587; see also ASV, *Pio IX, Oggetti Vari*, no. 1212. The signatories were Moore (*MP, Mayo co.*); Swift (*MP, Sligo*); Duffy (*MP, New Ross*); Maguire (*MP, Dungarvan*); McMahon (*MP, Wexford*); Brady (*MP, Leitrim*).

7. Lucas (*MP, Meath, Founder of* Tablet) to Anon. (*Lucas, wife*), 24 Jan. 1855: NLI, MS. 3738; see also Lucas, op. cit., vol. 2, pp. 122–5; Diary of Bernard Smith, 24 Jan. 1855: BAR, *Smith Papers*.

8. Lucas to Anon. (*Lucas*), 24 Jan. 1855: NLI, MS. 3738; see also Lucas, op. cit., vol. 2, p. 123.

9. Lucas, op. cit., vol. 2, p. 125, ibid, p. 125.

10. Lucas, op. cit., vol. 2, p. 124, ibid, p. 124.

11. ibid.

12. ibid, p. 123.

13. ibid.

14. Lucas to Duffy, 27 Jan. 1855: NLI, MS. 3738; see also Lucas, op. cit., vol. 2, p. 125.

15. Lucas to Anon. (*Lucas*), 24 Jan. 1855: NLI, MS. 3738; see also Lucas, op. cit., vol. 2, p. 125.

16. Prop. to MacHale (*Abp., Tuam*), 27 Jan. 1855: ACPF, CP, vol. 158, f. 85; ASV, *Pio IX, Oggetti Vari*, no. 1125.

17. MacHale to Prop., 29 Jan. 1855: ACPF, CP, vol. 158, ff. 86–7.

18. Memo, 31 Jan. 1855: ACPF, CP, vol. 158, f. 38.

19. Cullen to Pius IX, 2 Feb. 1855: ACPF, SC, *Irlanda*, vol. 32, f. 402; ibid, ACPF, CP, vol. 158, ff. 87–8; see also O'Reilly, op. cit., vol. 2, pp. 368–71.

20. ibid.

21. O'Reilly, op. cit., vol. 2, p. 368.

22. MacHale to Pius IX, 5 Feb. 1855: ACPF, CP, vol. 158, ff. 88 *(v)* –91; see also O'Reilly, op. cit., vol. 2, pp. 373–8.

23. O'Reilly, op. cit., vol. 2, p. 392, Lucas to MacHale, 13 Feb. 1855; MacHale to Durcan (*Bp., Achonry*), Derry (*Bp., Clonfert*), Browne (*Bp., Elphin*), O'Donnell (*Bp., Galway*), Feeny (*Bp., Killala*), Fallon (*Bp., Kilmacduagh & Kilfenora*), 5 Feb. 1855: ACPF, CP, vol. 158, f. 91 *(v)*; MacHale to Pius IX, 6 Feb. 1855: ACPF, CP, vol. 158, f. 91 *(v)*.

24. 'Osservazioni di Mons Cullen sulla risposta dell'Arcivescovo di Tuam', 17 Feb. 1855: ACPF, CP, vol 158, ff. 92–4.

25. Lucas to MacHale, 19 Feb. 1855: O'Reilly, op. cit., vol 2, p. 395; See Diary of Bernard Smith, 19 Feb. 1855: BAR, *Smith Papers*.

26. Mullally (*PP, Anacarty*), Cahill (*CC, Mullinahone*) O'Dwyer (*CC, Doon*), to clergy, Dec. 1854: ACPF, CP, vol. 158, f. 79 *(v)*; see also Rush (*PP, Ballinasloe*) to Cullen, 30 Nov. 1854: DDA, 332\2, no. 213; O'Brien (*PP, Waterford*), to Kirby, 16 Dec. 1854: ICAR, *Kirby Papers*, no. 1513; Haly (*Bp., Kildare & Leighlin*), to Kirby, 6 Jan. 1855: ICAR, *Kirby Papers*, no. 1526.

27. O'Dwyer to clergy, 12 December 1854:

DDA, 332\2, no. 220; ibid., ACPF, *CP*, vol. 158, f. 80.

28. O'Brien to Kirby (*Rec. Irish Coll., Rome*), 16 December 1854: ICAR, *Kirby Papers*, no. 1513; Dixon (*Abp., Armagh*),to Kirby, 19 January 1855: ICAR, *Kirby Papers*, no. 1535; Kilduff (*Bp., Ardagh & Clonmacnoise*), to Cullen, 24 January 1855: ICAR, *Kirby Papers*, no. 1537; Dixon to Smith (*Vice Rec. Irish Coll., Rome*), 8 February 1855: ICAR, *Kirby Papers*, no. 1546; Duffy, *League*, pp. 348–59.

29. Lyons (*Sec. Cullen*), to Cullen, 11 December 1854: DDA, 332\1, no. 13; Newman (*Rec. Cath. Univ. Ire.*) to Cullen, 29 January 1855; see also *FJ*, 15 February 1855; MacGrath, op. cit., p. 349.

30. They included priests from the dioceses of Achonry, Ardagh, Cashel, Clonfert, Cloyne, Down and Connor, Kerry, Killaloe, Limerick, Meath and Tuam. See 'To His Holiness Pope Pius IX. The Memorial of the undersigned Catholic priests of Ireland'; NLI, MS. 1587; ibid: DDA, 332\2, no. 225; ibid: ASV, Pio IX Oggetti Vari, no. 1212; ibid: ACPF, *CP*, vol. 158, ff. 365–7.

31. Duffy, op. cit., pp. 348–50.

32. ibid, p. 349.

33. ibid, pp. 349–59.

34. *Nation*, 24 February 1855; Duffy, op. cit., p. 351.

35. WT, 23 December 1854.

36. WT, 23 December 1854; *Nation*, 3 February 1855; Lucas, *Life*, vol. 2, p. 129.

37. See Meagher (*PP, Rathmines*) to Cullen, 8 December 1854: DDA, 332\1, no. 20.

38. Monsell (*MP, Limerick co.; Clerk of the Ordnance*), to Cullen, 18 February 1855: ASV, *Pio IX, Oggetti Vari*, no. 1125.

39. *Tablet*, 10 February 1855.

40. Monsell to Cullen, 18 February 1855: ASV, *Pio IX, Oggetti Vari*, no. 1125; see also Monsell to Cullen, 22 February 1855: ACPF, *CP*, vol. 128, ff. 181–4.

41. Lucas to MacHale, 19 February 1855: O'Reilly, op. cit., vol 2, pp. 395–9.

42. Lucas, op. cit., vol. 2, pp. 130–2.

43. ibid. p. 131.

44. ibid. pp. 137, 445.

45. 'Cum multa mala oriantur ex dissensionibus politicis inter clericos, ad grave Religionis detrimentum et ad fidelium scandalum, ut his in posterum praecaveatur, sacerdotibus alienae dioecesis vel paroeciae prohibemus in conventu publico de rebus politicis tractare seu suffragia populi rogare sine expressa licentia parochi loci. Meminerint vero sacerdotes omnes quod non possunt comminatione subtractionis sacramentorum populum cogere ad suffragia danda', ACPF, *Acta*, (*1855*), f. 201; see also ibid. f. 187.

46. '… i savii regolamenti … adottati per impedire che il clero s'inframischiasse con troppo fracasso e publicita nelle cose politiche', Kirby to Prop., 25 Nov. 1854: ACPF, *Acta*, vol. 219 (*1855*), f. 189; see also Cullen to Prop., 12 July 1853: ACPF, *SC, Irlanda*, vol. 31, f. 511.

47. Lyons to Bulwer (*Brit. Dip. Tuscany*), 11 Jan. 1855: PRO, FO, 43\60, no. 4.

48. *Acta et decreta Concilii Provincialis Armacani*, Dublin, 1855, p. 39.

49. Murray (*Sec. Cullen*) to Cullen, 17 Apr. 1855: ICAR, *NC, III*, 2, 1, no. 46.

50. Murray to Cullen, 17 Apr. 1855: ICAR, *NC, III*, 2, 1, no 46. The decrees were published in the *Nation*, 14 Apr. 1855.

51. ibid.

52. '*Relazione con sommario sopra alcuni provedimenti in bene del cattolicismo in Irlanda, 1855*', ACPF, *CP*, vol. 158, ff. 42–155.

53. ibid. f. 43.

54. Cullen to Prop, 25 Apr. 1855: ACPF, *CP*, vol. 158, ff. 53–74; Cullen to Prop, 8 May 1855: ACPF, *CP*, vol. 158, ff. 81–3; Cullen to Prop., 13 June 1855: ACPF, *SC, Irlanda*, vol. 32, ff. 482–5; ACPF, *CP*, vol. 158, ff. 345–60.

55. Cullen to Prop., 25 Apr. 1855: ACPF, *CP*, vol. 158, ff. 59, 62; see also Cullen to Prop., 8 May 1855: ACPF, *CP*, vol. 158, f. 82.

56. 'Non ho mai dettato e non credo che sia il mio dovere di dettare una linea di politica al clero. Ho inculcato a tutti d'esser pronti a difendere la fede e a promuovere la carità ma del resto non ho mai domandato come pensassero in cose meramente politiche. L'unica cosa in cui insisteva era, che tutti adempissero i loro doveri, e si comportassero con quella prudenza e moderazione che convengono agli ecclesiastici'; Cullen to Prop., 25 Apr. 1855: ACPF, *CP*, vol. 158, f. 63 (*v*).

57. Cullen to Prop., 25 Apr. 1855: ACPF, *CP*, vol. 158, f. 55 (*v*); Cullen to Prop., 8 May 1855: ACPF, *CP*, vol. 158, f. 81 (*v*)–2.

58. Cullen to Prop., 25 Apr. 1855: ACPF, CP, vol. 158, f. 55 (v).

59. 'Tutti desiderebbero certamente che avessimo in carica e specialmente nel Parlamento uomini di spirito independente, che senza farsi ligj d'alcuna fazione cercassero a promuovere gl'interessi del paese e della religione. Ma i capi della lega non si contentano d'una tal indipendenza: esigono assolutamente che i loro partigiani si mettano in diretta opposizione ad ogni governo, che non prometta di rimuovere tutti i gravami che pesano su i cattolici d'Irlanda, e siccome nessun governo ne'tempi attuali di eccitamento contro i cattolici potrebbe colla piu piccola speranza d'una felice riuscita metter la mano ad una tal opera, così si devono obbligare quei signori ad una perpetua ostilità ad ogni governo possibile ... Qualora tutti i cattolici s'unissero nell'adottare tali principj, sono persuaso che il governo Inglese in propria difesa dovrebbe cacciarli dal Parlamento e cominciar a rinnuovare le leggi penali'; Cullen to Prop., 25 Apr. 1855: ACPF, CP, vol. 158, f. 55 (v).

60. Cullen to Prop., 25 Apr. 1855: ACPF, CP, vol. 158, ff. 53–74.

61. 'Mi sono tenuto lontano dal governo senza assalirlo, e non ho voluto mai farmi ligio d'alcun partito popolare', Cullen to Prop., 8 May 1855: ACPF, CP, vol. 158, f. 83.

62. 'Quanto a me, non presi alcuna parte affatto in questa controversia perché vedeva, che se era da biasimare il Sig. Keogh da una parte per aver violato la sua promessa dall'altra parte si poteva allegare in suo favore, che la promessa era temeraria e dannosa, e perciò non obbligatoria'; Cullen to Prop., 8 May 1855: ACPF, CP, vol. 158, f. 81 (v).

63. 'Devo dire però che mi sembra un vantaggio incalcolabile d'avere cattolici in cariche giudiziali in Irlanda'; Cullen to Prop., 8 May 1855: ACPF, CP, vol. 158, f. 82.

64. 'Quindi non poteva non sentire gran piacere quando ho veduto promosso i sigg. Monsell, Fitzgerald, Ball, e qualche altro buon cattolico, a cariche importanti. Questi non avevano mai promesso di seguire la politica della continua opposizione'; Cullen to Prop., 8 May 1855: ACPF, CP, vol. 158, f. 82.

65. Monsell to Cullen, 18 Feb. 1855: ASV, Pio IX, Oggetti Vari, no. 1125; Monsell to Cullen, 22 Feb. 1855: ACPF, CP, vol. 128, ff. 181–4.

66. Monsell to Cullen, 18 Feb. 1855: ASV, Pio IX, Oggetti Vari, no. 1125; see also Monsell to Cullen, 22 Feb. 1855: ACPF, CP, vol. 128, ff. 181–4; Cullen to Monsell, 10 (March) 1855: NLI, MS. 8317.

67. Monsell to Cullen, 18 Feb. 1855: ASV, Pio IX, Oggetti Vari, no. 1125; see also Monsell to Cullen, 22 Feb. 1855: ACPF, CP, vol. 128, ff. 181–4.

68. Cullen to Monsell, 10 (March) 1855: NLI, MS. 8317; see also Cullen to Monsell, 11 Apr. 1855: NLI, MS. 8317.

69. ACPF, CP, vol. 158, f. 48.

70. ACPF, CP, vol. 158 ff. 49–50; Lyons to Marquis of Normandy, 16 June 1855: FO, 170\70.

71. ACPF, CP, vol. 158, f. 49.

72. Diary of Bernard Smith, 19 June 1855: BAR, Smith Papers.

73. ibid.

74. Cullen to Prop., 1 July 1855: ACPF, Acta, vol. 219 (1855), f. 809 (v).

75. Nation, 23 June 1855; see also Cullen to Prop., 28 July 1855: ACPF, SC Irlanda vol. 32, f. 509; ACPF, Acta, vol. 219 (1855), f. 809 (v).

76. Cullen to Kirby, 24 June 1855: ICAR, NC, III, 2, 1, no. 51; Cullen to Kirby, 26 June 1855: ICAR, NC, III, 2, 1, no. 52; Cullen to Prop., 1 July 1855: ACPF, Acta, vol. 219 (1855), f. 809 (v); Cullen to Prop., 23 July 1855: ACPF, Acta, vol. 219 (1855), ff. 810 (v) –11; Cullen to Prop., 28 July 1855: ACPF, SC, Irlanda, vol. 32, f. 509.

77. Cullen to Kirby, 1 July 1855: ICAR, NC, III, 2, 1, no. 54; see also Cullen to Prop., 1 July 1855: ACPF, Acta, vol. 219 (1855), f. 809 (v); Cullen to Prop., 23 July 1855: ACPF, Acta, vol. 219, ff. 810 (v) –11.

78. Cullen to Prop., 28 July 1855: ACPF, SC, Irlanda, vol. 32, f. 509 (v) –10; Cullen to Kirby, 28 July 1855: ICAR, NC, III, 2, 1, no. 60; Cullen to Pius IX, 31 Aug. 1855: ICAR, NC, III, 2, 1, no. 65.

79. Cullen to Prop., 28 July 1855: ACPF, SC, Irlanda, vol. 32, f. 510.

80. Cullen to Kirby, 1 July 1855: ICAR, NC, III, 2, 1, no. 54; Cullen to Prop., 1 July 1855: ACPF, Acta, vol. 219 (1855), f. 809 (v); Cullen to Prop., 23 July 1855: ACPF, Acta,

vol. 219 (*1855*), f. 810 (*v*) −11; Cullen to Prop., 28 July 1855: ACPF, SC Irlanda, vol. 32, f. 509 (*v*).

81. Cullen to Prop., 1 July 1855: ACPF, *Acta*, vol. 219 (*1855*), f. 809 (*v*); Cullen to Prop., 28 July 1855: ACPF, *SC, Irlanda*, vol. 32, f. 509 (*v*); Cullen to Kirby, 16 July 1855: ICAR, *NC, III*, 2, 1, no. 57; Cullen to Prop., 23 July 1855: ACPF, *Acta*, vol. 219 (*1855*) f. 810 (*v*); *Tablet*, 30 June, 7 July 1855.

82. Cullen to Prop., 1 July 1855: ACPF, *Acta*, vol. 219 (*1855*), f. 809 (*v*); Cullen to Prop., 28 July 1855: ACPF, *SC, Irlanda*, vol. 32, f. 510.

83. Cullen to Kirby, 1 July 1855: ICAR, *NC, III*, 2, 1, no. 54; see also Cullen to Prop., 28 July 1855: ACPF, *SC, Irlanda*, vol. 32, f. 510.

84. Cullen to Kirby, 16 July 1855: ICAR, *NC, III*, 2, 1, no. 57; Cullen to Kirby, 21 July 1855: ICAR, *NC, III*, 2, 1, no. 58.

85. Cullen to Prop., 28 July 1855: ACPF, *SC, Irlanda*, vol. 32, ff. 509, 511.

86. Cullen to Kirby, 6 July 1855: ICAR, *NC, III*, 2, 1, no. 55.

87. Cullen to Kirby, 30 June 1855: ICAR, *NC, III*, 2, 1, no. 53.

88. Cullen to Kirby, 16 July 1855: ICAR, *NC, III*, 2, 1, no. 57; Cullen to Kirby, 21 July 1855: ICAR, *NC, III*, 2, 1, no. 58; Cullen to Kirby, 28 July 1855: ICAR, *NC, III*, 2, 1, no. 60; Cullen to Kirby, 9 Aug. 1855: ICAR, *NC, III*, 2, 1, no. 62; Cullen to Prop., 11 Aug. 1855: ACPF, *SC, Irlanda*, vol. 32, f. 517; Cullen to Kirby, 24 Aug. 1855: ICAR, *NC, III*, 2, 1, no. 64; Cullen to Kirby, 2 Sept. 1855: ICAR, *NC, III*, 2, 1, no. 66; Cullen to Kirby, 3 Sept. 1855: ICAR, *NC, III*, 2, 1, no. 67; Cullen to Prop., n.d. (*1855, undelievered*): ICAR, *NC, III*, 2, 1, no. 69; see also Kirby to Prop., 19 Aug. 1855: ACPF, *SC, Irlanda*, vol. 32, f. 529; Anon. (*Kirby*) to Prop. n.d.: ACPF, *SC, Irlanda*, vol. 32, f. 513.

89. Cullen to Prop., 28 July 1855: ACPF, *SC, Irlanda*, vol. 32, f. 511; Cullen to Kirby, 9 Aug. 1855: ICAR, *NC, III*, 2, 1, no. 62; Cullen to Kirby, 9 Aug. 1855: ICAR, *NC, III*, 2, 1, no. 62; Cullen to Kirby, 23 Sept. 1855: ICAR, *NC, III*, 2, 1, no. 76.

90. Cullen to Pius IX, 31 Aug. 1855: ICAR, *NC, III*, 2, 1, no. 65.

91. Cullen to Prop., 23 July 1855: ACPF, *Acta*, vol. 219 (*1855*), f. 811; see also Cullen to Kirby, 9 Aug. 1855: ICAR, *NC, III*, 2, 1,

no. 62; Cullen to Prop., 11 Aug. 1855: ACPF, *SC, Irlanda*, f. 517; Cullen to Pius IX, 31 Aug. 1855: ICAR, *NC, III*, 2, 1, no. 65; Cullen to Kirby, 2 Sept. 1855: ICAR, *NC, III*, 2, 1, no. 66; *Tablet*, 11 Aug., 1 Sept. 1855.

92. Cullen to Kirby, 16 July 1855: ICAR, *NC, III*, 2, 1, no. 57; Cullen to Prop., 28 July 1855: ACPF, *SC, Irlanda*, vol. 32, ff. 509 (*v*) −10; Cullen to Pius IX, 31 Aug. 1855: ICAR, *NC, III*, 2, 1, no. 65; see also *Tablet*, 30 June, 7 July 1855.

93. 'Tendano a sturbare gli animi del popolO'; Cullen to Prop., 11 Aug. 1855: ACPF, *SC, Irlanda*, vol. 32, f. 517.

94. Cullen to Kirby, 3 Sept. 1855: ICAR, *NC, III*, 2, 1, no. 67; Cullen to Prop., n.d. (*1855, undelievered*): ICAR, *NC, III*, 2, 1, no. 69.

95. Cullen to Kirby, 24 Aug. 1855: ICAR, *NC, III*, 2, 1, no. 64; Cullen to Pius IX, 31 Aug. 1855: ICAR, *NC, III*, 2, 1, no. 65; see also Cullen to Kirby, 9 Aug. 1855: ICAR, *NC, III*, 2, 1, no. 62.

96. Cullen to Prop., 28 July 1855: ACPF, *SC, Irlanda*, vol. 32, f. 509 (*v*); see also Cullen to Kirby, 24 Aug. 1855: ICAR, *NC, III*, 2, 1, no. 64.

97. Cullen to Kirby, 28 July 1855: ICAR, *NC, III*, 2, 1, no. 60; see also Cullen to Kirby, 9 Aug. 1855: ICAR, *NC, III*, 2, 1, no. 62; Cullen to Prop., n.d. (*1855, undelievered*): ICAR, *NC, III*, 2, 1, no. 69.

98. Cullen to Prop., n.d. (*1855, undelievered*): ICAR, *NC, III*, 2, 1, no. 69.

99. Cullen to Kirby, 9 Aug. 1855: ICAR, *NC, III*, 2, 1, no, 62; see also Cullen to Prop., n.d. (*1855, undelievered*): ICAR, *NC, III*, 2, 1, no. 69.

100. Cullen to Kirby, 9 Aug. 1855: ICAR, *NC, III*, 2, 1, no. 62.

101. Cullen to Prop., n.d. (*1855, undelievered*): ICAR, *NC, III*, 2, 1, no. 69; see also Cullen to Kirby, 24 Aug. 1855: ICAR, *NC, III*, 2, 1, no. 64.

102. Cullen to Kirby, 3 Sept. 1855: ICAR, *NC, III*, 2, 1, no. 67; Cullen to Prop., n.d. (*1855, undelievered*): ICAR, *NC, III*, 2, 1, no. 69.

103. Cullen to Kirby, 6 July 1855: ICAR, *NC, III*, 2, 1, no. 55; Cullen to Kirby, 16 July 1855: ICAR, *NC, III*, 2, 1, no. 57; Cullen to Kirby, 21 July 1855: ICAR, *NC, III*, 2, 1, no. 58; Cullen to Kirby, 3 Sept. 1855: ICAR, *NC, III*, 2, 1, no. 68; see also Cullen to

Kirby, 29 Nov. 1855: ICAR, *NC, III*, 2, 1, no. 86

104. Cullen to Kirby, 6 July 1855: ICAR, *NC, III*, 2, 1, no. 55; Cullen to Kirby, 28 July 1855: ICAR, *NC, III*, 2, 1, no. 60; Cullen to Prop., 28 July 1855: ACPF, *SC, Irlanda*, vol. 32, f. 510; Cullen to Pius IX, 31 Aug. 1855: ICAR, *NC, III*, 2, 1, no. 65; Cullen to Kirby, 3 Sept. 1855: ICAR, *NC, III*, 2, 1, no. 68; Cullen to Kirby, 20 Sept. 1855: ICAR, *NC, III*, 2, 1, no. 74; Anon. (*Kirby*) to Prop., n.d.: ACPF, *SC, Irlanda*, vol. 32, f. 546; see also *Tablet*, 11 Aug. 1855; *Nation,* 18 Aug., 10 Nov. 1855.

105. Cullen to Kirby, 6 July 1855: ICAR, *NC, III*, 2, 1, no. 55; Cullen to Kirby, 28 July 1855: ICAR, *NC, III*, 2, 1, no. 60; Cullen to Pius IX, 31 Aug. 1855: ICAR, *NC, III*, 2, 1, no. 65; Cullen to Kirby, 3 Sept. 1855: ICAR, *NC, III*, 2, 1, no. 68; *Tablet*, 11 Aug. 1855; *FJ*, 23 Aug. 1855.

106. Lucas to MacHale, 30 July 1855; O'Reilly, op. cit., vol. 2, p. 403.

107. Cullen to Kirby, 28 July 1855: ICAR, *NC, III*, 2, 1, no. 60.

108. Cullen to Kirby, 20 Sept. 1855: ICAR, *NC, III*, 2, 1, no. 74; see also Cullen to Kirby, 23 Sept. 1855: ICAR, *NC, III*, 2, 1, no. 76; Cullen to Anon. (*Kirby*), n.d. (*1855*): ACPF, *SC, Irlanda*, vol. 32, f. 566 *(v)*; Anon. (*Kirby*) to Prop. n.d. (*Sept., 1855*): ACPF, *SC, Irlanda*, vol. 32, f. 546.

109. Cullen to Kirby, 28 July 1855: ICAR, *NC, III*, 2, 1, no. 60.

110. Cullen to Kirby, 6 July 1855: ICAR, *NC, III*, 2, 1, no. 55; Cullen to Kirby, 28 July 1855: ICAR, *NC, III*, 2, 1, no. 60; Cullen to Pius IX, 31 Aug. 1855: ICAR, *NC, III*, 2, 1, no. 65; Cullen to Kirby, 3 Sept. 1855: ICAR, *NC, III*, 2, 1, no. 68; Cullen to Kirby, 20 Sept. 1855: ICAR, *NC, III*, 2, 1, no. 74; Cullen to Anon. (*Kirby*), n.d. (*1855*): ACPF, *SC, Irlanda*, vol. 32, f. 566 *(v)*.

111. Cullen to Kirby, 20 Sept. 1855: ICAR, *NC, III*, 2, 1, no. 74; see also Anon. (*Kirby*) to Prop., n.d. (*Sept. 1855*): ACPF, *SC, Irlanda*, vol 32, f. 546.

112. Cullen to Anon. (*Kirby*), n.d. (*1855*): ACPF, *SC, Irlanda*, vol. 32, f. 566 *(v)*.

113. Cullen to Anon. (*Kirby*), n.d. (*1855*): ACPF, *SC, Irlanda*, vol. 32, f. 566 *(v)*.

114. Cullen to Kirby, 3 Sept. 1855: ICAR, *NC, III*, 2, 1, no. 68.

115. Lucas, op. cit., vol. 2, p. 455.

116. Cullen to Kirby, 2 Dec. 1855: ICAR, *NC, III*, 2, 1, no. 87; Lyons to Kirby, 5 Dec. 1855: ICAR, *NC, III*, 2, 1, no. 88; *Freeman's Journal & Catholic Register New York*, 8 Dec. 1855.

117. Cullen to Kirby, 29 Apr. 1856: ICAR, *NC, III*, 2, 1, no. 119; Cullen to Kirby, 5 May 1856: ICAR, *NC, III*, 2, 1, no. 120; ASV, *Pio IX, Oggetti Vari*, no. 1212; See Lucas, op. cit., vol. 2, pp. 139–441.

118. Cullen to Anon. (*Kirby*), 4 Oct. 1855: ICAR, *NC, III*, 2, 1, no. 80; see also Cullen to Anon. (*Kirby*), n.d. (*1855*): ACPF, *SC, Irlanda*, vol. 32, f. 567 *(v)*.

119. Cullen to Kirby, 23 Oct. 1855: ICAR, *NC, III*, 2, 1, no. 82.

120. Cullen to Prop., 24 Feb. 1856: ACPF, *SC, Irlanda*, vol. 32, f. 726 *(v)*.

121. *FJ*, 6 Nov. 1855.

122. Cullen to Kirby, 8 Dec. 1855: ICAR, *NC, III*, 2, 1, no. 90.

123. Cullen to Kirby, 29 Nov. 1855: ICAR, *NC, III*, 2, 1, no. 86; Cullen to Kirby, 2 Dec. 1855: ICAR, *NC, III*, 2, 1, no. 87; Cullen to Kirby, 10 Dec. 1855: ICAR, *NC, III*, 2, 1, no. 91; Anon. (*Kirby*) to Prop., n.d. (*Dec., 1855*): ACPF, *SC, Irlanda*, vol. 32, f. 683; Cullen to Prop., 24 Feb. 1856: ACPF, *SC, Irlanda*, vol. 32, f. 726 *(v)*.

124. Cullen to Kirby, 2 Dec. 1855: ICAR, *NC, III*, 2, 1, no. 87.

125. Anon. (*Kirby*) to Prop., n.d. (*Dec. 1855*): ACPF, *SC, Irlanda*, vol. 32, f. 683; see also *WRJ*, 1 Dec. 1855.

126. Cullen to Kirby, 23 Nov. 1855: ICAR, *NC, III*, 2, 1, no. 85.

127. Cullen to Kirby, 10 Dec. 1855: ICAR, *NC, III*, 2, 1, no. 91.

128. Cullen to Kirby, 23 Nov. 1855: ICAR, *NC, III*, 2, 1, no. 85; see also Cullen to Kirby, 29 Nov. 1855: ICAR, *NC, III*, 2, 1, no. 86; Cullen to Kirby, 2 Dec. 1855: ICAR, *NC, III*, 2, 1, no. 87; Anon. (*Kirby*) to Prop., n.d. (*Dec. 1855*): ACPF, *SC, Irlanda*, vol. 32, f. 683; Cullen to Anon. (*Kirby*), n.d. (*1855*): ACPF, *SC, Irlanda*, vol. 32, f. 567.

129. Cullen to Kirby, 22 Dec. 1855: ICAR, *NC, III*, 2, 1, no. 94; see also Cullen to Prop., 24 Feb. 1856: ACPF, *SC, Irlanda*, vol. 32, f. 727; Cullen to Kirby, 10 Dec. 1855: ICAR, *NC, III*, 2, 1, no. 91.

130. Cullen to Kirby, 10 Dec. 1855: ICAR, *NC, III*, 2, 1, no. 91.

278

131. Cullen to Kirby, 2 Dec. 1855: ICAR, *NC,* *III,* 2, 1, no. 87; see also Cullen to Kirby, 10 Dec. 1855: ICAR, *NC, III,* 2, 1, no. 91; Cullen to Kirby, 22 Dec. 1855: ICAR, *NC, III,* 2, 1, no. 94; Cullen to Kirby, 29 Dec. 1855: ICAR, *NC, III,* 2, 1, no. 95.

132. Dowling (*Relg. Pres. Castleknock Coll.*) to Moore, 17 Dec. 1855: NLI, MS. 893, f. 545; *Nation,* 22 Dec. 1855; see also Anon. (*Kirby*) to Prop., n.d (*Dec. 1855*): ACPF, *SC, Irlanda,* vol. 32, f. 682.

133. Anon. (*Kirby*) to Prop., n.d. (*Dec. 1855*): ACPF, *SC, Irlanda,* vol. 32, f. 682.

134. Cullen to Kirby, 22 Dec. 1855: ICAR, *NC, III,* 2, 1, no. 94; *Nation,* 22 Dec. 1855.

135. Murray to Kirby, 26 Oct. 1855: ICAR, *NC, III,* 2, 1, no. 84.

136. Cullen to Kirby, 29 Nov. 1855: ICAR, *NC, III,* 2, 1, no. 86.

137. Cullen to Kirby, 22 Dec. 1855: ICAR, *NC, III,* 2, 1, no. 94.

138. Lyons to Kirby, 5 Dec. 1855: ICAR, *NC, III,* 2, 1, no. 88.

139. Cullen to Kirby, 8 Dec. 1855: ICAR, *NC, III,* 2, 1, no. 90; Lyons to Kirby, 5 Dec. 1855: ICAR, *NC, III,* 2, 1, no. 88.

140. Cullen to Kirby, 3 Jan. 1856: ICAR, *NC, III,* 2, 1, no. 96; Cullen to Kirby, 11 Jan. 1856: ICAR, *NC, III,* 2, 1, no. 98; Cullen to Kirby, 21 Jan. 1856: ICAR, *NC, III,* 2, 1, no. 100; Cullen to Kirby, 28 Jan. 1856: ICAR, *NC, III,* 2, 1, no. 102.

141. Cullen to Kirby, 3 Jan. 1856: ICAR, *NC, III,* 2, 1, no. 96.

142. Cullen to Kirby, 5 Apr. 1856: ICAR, *NC, III,* 2, 1, no. 113.

Chapter Seven

1. *FJ,* 18 Feb., 3 Apr. 1856. *Nation,* 10 Nov. 1855.

2. Anon. (*Kirby, Rec. Irish Coll., Rome*) to Prop., n.d. (*1856*): ACPF, *SC, Irlanda,* vol. 32, f. 730.

3. *FJ,* 10 Mar. 1856, 14 Apr. 1856.

4. *FJ,* 12 Mar. 1856.

5. *FJ,* 10, 19 Mar. 1856, 14 Apr. 1856.

6. Cullen to Monsell (*MP, Limerick co., Clerk of the Ordnance*) 11 Apr. 1856: NLI, MS. 8317.

7. Cullen to Kirby, 15 May 1856: ICAR, *NC, III,* 2, 1, no. 121.

8. ibid.

9. Cullen to Kirby, 13 Apr. 1856: ICAR, *NC, III,* 2, 1, no. 116.

10. Cullen to Kirby, 25 Mar. 1856: ICAR, *NC, III,* 2, 1, no. 111; Cullen to Kirby, 5 Apr. 1856: ICAR, *NC, III,* 2, 1, no. 113; Cullen to Monsell, 11 Apr. 1855: NLI, MS. 8317, *Monsell Papers*; Cullen to Kirby, 5 May 1856: ICAR, *NC, III,* 2, 1, no. 120; Cullen to Kirby, 15 May 1856: ICAR, *NC, III,* 2, 1, no. 121; Cullen to Kirby, 8 June 1856: ICAR, *NC, III,* 2, 1, no. 123; Cullen to Kirby, 5 Sept. 1856: ICAR, *NC, III,* 2, 1, no. 138; Cullen to Kirby, 30 Sept. 1856: ICAR, *NC, III,* 2, 1, no. 142; Cullen to Kirby, 17 Dec. 1856: ICAR, *NC, III,* 2, 1, no. 155.

11. Cullen to Kirby, 13 Apr. 1856: ICAR, *NC, III,* 2, 1, no. 116; see also Cullen to Kirby, 20 Apr. 1856: ICAR, *NC, III,* 2, 1, no. 117; Cullen to Kirby, 25 Apr. 1856: ICAR, *NC, III,* 2, 1, no. 118; Cullen to Kirby, 5 May 1856: ICAR, *NC, III,* 2, 1, no. 120; Cullen to Kirby, 15 May 1856: ICAR, *NC, III,* 2, 1, no. 121; Cullen to Kirby, 5 Sept. 1856: ICAR, *NC, III,* 2, 1, no. 138; Cullen to Kirby, 17 Dec. 1856: ICAR, *NC, III,* 2, 1, no. 155.

12. Anon. (*Kirby*) to Prop., n.d. (*1856*): ACPF, *SC, Irlanda,* vol. 32, ff. 773, 775; *Nation,* 22 Mar. 1856.

13. Cullen to Prop., 25 Apr. 1856: ACPF, *SC, Irlanda,* vol. 32, f. 786; see also E.D. Steele, 'Cardinal Cullen and Irish Nationality' in *IHS,* vol. xix, no. 75 (*Mar. 1975*): pp. 245–6.

14. Cullen to Kirby, 29 Nov. 1855: ICAR, *NC, III,* 2, 1, no. 86.

15. Cullen to Kirby, 5 May 1856: ICAR, *NC, III,* 2, 1, no. 120.

16. Cullen to Kirby, 31 Jan. 1856: ICAR, *NC, III,* 2, 1, no. 103.

17. *Nation,* 20 Jan. 1856; see also Cullen to Kirby, 21 Jan. 1856: ICAR, *NC, III,* 2, 1, no. 100; Cullen to Kirby, 28 Jan. 1856: ICAR, *NC, III,* 2, 1, no. 102; Moore (*MP, Mayo*), to Maher (*PP, Carlow–Graigue, Rel. Cullen*), 18 Apr. 1856, *Nation,* 19 Apr. 1856; Cullen to Kirby, 20 Apr. 1856: ICAR, *NC, III,* 2, 1, no. 117; Cullen to Kirby, 25 Apr. 1856: ICAR, *NC, III,* 2, 1, no. 118; Moore, op. cit., pp. 250–2.

18. Cullen to Kirby, 25 Oct. 1856: ICAR, *NC, III,* 2, 1, no. 145; see also Cullen to Kirby, 2 Nov. 1856: ICAR, *NC, III,* 2, 1, no. 147.

19. Cullen to Kirby, 29 Dec. 1855: ICAR, *NC, III,* 2, 1, no. 95.

20. Cullen to Kirby, 29 Dec. 1855: ICAR, NC, III, 2, 1, no. 95; Cullen to Prop., 24 Feb. 1856: ACPF, SC, Irlanda, vol. 32, f. 726 (v).

21. Cullen to Prop., 24 Feb. 1856: ACPF, SC, Irlanda, vol. 32, f. 726–7; Prop. to Cullen, 16 May 1856: ACPF, Acta, vol. 221 (1857), f. 47.

22. Cullen to Kirby, 8 June 1856: ICAR, NC, III, 2, 1, no. 123; Cullen to Prop., 26 July 1856: ACPF, SC, Irlanda, vol. 32, f. 879.

23. Cullen to Kirby, 8 June 1856: ICAR, NC, III, 2, 1, no. 123.

24. Cullen to Prop., 26 July 1856: ACPF, SC, Irlanda, vol. 32, f. 879.

25. Lyons (Sec. Cullen), to Kirby, 27 June 1856: ICAR, NC, III, 2, 1, no. 126.

26. Cullen to Kirby, 5 Sept. 1856: ICAR, NC, III, 2, 1, no. 138.

27. Cullen to Kirby, 15 Sept. 1856: ICAR, NC, III, 2, 1, no. 140.

28. Cullen to Kirby, Oct. 1856: ICAR, NC, III, 2, 1, no. 146.

29. Cullen to Kirby, 17 Jan. 1857: ICAR, NC, III, 2, 2, no. 2

30. ibid.

31. 'E però troppo vero che qualche Vescovo e prete invece di pensare a veri interessi della religione amano piuttosto d'occuparsi di alcuni progetti politici che non si realizzeranno mai, e che solamente servono a pascere il popolo di vane speranze, promettendo ad esso d'ottenere dal Parlamento un diritto permanente a'terreni di cui sono gli affittajuoli, cosa a cui il Parlamento non consentirá mai.', Cullen to Prop., 6 Feb. 1857: ACPF, Acta, vol. 221 (1857), f. 122.

32. Cullen to Kirby, 21 Feb. 1857: ICAR, NC, III, 2, 2, no. 9.

33. Cullen to Kirby, 28 Feb. 1857: ICAR, NC, III, 2, 2, no. 10.

34. FJ, 17, 18 Feb. 1857.

35. Cullen to Kirby, 16 Mar. 1857: ICAR, NC, III, 2, 2, no. 12; see also TFP, 13 Mar. 1857.

36. Cullen to Kirby, 16 Mar. 1857: ICAR, NC, III, 2, 2, no. 12.

37. Moore to MacHale (Abp., Tuam), 14 Mar. 1857: NLI, MS. 893, f. 554; Cullen to Kirby, 28 Mar. 1857: ICAR, NC, III, 2, 2, no. 13; TFP, 17 Mar. 1857.

38. Cullen to Kirby, 28 Mar. 1857: ICAR, NC, III, 2, 2, no. 13.

39. 'Spero che in questa diocesi il Clero agirà con moderazione, ajutando a far eleggere soggetti buoni senza pero compromettere là dignita del proprio stato', Cullen to Prop., 7 Mar. 1857: ACPF, Acta, vol. 221 (1857), f. 127 (v).

40. 'In questa occasione avremo i soliti sconvolgimenti, e temo che qualche prete potrà prendere una parte troppo violenta nel movimento generale', Cullen to Prop., 7 Mar. 1857: ACPF, Acta, vol. 221 (1857), f. 127 (v).

41. FJ, 6 Nov. 1855.

42. FJ, 26, 27, 28 Mar. 1857.

43. FJ, 28 Mar. 4 Apr. 1857.

44. FJ, 26 Mar. 1857.

45. Cullen to Kirby, 28 Mar. 1857: ICAR, NC, III, 2, 2, no. 13.

46. DE, 25 Mar. 1857.

47. FJ, 21 Mar. 1857.

48. DE, 1 Apr. 1857.

49. Cullen to Kirby, 26 Feb. 1857: ICAR, NC, III, 2, 2, no. 19; Cullen to Prop., 21 Aug. 1857: ACPF, SC, Irlanda, vol. 33, f. 408 (v); Anon (Kirby) to Prop., n.d. (1857): ACPF, SC, Irlanda, vol. 33, f. 384; see also LR, 3, 24 Mar. 1857; FJ, 6 Apr. 1857; TFP, 7 Apr. 1857.

50. FJ, 6 Apr. 1857; Anon. (Kirby) to Prop., n.d. (1857): ACPF, SC, Irlanda, vol. 33, f. 384; see also Cullen to Prop., 21 Aug. 1857: ACPF, SC, Irlanda, vol. 33, f. 409.

51. FJ, 6, 11 Apr. 1857.

52. Blake (MP, Galway borough) to Moore, 25 Mar. 1857: NLI, MS. 894, f. 565.

53. Cullen to Kirby, 14 Apr. 1857: ICAR, NC,, III, 2, 2, no. 15; see also Cullen to Kirby, 25 Apr. 1857: ICAR, NC, III, 2, 2, no. 17; Cullen to Prop., 29 Mar. 1857: ACPF, Acta, vol. 221 (1857), f. 134 (v).

54. Murray (CC, Shane Hill) to Murray (Sec. Cullen), 14 Apr. 1857: ACPF, SC, Irlanda, vol. 33, ff. 24 (v) –5; Cullen to Kirby, 14 Apr. 1857: ICAR, NC, III, 2, 2, no. 15; Cullen to Kirby, 25 Apr. 1857: ICAR, NC, III, 2, 2, no. 17; Cullen to Kirby, 26 Feb. 1857: ICAR, NC, III, 2, 2, no. 19; Cullen to Kirby, 21 May 1857: ICAR, NC, III, 2, 2, no. 25; Cullen to Kirby, 28 May 1857: ICAR, NC, III, 2, 2, no. 28; see also Cullen to Prop., 29 May 1857: ACPF, SC, Irlanda, vol. 33, f. 294; Drogheda elect. pet., H.C. 1857 (sess. 2), vol. 6. pp. 26–7; Mayo elect. pet., H.C. 1857 (sess. 2), vol. 7, pp. 399, 415.

55. CE, 30 Mar. 1857.

56. See Cullen to Prop., 29 May 1857: ACPF, *SC, Irlanda*, vol. 33, f. 294; Cullen to Kirby, 14 Apr. 1857: ICAR, *NC, III*, 2, 2, no. 15; Anon. (*Kirby*) to Prop., n.d. (*1857*): ACPF, *SC, Irlanda*, vol. 33, f. 384; *Mayo elect. pet.*, H.C. (*sess. 2*), 1857, vol. 7, p. 399.

57. *WG*, 9 Apr. 1857.

58. *FJ*, 4, 11 Apr. 1857; CT, 4 Apr. 1857.

59. *LR*, 3, 24 Mar. 1857; *FJ*, 6 Apr. 1857; *TFP*, 7 Apr. 1857; see also Cullen to Prop., 21 July 1857: ACPF, *SC, Irlanda*, vol. 33, f. 383; Cullen to Kirby, 12 July 1857: ICAR, *NC, III*, 2, 2, no. 33; Cullen to Prop., 21 Aug. 1857: ACPF, *SC, Irlanda*, vol. 33, ff 408 (*v*) 9; *Mayo elect. pet.*, H.C. 1857 (*sess. 2*), vol. 7, pp. 399, 415, 516.

60. Cullen to Kirby, 28 Mar. 1857: ICAR, *NC, III*, 2, 2, no. 13; Cullen to Kirby, 14 Apr. 1857: ICAR, *NC, III*, 2, 2, no. 15; Cullen to Kirby, 25 Apr. 1857: ICAR, *NC, III*, 2, 2, no. 17; Cullen to Prop., n.d. (*1857*): ACPF, *SC, Irlanda*, vol. 33, f. 232.

61. Cullen to Kirby, 14 Apr. 1857: ICAR, *NC, III*, 2, 2, no. 15.

62. Cullen to Prop., n.d. (*1857*): ACPF, *SC, Irlanda*, vol. 33, f. 232; Cullen to Kirby, 25 Apr. 1857: ICAR, *NC, III*, 2, 2, no. 17.

63. Cullen to Kirby, 25 Apr. 1857: ICAR, *NC, III*, 2, 2, no. 17.

64. Cullen to Kirby n.d. (*1857*): ICAR, *NC, III*, 2, 2, no. 14.

65. 'Circular to the Clergy of Dublin Archdiocese', 25 Mar. 1857: DDA, 43\3; ibid: ACPF, *SC, Irlanda*, vol. 33, f. 233.

66. 'Circular to the Clergy of Dublin Archdiocese', 25 Mar. 1857: DDA, 43\3; ibid: ACPF, *SC, Irlanda*, vol. 33 f. 233; see also Cullen to Kirby, n.d. (*1857*): ICAR, *NC, III*, 2, 2, no. 14.

67. 'Circular to the Clergy of Dublin Archdiocese', 25 Mar. 1857: DDA, 43\3; ibid: ACPF, *SC, Irlanda*, vol. 33, f. 233.

68. ibid.

69. ibid.

70. ibid.

71. ibid.

72. ibid.

73. 'Non mi sono dichiarato per alcun partito ma ho cercato di persuadere i cattolici che nella scelta dei Membri del Parlamento devono pensare alle esigenze della carità e alla preservazione della religione', Cullen to Prop., 29 Mar. 1857: ACPF, *Acta*, vol. 221 (*1857*), f. 134 (*v*).

74. Cullen to Kirby, 28 Mar. 1857: ICAR, *NC, III*, 2, 2, no. 13.

75. *Nation*, 6 Dec. 1856.

76. Vaughan (*Bp., Killaloe*) to Cullen, 22 Feb. 1857: DDA, 339\5; O'Brien (*Bp., Waterford*) to Cullen, 2 Mar. 1857: DDA, 339\5; O'Brien to Cullen, 8 Mar. 1857: DDA, 339\5; O'Brien to Cullen, 18 Mar. 1857: DDA, 339\5; Dixon (*Abp., Armagh*) to Cullen, 5 Aug. 1857: DDA, 339\5.

77. *FJ*, 18 Apr. 1857, *Nation*, 18 Apr. 1857.

78. Cullen to Kirby, 28 May 1857: ICAR, *NC, III*, 2, 2, no. 28.

79. *FJ*, 18 Apr. 1857, DEM, 22 Apr. 1857, gives the party 12 seats; DEP, 21 Apr. 1857 gives it 14; *Tablet*, 18 Apr. 1857 gives it 16; *Nation*, 18 Apr. 1857 gives it 18.

80. Cullen to Kirby, 25 Apr. 1857: ICAR, *NC, III*, 2, 2, no. 17; see also Cullen to Kirby, 12 July 1857: ICAR, *NC, III*, 2, 2, no. 33; Cullen to Kirby, 5 May 1857: ICAR, *NC, III*, 2, 2, no. 21.

81. *Mayo elect. pet.*, H.C. 1857 (*sess. 2*), vol. 7; Cullen to Prop., 21 Aug. 1857: ACPF, *SC, Irlanda*, vol. 33, f. 409 (*v*); see also Cullen to Prop., 29 May 1857: ACPF, *SC, Irlanda*, vol. 33, f. 294.

82. Cullen to Kirby, 21 May 1857: ICAR, *NC, III*, 2, 2, no. 25.

83. Cullen to Kirby, 21 May 1857: ICAR, *NC, III*, 2, 2, no. 25; see also Cullen to Prop., 29 May 1857: ACPF, *SC, Irlanda*, vol. 33, f. 294; Cullen to Kirby, 5 July 1857: ICAR, *NC, III*, 2, 2, no. 30; Cullen to Kirby, 8 July 1857: ICAR, *NC, III*, 2, 2, no. 32; Cullen to Kirby, 12 July 1857: ICAR, *NC, III*, 2, 2, no. 33; Cullen to Prop., 21 July 1857: ACPF, *SC, Irlanda*, vol. 33, f. 383; Cullen to Kirby, 22 July 1857: ICAR, *NC, III*, 2, 2, no. 35; Cullen to Kirby, 27 July 1857: ICAR, *NC, III*, 2, 2, no. 36; Cullen to Prop., 21 Aug. 1857: ACPF, *SC, Irlanda*, vol. 33, f. 410.

84. 'i preti coll'immischiarsi con troppa violenza nelle cose politiche e col trattarle dall'Altare, non fanno altro che distruggere la propria influenza anche coi Cattolici ed attirarsi un mondo di guai. Mentre si cercava d'ottenere la Emancipazione de' Cattolici, tutti erano d'accordo, clero e laici, e se si commetteva dal clero qualche violenza si tollerava: ma adesso quando si trattano questioni libere sulle quali sono divisi i Cattolici ed anche i preti medesimi,

un parroco ed altro prete non può toccarla nella Chiesa, senza offendere molti della sua greggia. In Mayo sono persuaso, che per molti anni non si scorderanno le dissensioni teste eccitate tra il clero e il popolo, e non so come i preti e i laici potranno amministrare o ricevere i sacramenti dopo che gli uni hanno insultato o strapazzato gli altri', Cullen to Prop., 21 Aug. 1857: ACPF, *SC, Irlanda*, vol. 33, f. 408 *(v)*.

85. Cullen to Kirby, 21 May 1857: ICAR, *NC, III*, 2, 2, no. 25; see also Cullen to Prop., 29 May 1857: ACPF, *SC, Irlanda*, vol. 33, f. 294; Cullen to Prop., 21 July 1857: ACPF, *SC, Irlanda*, vol. 33, f. 383; Cullen to Kirby, 12 July 1857: ICAR, *NC, III*, 2, 2, no. 33; Cullen to Kirby, 22 July 1857: ICAR, *NC, III*, 2, 2, no. 35; Cullen to Kirby, 27 July 1857: ICAR, *NC, III*, 2, 2, no. 36; Cullen to Prop., 21 Aug. 1857: ACPF, *SC, Irlanda*, vol. 33, f. 410.

86. 'Forse impareranno dal parlamento, ciò che non hanno voluto apprendere dalle istruzioni della S. Sede', Cullen to Prop., 21 July 1857: ACPF, *SC, Irlanda*, vol. 33, f. 383.

87. 'se non si fa qualche passo per moderare quei preti violenti che calpestano le regole gia fatte, verrà ben presto il momento in cui il Parlamento cercherà di spogliare il clero d'ogni influenza, e farà leggi assai stringenti per impedirlo dal prendere alcuna parte nell'elezione', Cullen to Prop., 21 July 1857: ACPF, *SC, Irlanda*, vol. 33, f. 383; see also Cullen to Kirby, 21 May 1857: ICAR, *NC, III*, 2, 2, no. 25; Anon. (*Kirby*) to Prop., n.d. (*1857*): ACPF, *SC, Irlanda*, vol. 33, f. 384 *(v)*; Cullen to Prop., 21 Aug. 1857: ACPF, *SC, Irlanda*, vol. 33, f. 410; Cullen to Kirby, 27 July 1857: ICAR, *NC, III*, 2, 2, no. 36.

88. The Corrupt Practices Act, 1858 (*21 and 22 Vict., c. 87*).

89. Cullen to Kirby, 6 Dec. 1857: ICAR, *NC, III*, 2, 2, no. 52; see also Cullen to Kirby, 22 Dec. 1857: ICAR, *NC, III*, 2, 2, no. 56; Cullen to Kirby, 29 Dec. 1857: ICAR, *NC, III*, 2, 2, no. 57.

90. Cullen to Prop., 20 Mar. 1858: ACPF, *SC, Irlanda*, vol. 33, f. 635; Cullen to Kirby, 28 Mar. 1858: ICAR, *NC, III*, 2, 2, no. 67.

91. Cullen to Kirby, 5 Feb. 1858: ICAR, *NC, III*, 2, 2, no. 61; *Mayo elect. pet.*, H.C. 1857 (*sess. 2*), vol. 7, pp. 399, 415, 516, 614.

92. Cullen to Kirby, 5 Feb. 1858: ICAR, *NC, III*, 2, 2, no. 61; Cullen to Kirby, 13 Feb. 1858: ICAR, *NC, III*, 2, 2, no. 63; Cullen to Kirby, 26 Feb. 1858: ICAR, *NC, III*, 2, 2, no. 64.

93. Cullen to Kirby, 26 Feb. 1858: ICAR, *NC, III*, 2, 2, no. 64.

94. *Parl. Deb.* ser. 3, cl, 2015.

95. In 1861 the proportion was 28.4 per cent: 'Return stating the numbers and religious denominations of all the soldiers in Her Majesty's land and marine forces', H.C. 1864 (*382*), xxxv.

96. *CE*, 6 Oct. 1858.

97. *CE*, 21 Mar. 1859.

98. Cullen to Kirby, 13 Feb. 1858: ICAR, *NC, III*, 2, 2, no. 63.

99. *MN*, 12 May 1858.

100. Anon. (*Cullen*) to Anon. (*Kirby*), 27 Mar. 1858: ICAR, *NC, III*, 2, 2, no. 66.

101. ibid.

102. Cullen to Kirby, 22 July 1857: ICAR, *NC, III*, 2, 2, no. 35; Cullen to Kirby, 27 July 1857: ICAR, *NC, III*, 2, 2, no. 36.

103. Cullen to Kirby, 22 Dec. 1857: ICAR, *NC, III*, 2, 2, no. 56.

104. Cullen to Kirby, 19 May 1858: ICAR, *NC, III*, 2, 2, no. 76.

105. Anon. (*Cullen*) to Kirby, 27 June 1858: ICAR, *NC, III*, 2, 2, no. 80.

106. ibid.

107. Lyons to Kirby, 1 July 1858: ICAR, *NC, III*, 2, 2, no. 82; Anon. (*Kirby*) to Prop., n.d. (*1858*): ACPF, *SC, Irlanda*, vol. 33, f. 742.

108. Cullen to Kirby, 6 July 1858: ICAR, *NC, III*, 2, 2, no. 85.

109. Cullen to Kirby, 15 July 1858: ICAR, *NC, III*, 2, 2, no. 86.

110. Cullen to Kirby, 24 July 1858: ICAR, *NC, III*, 2, 2, no. 87.

111. Cullen to Kirby, 13 Aug. 1858: ICAR, *NC, III*, 2, 2, no. 92; Cullen to Kirby, 31 Aug. 1858: ICAR, *NC, III*, 2, 2, no. 95.

112. Cullen to Kirby, 5 Aug. 1858: ICAR, *NC, III*, 2, 2, no. 90; Talbot (*Papal Chamberlain*) to Prop., 12 Aug. 1858: ACPF, *SC, Irlanda*, vol. 33, f. 756 *(v)*.

113. Lyons to Kirby, 14 Aug. 1858: ICAR, *NC, III*, 2, 2, no. 93.

114. Cullen to Kirby, 24 Sept. 1858: ICAR, *NC, III*, 2, 2, no. 101; Cullen to Prop., 25 Sept. 1858: ACPF, *SC, Irlanda*, vol. 33 f. 780; Cullen to Kirby, 6 Oct. 1858: ICAR, *NC, III*, 2, 2, no. 102.

115. *Nation,* 25 Mar. 1859, *Tablet,* 2, 9 Apr. 1859, CE, 2 May 1859.

116. Detective Report, 18 Aug. 1859: NLI, MS. 7636, *Larcom Papers.*

117. K.T. Hoppen, 'Tories, Catholics and the General Election of 1859', *Historical Journal,* vol. 13, (1970), pp. 48–67; E.R. Norman, *The Catholic Church and Ireland in the Age of Rebellion,* London, 1965, pp. 37–8.

118. *FJ,* 21 May 1859.

119. Cullen to Kirby, 19 May 1859: ICAR, *NC, III,* 2, 2, no. 115; Cullen to Kirby, 25 May 1859: ICAR, *NC, III,* 2, 2, no. 116a; Cullen to Kirby, 27 May 1859: ICAR, *NC, III,* 2, 2, no. 116b.

120. See Cullen to Kirby, 29 May 1859: ICAR, *NC, III,* 2, no. 117; Cullen to Kirby, 3 June 1859: ICAR, *NC, III,* 2, 2, no. 119; Cullen to Monsell, 14 June 1859: NLI, MS. 8317, *Monsell Papers;* see also Dixon to Wiseman (*Abp. Westminster*) 7 May 1859: WDA, W3\36, no. 55; Anon. (*Kirby*) to Prop., 5 July 1859: ACPF, *SC, Irlanda,* vol. 33, f. 928.

Chapter Eight

1. Cullen to Kirby (*Rec. Irish Coll., Rome*) 31 Oct. 1861: ICAR, *NC, III,* 2, 3, no. 171; see also Cullen to Prop., 16 Nov. 1861: ACPF, *SC, Irlanda,* vol. 34, ff. 190–2.

2. ibid.

3. Cullen to Prop., 16 Nov. 1861: ACPF, *SC, Irlanda,* vol. 34, ff. 190–2; Cullen to Kirby, 10 Dec. 1861: ICAR, *NC, III,*, 2, 3, no. 178.

4. Cullen to Kirby, 5 Apr. 1861: ICAR, *NC, III,* 2, 3, no. 143.

5. W. D'Arcy, *The Fenian Movement in the United States,* Washington, 1947, p. 5.

6. Cullen to Kirby, n.d. (*Apr. 1864*): ACPF, *SC, Irlanda,* vol 35, f. 47; Cullen to Prop., 1 Apr. 1864: ACPF, *SC, Irlanda,* vol. 35, f. 43.

7. J. Denieffe, *A Personal Narrative of the Irish Revolutionary Brotherhood,* New York, 1904, p. 3.

8. WFJ, 13 Oct. 1882; see also ibid., 1, 8 Dec. 1883.

9. WFJ, 17 Nov. 1883.

10. WFJ, 9 Feb. 1884; R.V. Comerford, *The Fenians in Context, Irish Politics and Society 1848–82,* Dublin, 1985, p. 40.

11. Denieffe, op. cit., pp. 156–7.

12. J. O'Leary, *Recollections of Fenians and Fenianism,* London, 1896, vol. 2, p. 81. Denieffe, op. cit., p. 22.

13. Moran, op. cit., vol. 1, p. 576.

14. IP, 26 Mar. 1864, 16 Aug. 1865; O'Leary, op. cit., vol. 1, p. 123.

15. C. Townshend, *Political Violence in Ireland: Government and Resistence since 1848,* Oxford, 1983, p. 25.

16. *Irishman,* 8 Jan., 12 Mar. 1859.

17. A.M. Sullivan, op. cit., p. 36.

18. CJ, 14 Mar. 1859.

19. O'Sullivan (*PP, Kenmare*) to Naas (*Lord Lieut.*) 5 Oct. 1858, in C.J. Rutherford, *The Fenian Conspiracy,* London, 1877, vol. 1, p. 118.

20. DA, 5 Mar. 1859.

21. R.R. Green, 'The Beginnings of Fenianism': T.W. Moody, *The Fenian Movement,* Cork, 1968, pp. 17–18.

22. CE, 10 Dec. 1858; WFJ, 9 Feb. 1884.

23. CJ, 14 Mar. 1859; CE, 14 Mar. 1859.

24. *Cork Constitution,* 4 Nov. 1858; WFJ, 3 Nov. 1883.

25. WFJ, 3 Mar. 1859.

26. Rutherford, op. cit., pp. 62–5.

27. *Cork Constitution,* 16, 29 Nov. 1858.

28. Ryan, op. cit., p. 160; Denieffe, op. cit., p. 46.

29. D'Arcy, op. cit., pp. 25, 27, 52.

30. Cullen to Kirby, 3 Feb. 1860: ICAR, *NC, III,* 2, 3, no. 8; Cullen to Kirby, n.d. (*Feb. 1860*): ICAR, *NC, III,* 2, 3, no. 14.

31. Cullen to Kirby, 3 Feb. 1860: ICAR, *NC, III,* 2, 3, no. 8; Cullen to Kirby, 15 Feb. 1861: ICAR, *NC, III,* 2, 3, no. 133.

32. Cullen to Kirby, 3 Feb. 1860: ICAR, *NC, III,* 2, 3, no. 8; Cullen to Kirby, n.d. (*Feb. 1860*): ICAR, *NC, III,* 2, 3, no. 14; Cullen to Monsell (*MP, Limerick co.*) 14 June 1859: NLI, MS. 8317 (3), *Monsell Papers.*

33. Cullen to Kirby, 7 Dec. 1860: ICAR, *NC, III,* 2, 3, no. 110; Cullen to Kirby, 3 Feb. 1860: ICAR, *NC, III,* 2, 3, no. 8; Cullen to Kirby, n.d. (*Feb. 1860*): ICAR, *NC, III,* 2, 3, no. 14; Cullen to Kirby, 1 May 1860: ICAR, *NC, III,* 2, 3, no. 38; Cullen to Kirby, 15 Feb. 1861: ICAR, *NC, III,* 2, 3, no. 133; Cullen to Kirby, 5 Apr. 1861: ICAR, *NC, III,* 2, 3, no. 143.

34. FJ, 9 Feb. 1860.

35. FJ, 5 Dec. 1860, 2, 7 Jan. 1861; Cullen to Kirby, 15 Feb. 1861: ICAR, *NC, III,* 2, 3, no. 133; Sullivan, op. cit., pp. 242–3; Moore, op. cit., pp. 275–80; ICD, 1862, p. 211.

36. Cullen to Kirby, Mar. 1860: ICAR, *NC, III,* 2, 3, no. 30; Cullen to Kirby, 27 Apr. 1860:

ICAR, *NC, III*, 2, 3, no. 34; Cullen to Kirby, 19 Oct. 1860: ICAR, *NC, III*, 2, 3, no. 96; Cullen to Kirby, 7 Dec. 1860: ICAR, *NC, III*, 2, 3, no. 110; Cullen to Kirby, 21 Dec. 1860: ICAR, *NC, III*, 2, 3, no. 117; Cullen to Prop., 9 Feb. 1861: ACPF, *SC, Irlanda*, vol. 34, f. 33 (*v*); Cullen to Kirby, 15 Feb. 1861: ICAR, *NC, III*, 2, 3, no. 133; Cullen to Kirby, n.d. (*Mar. 1861*): ICAR, *NC, III*, 2, 3, no. 140; Cullen to Kirby, 5 Apr. 1861: ICAR, *NC, III*, 2, 3, no. 143; Cullen to Kirby, 9 Apr. 1861: ICAR, *NC, III*, 2, 3, no. 144; Cullen to Kirby, 1 May 1861: ICAR, *NC, III*, 2, 3, no. 151; Cullen to Kirby, n.d. (*May 1861*): ICAR, *NC, III*, 2, 3, no. 153; Cullen to Talbot (*Papal Chamberlain*), 3 Nov. 1861: VECAR, *Talbot Papers*, no. 1574.

37. *Nation*, 2 May 1863.

38. Cullen to Kirby, 19 Oct. 1860: ICAR, *NC, III*, 2, 3, no. 96.

39. Cullen to Kirby, 9 Apr. 1861: ICAR, *NC, III*, 2, 3, no. 144.

40. Cullen to Kirby, n.d. (*May 1861*): ICAR, *NC, III*, 2, 3, no. 153; Cullen to Kirby, 28 May 1861: ICAR, *NC, III*, 2, 3, no. 154.

41. Cullen to Kirby, 3 May 1861: ICAR, *NC, III*, 2, 3, no. 163.

42. Cullen to Kirby, 7 June 1861: ICAR, *NC, III*, 2, 3, no. 155.

43. Cullen to Monsell, 8 July 1861: NLI, MS. 8317, (*3*), *Monsell Papers*.

44. Cullen to Kirby, 15 Feb. 1861: ICAR, *NC, III*, 2, 3, no. 133.

45. Cullen to Kirby, 5 Apr. 1861: ICAR, *NC, III*, 2, 3, no. 143; see also Cullen to Kirby, 15 Feb. 1861: ICAR, *NC, III*, 2, 3, no. 133.

46. Cullen to Kirby, 5 Apr. 1861: ICAR, *NC, III*, 2, 3, no. 143.

47. ibid.

48. ibid.

49. Moran, op. cit., pp. 830–56; *FJ*, 24 Apr. 1862.

50. Moran, op. cit., p. 839.

51. Cullen to Kirby, 5 Apr. 1861: ICAR, *NC, III*, 2, 3, no. 143.

52. Cullen to Kirby, 31 Oct. 1861: ICAR, *NC, III*, 2, 3, no. 171; see also Cullen to Prop, 16 Nov. 1861: ACPF, *SC, Irlanda*, vol. 34, f. 190.

53. Cullen to Prop., 16 Nov. 1861: ACPF, *SC, Irlanda*, vol. 34, f. 190 (*v*).

54. 'Alcuni matti americani ed irlandesi', Cullen to Prop., 16 Nov. 1861: ACPF, *SC, Irlanda*, vol. 34, f. 190 (*v*); see also Cullen to Kirby, 10 Dec. 1861: ICAR, *NC, III*, 2, 3, no. 178; Cullen to Prop., 1 Apr. 1864: ACPF, *SC, Irlanda*, vol. 35, f. 43.

55. Murray (*Sec. Cullen*) to Kirby, 8 Nov. 1861: ICAR, *NC, III*, 2, 3, no. 173; Cullen to Prop., 16 Nov. 1861: ACPF, *SC, Irlanda*, vol. 34, f. 190 (*v*); Cullen to Prop., 1 Apr. 1864: ACPF, *SC, Irlanda*, vol. 35, f. 43.

56. Murray to Kirby, 8 Nov. 1861: ICAR, *NC, III*, 2, 3, no. 173; Cullen to Prop., 16 Nov. 1861: ACPF, *SC, Irlanda*, vol. 34, f. 190 (*v*).

57. Cullen to Kirby, 31 Oct. 1861: ICAR, *NC, III*, 2, 3, no. 171; Cullen to Kirby, 11 Oct. 1862: ICAR, *NC, III*, 3, 1, no. 56; Cullen to Prop., 26 Oct. 1863: ACPF, *SC, Irlanda*, vol. 35, f. 121 (*v*); Anon. (*Moran, Vice Rec. Coll., Rome, Rel. Cullen*) to Prop., n.d.: ACPF, *SC, Irlanda*, vol. 35, f. 51 (*v*).

58. Cullen to Prop., 16 Nov. 1861: ACPF, *SC, Irlanda*, vol. 34, f. 190 (*v*); Cullen to Kirby, 10 Dec. 1861: ICAR, *NC, III*, 2, 3, no. 178.

59. Cullen to Kirby, 10 Dec. 1861: ICAR, *NC, III*, 2, 3, no. 178.

60. Cullen to Kirby, 31 Oct. 1861: ICAR, *NC, III*, 2, 3, no. 171; see also Kirby, 8 Nov. 1861: ICAR, *NC, III*, 2, 3, no. 173.

61. Cullen to Kirby, 31 Oct. 1861: ICAR, *NC, III*, 2, 3, no. 171; Murray to Kirby, 8 Nov. 1861: ICAR, *NC, III*, 2, 3, no. 173; Cullen to Prop., 16 Nov. 1861: ACPF, *SC, Irlanda*, vol. 34, ff. 190 (*v*) –1; Cullen to Kirby, 10 Dec. 1861: ICAR, *NC, III*, 2, 3, no. 178.

62. MacManus (*funeral committ.*) to Cullen, 15 Oct. 1861: DDA, 340\2, no. 122; Ryan (*funeral committ.*) to Cullen, 16 Oct. 1861: DDA, 340\2, no. 122; McManus to Cullen, Oct. 1861: DDA, 340\2, no. 122; Cullen to Kirby, 31 Oct. 1861: ICAR, *NC, III*, 2, 3, no. 171; see also Cullen to Prop. 16 Nov. 1861: ACPF, *SC, Irlanda*, vol. 34, f. 191.

63. Murray to Ryan, 18 Oct. 1861: DDA, 334\1, (*iv*), no. 6; Cullen to Kirby, 31 Oct. 1861: ICAR, *NC, III*, 2, 3, no. 171; Murray to Kirby, 8 Nov. 1861: ICAR, *NC, III*, 2, 3, no. 173; Cullen to Prop., 16 Nov. 1861: ACPF, *SC, Irlanda*, vol. 34, f. 191.

64. Cullen to Kirby, 31 Oct. 1861: ICAR, *NC, III*, 2, 3, no. 171.

65. ibid.

66. Murray to Ryan, 18 Oct. 1861: DDA, 334\1 (*iv*), no. 6; Cullen to Kirby, 31 Oct. 1861: ICAR, *NC, III*, 2, 3, no. 171; Cullen

to Prop., 16 Nov. 1861: ACPF, *SC, Irlanda*, vol. 34, f. 191.

67. McManus to Cullen, 19 Oct. 1861: DDA, 340\2, no. 123; McManus to Cullen, 21 Oct. 1861: DDA, 340\2, no. 124; Cullen to Prop., 16 Nov. 1861: ACPF, *SC, Irlanda*, vol. 34, f. 191.

68. Murray to Ryan, 26 Oct. 1861: DDA, 334\1, *(iv)*, no. 7; Cullen to Kirby, 31 Oct. 1861: ICAR, *NC, III*, 2, 3, no. 171; Cullen to Kirby, 12 Nov. 1861: ICAR, *NC, III*, 2, 3, no. 174; Gillooly (*Bp., Elphin*) to Cullen, 16 Nov. 1861: DDA, 334\1, *(i)*, no. 111; Cullen to Prop., 16 Nov. 1861: ACPF, *SC, Irlanda*, vol. 34, f. 191; Cullen to Kirby, 10 Dec. 1861: ICAR, *NC, III*, 2, 3, no. 178.

69. Cullen to Kirby, 31 Oct. 1861: ICAR, *NC, III*, 2, 3, no. 171; Cullen to Prop., 16 Nov. 1861: ACPF, *SC, Irlanda*, vol. 34, f. 191; O'Brien (*Bp., Waterford*) to Cullen, 11 Apr. 1862: DDA, 340\4, *(ii)*, no. 162.

70. Police Report: SPO, CSO, RP, 1861\8418; Stephens (*Fen.*) to O'Mahony (*Fen.*) n.d. in Ryan, op. cit., p. 176.

71. *FJ*, 6, 10 Nov. 1861.

72. Cullen to Kirby, 10 Dec. 1861: ICAR, *NC, III*, 2, 3, no. 178.

73. Cullen to Kirby, 12 Nov. 1861: ICAR, *NC, III*, 2, 3, no. 174.

74. Cullen to Kirby, 17 Nov. 1861: ICAR, *NC, III*, 2, 3, no. 176.

75. Police Report: SPO, CSO, RP, 1861\8418; *FJ*, 11 Nov. 1861; Cullen to Kirby, 12 Nov. 1861: ICAR, *NC, III*, 2, 3, no. 174;

76. Cullen to Kirby, 12 Nov. 1861: ICAR, *NC, III*, 2, 3, no. 174; Cullen to Prop., 16 Nov. 1861: ACPF, *SC, Irlanda*, vol. 34, f. 191 *(v)*.

77. Cullen to Kirby, 12 Nov. 1861: ICAR, *NC, III*, 2, 3, no. 174; Cullen to Prop., 16 Nov. 1861: ACPF, *SC, Irlanda*, vol. 34, ff. 191 *(v)* −2; Cullen to Prop., 7 Oct. 1862: ACPF, *SC, Irlanda*, vol. 34, f. 532 *(v)*; Cullen to Prop., 1 Apr. 1864: ACPF, *SC, Irlanda*, vol. 35, f. 43.

78. Delany (*Bp., Cork*) to Murray, 10 Nov. 1861: DDA, 340\1, no. 150; see also Cullen to Prop., 16 Nov. 1861: ACPF, *SC, Irlanda*, vol. 34, ff. 191 *(v)* −2; Cullen to Kirby, 17 Nov. 1861: ICAR, *NC, III*, 2, 3, no. 176; Cullen to Prop., 29 Nov. 1861: ACPF, *SC, Irlanda*, vol. 34, f. 208; Anon. (*Moran*) to Prop., 16 Mar. 1864: ACPF, *SC, Irlanda*, vol. 35, f. 51 *(v)*.

79. *FJ*, 11 Nov. 1861.

80. Cullen to Prop., 16 Nov. 1861: ACPF, *SC, Irlanda*, vol. 34, f. 191 *(v)*; Cullen to Prop., 21 June 1863: ACPF, *SC, Irlanda*, vol. 35, f. 134; Anon. (*Kirby*) to Prop., n.d.: ACPF, *SC, Irlanda*, vol. 35, f. 56.

81. Cullen to Kirby, 3 Mar. 1860: ICAR, *NC, III*, 2, 3, no. 19.

82. Delany to Murray, 10 Nov. 1861: DDA, 340\1, no. 150; Cullen to Kirby, 12 Nov. 1861: ICAR, *NC, III*, 2, 3, no. 174; Cullen to Prop., 16 Nov. 1861: ACPF, *SC, Irlanda*, vol. 34, f. 191 *(v)*; Cullen to Kirby 17 Nov. 1861: ICAR, *NC, III*, 2, 3, no. 176; Cullen to Prop., 21 June 1863: ACPF, *SC, Irlanda*, vol. 35, f. 134; Anon. (*Cullen*) to Prop., n.d.: ACPF, *SC, Irlanda*, vol. 35, f. 92 *(v)*.

83. *FJ*, 6 Nov. 1861; Murray to Kirby, 8 Nov. 1861: ICAR, *NC, III*, 2, 3, no. 173; Cullen to Kirby, 12 Nov. 1861: ICAR, *NC, III*, 2, 3, no. 174; Cullen to Prop., 16 Nov. 1861: ACPF, *SC, Irlanda*, vol. 34, f. 191 *(v)*; Cullen to Kirby, 17 Nov. 1861: ICAR, *NC, III*, 2, 3, no. 176.

84. Cullen to Kirby, 12 Nov. 1861: ICAR, *NC, III*, 2, 3, no. 174.

85. Murray to Kirby, 8 Nov. 1861: ICAR, *NC, III*, 2, 3, no. 173.

86. *FJ*, 6 Nov. 1861; Delany to Murray, 10 Nov. 1861: DDA, 340\1, no. 150; Furlong (*Bp., Ferns*) to Cullen, 11 Nov. 1861: DDA, 334\1, *(i)*, no. 105; Gillooly to Cullen, 16 Nov. 1861: DDA, 334\1, *(i)*, no. 111.

87. Cullen to Kirby, 12 Nov. 1861: ICAR, *NC, III*, 2, 3, no. 174.

88. Cullen to Kirby, 17 Nov. 1861: ICAR, *NC, III*, 2, 3, no. 176.

89. Cullen to MacHale (*Abp., Tuam*), 9 November 1861: ACPF, *SC, Irlanda*, vol. 34, f. 201. Cullen to Kirby, 12 Nov. 1861: ICAR, *NC, III*, 2, 3, no. 174; Cullen to Prop., 16 Nov. 1861: ACPF, *SC, Irlanda*, vol. 34, f. 191 *(v)*.

90. MacHale to Cullen, 11 Nov. 1861: DDA, 334\1, *(i)*, no. 104; Cullen to Kirby, 12 Nov. 1861: ICAR, *NC, III*, 2, 3, no. 174; Cullen to Prop., 16 Nov. 1861: ACPF, *SC, Irlanda*, vol. 34, f. 192; Cullen to Kirby, 27 Nov. 1861: ACPF, *SC, Irlanda*, vol. 34, ff. 197−201.

91. Cullen to Prop., 16 Nov. 1861: ACPF, *SC, Irlanda*, vol. 34, f. 192; Cullen to Kirby, 17 Nov. 1861: ICAR, *NC, III*, 2, 3, no. 176.

92. Furlong to Cullen, 7 Nov. 1861: DDA, 334\1, (i), no. 102; Dixon (Abp., Armagh) to Cullen, 7 Nov. 1861: DDA, 334\1, (i), no. 103; Furlong to Cullen, 11 Nov. 1861: DDA, 334\1, no. 105; Cullen to Kirby, 12 Nov. 1861: ICAR, NC, III, 2, 3, no 174; Mansfield (lay corr.) to Cullen, 12 Nov. 1861: DDA, 340\2, no. 131; MacNally (Bp., Clogher) to Cullen, 13 Nov. 1861: DDA, 334\1 (i), no. 107; Furlong to Cullen, 15 Nov. 1861: DDA, 334\1, (i), no. 110; Gillooly to Cullen, 16 Nov. 1861: DDA, 334\1, no. 111; Cullen to Kirby 17 Nov. 1861: ICAR, NC, III, 2, 3, no. 176; Stokes (lay corr.) to Cullen, 17 Nov. 1861: DDA, 340\2, no. 135; More O'Ferrall (MP, Kildare co.) to Cullen, 1 Dec. 1861: DDA, 340\2, no. 144; Cullen to Kirby, 27 Nov. 1861: ACPF, SC, Irlanda, vol. 34, f. 197; Redmond (PP, Arklow) to Cullen, 29 Sept. 1865: DDA, 327\2, (iii), no. 20.

93. Cullen to Kirby, 12 Nov. 1861: ICAR, NC, III, 2, 3, no. 174; Cullen to Prop., 16 Nov. 1861: ACPF, SC, Irlanda, vol. 34, ff. 190–2; Cullen to Kirby, 17 Nov. 1861: ICAR, NC, III, 2, 3, no. 176; Cullen to Kirby, 27 Nov. 1861: ACPF, SC, Irlanda, vol. 34, f. 197; Cullen to Kirby, 27 Dec. 1861: ICAR, NC, III, 2, 3, no. 181; Cullen to Kirby, n.d. (Dec. 1861): ICAR, NC, III, 2, 3, no. 182.

94. Cullen to Kirby, 26 November 1861: ICAR, NC, III, 2, 3, no. 177; Cullen to Kirby, n.d. (Dec. 1861): ICAR, NC, III, 2, 3, no. 182; Anon. (Cullen) to Prop., n.d.: ACPF, SC, Irlanda, vol. 35, f. 92.

95. Cullen to Kirby, 26 Nov. 1861: ICAR, NC, III, 2, 3, no. 177; Cullen to Kirby, 27 Nov. 1861: ACPF, SC, Irlanda, vol. 34, f. 197.

96. Cullen to Prop., 5 Dec. 1861: ACPF, SC, Irlanda, vol. 34, f. 210 (v); Cullen to Kirby, 10 Dec. 1861: ICAR, NC, III, 2, 3, no. 178.

97. Cullen to Kirby, 5 Apr. 1861: ICAR, NC, III, 2, 3, no. 143.

98. 'Mi sembra ancora che sia cosa non solamente sciocca di parlare in questo paese di rivoluzione mentre il popolo è così debole e sprovveduto d'armi, ma anche destruttiva della religione', Cullen to Prop., 29 Nov. 1861: ACPF, SC, Irlanda, vol. 34, f. 208; see also Cullen to Kirby, 31 Oct. 1861: ICAR, NC, III, 2, 3, no. 171; Cullen to Prop., 16 Nov. 1861: ACPF, SC, Irlanda, vol. 34, f. 191 (v).

99. Cullen to Prop., 16 Nov. 1861: ACPF, SC, Irlanda, vol. 34, f. 190 (v); Cullen to Prop., 29 Nov. 1861: ACPF, SC, Irlanda, vol. 34, f. 208.

100. Cullen to Prop., 16 Nov. 1861: ACPF, SC, Irlanda, vol. 34, f. 191 (v).

101. ibid

102. Cullen to Kirby, 10 Dec. 1861: ICAR, NC, III, 2, 3, no. 178.

103. Cullen to Kirby, 12 Nov. 1861: ICAR, NC, III, 2, 3, no. 174; Cullen to Prop., 16 Nov. 1861: ACPF, SC, Irlanda, vol. 34, f. 191 (v).

104. Cullen to Prop., 29 Nov. 1861: ACPF, SC, Irlanda, vol. 34, f. 208; Cullen to Kirby, n.d. (Dec. 1861): ICAR, NC, III, 2, 3, no. 179; Cullen to Kirby, 27 Dec. 1861: ICAR, NC, III, 2, 3, no. 181; Moran, op. cit., vol. 1, p. 869; CT, 7 Dec. 1861.

105. 'E meglio soffire i mali attuali, che ingolfarci nei mali infinitamente peggiori della rivoluzione, e dell'incredulita dà cui siamo sinora restati così liberi', Cullen to Prop., 29 Nov. 1861: ACPF, SC, Irlanda, vol. 34, f. 208.

106. Furlong to Cullen, 2 Nov. 1861: DDA, 334\1, (i), no. 100; Furlong to Cullen, 7 Nov. 1861: DDA, 334\1, (i), no. 102; Walshe (Bp., Kildare & Leighlin) to Cullen, 2 Dec. 1861: DDA, 334\1, no. 115; Cullen to Prop., 5 Dec. 1861: ACPF, SC, Irlanda, vol. 34, f. 210 (v); Cullen to Kirby, 27 Dec. 1861: ICAR, NC, III, 2, 3, no. 181; Cullen to Kirby, 17 Jan. 1862: ICAR, NC, III, 3, 1, no. 2; Redmond to Cullen, 9 Mar. 1862: DDA, 340\4, (i), no. 9; Anon. to Cullen, 10 Mar. 1862: DDA, 340\5, no. 42; Redmond to Cullen, 13 Mar. 1862: DDA, 340\4, (i), no. 11; Cullen to Prop., 21 Mar. 1862: ACPF, SC, Irlanda, vol. 34, f. 353 (v); O'Brien to Cullen, 24 Mar. 1862: DDA, 340\4, (ii), no. 160; O'Brien to Cullen, 31 Mar. 1862: DDA, 340\4, (ii), no. 161; O'Brien to Cullen, 11 Apr. 1862: DDA, 340\4, (ii), no. 162; Cullen to Kirby, 15 Apr. 1862: ICAR, NC, III, 3, 1, no. 27; O'Brien to Cullen, 16 Apr. 1862: DDA, 340\4, (ii), no. 163; Redmond to Cullen, 30 Aug. 1862: DDA, 340\4, (i), no. 24; Redmond to Cullen, 11 Oct. 1862: DDA, 340\4, (i), no. 31; Lavelle (PP, Partry) to Cullen, n.d. (1862): DDA, 340\6, no. 72.

107. Cullen to Kirby, 17 Nov. 1861: ICAR, NC, III, 2, 3, no. 176; O'Brien to Cullen,

24 Mar. 1862: DDA, 340\4, *(ii)*, no. 160; O'Brien to Cullen, 31 Mar. 1862: DDA, 340\4, *(ii)*, no. 161; O'Brien to Cullen, 11 Apr. 1862: DDA, 340\4, *(ii)*, no. 162.

108. Cullen to Kirby, 22 Apr. 1862: ICAR, *NC, III*, 3, 1, no. 30; see also Cullen to Kirby, 10 Dec. 1861: ICAR, *NC, III*, 2, 3, no. 178; Cullen to Prop., 28 Feb. 1862: ACPF, *SC, Irlanda*, vol. 35, f. 142; Cullen to Kirby, n.d.: ICAR, *NC, III*, 3, 1, no. 28.

109. Cullen to Kirby, 5 Apr. 1861: ICAR, *NC, III*, 2, 3, no. 143; Cullen to Kirby, 10 Dec. 1861: ICAR, *NC, III*, 2, 3, no. 178; Cullen to Monsell, 8 Jan. 1862: NLI, MS. 8317 *(3)*, *Monsell Papers*; Cullen to Prop., 28 Feb. 1862: ACPF, *SC, Irlanda*, vol. 35, f. 142; Cullen to Prop. 21 Mar. 1862: ACPF, *SC, Irlanda*, vol. 34, f. 353 *(v)*; Cullen to Kirby, 1 Apr. 1862: ICAR, *NC, III*, 3, 1, no. 21; Cullen to Prop., 11 Apr. 1862: ACPF, *SC, Irlanda*, vol. 35, f. 139; Cullen to Kirby, 15 Apr. 1862: ICAR, *NC, III*, 3, 1 no. 27; Anon. (*Kirby*) to Prop. n.d. (*Apr. 1862*): ACPF, *SC, Irlanda*, vol. 34, f. 362; Cullen to Kirby, n.d.: ICAR, *NC, III*, 3, 1, no. 28; Cullen to Kirby, 11 Mar. 1863: ICAR, *NC, III*, 3, 1, no. 77; Cullen to Kirby, 23 Oct. 1863: ACPF, *SC, Irlanda*, vol. 34, f. 873; Cullen to Prop., 8 Apr. 1864: ACPF, *SC, Irlanda*, vol. 34, f. 1166 *(v)*.

110. Cullen to Prop., 16 Nov. 1861: ACPF, *SC, Irlanda*, vol. 34, ff. 190 *(v)* −1; Cullen to Kirby, 29 Nov. 1861: ACPF, *SC, Irlanda*, vol. 34, f. 208; Cullen to Kirby, 10 Dec. 1861: ICAR, *NC, III*, 2, 3, no. 178; Cullen to Kirby, 27 Dec. 1861: ICAR, *NC, III*, 2, 3, no. 181; Cullen to Kirby, 17 Jan. 1862: ICAR, *NC, III*, 3, 1, no. 2; Cullen to Kirby, 28 Jan. 1862: ACPF, *SC, Irlanda*, vol. 35, f. 144 *(v)*; Cullen to Kirby, 21 Feb. 1862: ICAR, *NC, III*, 3, 1, no. 11; Cullen to Prop., 28 Feb. 1862: ACPF, *SC, Irlanda*, vol. 35, ff. 141 *(v)* −2; Cullen to Kirby, 21 Mar. 1862: ICAR, *NC, III*, 3, 1, no. 17; Cullen to Prop., 21 Mar. 1862: ACPF, *SC, Irlanda*, vol. 34, f. 353 *(v)*; Cullen to Kirby, 1 Apr. 1862: ICAR, *NC, III*, 3, 1, no. 21; Cullen to Moran, 4 Apr. 1862: ICAR, *NC, III*, 3, 1, no. 22; Cullen to Kirby, 6 Apr. 1862: ICAR, *NC, III*, 3, 1, no. 23; Cullen to Prop., 11 Apr. 1862: ACPF, *SC, Irlanda*, vol. 35, f. 139; Cullen to Kirby, n.d.: ICAR, *NC, III*, 3, 1, no. 26; Cullen to Kirby, 15 Apr. 1862:

ICAR, *NC, III*, 3, 1, no. 27; Cullen to Kirby, n.d.: ICAR, *NC, III*, 3, 1, no. 28; Cullen to Prop., 13 Mar. 1863: ACPF, *SC, Irlanda*, vol. 34, f. 909 *(v)*; Cullen to Prop., 21 June 1863: ACPF, *SC, Irlanda*, vol. 35, f. 134 *(v)*; Anon. (*Kirby*) to Prop., n.d. (*Apr. 1862*): ACPF, *SC, Irlanda*, vol. 34, f. 362; Anon. (*Kirby*) to Prop., n.d. (*Nov. 1863*): ACPF, *SC, Irlanda*, vol. 35, f. 120; Cullen to Prop., 8 Apr. 1864: ACPF, *SC, Irlanda*, vol. 34, f. 1167; O'Brien to Cullen, 16 Apr. 1862: DDA, 340\4, *(ii)*, no. 163.

111. Cullen to Kirby, 10 Dec. 1861: ICAR, *NC, III*, 2, 3, no. 178; Cullen to Monsell, 8 Jan. 1862: NLI, MS. 8317 *(3)*, *Monsell Papers*; Cullen to Prop., 21 Mar. 1862: ACPF, *SC, Irlanda*, vol. 34, f. 353 *(v)*; Cullen to Moran, 4 Apr. 1862: ICAR, *NC, III*, 3, 1, no. 22; Cullen to Kirby, 15 Apr. 1862: ICAR, *NC, III*, 3, 1, no. 27; Anon. to Cullen, 21 Aug. 1862: DDA, 340\6, no. 18; Cullen to Kirby, 11 Mar. 1863: ICAR, *NC, III*, 3, 1, no. 77.

112. Cullen to Kirby, 21 Feb. 1862: ICAR, *NC, III*, 3, 1, no. 11; Cullen to Kirby, 6 Apr. 1862: ICAR, *NC, III*, 3, 1, no. 23; Cullen to Kirby, n.d.: ICAR, *NC, III*, 3, 1, no. 26; Cullen to Kirby, 15 Apr. 1862: ICAR, *NC, III*, 3, 1, no. 27.

113. Cullen to Kirby, 17 Jan. 1862: ICAR, *NC, III*, 3, 1, no. 2; Cullen to Prop., 29 Nov. 1861: ACPF, *SC, Irlanda*, vol. 34, f. 208; Cullen to Kirby, 28 Jan. 1862: ACPF, *SC, Irlanda*, vol. 35, f. 144 *(v)*; Cullen to Kirby, 21 Feb. 1862: ICAR, *NC, III*, 3, 1, no. 11; Cullen to Prop., 28 Feb. 1862: ACPF, *SC, Irlanda*, vol. 35, f. 142; Cullen to Prop., 21 Mar. 1862: ACPF, *SC, Irlanda*, vol. 34, f. 353 *(v)*; Cullen to Kirby, 1 Apr. 1862: ICAR, *NC, III*, 3, 1, no. 21; Cullen to Kirby, 6 Apr. 1862: ICAR, *NC, III*, 3, 1, no. 23; Cullen to Prop., 11 Apr. 1862: ACPF, *SC, Irlanda*, vol. 35, f. 139; Cullen to Kirby, 15 Apr. 1862: ICAR, *NC, III*, 3, 1, no. 27; Anon. (*Kirby*) to Prop., n.d. (*Apr. 1862*): ACPF, *SC, Irlanda*, vol. 34, f. 362; Cullen to Kirby, n.d.: ICAR, *NC, III*, 3, 1, no. 28; Cullen to Kirby, 24 Mar. 1863: ICAR, *NC, III*, 3, 1, no. 79.

114. Cullen to Kirby, 1 Apr. 1862: ICAR, *NC, III*, 3, 1, no. 21; Cullen to Kirby, n.d.: ICAR, *NC, III*, 3, 1, no. 28; Cullen to Kirby, 10 Dec. 1861: ICAR, *NC, III*, 2, 3, no. 178;

Cullen to Prop., 21 Mar. 1862: ACPF, *SC, Irlanda*, vol. 34, f. 353 *(v)*; Cullen to Prop., 13 Mar. 1863: ACPF, *SC, Irlanda*, vol. 34, f. 909 *(v)*; Cullen to Prop., 9 Sept. 1864: ACPF, *SC, Irlanda*, vol. 34, f. 1325.

115. Cullen to Kirby, 5 Apr. 1861: ICAR, *NC, III*, 2, 3, no. 143.

116. Cullen to Monsell, 8 Jan. 1862: NLI, MS. 8317 (3), *Monsell Papers*; McDonald *(Ad., Dundee)* to Cullen, 15 Feb. 1862: DDA, 340\4, *(ii)*, no. 23; Cullen to Kirby, 21 Feb. 1862: ICAR, *NC, III*, 3, 1, no. 11; Cullen to Prop., 28 Feb. 1862: ACPF, *SC, Irlanda*, vol. 35, f. 141 *(v)*; Goss *(Bp., Liverpool)* to Cullen, 8 Mar. 1862: DDA, 340\3, *(ii)*, no. 5(a); Cullen to Prop., 21 Mar. 1862: ACPF, *SC, Irlanda*, vol. 34, f. 353 *(v)*; Cullen to Kirby, 23 Oct. 1863: ACPF, *SC, Irlanda*, vol. 34, f. 873; Cullen to Kirby, n.d.: ICAR, *NC, III*, 3, 1, no. 26.

117. Cullen to Kirby, 27 Dec. 1861: ICAR, *NC, III*, 2, 3, no. 181; Cullen to Kirby, 21 Feb. 1862: ICAR, *NC, III*, 3, 1, no. 11.

Chapter Nine

1. Cullen to Kirby *(Rec. Irish Coll., Rome)*, 15 Apr. 1862: ICAR, *NC, III*, 3, 1, no. 27; see also Cullen to Monsell *(MP, Limerick co.)*, 8 Jan. 1862: NLI, MS. 8317 (3), *Monsell Papers*; Cullen to Kirby, 23 Oct. 1863: ACPF, *SC, Irlanda*, vol. 34, f. 873 *(v)*.

2. Cullen to Kirby, n.d.: ICAR, *NC, III*, 3, 1, no. 28.

3. Cullen to Kirby, 10 Dec. 1861: ICAR, *NC, III*, 2, 3, no. 178; Cullen to Monsell, 8 Jan. 1862: NLI, MS. 8317 (3), *Monsell Papers*; Cullen to Prop., 21 Mar. 1862: ACPF, *SC, Irlanda*, vol. 34, f. 353 *(v)*; Cullen to Prop., 11 Apr. 1862: ACPF, *SC, Irlanda*, vol. 35, f. 139 *(v)*; Cullen to Kirby, 15 Apr. 1862: ICAR, *NC, III*, 3, 1, no. 27; Cullen to Prop., 8 Apr. 1864: ACPF, *SC, Irlanda*, vol. 34, f. 1167.

4. Cullen to Kirby, 1 Apr. 1862: ICAR, *NC, III*, 3, 1, no. 21.

5. Cullen to Prop., 28 Feb. 1862: ACPF, *SC, Irlanda*, vol. 35, f. 142 *(v)*; Cullen to Prop., 11 Apr. 1862: ACPF, *SC, Irlanda*, vol. 35, f. 139.

6. Moran, op. cit., vol. 1, pp. 863–73; *CT*, 7 Dec. 1861; see also Cullen to Prop., 5 Dec. 1861: ACPF, *SC, Irlanda*, vol. 34, f. 210 *(v)*; Cullen to Kirby, 10 Dec. 1861: ICAR, *NC, III*, 2, 3, no. 178.

7. Cullen to Kirby, 10 Dec. 1861: ICAR, *NC, III*, 2, 3, no. 178; Cullen to Kirby, 27 Dec. 1861: ICAR, *NC, III*, 2, 3, no. 181; Cullen to Kirby, n.d.: ICAR, *NC, III*, 3, 1, no. 28.

8. Moran, op. cit., vol. 1, p. 869; see also *CT*, 7 Dec. 1861.

9. Cullen to Kirby, 27 Dec. 1861: ICAR, *NC, III*, 2, 3, no. 181; Cullen to Kirby, n.d. *(Dec. 1861)*: ICAR, *NC, III*, 2, 3, no. 179; Cullen to Monsell, 8 Jan. 1862: NLI, MS. 8317 (3), *Monsell Papers*.

10. Cullen to Kirby, 17 Jan. 1862: ICAR, *NC, III*, 3, 1, no. 2.

11. Cullen to Kirby, 17 Jan. 1862: ICAR, *NC, III*, 3, 1, no. 2; MacHale *(Abp., Tuam)* to Prop., 19 Jan. 1862: ACPF, *SC, Irlanda*, vol. 34, ff. 283, 285.

12. Cullen to Kirby, 17 Jan. 1862: ICAR, *NC, III*, 3, 1, no. 2; Cullen to Kirby, 28 Jan. 1862: ACPF, *SC, Irlanda*, vol. 35, f. 144.

13. Cullen to Kirby, 17 Jan. 1862: ICAR, *NC, III*, 3, 1, no. 2; Cullen to Kirby, 28 Jan. 1862: ACPF, *SC, Irlanda*, vol. 35, f. 144 *(v)*; Cullen to Kirby, 29 Jan. 1862: ICAR, *NC, III*, 3, 1, no. 3; Cullen to Kirby, 31 Jan. 1862: ICAR, *NC, III*, 3, 1, no. 4; MacHale to Cullen, 30 Jan. 1862: DDA, 340\3, *(i)*, no. 12; Cullen to Kirby, 14 Feb. 1862: ICAR, *NC, III*, 3, 1, no. 6.

14. Cullen to Kirby, 29 Jan. 1862: ICAR, *NC, III*, 3, 1, no. 3.

15. 'Io sarò ridotto alla necessità di sospendere publicamente il lupetto che viene a divorare le mie pecorelle', Cullen to Kirby, 28 Jan. 1862: ACPF, *SC, Irlanda*, vol. 35, f. 144 *(v)*; see also Cullen to Kirby, 29 Jan. 1862: ICAR, *NC, III*, 3, 1, no. 3.

16. Cullen to Monsell, 8 Jan. 1862: NLI, MS. 8317 (3), *Monsell Papers*; see also Butler *(Coadj. Bp., Limerick)* to Cullen, 21 Jan. 1862: DDA, 340\3, *(i)* no. 9; Dixon *(Abp., Armagh)* to Prop., 1 Feb. 1862: DDA, 340\3, no. 14.

17. Cullen to Kirby, 21 Feb. 1862: ICAR, *NC, III*, 3, 1, no. 11; Cullen to Prop., 21 Mar. 1862: ACPF, *SC, Irlanda*, vol. 34, f. 353 *(v)*.

18. Cullen to Kirby, 21 Feb. 1862: ICAR, *NC, III*, 3, 1, no. 11; Cullen to Prop., 21 Mar. 1862: ACPF, *SC, Irlanda*, vol. 34, f. 353 *(v)*; Cullen to Kirby, n.d.: ICAR, *NC, III*, 3, 1, no. 28; Murphy *(lay corr.)* to Cullen, 18 Mar. 1862: DDA, 340\5, no. 47; Anon. to Cullen, 29 *(March)* 1862: DDA, 340\5, no. 54.

19. 'Il Sigr. Lavelle si fa l'apostolo di quella società', Cullen to Prop, 21 Mar. 1862: ACPF, SC, Irlanda, vol. 34, f. 353 (v); see also Cullen to Kirby, 21 Mar. 1862: ICAR, NC, III, 3, 1, no. 17; Flannery (Bp., Killaloe) to Cullen, 6 Apr. 1862: DDA, 340\3, (i), no. 57; Cullen to Kirby, 15 Apr. 1862: ICAR, NC, III, 3, 1, no. 27; Cullen to Kirby, n.d.: ICAR, NC, III, 3, 1, no. 28.

20. Cullen to Kirby, 10 Dec. 1861: ICAR, NC, III, 2, 3, no. 178; see also Cullen to Kirby, 25 Feb. 1862: ICAR, NC, III, 3, 1, no. 12; Cullen to Prop., 21 Mar. 1862: ACPF, SC, Irlanda, vol. 34, f. 353 (v).

21. Cullen to Kirby, 16 Feb. 1862: ICAR, NC, III, 3, 1, no. 9; Cullen to Kirby, 21 Feb. 1862: ICAR, NC, III, 3, 1, no. 11.

22. ibid.

23. MacHale to Cullen, 11 Nov. 1861: DDA, 334\1, no. 105; Cullen to Kirby, 14 Feb. 1862: ICAR, NC, III, 3, 1, no. 6; Cullen to Kirby, 16 Feb. 1862: ICAR, NC, III, 3, 1, no. 9; Cullen to Kirby, 21 Feb. 1862: ICAR, NC, III, 3, 1, no. 11; Cullen to Kirby, 25 Feb. 1862: ICAR, NC, III, 3, 1, no. 12; Cullen to Prop., 28 Feb. 1862: ACPF, SC, Irlanda, vol. 35, f. 141 (v); Cullen to Kirby, n.d.: ICAR, NC, III, 3, 1, no. 28.

24. FJ, 5, 10 Mar. 1862; Cullen to Kirby, 6 Apr. 1862: ICAR, NC, III, 3, 1, no. 23.

25. Cullen to Kirby, 16 Mar. 1862: ICAR, NC, III, 3, 1, no. 14; see also Cullen to Prop., 11 Apr. 1862: ACPF, SC, Irlanda, vol. 35, f. 139; Cullen to Kirby, n.d.: ICAR, NC, III, 3, 1, no. 26.

26. Farrell (PP, Thomas St.) to O'Donoghue (MP, Tipperary), 7 Mar. 1862: DDA, 340\4, (ii), no. 30; Goss (Abp., Liverpool) to Cullen, 8 Mar. 1862: DDA, 340\3, (ii), no. 5 (a); Cullen to Kirby, 16 Mar. 1862: ICAR, NC, III, 3, 1, no. 14; Cullen to Prop., 21 Mar. 1862: ACPF, SC, Irlanda, vol. 34, f. 353 (v); Cullen to Kirby, n.d.: ICAR, NC, III, 3, 1, no. 28.

27. Cullen to Kirby, 21 Mar. 1862: ICAR, NC, III, 3, 1, no. 17; see also Gastaldi (PP, Cardiff) to Cullen, 27 Mar. 1861: DDA, 340\4, (ii), no. 36; Cullen to Kirby, 1 Apr. 1862: ICAR, NC, III, 3, 1, no. 21; Anon. (Kirby) to Prop., n.d. (Apr. 1862): ACPF, SC, Irlanda, vol. 34, f. 362.

28. Cullen to Kirby, 1 Apr. 1862: ICAR, NC, III, 3, 1, no. 21; Cullen to Moran (Vice Rec. Irish Coll., Rome, Rel. Cullen), 4 Apr. 1862: ICAR, NC, III, 3, 1, no. 22; Cullen to Kirby, 6 Apr. 1862: ICAR, NC, III, 3, 1, no. 23; Anon. (Kirby) to Prop., n.d. (Apr. 1862): ACPF, SC, Irlanda, vol. 34, f. 362.

29. Cullen to Kirby, 6 Apr. 1862: ICAR, NC, III, 3, 1, no. 23.

30. ibid.

31. Cullen to Prop., 21 Mar. 1862: ACPF, SC, Irlanda, vol. 34, ff. 353 (v) −4; Cullen to Kirby, 15 Apr. 1862: ICAR, NC, III, 3, 1, no. 27; Cullen to Kirby, n.d.: ICAR, NC, III, 3, 1, no. 28.

32. Cullen to Kirby, 28 Jan. 1862: ACPF, SC, Irlanda, vol. 35, f. 145; Cullen to Kirby, 14 Feb. 1862: ICAR, NC, III, 3, 1, no. 6; Cullen to Prop., 28 Feb. 1862: ACPF, SC, Irlanda, vol. 35, f. 142 (v); Cullen to Kirby, n.d.: ICAR, NC, III, 3, 1, no. 64; Cullen to Kirby, 11 Nov. 1862: ICAR, NC, III, 3, 1, no. 65; Cullen to Kirby, 16 Dec. 1862: ICAR, NC, III, 3, 1, no. 71.

33. Cullen to Kirby, 28 Jan. 1862: ACPF, SC, Irlanda, vol. 35, f. 145 (v); Cullen to Kirby, 29 Jan. 1862: ICAR, NC, III, 3, 1, no. 3; Cullen to Kirby, 14 Feb. 1862: ICAR, NC, III, 3, 1, no. 6; Cullen to Kirby, n.d. (Mar. 1862): ICAR, NC, III, 3, 1, no. 26; Cullen to Kirby, 16 Feb. 1862: ICAR, NC, III, 3, 1, no. 9; Cullen to Kirby, 21 Feb. 1862: ICAR, NC, III, 3, 1, no. 11; Cullen to Kirby, 21 Mar. 1862: ICAR, NC, III, 3, 1, no. 17; Cullen to Kirby, 16 Mar. 1862: ICAR, NC, III, 3, 1, no. 14; Cullen to Prop., 11 Apr. 1862: ACPF, SC, Irlanda, vol. 35, f. 140 (v); Cullen to Kirby, 17 July 1862: ICAR, NC, III, 3, 1, no. 50; Cullen to Prop., 7 Oct. 1862: ACPF, SC, Irlanda, vol. 34, f. 534 (v); Cullen to Kirby, n.d. (1862): ICAR, NC, III, 3, 1, no. 64; Cullen to Kirby, 28 Nov. 1862: ICAR, NC, III, 3, 1, no. 66; Cullen to Prop., 28 Nov. 1862: ACPF, SC, Irlanda, vol. 34, f. 570.

34. Cullen to Prop., 28 Feb. 1862: ACPF, SC, Irlanda, vol. 35, f. 142 (v); Cullen to Kirby, 14 Feb. 1862: ICAR, NC, III, 3, 1, no. 6; Cullen to Prop., 11 Apr. 1862: ACPF, SC, Irlanda, vol. 35, f. 140 (v).

35. 'La cosa riuscerebbe meglio se non fosse per la gran miseria che ci prevale. Il popolo soffre assai e non c'è mezzo per aiutarlo − Il governo è determinato di non fare niente.', Cullen to Kirby, 28 Jan. 1862:

ACPF, *SC, Irlanda*, vol. 35, f. 145; see also Cullen to Prop., 28 Feb. 1862: ACPF, *SC, Irlanda*, vol. 35, f. 142 *(v)*.

36. Cullen to Kirby 29 Jan. 1862: ICAR, *NC, III*, 3, 1, no. 3; Cullen to Prop., 21 Mar. 1862: ACPF, *SC, Irlanda*, vol. 34, f. 353; Cullen to Kirby, 17 July 1862: ICAR, *NC, III*, 3, 1, no. 50; Cullen to Prop., 28 Nov. 1862: ACPF, *SC, Irlanda*, vol. 34, f. 570; Cullen to Kirby, 16 Dec. 1862: ICAR, *NC, III*, 3, 1, no. 71.

37. Cullen to Kirby, 1 Apr. 1862: ICAR, *NC, III*, 3, 1, no. 21; Cullen to Prop., 11 Apr. 1862: ACPF, *SC, Irlanda*, vol. 35, f. 139 *(v)*.

38. Cullen to Kirby, 28 Jan. 1862: ACPF, *SC, Irlanda*, vol. 35, f. 145; see also Cullen to Kirby, 29 Jan. 1862: ICAR, *NC, III*, 3, 1, no. 3.

39. *ICD*, 1863, p. 247.

40. Cullen to Prop., 21 Mar. 1862: ACPF, *SC, Irlanda*, vol. 34 f. 353 *(v)*; Cullen to Moran, 4 Apr. 1862: ICAR, *NC, III*, 3, 1, no. 22; Cullen to Kirby, 6 Apr. 1862: ICAR, *NC, III*, 3, 1, no. 23; Cullen to Prop., 11 Apr. 1862: ACPF, *SC, Irlanda*, vol. 35, f. 139 *(v)*.

41. Cullen to Moran, 4 Apr. 1862: ICAR, *NC, III*, 3, 1, no. 22; Cullen to Kirby, 6 Apr. 1862: ICAR, *NC, III*, 3, 1, no. 23.

42. Cullen to Kirby, 6 Apr. 1862: ICAR, *NC, III*, 3, 1, no. 23.

43. Cullen to Kirby, 21 Feb. 1862: ICAR, *NC, III*, 3, 1, no. 11; Cullen to Kirby, 21 Mar. 1862: ICAR, *NC, III*, 3, 1, no. 17; Cullen to Kirby, 1 Apr. 1862: ICAR, *NC, III*, 3, 1, no. 21; Cullen to Moran, 4 Apr. 1862: ICAR, *NC, III*, 3, 1, no. 22; Cullen to Kirby, 6 Apr. 1862: ICAR, *NC, III*, 3, 1, no. 23; Cullen to Kirby, 11 Apr. 1862: ICAR, *NC, III*, 3, 1, no. 25; Cullen to Kirby, n.d. (*Apr. 1862*): ICAR, *NC, III*, 3, 1, no. 26; Cullen to Kirby, n.d. (*Apr. 1862*): ICAR, *NC, III*, 3, 1, no. 28; Anon. (*Kirby*) to Prop., n.d. (*Apr. 1863*): ACPF, *SC, Irlanda*, vol. 34, f. 671; Cullen to Kirby, n.d. (*Sept. 1863*): ICAR, *NC, III*, 3, 1, no. 85; Cullen to Kirby, 23 Oct. 1863: ACPF, *SC, Irlanda*, vol. 34, f. 873; Anon. (*Cullen*) to Prop, n.d. (*1863*): ACPF, *SC, Irlanda*, vol. 35, f. 92.

44. Cullen to Kirby, n.d.: ICAR, *NC, III*, 3, 1, no. 28.

45. Cullen to Kirby, 15 Apr. 1862: ICAR, *NC, III*, 3, 1, no. 27; see also Cullen to Kirby, 21 Feb. 1862: ICAR, *NC, III*, 3, 1, no. 11.

46. Cullen to Kirby, 6 Apr. 1862: ICAR, *NC, III*, 3, 1, no. 23; Cullen to Prop., 11 Apr. 1862: ACPF, *SC, Irlanda*, vol. 35, f. 139 *(v)*; Cullen to Kirby, 11 Apr. 1862: ICAR, *NC, III*, 3, 1, no. 25; Cullen to Kirby, 15 Apr. 1862: ICAR, *NC, III*, 3, 1, no. 27; Anon. (*Kirby*) to Prop., n.d. (*Apr. 1863*): ACPF, *SC, Irlanda*, vol. 34, f. 671; Cullen to Prop., 21 June 1863: ACPF, *SC, Irlanda*, vol. 35, f. 134; Anon. (*Kirby*) to Prop., n.d. (*1863*): ACPF, *SC, Irlanda*, vol. 35, f. 188; Cullen to Prop., 8 Apr. 1864: ACPF, *SC, Irlanda*, vol. 34, f. 1167; Cullen to Prop., 12 Aug. 1864: ACPF, *SC, Irlanda*, vol. 34, f. 1291; *Irishman*, 10 Apr. 1862.

47. Cullen to Kirby, 11 Apr. 1862: ICAR, *NC, III*, 3, 1, no. 25; Anon. (*Kirby*) to Prop., n.d. (*Apr. 1863*): ACPF, *SC, Irlanda*, vol. 34, f. 671.

48. Cullen to Kirby, n.d. (*1862*): ICAR, *NC, III*, 3, 1, no. 26; see also Cullen to Kirby, 6 Apr. 1862: ICAR, *NC, III*, 3, 1, no. 23.

49. Cullen to Kirby, n.d. (*1862*): ICAR, *NC, III*, 3, 1, no. 26; Cullen to Kirby, 15 Apr. 1862: ICAR, *NC, III*, 3, 1, no. 27.

50. ibid.

51. Cullen to Kirby, 15 Apr. 1862: ICAR, *NC, III*, 3, 1, no. 27; Cullen to Kirby, 22 Apr. 1862: ICAR, *NC, III*, 3, 1, no. 30.

52. Cullen to Kirby, n.d. (*1862*): ICAR, *NC, III*, 3, 1, no. 26.

53. 'Se non si potrà arrestare il corso di queste pazzie, la religione soffrirà assai', Cullen to Prop., 11 Apr. 1862: ACPF, *SC, Irlanda*, vol. 35, f. 139.

54. Cullen to Kirby, 22 Apr. 1862: ICAR, *NC, III*, 3, 1, no. 30; see also Cullen to Prop., 11 Apr. 1862: ACPF, *SC, Irlanda*, vol. 35, f. 139.

55. Cullen to Kirby, 11 Apr. 1862: ICAR, *NC, III*, 3, 1, no. 25; MacEvilly (*Bp., Galway*) to Cullen, 11 Apr. 1862: DDA, 340\3, *(i)*, no. 63; Cullen to Kirby, 22 Apr. 1862: ICAR, *NC, III*, 3, 1, no. 30.

56. Cullen to Kirby, 15 Apr. 1862: ICAR, *NC, III*, 3, 1, no. 27.

57. ibid.

58. Cullen to Kirby, n.d. (*1862*): ICAR, *NC, III*, 3, 1, no. 28.

59. MacHale to Prop., 14 Apr. 1862: ACPF, *SC, Irlanda*, vol. 34, ff. 369–70.

60. Cullen to Kirby, n.d. (*1862*): ICAR, *NC, III*, 3, 1, no. 28.

61. Cullen to Kirby, 9 May 1862: ICAR, *Kirby Papers*, 1862, no. 77; see also Cullen to Kirby, 1 Apr. 1862: ICAR, *NC, III*, 3, 1, no. 21.

62. Cullen to Kirby, 9 May 1862: ICAR, *Kirby Papers*, 1862, no. 77.

63. *FJ*, 27 May 1862; *ICD*, 1863, pp. 268–9.

64. ibid.

65. Moran, op. cit., vol. ii, p. 143; *FJ*, 26, 27 May 1862; CT, 26 May 1862.

66. ibid.

67. Cullen to Kirby, 26 Oct. 1862: ICAR, *NC, III*, 3, 1, no. 59.

68. Cullen to Kirby, 1 Apr. 1862: ICAR, *NC, III*, 3, 1, no. 21; Cullen to Kirby, 22 Apr. 1862: ICAR, *NC, III*, 3, 1, no. 30; Cullen to Kirby, 4 July 1862: ICAR, *NC, III*, 3, 1, no. 49; Quinn (*PP, Athy*), to Cullen, 23 July 1862: DDA, 340\4, *(ii)*, no. 62.

69. Murray (*Sec. Cullen*) to Cullen, 27 May 1862: DDA, 340\3, *(iii)*, no. 5; Murray to Cullen, 3 June 1862: DDA, 340\3, *(iii)*, no. 7; Murray to Cullen, 6 June 1862: DDA, 340\3, *(iii)*, no. 8.

70. MacEvilly to Cullen, 2 Oct. 1862: DDA, 340\3, no. 96; Ullathorne (*Bp., Birmingham*) to Cullen, 16 Oct. 1862: DDA, 340\3, *(ii)*, no. 21; Goss to Cullen, 17 Oct. 1862: DDA, 340\3, *(ii)*, no. 22; Grant (*Bp., Southark*) to Cullen, 18 Nov. 1862: DDA, 340\3, *(ii)*, no. 25.

71. MacHale to Cullen, 29 Sept. 1862: DDA, 340\3, *(i)*, no. 94.

72. Cullen to Kirby, 5 Feb. 1863: ICAR, *NC, III*, 3, 1, no. 73; Cullen to Kirby, 26 Feb. 1863: ICAR, *NC, III*, 3, 1, no. 76; Anon. (*Kirby*) to Prop., n.d. (*Feb. 1863*): ACPF, *SC, Irlanda*, vol. 34, f. 613 *(v)*; Cullen to Prop., 13 Mar. 1863: ACPF, *SC, Irlanda*, vol. 34, f. 909; Cullen to Prop., 26 May 1863: ACPF, *SC, Irlanda*, vol. 34, f. 902; Cullen to Prop., 28 June 1863: ACPF, *SC, Irlanda*, vol. 35, f. 136 *(v)*; Cullen to Kirby, 23 Oct. 1863: ACPF, *SC, Irlanda*, vol. 34, f. 873; Cullen to Prop., 27 Nov. 1863: ACPF, *SC, Irlanda*, vol. 34, f. 985 *(v)*.

73. Cullen to Prop., 13 Mar. 1863: ACPF, *SC, Irlanda*, vol. 34, f. 909 *(v)*.

74. Cullen to Kirby, 11 Mar. 1863: ICAR, *NC, III*, 3, 1, no. 77.

75. ibid.

76. Cullen to Kirby, 24 Mar. 1863: ICAR, *NC, III*, 3, 1, no. 79.

77. Cullen to Kirby, 11 Mar. 1863: ICAR, *NC, III*, 3, 1, no. 77; Redmond (*PP, Arklow*) to Cullen, 13 Mar. 1863: DDA, 340\8, *(ii)*, no. 15; Cullen to Kirby, 24 Mar. 1863: ICAR, *NC, III*, 3, 1, no. 79.

78. Cullen to Kirby, 5 Feb. 1863: ICAR, *NC, III*, 3, 1, no. 73; Anon. (*Kirby*) to Prop. n.d. (*Feb. 1863*): ACPF, *SC, Irlanda*, vol. 34, f. 613; Dixon to Cullen, 9 Feb. 1863: DDA, 340\7, *(i)*, no. 19; Walsh (*Bp., Ossory*) to Cullen, 26 Feb. 1863: DDA, 340\7, *(i)*, no. 26; Walshe (*Bp., Kildare & Leighlin*) to Cullen, 27 Feb. 1863: DDA, 340\7, *(i)*, no. 23; Furlong (*Bp., Ferns*) to Cullen, 2 Mar. 1863: DDA, 340\7, *(i)*, no. 25; Gillooly (*Bp., Elphin*) to Cullen, 3 Mar. 1863: DDA, 340\7, *(i)*, no. 26; Dixon to Cullen, 5 Mar. 1863: DDA, 340\7, *(i)*, no. 27; Dixon to Cullen, 7 Mar. 1863: DDA, 340\7, *(i)*, no. 28; Walsh to Cullen, 7 Mar. 1863: DDA, 340\7, *(i)*, no. 29; Furlong to Cullen, 8 Mar. 1863: DDA, 340\7, *(i)*, no. 30; Walshe to Cullen, 8 Mar. 1863: DDA, 340\7, *(i)*, no. 31; Cullen to Kirby, 11 Mar. 1863: ICAR, *NC, III*, 3, 1, no. 77; CT, 28 Mar. 1863.

79. Cullen to Kirby, 26 Feb. 1863: ICAR, *NC, III*, 3, 1, no. 76; see also Cullen to Kirby, 5 Feb. 1863: ICAR, *NC, III*, 3, 1, no. 73; Anon. (*Kirby*) to Prop. n.d. (*Feb. 1863*): ACPF, *SC, Irlanda*, vol. 34, f. 613; Walshe to Cullen, 8 Mar. 1863: DDA, 340\7, *(i)*, no. 31; Cullen to Kirby, 11 Mar. 1863: ICAR, *NC, III*, 3, 1, no. 77.

80. Cullen to Kirby, 5 Feb. 1863: ICAR, *NC, III*, 3, 1, no. 73; Dixon to Cullen, 7 Mar. 1863: DDA, 340\7, *(i)*, no. 28.

81. Cullen to Kirby, 11 Mar. 1863: ICAR, *NC, III*, 3, 1, no. 77; see also Cullen to Kirby, 5 Feb. 1863: ICAR, *NC, III*, 3, 1, no. 73; Dixon to Cullen, 20 Mar. 1863: DDA, 340\7, *(i)*, no. 34; Walshe to Cullen, 24 Mar. 1863: DDA, 340\7, *(i)*, no. 36; Furlong to Cullen, 24 Mar. 1863: DDA, 340\7, *(i)*, no. 37; Furlong to Cullen, 1 Apr. 1863: DDA, 340\7, *(i)*, no. 45.

82. Redmond to Cullen, 13 Mar. 1863: DDA, 340\8, *(ii)*, no. 15; Dixon to Cullen, 13 Mar. 1863: DDA, 340\7, *(i)*, no. 33; Cullen to Kirby, 24 Mar. 1863: ICAR, *NC, III*, 3, 1, no. 79; Delaney (*Bp., Cork*) to Kirby, 28 Mar. 1863: ICAR, *Kirby Papers*, 1863, no. 105; Cornthwaite (*Bp., Beverley*)

to Cullen, 20 Apr. 1863: DDA, 340\7, *(ii)*, no. 19; Quinn to Cullen, 1 May 1863: DDA, 340\8, *(i)*, no. 66; Redmond to Cullen, 4 May 1863: DDA, 340\8, *(ii)*, no. 27.

83. Cullen to Kirby, 24 Mar. 1863: ICAR, *NC, III*, 3, 1, no. 79.

84. Cullen to Kirby, 24 Mar. 1863: ICAR, *NC, III*, 3, 1, no. 79; see also Brown (*Bp., Shrewsbury*) to Cullen, 28 May 1863: DDA, 340\7, *(ii)*, no. 24; Cullen to Prop., 21 June 1863: ACPF, *SC, Irlanda*, vol. 35, f. 134; Cullen to Prop., 28 June 1863: ACPF, *SC, Irlanda*, vol. 35, f. 136.

85. Brown to Cullen, 28 May 1863: DDA, 340\7, *(ii)*, no. 24; Cullen to Prop., 21 June 1863: ACPF, *SC, Irlanda*, vol. 35, f. 134.

86. Cullen to Kirby, 24 Mar. 1863: ICAR, *NC, III*, 3, 1, no. 79; see also Cullen to Kirby, 31 Mar. 1863: ICAR, *Kirby Papers*, 1863, no. 110; Cullen to Kirby, 22 May 1863: ICAR, *Kirby Papers*, 1863, no. 152.

87. Cullen to Prop., 21 June 1863: ACPF, *SC, Irlanda*, vol. 35, f. 134.

88. Cullen to Prop., 16 Nov. 1861: ACPF, *SC, Irlanda*, vol. 34, f. 191 *(v)*.

89. 'E una cosa da deplorarsi che uomini come il Lavelle e i fratelli di. S. Patrizio cerchino di spingere il popolo a mene rivoluzionarie', Cullen to Prop., 28 June 1863: ACPF, *SC, Irlanda*, vol. 35, f. 136 *(v)*.

90. 'Io non cesso di dire ai cattolici che è una vera pazzia di parlare di rivoluzioni, poichè il popolo qui è senza armi, senza denaro e senza alcun mezzo di resistenza di modo che qualunque movimento popolare non farebbe altro che dare ai nostri nemici l'occasione di rovinarci totalmente. Disgraziatamente vi sono dei pazzi che non vogliono sentire un consiglio così ragionevole', Cullen to Prop., 13 Mar. 1863: ACPF, *SC, Irlanda*, vol. 34, f. 909 *(v)*; see also Cullen to Prop., 28 June 1863: ACPF, *SC, Irlanda*, vol. 35, f. 136 *(v)*.

91. Cullen to Kirby, 11 Mar. 1863: ICAR, *NC, III*, 3, 1, no. 77.

92. Cullen to Prop., 12 May 1863: ACPF, *SC, Irlanda*, vol. 34, f. 704.

93. Moran, op. cit., vol. 2, p. 192–3; see also CT, 20 June 1863.

94. *GFP*, 13 June 1863; CT, 20 June 1863; Cullen to Kirby 21 June 1863: ICAR, *Kirby Papers*, 1863, no. 171; Cullen to Prop.,

21 June 1863: ACPF, *SC, Irlanda*, vol. 35, f. 134; Cullen to Kirby, 3 July 1863: ICAR, *Kirby Papers*, 1863, no. 180.

95. Cullen to Prop., 21 June 1863: ACPF, *SC, Irlanda*, vol. 35, f. 134; Cullen to Kirby, 21 June 1863: ICAR, *Kirby Papers*, 1863, no. 171; Cullen to Kirby, 3 July 1863: ICAR, *Kirby Papers*, 1863, no. 180; Cullen to Prop., 28 June 1863: ACPF, *SC, Irlanda*, vol. 35, f. 136.

96. Cullen to Prop., 21 June 1863: ACPF, *SC, Irlanda*, vol. 35, f. 134 *(v)*; Cullen to Prop., 28 June 1863: ACPF, *SC, Irlanda*, vol. 35, f. 136.

97. Moran to Prop., 12 Aug. 1863: ACPF, *SC, Irlanda*, vol. 34, f. 813 *(v)*.

98. *San Francisco Irish News*, 6 June 1863; CT, 25 July 1863.

99. *Tablet*, 8 Aug. 1863.

100. ibid.

101. Cullen to Prop., 21 June 1863: ACPF, *SC, Irlanda*, vol. 35, f. 134 *(v)*; Cullen to Kirby, 9 Aug. 1863: ICAR, *Kirby Papers*, 1863, no. 203; Cullen to Prop., 11 Aug. 1863: ACPF, *SC, Irlanda*, vol. 34, f. 804; Anon. (*Kirby*) to Prop., n.d. (*Aug. 1863*): ACPF, *SC, Irlanda*, vol. 34, f. 805; ACPF, *Acta*, vol. 228, (*1864*), ff. 96–110.

102. *ICD*, 1864, p. 286; see also Cullen to Kirby, 9 Aug. 1863: ICAR, *Kirby Papers*, 1863, no. 203; Cullen to Prop., 11 Aug. 1863: ACPF, *SC, Irlanda*, vol. 34, f. 804; Anon (*Kirby*) to Prop., n.d. (*Aug. 1863*): ACPF, *SC, Irlanda*, vol. 34, f. 805; Cullen to Prop., 9 Sept. 1863: ACPF, *SC, Irlanda*, vol. 35, f. 106; CT, 19 Sept. 1863.

103. 'Tutti i vescovi ... eccettuati l'arcivescovo di Tuam e il vescovo di Clonfert erano unanimi nel condannare le lettere del prete Lavelle, dichiarandole sovvenire dell'autorità ecclesiastica e civile', Cullen to Prop., 11 Aug. 1863: ACPF, *SC, Irlanda*, vol. 34, f. 804; see also Cullen to Kirby, 9 Aug. 1863: ICAR, *Kirby Papers*, 1863, no. 203; Cullen to Kirby, 11 Aug. 1863: ICAR, *Kirby Papers*, 1863, no. 204; Anon (*Kirby*) to Prop., n.d. (*Aug. 1863*): ACPF, *SC, Irlanda*, vol. 34, f. 805; Cullen to Prop., 30 Aug. 1863: ACPF, *Acta*, vol. 228, (*1864*) f. 104; Cullen to Prop., 9 Sept. 1863: ACPF, *SC, Irlanda*, vol. 35, ff. 105(v) 7; CT, 19 Sept. 1863.

104. *ICD*, 1864, pp. 285–7; CT, 19 Sept. 1863.

105. Cullen to Kirby, 9 Aug. 1863: ICAR, *Kirby Papers*, 1863, no. 203; Cullen to Kirby, 11 Aug. 1863: ICAR, *Kirby Papers*, 1863, no. 204; Cullen to Prop., 11 Aug. 1863: ACPF, *SC, Irlanda*, vol. 34, f. 804; Anon. (*Kirby*) to Prop., n.d. (*Aug. 1863*): ACPF, *SC, Irlanda*, vol. 34, f. 805; Cullen to Prop., 30 Aug. 1863: ACPF, *Acta*, vol. 228, (*1864*) f. 104; Cullen to Prop., 9 Sept. 1863: ACPF, *SC, Irlanda*, vol. 35, f. 105 (*v*); CT, 19 Sept. 1863.

106. Cullen to Kirby, 9 Aug. 1863: ICAR, *Kirby Papers*, 1863, no. 203; Cullen to Prop., 11 Aug. 1863: ACPF, *SC, Irlanda*, vol. 34, f. 804; Anon. (*Kirby*) to Prop., n.d. (*Aug. 1863*): ACPF, *SC, Irlanda*, vol. 34, f. 805; Cullen to Prop., 30 Aug. 1863: ACPF, *Acta*, vol. 228, (*1864*) f. 104; Cullen to Prop., 9 Sept. 1863: ACPF, *SC, Irlanda*, vol. 35, f. 105 (*v*); CT, 19 Sept. 1863.

107. CT, 3 Oct. 1863.

108. Cullen to Prop., 3 Nov. 1863: ACPF, *SC, Irlanda*, vol. 35, f. 7 (*v*).

109. Moran to Prop., 12 Aug. 1863: ACPF, *SC, Irlanda*, vol. 34, f. 814.

110. ibid.

111. Cullen to Kirby, 4 Sept. 1863: ICAR, *Kirby Papers*, 1863, no. 227; Cullen to Prop., 9 Sept. 1863: ACPF, *SC, Irlanda*, vol. 35, f. 105 (*v*); Cullen to Kirby, n.d. (*Sept. 1863*): ICAR, *NC, III*, 3, 1, no. 85.

112. Cullen to Kirby, 4 Sept. 1863: ICAR, *Kirby Papers*, 1863, no 227; Cullen to Kirby, 23 Oct. 1863: ACPF, *SC, Irlanda*, vol. 34, f. 873 (*v*).

113. 'La ... rovina dell'Irlanda', Moran to Prop., 12 Aug. 1863: ACPF, *SC, Irlanda*, vol. 34, f. 814; see also Cullen to Kirby, 4 Sept. 1863: ICAR, *Kirby Papers*, 1863, no. 227; Cullen to Prop., 9 Sept. 1863: ACPF, *SC, Irlanda*, vol. 35, f. 105 (*v*); Cullen to Kirby, n.d. (*Sept. 1863*): ICAR, *NC, III*, 3, 1, no. 85; Cullen to Kirby, 2 Oct. 1863: ICAR, *Kirby Papers*, 1863, no. 252.

114. Cullen to Kirby, n.d. (*Sept. 1863*): ICAR, *NC, III*, 3, 1, no. 85; MacEvilly to Cullen, 15 Sept. 1863: DDA, 340\7, (*i*), no. 122; MacEvilly to Cullen, 9 Oct. 1863: DDA, 340\7, (*i*), no. 136.

115. Redmond to Cullen, 23 Oct. 1863: ICAR, *NC, III*, 3, 1, no. 88; Cullen to Kirby, 26 Oct. 1863: ACPF, *SC, Irlanda*, vol. 35, f. 122; Redmond to Cullen, 6 Nov. 1863: DDA, 340\8, (*ii*), no. 63; Redmond to Cullen, 8 Nov. 1863: DDA, 340\8, (*ii*), no. 64.

116. 'Minacciano di venire dall'America con 200,000 uomini ad invader l'Irlanda ... L'Oggetto dei fratelli è di eccitare turbolenze nell'Irlanda, e poi ancora d'attirare i nostri poveri contadini all'armata americana per esservi massacrati. Il nostro gov. machiavelliano che è ora potentissimo, non vedrebbe di mal occhio una ribellione in Irlanda, perchè potrebbe sopprimerla in un momento, e perchè darebbe occasione a rubare di nuovo le chiese e conventi, e di confiscare ciò che i Cattolici hanno guadagnatO', Cullen to Kirby, 23 Oct. 1863: ACPF, *SC, Irlanda*, vol. 34, f. 873.

117. Cullen to Kirby, 23 Oct. 1863: ACPF, *SC, Irlanda*, vol. 34, f. 873. He also reiterated his assertion that the whole Fenian movement was a plot to mislead the people. ibid.(*v*).

118. Cullen to Kirby, 23 Oct. 1863: ACPF, *SC, Irlanda*, vol. 34, f. 874; Cullen to Prop., 3 Nov. 1863: ACPF, *SC, Irlanda*, vol. 35, f. 117 (*v*); Cullen to Prop., 27 Nov. 1863: ACPF, *SC, Irlanda*, vol. 34, f. 985–6; Anon. (*Kirby*) to Prop., n.d. (*Nov. 1863*): ACPF, *SC, Irlanda*, vol. 35, f. 120.

119. Capalti (*Sec. Prop.*) to Prop., n.d. (*Sept. 1863*): ACPF, *SC, Irlanda*, vol. 34, f. 820.

120. Pius IX to MacHale, 24 Sept. 1863: ICAR, *NC, III*, 3, 1, no. 84; ibid,: ACPF, *SC, Irlanda*, vol. 35, ff. 130–2; Capalti to Prop., n.d. (*Sept. 1863*): ACPF, *SC, Irlanda*, vol. 34, f. 820.

121. Pius IX to MacHale, 24 Sept. 1863: ICAR, *NC, III*, 3, 1,no. 84; ibid,: ACPF, *SC, Irlanda*, vol. 35, ff. 130–2; Cullen to Kirby, 9 Oct. 1863: ICAR, *Kirby Papers*, 1863, no. 261; MacEvilly to Cullen, 18 Oct. 1863: DDA, 340\7, (*i*), no. 138; Cullen to Kirby, 20 Oct. 1863: ICAR, *Kirby Papers*, 1863, no. 272; *Nation*, 5 Sept. 1863; CT, 12 Sept. 1863, 10 Oct. 1863.

122. *Conn. Pat.*, 24 Oct. 1863; *FJ*, 26 Oct. 1863; CT, 31 Oct. 1863; TMN, 4 Nov. 1863; see also Cullen to Kirby, 26 Oct. 1863: ACPF, *SC, Irlanda*, vol. 35, f. 121; Cullen to Kirby, 3 Nov. 1863: ICAR, *Kirby Papers*, 1863, no. 282; Cullen to Kirby, 17 Nov. 1863: ICAR, *Kirby Papers*, 1863, no. 300; Cullen to Prop. n.d.: ACPF, *SC, Irlanda*, vol. 35, ff. 92; Anon. (*Kirby*) to Prop. n.d. (*Nov. 1863*):

ACPF, *SC, Irlanda*, vol. 35, f. 93; Anon. (*Kirby*) to Prop., n.d. (*Nov. 1863*): ACPF, *SC, Irlanda*, vol. 35, f. 120; Moran to Prop. 19 Nov. 1863: ACPF, *SC, Irlanda*, vol. 35, f. 118.

123. 'E una scaltra difesa di tutte le cose le più scandalose che sinora aveva pubblicato', Cullen to Prop., n.d.: ACPF, *SC, Irlanda*, vol. 35, f. 92; see also Cullen to Kirby, 17 Nov. 1863: ICAR, *Kirby Papers*, 1863, no. 300.

124. Cullen to Kirby, 26 Oct. 1863: ACPF, *SC, Irlanda*, vol. 35, f. 121; Anon. (*Kirby*) to Prop., n.d.: ACPF, *SC, Irlanda*, vol. 35, f. 93; Anon. (*Kirby*) to Prop., n.d. (*Nov. 1863*): ACPF, *SC, Irlanda*, vol. 35, f. 120.

125. Cullen to Kirby, 26 Oct. 1863: ACPF, *SC, Irlanda*, vol. 35, f. 121; Anon. (*Kirby*) to Prop., n.d. (*Nov. 1863*): ACPF, *SC, Irlanda*, vol. 35, f. 120; Cullen to Prop., n.d. (*1863*): ACPF, *SC, Irlanda*, vol. 35, f. 92; Dixon to Cullen, 30 Oct. 1863: DDA, 340\7, *(i)*, no. 141.

126. 'alcune spiegazioni', Anon. (*Kirby*) to Prop., n.d.: ACPF, *SC, Irlanda*, vol. 35, f. 93.

127. Moran to Prop., 19 Nov. 1863: ACPF, *SC, Irlanda*, vol. 35, f. 118.

128. *Irishman*, 31 Oct. 1863; Cullen to Prop., 3 Nov. 1863: ACPF, *SC, Irlanda*, vol. 35, f. 117.

129. *Irishman*, 31 Oct. 1863; see also Cullen to Prop., 3 Nov. 1863: ACPF, *SC, Irlanda*, vol. 35, f. 117; Cullen to Kirby, 3 Nov. 1863: ICAR, *Kirby Papers*, 1863, no. 282; Moran to Prop., 19 Nov. 1863: ACPF, *SC, Irlanda*, vol. 35, f. 118; Cullen to Kirby, 27 Nov. 1863: ICAR, *Kirby Papers*, 1863, no. 307; Woodlock (*Rec. Cath. Univ. Ire.*) and Forde (*PP, Booterstown*) to Prop., 27 Nov. 1863: ACPF, *SC, Irlanda*, vol. 34, f. 983 *(v)*.

130. Cullen to Prop., 3 Nov. 1863: ACPF, *SC, Irlanda*, vol. 35, f. 117 *(v)*; Cullen to Kirby, 17 Nov. 1863: ICAR, *Kirby Papers*, 1863, no. 300; Cullen to Prop., n.d.: ACPF, *SC, Irlanda*, vol. 35, f. 92 *(v)*; Anon. (*Kirby*) to Prop., n.d. (*Nov. 1863*): ACPF, *SC, Irlanda*, vol. 35, f. 120.

131. Anon. (*Kirby*) to Prop., n.d. (*Nov. 1863*): ACPF, *SC, Irlanda*, vol. 35, f. 120.

132. Cullen to Kirby, 3 Nov. 1863: ICAR, *Kirby Papers*, 1863, no. 282; Cullen to Prop., 3 Nov. 1863: ACPF, *SC, Irlanda*, vol. 35, f. 117; see also Cullen to Prop n.d.: ACPF, *SC, Irlanda*, vol. 35, f. 92; Moran to Prop.,

19 Nov. 1863: ACPF, *SC, Irlanda*, vol. 35, f. 118; Anon. (*Kirby*) to Prop., n.d. (*Nov. 1863*): ACPF, *SC, Irlanda*, vol. 35, f. 120.

133. Cullen to Prop., 3 Nov. 1863: ACPF, *SC, Irlanda*, vol. 35, f. 117*(v)*.

134. ibid.

135. Cullen to Prop., 3 Nov. 1863: ACPF, *SC, Irlanda*, vol. 35, f. 117 *(v)*; Moran to Prop., 19 Nov. 1863: ACPF, *SC, Irlanda*, vol. 35, f. 118; Cullen to Prop., n.d. (1863): ACPF, *SC, Irlanda*, vol. 35, f. 92 *(v)*.

136. Barnabò (*Sec. Prop.*) to Prop., 12 Nov. 1863: ACPF, *SC, Irlanda*, vol. 34, f. 968; see also Kirby to Prop., n.d. (*Nov. 1863*): ACPF, *SC, Irlanda*, vol. 35, f. 120 *(v)*.

137. Pius IX to MacHale, 26 Nov. 1863: ACPF, *SC, Irlanda*, vol. 35, f. 90; see also Cullen to Kirby, 11 Dec. 1863: ICAR, *Kirby Papers*, 1863, no. 322; Cullen to Kirby, 18 Dec. 1863: ICAR, *Kirby Papers*, 1863, no. 331.

138. Cullen to Kirby, 27 Nov. 1863: ICAR, *Kirby Papers*, 1863, no. 307; Cullen to Prop., 27 Nov. 1863: ACPF, *SC, Irlanda*, vol. 34, f. 986.

139. Cullen to Kirby, 3 Dec. 1863: ICAR, *Kirby Papers*, 1863, no. 316.

140. 'E molto da desiderarsi che si metta fine alla carriera di quel prete, altrimenti egli indebolirà a fede del popolo, ecciterà uove dissensioni nel paese, e darà ccasione ai nostri nemici di continuare le loro soverchierie verso i poveri. L'affare sta adesso nelle mani di Roma e spero che si porterà buon esito senza cagionare altri mali in questo regnO', Cullen to Prop., 27 Nov. 1863: ACPF, *SC, Irlanda*, vol. 34, f. 986; see also Cullen to Kirby, 27 Nov. 1863: ICAR, *Kirby Papers*, 1863, no. 307.

141. Woodlock and Forde to Prop., 27 Nov. 1863: ACPF, *SC, Irlanda*, vol. 34, ff. 983–4; MacEvilly to Cullen, 5 Dec. 1863: DDA, 340\7, *(i)*, no. 152; MacEvilly to Cullen, 11 Dec. 1863: DDA, 340\7, *(i)*, no. 154.

142. Cullen to Kirby, 11 Dec. 1863: ICAR, *Kirby Papers*, 1863, no. 322; Gillooly to Cullen, 14 Dec. 1863: DDA, 340\7, *(i)*, no. 156.

143. Cullen to Prop., 15 Jan. 1864: ACPF, *SC, Irlanda*, vol. 34, f. 1046 *(v)*; Cullen to Prop., 28 Jan. 1864: ACPF, *SC, Irlanda*, vol. 34, ff. 1062 *(v)* –3; Cullen to Kirby, 27 Mar. 1864: ACPF, *SC, Irlanda*, vol. 35, f. 47; Anon. (*Kirby*) to Prop., n.d. (*Apr. 1864*): ACPF, *SC, Irlanda*, vol. 35, f. 56.

144. Cullen to Prop., 15 Jan. 1864: ACPF, *SC, Irlanda*, vol. 34, f. 1046 *(v)*.

Chapter Ten

1. *IP,* 28 Nov. 1863.
2. Cullen to Prop., 12 Aug. 1864: ACPF, *SC, Irlanda*, vol. 34, f. 1292.
3. *IP,* 27 Feb., 14 May, 4, 14 June, 16 Sept., 5, 19 Nov., 17 Dec. 1864, 6 May, 16 Sept. 1865.
4. *IP,* 16 Sept. 1865.
5. *IP,* 21 May 1864.
6. *IP,* 24 Feb. 1864, 7 Jan., 14 Jan., 4 Feb., 18 Mar., 8 Apr. 1865.
7. *IP,* 9 Apr. 1864.
8. *IP,* 16, 23 Jan., 7 May 1864; see also *Nation,* 26 Mar. 1864.
9. *IP,* 6 Feb. 1864.
10. Cullen to Prop., 28 Jan. 1864: ACPF, *SC, Irlanda*, vol. 34, f. 1063; Cullen to Prop., 18 Mar. 1864: ACPF, *SC, Irlanda*, vol. 34, f. 1243; Cullen to Prop., 1 Apr. 1864: ACPF, *SC, Irlanda*, vol. 35, f. 45; Cullen to Prop., 8 Apr. 1864: ACPF, *SC, Irlanda*, vol. 34, f. 1166 *(v)*; Cullen to Prop., 24 Febrary 1865: ACPF, *SC, Irlanda*, vol. 35, f. 206; Cullen to Prop., 17 Sept. 1865: ACPF, *SC, Irlanda*, vol. 35, f. 414 *(v)*; Cullen to Kirby *(Rec. Irish Coll., Rome)*, 1 Oct. 1865: ICAR, *NC, III*, 3, 1, no. 120.
11. 'Gli articoli d'esso oltre d'esser rivoluzionari spesso ... assaliscono il governo temporale del Papa e lodano Garibaldi e ogni giorno prendono a screditare il clero cattolico e di sminuirne l'influenza', Cullen to Prop., 12 Aug. 1864: ACPF, *SC, Irlanda*, vol. 34, f. 1291 *(v)*.
12. Cullen to Prop., 18 Mar. 1864: ACPF, *SC, Irlanda*, vol. 34, f. 1243 *(v)*.
13. Cullen to Prop., 8 Mar. 1864: ACPF, *SC, Irlanda*, vol. 35, f. 53 *(v)*; Cullen to Prop., 1 Apr. 1864: ACPF, *SC, Irlanda*, vol. 35, f. 45; Cullen to Prop., 15 Apr. 1864: ACPF, *SC, Irlanda*, vol. 34, f. 1160; Cullen to Prop., 12 Aug. 1864: ACPF, *SC, Irlanda*, vol. 34, f. 1291 *(v)*; Cullen to Prop., 23 Dec. 1864: ACPF, *SC, Irlanda*, vol. 34, f. 1382; Cullen to Prop., 17 Sept. 1865: ACPF, *SC, Irlanda*, vol. 35, f. 414 *(v)*; Cullen to Kirby, 1 Oct. 1865: ICAR, *NC, III*, 3, 1, no. 120; Cullen to Prop., 18 Dec. 1865: ACPF, *SC*, vol. 35, f. 451 *(v)*.
14. Cullen to Prop., 2 Mar. 1864: ACPF, *SC, Irlanda*, vol. 34, f. 1085 *(v)*; Cullen to Prop.,

8 Mar. 1864: ACPF, *SC, Irlanda*, vol. 35, f. 53 *(v)*; Moran *(Vice Rec. Irish Coll., Rome)* to Prop., 8 Mar. 1864: ACPF, *SC, Irlanda*, vol. 35, f. 21; Cullen to Prop., 25 Mar. 1864: ACPF, *SC, Irlanda*, vol. 35, f. 49 *(v)*; Cullen to Kirby, 27 Mar. 1864: ACPF, *SC, Irlanda*, vol. 35, f. 47; Cullen to Prop., 15 Apr. 1864: ACPF, *SC, Irlanda*, vol. 34, f. 1160; Cullen to Prop., 20 May 1864: ACPF, *SC, Irlanda*, vol. 34, f. 1177 *(v)*; Cullen to Kirby, 30 June 1864: ACPF, *SC, Irlanda*, vol. 34, f. 1222; Anon *(Kirby)* to Prop., n.d. *(Aug. 1864)*: ACPF, *SC, Irlanda*, vol. 34, f. 1278; Cullen to Prop., 9 Sept. 1864: ACPF, *SC, Irlanda*, vol. 34, f. 1325; Moran to Prop., n.d. *(Mar. 1865)*: ACPF, *SC, Irlanda*, vol. 35 f. 9; Cullen to Prop., 9 Oct. 1865: ACPF, *SC, Irlanda*, vol. 35, f. 405 *(v)*; Cullen to Prop., 18 Dec. 1865: ACPF, *SC, Irlanda*, vol. 35, f. 451 *(v)*; Anon. *(Memo)* to Prop., n.d.: ACPF, *SC, Irlanda*, vol. 35, f. 15 *(v)*; *Conn. Pat.*, 20 Feb., 5, 16 Mar., 3 Sept. 1864; 20 Mar., 22 Apr. 1865.

15. 'Molti giornali. direttamente o indirettamente assaliscono il clero e cercano a desseminare la zizzania nel paese. L'argomento dei giornali è he l'Irlanda non potrà ai divenir quale deve essere senza una rivoluzione, e senza scuoter il giogo dell'Inghilterra. ... I medesimi giornali scrivono continuamente contro di me perchè ondanno le società egrete e cerco d'impedire movimenti rivoluzionari che non potrebbero aver luogo senza portare rovina ed esterminio a questo paese, poichè l popolo qui non ha la più iccola pretensione di poter resistere per una settimana alla potenza d'Inghilterra. Perchè o faccio queste cose scrivono che io sono un prete politico e m'ingerisco in cose che non m'appartengono', Cullen to Prop., 18 Mar. 1864: ACPF, *SC, Irlanda*, vol. 34, ff. 1243 *(v)* –4; see also Cullen to Prop., 6 Mar. 1866: ACPF, *SC, Irlanda*, vol. 35, f. 612.

16. Cullen to Prop., 15 Jan. 1864: ACPF, *SC, Irlanda*, vol. 34, f. 1046 *(v)*; Cullen to Prop., 25 Mar. 1864: ACPF, *SC, Irlanda*, vol. 35, f. 50.

17. *IP,* 2, 24 Apr., 7 May, 6 Aug. 1864, 18 Mar., 20 May, 8 July, 19 Aug. 1865; SPO, CSO, RP, 1865\10377, 3665; 1867\4222, 12514, 13503; Resident Magistrates Report, 19 July 1866: NLI, MS. 7590, *Larcom Papers*; De

Gernon (*lay corr.*) to Larcom (*Under Sec., Ire.*), 23 Nov. 1866: NLI, MS. 7590, Larcom Papers; M. O'Connor, 'Sogarth Aroon', in *IER*, 1869, p. 550; P. O'Leary, *Mo Sceal Fein*, London, 1970, p. 83.

18. *IP*, 2 Apr., 22 Oct. 1864, 17, 24, 31 Dec. 1864, 14, 21 Jan., 4, 11, 25 Feb., 1, 8, 15, 18 Mar., Apr., 6, 13, 20 May 1865, 10 June, 1 July, 19 Aug., 16 Sept. 1865; O'Leary, op. cit. pp. 81–3.

19. Cullen to Prop., 8 Apr. 1864: ACPF, *SC, Irlanda*, vol. 34, f. 1166 (*v*).

20. *FJ*, 15 Feb. 1864; Moran, op. cit., vol. 2, pp. 237–66.

21. Cullen to Prop., 25 March 1864: ACPF, *SC, Irlanda*, vol. 35, f.50; Moran, op. cit., vol. 2, pp. 248–54; *Conn. Pat.* 16 Mar. 1864.

22. Cullen to Kirby, 29 Dec. 1863: ICAR, *Kirby Papers*, 1863, no. 344.

23. MacEvilly (*Bp., Galway*) to Cullen, 27 Dec. 1863: DDA, 340\7, (*i*), no. 160.

24. Cullen to Kirby 29 Dec. 1863: ICAR, *Kirby Papers*, 1863, no. 344; Kirby to Prop., n.d. (Jan. 1864): ACPF, *SC, Irlanda*, vol. 35, f. 75

25. ibid.

26. Cullen to Prop., 15 Jan. 1864: ACPF, *SC, Irlanda*, vol. 34, f. 1046 (*v*); Gaspare di S. Giovanni Battista (*Relg. Rome*) to Prop., 23 Jan. 1864: ACPF, *SC, Irlanda*, vol. 35, f. 63; Sisto di S. Francesco (*Relg. Rome*) to Prop., 25 Jan. 1864: ACPF, *SC, Irlanda*, vol. 35, f. 62.

27. Lavelle (*PP, Partry*) to Pius IX., 25 Jan. 1864: ACPF, *SC, Irlanda*, vol. 35, f. 74; Lavelle to Pius IX, Jan. 1864: ACPF, *SC, Irlanda*, vol. 35, f. 79–88; ibid.: ICAR, *Kirby Papers*, 1864, no. 14; Cullen to Prop., 12 Feb. 1864: ACPF, *SC, Irlanda*, vol. 34, f. 1070; *Conn. Pat.*, 5 Mar. 1864.

28. Sisto di S. Francesco to Prop., 25 Jan. 1864: ACPF, *SC, Irlanda*, vol. 35, f. 62.

29. Lavelle to Pius IX, 25 Jan. 1864: ACPF, *SC, Irlanda*, vol. 35, f. 74; Prop. to Cullen, 3 Feb. 1864: ACPF, *LDB*, vol. 355, f. 56; *Conn. Pat.*, 5 Mar. 1864.

30. Lavelle to Pius IX, Jan. 1864: ACPF, *SC, Irlanda*, vol. 35, f. 79–88; ibid.: ICAR, *Kirby Papers*, 1864, no. 14; Cullen to Kirby, 12 Feb. 1864: ICAR, *Kirby Papers*, 1864, no. 30; Kirby to Prop., 2 Apr. 1864: ACPF, *SC, Irlanda*, vol. 35, f. 77; *Conn. Pat.*, 5 Mar. 1864; Cullen to Prop., 8 Mar. 1864: ACPF, *SC, Irlanda*, vol. 35, f. 53; Anon. (*Moran*) to

31. 'La cause de la ruine de l'Irlande', Lavelle to Pius IX, Jan. 1864: ACPF, *SC, Irlanda*, vol. 35, f. 84 (*v*); ibid.: ICAR, *Kirby Papers*, 1864, no. 14.

32. *Conn. Pat.*, 5 Mar. 1864; *CT*, 12 Mar. 1864; see also Anon. (*Moran*) to Prop., 16 Mar. 1864: ACPF, *SC, Irlanda*, vol. 35, ff. 51–2.

33. Cullen to Prop., 15 Jan. 1864: ACPF, *SC, Irlanda*, vol. 34, f. 1046 (*v*); Cullen to Prop., 28 Jan. 1864: ACPF, *SC, Irlanda*, vol. 34, f. 1063.

34. Cullen to Prop., 28 Jan. 1864: ACPF, *SC, Irlanda*, vol. 34, ff. 1062 (*v*) –3; Cullen to Prop., 12 Feb. 1864: ACPF, *SC, Irlanda*, vol. 34, f. 1070; Cullen to Prop., 8 Mar. 1864: ACPF, *SC, Irlanda*, vol. 35, f. 53.

35. Cullen to Prop., 15 Jan. 1864: ACPF, *SC, Irlanda*, vol. 34, f. 1046 (*v*); Cullen to Prop., 28 Jan. 1864: ACPF, *SC, Irlanda*, vol. 34, f. 1062 (*v*) –3.

36. Cullen to Prop., 28 Jan. 1864: ACPF, *SC, Irlanda*, vol. 34, ff. 1062 (*v*) –3; Cullen to Prop., 18 Mar. 1864: ACPF, *SC, Irlanda*, vol. 34, f. 1244–5; Cullen to Prop., 25 Mar. 1864: ACPF, *SC, Irlanda*, vol. 35, f. 49.

37. *Conn. Pat.*, 13 Feb. 1864.

38. *IP*, 27 Feb. 1864; Cullen to Prop., 8 Mar. 1864: ACPF, *SC, Irlanda*, vol. 35, f. 53.

39. See Anon. (*Kirby*) to Prop., n.d. (*Mar. 1864*): ACPF, *SC, Irlanda*, vol. 35, f. 57.

40. ibid.

41. ibid.

42. McEvilly to Kirby, 26 Feb. 1864: ICAR, *Kirby Papers*, 1864, no. 44; MacEvilly to Cullen, 1 Mar. 1864: DDA, 320\3, (*i*), no. 9; Wiseman (*Abp., Westminster*) to Talbot (*Papal Chamberlain*), 1 Mar. 1864: VECAR, Talbot Papers, no. 1116; Cullen to Prop., 2 Mar. 1864: ACPF, *SC, Irlanda*, vol. 34, f. 1085 (*v*); Cullen to Kirby, 4 Mar. 1864: ICAR, *Kirby Papers*, 1864, no. 48; Moran to Prop., 8 Mar. 1864: ACPF, *SC, Irlanda*, vol. 35, f. 21.

43. Moran to Prop., 8 Mar. 1864: ACPF, *SC, Irlanda*, vol. 35, f. 21.

44. Prop. to Cullen, 3 Feb. 1864: ACPF, *LDB*, vol. 355, f. 56.

45. Moran to Prop., 8 Mar. 1864: ACPF, *SC, Irlanda*, vol. 35, f. 21.

46. Cullen to Prop., 2 Mar. 1864: ACPF, *SC, Irlanda*, vol. 34, f. 1085 (*v*).

47. *Conn. Pat.*, 5 Mar. 1864; Cullen to Prop., 8 Mar. 1864: ACPF, *SC, Irlanda*, vol. 35, f. 53; Anon. (*Moran*) to Prop., 16 Mar. 1864: ACPF, *SC, Irlanda*, vol. 35, ff. 51–2.

48. *Conn. Pat.*, 5 Mar. 1864; CT, 12 Mar. 1864; Gillooly to Cullen, 8 Mar. 1864: DDA, 320\3, (i), no. 11; Furlong (*Bp., Ferns*) to Cullen, 9 Mar. 1864: DDA, 320\3, (i), no. 12; Kirby to Moriarty (*Bp., Kerry*), n.d. (*Apr. 1864*): KDA, Moriarty XV, no. 33, *Moriarty Papers*.

49. *Conn. Pat.*, 5 Mar. 1864; CT, 12 Mar. 1864.

50. 'Sarebbe bene di sapere, se egli l'abbia mai presentato', Cullen to Prop., 8 Mar. 1864: ACPF, *SC, Irlanda*, vol. 35, f. 53.

51. Lavelle to Pius IX, Jan. 1864: ACPF, *SC, Irlanda*, vol. 35, f. 79–88; ibid.: ICAR, *Kirby Papers*, 1864, no. 14.

52. Prop. to Cullen, 10 Mar. 1864: ACPF, *LDB*, vol. 355, f. 117; Cullen to Prop., 18 Mar. 1864: ACPF, *SC, Irlanda*, vol. 34, f. 1245.

53. Cullen to Prop., 18 Mar. 1864: ACPF, *SC, Irlanda*, vol. 34, f. 1245; Cullen to Prop., 25 Mar. 1864: ACPF, *SC, Irlanda*, vol. 35, f. 49; Cullen to Prop., 8 Apr. 1864: ACPF, *SC, Irlanda*, vol. 34, f. 1166; Cullen to Prop., 12 Apr. 1864: ACPF, *SC, Irlanda*, vol. 35, f. 37; Anon. (*Kirby*) to Prop., n.d. (*Mar. 1864*): ACPF, *SC, Irlanda*, vol. 34, f. 1107.

54. Cullen to Prop., 18 Mar. 1864: ACPF, *SC, Irlanda*, vol. 34, f. 1245; Anon. (*Kirby*) to Prop., n.d. (*Mar. 1864*): ACPF, *SC, Irlanda*, vol. 34, f. 1107.

55. 'Indubbiamente questo è un gravissimo scandalo in Irlanda ove i cattolici sono così ben disposti a rispettar la S. Sede. Ma nel cercare d'indurre Monisgr MacHale a dare saggio d'ubbedienza, bisognerà essere assai cauto a non spingere quel Prelato che non è distinto per la virtù e l'umiltà ad offrire una resistenza pubblica che potrebbe essere d'origine di maggiori mali', Cullen to Prop., 9 Sept. 1864: ACPF, *SC, Irlanda*, vol. 34, f. 1326-(v).

56. Cullen to Prop., 23 Dec. 1864: ACPF, *SC, Irlanda*, vol. 34, ff. 1382 (v) –83.

57. Anon. (*Moran*) to Prop., 16 Mar. 1864: ACPF, *SC, Irlanda*, vol. 35, ff. 51–2; Cullen to Prop., 25 Mar. 1864: ACPF, *SC, Irlanda*, vol. 35, f. 49–50; Cullen to Prop., 27 Mar. 1864: ACPF, *SC, Irlanda*, vol. 35, f. 47; Cullen to Prop., 1 Apr. 1864: ACPF, *SC, Irlanda*, vol. 35, f. 46 (v); Kirby to Prop.

2 Apr. 1864: ACPF, *SC, Irlanda*, vol. 35, f. 77; Kirby to Prop. 4 Apr. 1864: ACPF, *SC, Irlanda*, vol. 35, f. 22; Cullen to Prop., 12 Apr. 1864: ACPF, *SC, Irlanda*, vol. 35, ff. 37–8; Cullen to Kirby, 15 Apr. 1864: ICAR, *Kirby Papers*, 1864, no. 86.

58. 'i cattolici buoni cominciano a dimandare se non v'è lcun potere nella chiesa per tener in ordine o per punire un prete che calpesta tutte le leggi', Cullen to Prop., 25 Mar. 1864: ACPF, *SC, Irlanda*, vol. 35, f. 49; see also Cullen to Prop., 1 Apr. 1864: ACPF, *SC, Irlanda*, vol. 35, f. 46.

59. Cullen to Prop., 18 Mar. 1864: ACPF, *SC, Irlanda*, vol. 34, f. 1245; Cullen to Prop., 25 Mar. 1864: ACPF, *SC, Irlanda*, vol. 35, f. 49 (v); Cullen to Kirby, 27 Mar. 1864: ACPF, *SC, Irlanda*, vol. 35, f. 47 (v); Cullen to Prop., 1 Apr. 1864: ACPF, *SC, Irlanda*, vol. 35, f. 46; Cullen to Prop., 8 Apr. 1864: ACPF, *SC, Irlanda*, vol. 34, f. 1166; Cullen to Prop., 12 Apr. 1864: ACPF, *SC, Irlanda*, vol. 35, f. 37; Cullen to Prop., 9 Sept. 1864: ACPF, *SC, Irlanda*, vol. 34, f. 1326 (v).

60. Cullen to Prop., 12 Apr. 1864: ACPF, *SC, Irlanda*, vol. 35, f. 37.

61. 'i vescovi che li condannano sono meri schiavi del governo, o uomini fanatici ed ignoranti', Cullen to Prop., 15 Apr. 1864: ACPF, *SC, Irlanda*, vol. 34, f. 1160.

62. Redmond (*PP, Arklow*) to Cullen, 17 Jan. 1864: DDA, 320\5, (ii), no. 1; Cullen to Prop., 29 Mar. 1864: ACPF, *SC, Irlanda*, vol. 34, f. 1121; Cullen to Prop., 12 Apr. 1864: ACPF, *SC, Irlanda*, vol. 35, f. 37.

63. Cullen to Kirby, 27 Mar. 1864: ACPF, *SC, Irlanda*, vol. 35, f. 47 (v)

64. Cullen to Prop., 6 Dec. 1866: ACPF, *SC, Irlanda*, vol. 35, f. 864 (v); Cullen to Prop., 28 Jan. 1864: ACPF, *SC, Irlanda*, vol. 34, f. 1063; Cullen to Kirby, 27 Mar. 1864: ACPF, *SC, Irlanda*, vol. 35, ff. 47–8; Cullen to Prop., 1 Apr. 1864: ACPF, *SC, Irlanda*, vol. 35, f. 43; Cullen to Prop., 15 Apr. 1864: ACPF, *SC, Irlanda*, vol. 34, f. 1158; Cullen to Prop., 1 Apr. 1864: ACPF, *SC, Irlanda*, vol. 35, f. 46.

65. Cullen to Prop., 1 Apr. 1864: ACPF, *SC, Irlanda*, vol. 35, f. 46; Cullen to Prop., 15 Jan. 1864: ACPF, *SC, Irlanda*, vol. 34, f. 1047; see also O'Brien (*Bp., Waterford*) to Cullen, 3 Mar. 1864: DDA, 320\3, (i), no. 10.

66. Cullen to Prop., 15 Jan. 1864: ACPF, *SC, Irlanda*, vol. 34, f. 1046 *(v)*; Cullen to Prop., 1 Apr. 1864: ACPF, *SC, Irlanda*, vol. 35, f. 46; Cullen to Prop., 8 Apr. 1864: ACPF, *SC, Irlanda*, vol. 34, f. 1167; Cullen to Prop., 15 Apr. 1864: ACPF, *SC, Irlanda*, vol. 34, f.1159; Cullen to Prop., 12 Aug. 1864: ACPF, *SC, Irlanda*, vol. 34, ff. 1291 *(v)* –2; Cullen to Prop., 9 Sept. 1864: ACPF, *SC, Irlanda*, vol. 34, f. 1325.

67. Cullen to Prop. 15 Jan. 1864: ACPF, *SC, Irlanda*, vol. 34, f. 1046 *(v)*; Cullen to Prop., 25 Mar. 1864: ACPF, *SC, Irlanda*, vol. 35, f. 50; Cullen to Prop., 1 Apr. 1864: ACPF, *SC, Irlanda*, vol. 35, ff. 43–6; Cullen to Prop., 8 Apr. 1864: ACPF, *SC, Irlanda*, vol. 34, ff. 1166 *(v)* –7; Cullen to Prop., 15 Apr. 1864: ACPF, *SC, Irlanda*, vol. 34, ff. 1158–61; Cullen to Prop., 12 Aug. 1864: ACPF, *SC, Irlanda*, vol. 34, ff. 1291–2; Cullen to Prop., 23 Dec. 1864: ACPF, *SC, Irlanda*, vol. 34, ff. 1382–3; Cullen to Prop., 6 Jan. 1865: ACPF, *SC, Irlanda*, vol. 35, f. 173 *(v)*; Cullen to Prop., 17 Sept. 1865: ACPF, *SC, Irlanda*, vol. 35, ff. 414–15; Cullen to Prop., 29 Sept. 1865: ACPF, *SC, Irlanda*, vol. 35, f. 401; Cullen to Prop., 9 Oct. 1865: ACPF, *SC, Irlanda*, vol. 35, f. 405; Cullen to Prop., 13 Oct. 1865: ACPF, *SC, Irlanda*, vol. 35, f. 408; Cullen to Prop., 10 Dec. 1865: ACPF, *SC, Irlanda*, vol. 35, f. 452; Cullen to Prop., 18 Dec. 1865: ACPF, *SC, Irlanda*, vol. 35, f. 451; Cullen to Prop., 12 Jan. 1866: ACPF, *SC, Irlanda*, vol. 35, f. 630; Cullen to Prop., 18 Feb. 1866: ACPF, *SC, Irlanda*, vol. 35, f. 609; Cullen to Prop., 6 Mar. 1866: ACPF, *SC, Irlanda*, vol. 35, f. 612; Cullen to Prop., 23 Mar. 1866: ACPF, *SC, Irlanda*, vol. 35, f. 624 *(v)*; Cullen to Prop., 5 Mar. 1867: ACPF, *SC, Irlanda*, vol. 35, f. 984 *(v)*; Cullen to Prop., 15 Mar. 1867: ACPF, *SC, Irlanda*, vol. 35, f. 992; Cullen to Prop., 16 Dec. 1867: ACPF, *SC, Irlanda*, vol. 35, f. 1331 *(v)*; Cullen to Kirby, 16 May 1869: ICAR, *NC, III*, 3, 2, no. 67; Anon. (*Kirby*) to Prop., n.d. (*1867*): ACPF, *SC, Irlanda*, vol. 35, f. 919; see also Duggan (*Bp., Chicago*) to Cullen, 9 Mar. 1864: DDA, 320\3, *(ii),* no. 8; Duggan to Cullen, 25 Apr. 1864: DDA, 320\3, *(ii),* no. 16; Dease (*lay. corr.*) to Cullen, 23 Feb. 1866: DDA, 327\7, no. 33; 'A Scotch Priest' to Cullen, 23 May 1867: DDA, 334\5, *(i),* no. 57; *FJ*, 15 Mar. 1867, 27 Jan. 1868.

68. Cullen to Kirby, 27 Mar. 1864: ACPF, *SC, Irlanda*, vol. 35, f. 47 *(v)*; Cullen to Prop., 15 Apr. 1864: ACPF, *SC, Irlanda*, vol. 34, f. 1161; Cullen to Prop., 6 Jan. 1865: ACPF, *SC, Irlanda*, vol. 35, f. 173 *(v)*; Cullen to Prop., 17 Sept. 1865: ACPF, *SC, Irlanda*, vol. 35, f. 415; Cullen to Prop., 29 Sept. 1865: ACPF, *SC, Irlanda*, vol. 35, f. 401; Cullen to Prop., 9 Oct. 1865: ACPF, *SC, Irlanda*, vol. 35, f. 405; Cullen to Prop., 10 Dec. 1865: ACPF, *SC, Irlanda*, vol. 35, f. 452 *(v)*; Cullen to Prop., 18 Dec. 1865: ACPF, *SC, Irlanda*, vol. 35, f. 451; Cullen to Prop., 29 Dec. 1865: ACPF, *SC, Irlanda*, vol. 35, f. 470; Cullen to Prop., 12 Jan. 1866: ACPF, *SC, Irlanda*, vol. 35, f. 630; Cullen to Prop., 18 Feb. 1866: ACPF, *SC, Irlanda*, vol. 35, f. 609; Cullen to Prop., 6 Mar. 1866: ACPF, *SC, Irlanda*, vol. 35, f. 612; see also Duggan to Cullen, 9 Mar. 1864: DDA, 320\3, *(ii),* no. 8.

69. Cullen to Prop., 29 Mar. 1864: ACPF, *SC, Irlanda*, vol. 34, f. 1121 *(v)*; Cullen to Prop., 1 Apr. 1864: ACPF, *SC, Irlanda*, vol. 35, f. 46 *(v)*; Cullen to Prop., 12 Apr. 1864: ACPF, *SC, Irlanda*, vol. 35, f. 38; Cullen to Prop., 15 Apr. 1864: ACPF, *SC, Irlanda*, vol. 34, f. 1160 *(v)*; Cullen to Prop., 20 May 1864: ACPF, *SC, Irlanda*, vol. 34. ff. 1177 *(v)* –8; Cullen to Prop, 12 Aug. 1864: ACPF, *SC, Irlanda*, vol. 34, f. 1292; Cullen to Prop., 29 Dec. 1865: ACPF, *SC, Irlanda*, vol. 35, f. 470; Cullen to Prop., 6 Mar. 1866: ACPF, *SC, Irlanda*, vol. 35, f. 612; see also Anon. (*Kirby*) to Prop., n.d. (*Apr. 1864*): ACPF, *SC, Irlanda*, vol. 35, f. 56.

70. Cullen to Prop., 12 Apr. 1864: ACPF, *SC, Irlanda*, vol. 35, f. 38; Cullen to Prop., 20 May 1864: ACPF, *SC, Irlanda*, vol. 34, f. 1178; Cullen to Kirby, 30 June 1864: ACPF, *SC, Irlanda*, vol. 34, f. 1222 *(v)*; Cullen to Prop., 17 Sept. 1865: ACPF, *SC, Irlanda*, vol. 35, f. 414; Cullen to Prop., 10 Dec. 1865: ACPF, *SC, Irlanda*, vol. 35, ff. 452 *(v)* –53; Cullen to Prop., 15 Mar. 1867: ACPF, *SC, Irlanda*, vol. 35, f. 992.

71. 'In primo luogo ... non possono fare niente, non essendosi in Irlanda nè rmi, nè unizioni da guerra, nè enaro, e secondo, perchè n un vero spirito di Macchiavelismo alcuni signori desiderano che si preservino questa fratellanza, perchè er mezzo di essa si indeboliscono.. i poveri cattolici', Cullen

298

to Prop., 15 Jan. 1864: ACPF, *SC, Irlanda*, vol. 34, ff. 1046 *(v)* –1047.

72. 'tanto è 'odio loro contro la religione cattolica, che sembrino esultare nella distruzione della povera gente', Cullen to Prop., 20 May 1864: ACPF, *SC, Irlanda*, vol. 34, f. 1178.

73. 'Bisogna dire che qui non si può ire tanto contro il nostro popolo se si lascia attirare alle società egrete, poichè iene spinto a tali cose 10 dal cattivo trattamento che riceve dal governo e 20 dall'esempio che si da dai nostri primi ministri e dal popolo inglese, i quali in questi giorni non fanno altro che difender Mazzini e dare feste a Garibaldi', Cullen to Prop., 12 Apr. 1864: ACPF, *SC, Irlanda*, vol. 35, f. 38; see also Cullen to Prop., 18 Mar. 1864: ACPF, *SC, Irlanda*, vol. 34, f. 1244; Cullen to Prop., 29 Mar. 1864: ACPF, *SC, Irlanda*, vol. 34, f. 1121; Cullen to Prop., 15 Apr. 1864: ACPF, *SC, Irlanda*, vol. 34, f. 1161.

74. Cullen to Prop., 1 Apr. 1864: ACPF, *SC, Irlanda*, vol. 35, f. 45; see also Murray (*Sec. Cullen*) to Cullen, 13 Mar. 1864: DDA, 320\3, *(iii)*, no. 3.

75. Duggan to Cullen, 12 Feb. 1864: DDA, 320\3, *(ii)*, no. 3; Duggan to Prop., n.d. (*Feb. 1864*): ACPF, *SC, Irlanda*, vol. 34, ff. 1064–65; Duggan to Cullen, 9 Mar. 1864: DDA, 320\3, *(ii)*, no. 8; O'Hara (*PP, Syracuse*) to Prop., 30 Mar. 1864: ACPF, SC, America Centrale, vol. 20, f. 753; Duggan to Cullen, 25 Apr. 1864: DDA, 320\3, *(ii)*, no. 16; Prop. to Duggan, 23 May 1864: ACPF, *LDB*, (*1864*), vol. 355, f. 237; Prop. to Monaco la Valletta (*Assess. of Holy Office*), 24 May 1864: ACPF, *LDB*, (*1864*), vol. 355, f. 259; Anon. to Prop., n.d.: ACPF, *SC, Irlanda*, vol. 35, f. 19.

76. Cullen to Prop., 28 Jan. 1864: ACPF, *SC, Irlanda*, vol. 34, f. 1063; Cullen to Prop., 15 Apr. 1864: ACPF, *SC, Irlanda*, vol. 34, ff. 1158–61.

77. Duggan to Cullen, 9 Mar. 1864: DDA, 320\3, *(ii)*, no. 8; Duggan to Cullen, 25 Apr. 1864: DDA, 320\3, *(ii)*, no. 16; Dease (*lay corr.*) to Cullen, 23 Feb. 1866: DDA, 327\7, no. 33; *FJ*, 15 Mar. 1867; Lynch (*Coadj. wst. dist. Scotland*) to Cullen, 21 Mar. 1867: DDA, 334\4, *(iii)*, no. 13; 'A Scotch Priest' to Cullen, 23 May 1867: DDA, 334\5, *(i)*, no. 57; *FJ*, 27 Jan. 1868.

78. *The Fenian*, 12 Mar. 1864; Cullen to Prop 1 Apr. 1864: ACPF, *SC, Irlanda*, vol. 35 f. 45; Cullen to Prop., 8 Apr. 1864: ACPF, *SC, Irlanda*, vol. 34, f. 1166 *(v)*; Cullen to Prop., 15 Apr. 1864: ACPF, *SC, Irlanda*, vol. 34, ff. 1159 *(v)* –60.

79. 'Mi sono convinto che la fratellanza è on solamente illegale o contraria alle leggi di questo regno, ma che è ncora cattiva in se e degna da condannarsi, 10 perchè adunandosi persone d'ogni religione l'espone al pericolo di perder la fede; 20 perchè ette i membri in ostilità l clero; 30 perchè erca a sovvertir un governo riconosciuto e 40 perchè lmeno in Irlanda (e forse anche in America) i membri sono legati da giuramenti amministrati senza alcuna autorità egittima', Cullen to Prop., 1 Apr. 1864: ACPF, *SC, Irlanda*, vol. 35, f. 44 *(v)*.

80. 'Una decisione su questo punto sarebbe assai da desiderarsi per mantener l'uniformità i pratica nel clero d'Irlanda', Cullen to Prop., 1 Apr. 1864: ACPF, *SC, Irlanda*, vol. 35, f. 44 *(v)*; see also Cullen to Prop., 15 Apr. 1864: ACPF, *SC, Irlanda*, vol. 34, f. 1160.

81. Cullen to Prop., 1 Apr. 1864: ACPF, *SC, Irlanda*, vol. 35, f. 45.

82. 'I liberi muratori fanno lo stesso radanendosi qui pubblicamente, e dando anche inviti ai loro pranzi e balli, eppure non cessano di costituire una società egreta', Cullen to Prop, 1 Apr. 1864: ACPF, *SC, Irlanda*, vol. 35, f. 45 *(v)*.

83. Cullen to Prop., 15 Jan. 1864: ACPF, *SC, Irlanda*, vol. 34, ff. 1047; Cullen to Prop., 29 Mar. 1864: ACPF, *SC, Irlanda*, vol. 34, f. 1121 *(v)*; Cullen to Prop., 1 Apr. 1864: ACPF, *SC, Irlanda*, vol. 35, f. 46; Cullen to Prop., 12 Apr. 1864: ACPF, *SC, Irlanda*, vol. 35, f. 37; Cullen to Prop., 15 Apr. 1864: ACPF, *SC, Irlanda*, vol. 34, ff. 1160 *(v)* –61.

84. Cullen to Prop., 25 Mar. 1864: ACPF, *SC, Irlanda*, vol. 35, f. 49; Cullen to Prop., 29 Mar. 1864: ACPF, *SC, Irlanda*, vol. 34, f. 1121 *(v)*; Cullen to Prop., 1 Apr. 1864: ACPF, *SC, Irlanda*, vol. 35, f. 45; Cullen to Prop., 12 Apr. 1864: ACPF, *SC, Irlanda*, vol. 35, f. 37; Cullen to Prop., 15 Apr. 1864: ACPF, *SC, Irlanda*, vol. 34, ff. 1159 *(v)* –61.

85. 'Il movimento cesserebbe ben presto se non fosse per l'incoraggiamento che riceve da Padre Lavelle, e qualche altro ecclesiastico',

Cullen to Prop., 1 Apr. 1864: ACPF, *SC, Irlanda*, vol. 35, f. 46 *(v)*; see also Cullen to Prop., 12 Apr. 1864: ACPF, *SC, Irlanda*, vol. 35, f. 37.

86. Cullen to Prop., 12 Apr. 1864: ACPF, *SC, Irlanda*, vol. 35, f. 38; see also Duggan to Cullen, 25 Apr. 1864: DDA, 320\3, *(ii)*, no. 16.

87. 'In pochi mesi tutti gli altri addetti a queste società e lascieranno, e comincieranno a pensare a qualche altra cosa', Cullen to Prop., 12 Apr. 1864: ACPF, *SC, Irlanda*, vol. 35, f. 38; see also Duggan to Cullen, 25 Apr. 1864: DDA, 320\3, *(ii)*, no. 16.

88. ACPF, *Acta*, vol. 228 *(1864)*, f. 100; Redmond to Cullen, 14 Apr. 1863: DDA, 320\5, *(ii)*, no. 9; Redmond to Cullen, 13 May 1863: DDA, 320\5, *(ii)*, no. 13; Redmond to Cullen, 25 Mar. 1863: DDA, 320\5, *(ii)*, no. 8; Dunne *(Pres. Carlow Coll.)* to Cullen, 13 Apr. 1864: DDA, 320\5, *(i)*, no. 35; Moran to Prop., 30 Apr. 1864: ACPF, *SC, Irlanda*, vol. 35, f. 26; Taylor *(PP, Kilbritain)* to Cullen, 1 May 1864: DDA, 320\5, *(i)*, no. 40.

89. Prop. to Cullen, 1 Apr. 1864: ACPF, *LDB*, vol. 355, f. 155; Prop. to MacHale *(Abp., Tuam)*, Dixon *(Abp., Armagh)*, Leahy *(Abp., Cashel)* and Cullen, 1 Apr. 1864: ACPF, *LDB*, vol. 355, ff. 155 *(v)* –156; Cullen to Prop., 8 Apr. 1864: ACPF, *SC, Irlanda*, vol. 34, f. 1166; MacHale to Prop., 10 Apr. 1864: ACPF, *SC, Irlanda*, vol. 35, f. 41.

90. Prop. to Lavelle, 1 Apr. 1864: ACPF, *LDB*, vol. 355, f. 155.

91. Cullen to Prop., 8 Apr. 1864: ACPF, *SC, Irlanda*, vol. 34, f. 1166; Murray to Moran, 15 Apr. 1864: DDA, 320\3, *(iii)*, no. 7.

92. Cullen to Prop., 15 Apr. 1864: ACPF, *SC, Irlanda*, vol. 34, f. 1160.

93. Lavelle to Fowler *(printer)*, 22 Mar. 1864: ACPF, *SC, Irlanda*, vol. 34, f. 1163; Dunne to Cullen, 9 Apr. 1864: DDA, 320\5, *(i)*, no. 32; Cullen to Prop., 12 Apr. 1864: ACPF, *SC, Irlanda*, vol. 35, f. 37 *(v)*; Cullen to Prop., 15 Apr. 1864: ACPF, *SC, Irlanda*, vol. 34, f. 1159 *(v)*; MacEvilly to Cullen, 19 Apr. 1864: DDA, 320\3, *(i)*, no. 19.

94. Cullen to Prop., 15 Apr. 1864: ACPF, *SC, Irlanda*, vol. 34 f. 1160*(v)*.

95. Pius IX to MacHale, 18 Apr. 1864: ACPF, *SC, Irlanda*, vol. 35, ff. 34–5; see also Furlong to Cullen, 25 Apr. 1864: DDA,

320\3, *(i)*, no. 20; Kirby to Moriarty, n.d. *(Apr. 1864)*: KDA, Moriarty XV, no. 33, *Moriarty Papers*; Keane *(Bp., Cloyne)* to Cullen, 18 May 1864: DDA, 320\3, *(i)*, no. 31; MacEvilly to Cullen, 10 Sept. 1864: DDA, 320\3, *(i)*, no. 54; ACPF, *Acta*, vol. 228, (1864), ff. 115–16.

96. Prop. to Cullen, 27 Apr. 1864: ACPF, LDB, vol. 355, f. 183; Grant *(Bp., Southark)* to Cullen, 13 May 1864: DDA, 320\3, *(ii)*, no. 20; Cullen to Prop., 20 May 1864: ACPF, *SC, Irlanda*, vol. 34. ff. 1177.

97. Cullen to Prop., 20 May 1864: ACPF, *SC, Irlanda*, vol. 34, ff. 1177; Cullen to Kirby, 30 June 1864: ACPF, *SC, Irlanda*, vol. 34, f. 1222; see also Ullathorne *(Bp., Birmingham)* to Cullen, n.d. *(June 1864)*: DDA, 320\3, *(ii)*, no. 21; Goss *(Bp., Liverpool)* to Cullen, 10 June 1864: DDA, 320\3, *(ii)*, no. 24; Ullathorne to Cullen 11 June 1864: DDA, 320\3, *(ii)*, no. 25; Duggan to Cullen, 16 June 1864: DDA, 320\3, *(ii)*, no. 27; Wood *(Bp., Philadelphia)* to Cullen, 7 Nov. 1864: DDA, 320\3, *(ii)*, no. 35; CT, 2 July 1864; *CP*, 3 Sept. 1864.

98. 'Sarà idotto a neinte il partito di Lavelle', Cullen to Kirby, 30 June 1864: ACPF, *Irlanda*, vol. 34, f. 1222 *(v)*; see also Cullen to Prop., 20 May 1864: ACPF, *SC, Irlanda*, vol. 34, f. 1177 *(v)*.

99. Cullen to Prop., 20 May 1864: ACPF, *SC, Irlanda*, vol. 34, ff. 1177 *(v)* –78.

100. Duggan to Cullen, 26 July 1864: DDA, 320\3, *(ii)*, no. 30.

101. Cullen to Prop., 20 May 1864: ACPF, *SC, Irlanda*, vol. 34, f. 1177; Cullen to Kirby, 30 June 1864: ACPF, *SC, Irlanda*, vol. 34, f. 1222; Geison *(Relg., Ohio)* to Cullen, 12 June 1864: DDA, 320\5, *(iii)*, no. 19; Cullen to Kirby, 26 July 1864: ACPF, *SC, Irlanda*, vol. 34, f. 1283; Cullen to Prop., 9 Sept. 1864: ACPF, *SC, Irlanda*, vol. 34, f. 1325; Cullen to Prop., 23 Dec. 1864: ACPF, *SC, Irlanda*, vol. 34, f. 1382.

102. Cullen to Kirby, 13 May 1864: ICAR, *Kirby Papers*, 1864, no. 97; McEvilly to Cullen, 14 June 1864: ICAR, *Kirby Papers*, 1864, no. 115; McEvilly to Kirby, 24 June 1864: ICAR, *Kirby Papers*, 1864, no. 123.

103. Moran to Prop., 2 June 1864: ACPF, *SC, Irlanda*, vol. 34, f. 1193; Cullen to Kirby, 26 July 1864: ACPF, *SC, Irlanda*, vol. 34, f. 1283; Cullen to Prop., 9 Sept. 1864: ACPF,

SC, Irlanda, vol. 34, f. 1325; GFP, 21 May 1864.

104. Moran to Prop., 2 June 1864: ACPF, SC, Irlanda, vol. 34, f. 1193; Cullen to Kirby, 30 June 1864: ACPF, SC, Irlanda, vol. 34, f. 1222; Cullen to Prop., 9 Sept. 1864: ACPF, SC, Irlanda, vol. 34, f. 1325.

105. Cullen to Prop., 20 May 1864: ACPF, SC, Irlanda, vol. 34, f. 1177; Cullen to Kirby, 24 May 1864: ICAR, Kirby Papers, 1864, no. 105; Moran to Prop., 2 June 1864: ACPF, SC, Irlanda, vol. 34, f. 1193; Cullen to Kirby, 17 June 1864: ICAR, Kirby Papers, 1864, no. 118; Cullen to Kirby, 30 June 1864: ACPF, SC, Irlanda, vol. 34, f. 1222; Cullen to Kirby, 19 July 1864: ICAR, Kirby Papers, 1864, no. 140; Cullen to Kirby, 6 Aug. 1864: ICAR, Kirby Papers, 1864, no. 151; Cullen to Prop., 9 Sept. 1864: ACPF, SC, Irlanda, vol. 34, f. 1325; Cullen to Prop., 23 Dec. 1864: ACPF, SC, Irlanda, vol. 34, f. 1382 (v); GFP, 21 May 1864; CT, 21 May 1864, 15 Oct. 1864; IP, 4 June 1864.

106. Cullen to Kirby, 26 July 1864: ACPF, SC, Irlanda, vol. 34, f. 1283; Cullen to Kirby, 30 June 1864: ACPF, SC, Irlanda, vol. 34, f. 1222; Cullen to Kirby, 26 July 1864: ACPF, SC, Irlanda, vol. 34, f. 1283; Cullen to Prop., 9 Sept. 1864: ACPF, SC, Irlanda, vol. 34, f. 1325.

107. Cullen to Kirby, 9 Sept. 1864: ICAR, Kirby Papers, 1864, no. 162.

108. Cullen to Kirby, 30 June 1864: ACPF, SC, Irlanda, vol. 34, f. 1222 (v); Cullen to Kirby, 26 July 1864: ACPF, SC, Irlanda, vol. 34, f. 1283; Cullen to Prop., 9 Sept. 1864: ACPF, SC, Irlanda, vol. 34, f. 1326; CT, 2 July 1864.

109. Prop. to Wiseman, Kyle (Vic. Apos., nrth. dist., Scotland), to Murdock (Vic. Apos., wst. dist., Scotland), Kenrick (Abp., St. Louis) and Duggan, 27 July 1864: ACPF, LDB, vol. 355, f. 343 (v).

110. CT, 2 July 1864; MacHale to Prop., 25 July 1864: ACPF, SC, Irlanda, vol. 34, f. 1260; Prop. to MacHale, 19 Aug. 1864: ACPF, LDB, vol. 355, f. 381; MacHale to Pius IX, 25 July 1864: ACPF, SC, Irlanda, vol. 34, f. 1270; MacHale to Pius IX, 5 Dec. 1864: ACPF, SC, Irlanda, vol. 35, ff. 153-7.

111. Cullen to Prop., 9 Sept. 1864: ACPF, SC, Irlanda, vol. 34, f. 1326 (v).

112. Cullen to Prop., 20 May 1864: ACPF, SC,

Irlanda, vol. 34, f. 1177; Cullen to Kirby, 30 June 1864: ACPF, SC, Irlanda, vol. 34, f. 1222.

113. Cullen to Prop., 12 Aug. 1864: ACPF, SC, Irlanda, vol. 34, f. 1292.

114. Ryan (Bp., Limerick) to Cullen, 24 Aug. 1864: DDA, 320\7, no. 12; Nation, 27 Aug. 1864; CT, 27 Aug. 1864; Conn. Pat., 3 Sept. 1864: Cullen to Prop., 9 Sept. 1864: ACPF, SC, Irlanda, vol. 34, f. 1325; Cullen to Kirby, 6 Nov. 1864: ICAR, Kirby Papers, 1864, no. 212; Cullen to Kirby, 8 Nov. 1864: ICAR, Kirby Papers, 1864, no. 216; MacEvilly to Cullen, 15 Dec. 1864: DDA, 320\3, (i), no. 73.

115. 'Memorial to Pius IX', 29 Nov. 1864: ACPF, SC, Irlanda, vol. 35, ff. 193-4; Ryan to Cullen, 24 Aug. 1864: DDA, 320\7, no. 12; McEvilly to Kirby, 4 Dec. 1864: ICAR, Kirby Papers, 1864, no. 241; Gillooly to Cullen, 4 Dec. 1864: DDA, 320\3, (i), no. 72; Cullen to Kirby, 9 Dec. 1864: ICAR, Kirby Papers, 1864, no. 246; MacEvilly to Cullen, 15 Dec. 1864: DDA, 320\3, (i), no. 73; Gillooly to Cullen, 18 Dec. 1864: DDA, 320\3, (i), no. 76; Kirby to Prop., n.d. (Dec. 1864): ACPF, SC, Irlanda, vol. 35, f. 191; 'Apologia for Lavelle' by James Murray, n.d.: ACPF, SC, Irlanda, vol. 34, ff. 1366-9.

116. Prop. to Monaco La Valletta (Assess. Holy Office), 22 Apr. 1864: ACPF, LDB, vol. 355, f. 205; Prop. to Cullen, 27 Apr. 1864: ACPF, LDB, vol. 355, f. 183; Prop. to Monaco La Valletta, 10 May 1864: ACPF, LDB, vol. 355, f. 253 (v); Prop. to Cullen, 20 May 1864: ACPF, LDB, vol. 355, ff. 233 (v) -4; Prop. to O'Hara, 20 May 1864: ACPF, LDB, (1864), vol. 355, f. 232; Prop. to Monaco La Valletta, 24 May 1864: ACPF, LDB, (1864), vol. 355, f. 259; Prop. to Duggan, 23 May 1864: ACPF, LDB, (1864), vol. 355, f. 237; ACPF, Acta, vol. 228 (1864), ff. 114-5.

117. ACPF, Acta, vol. 228 (1864), ff. 114-5.

118. Monaco la Valletta to Prop., 2 June 1864: ACPF, Acta, vol. 288 (1864), f. 437.

119. 'Societates occultae, de quibus in Pontificiis Constitutionibus sermo est, eae omnes intelliguntur, quae adversus Ecclesiam vel Gubernium sibi aliquid proponunt, exigant vel non exigant juramentum de secreto servando': ACPF, Acta, vol. 228, (1864),

f. 437; see also Prop. to O'Hara, 14 June 1864: ACPF, *LDB*, *(1864)*, vol. 355, f. 279 *(v)*; Prop. to Monaco La Valletta, 16 Mar. 1865: ACPF, *LDB*, *(1865)*, vol. 356, f. 719.

120. Prop. to Cullen, 6 June 1864: ACPF, *LDB*, vol. 355, f. 284; Prop. to Cullen, 7 June 1864: ACPF, *LDB*, vol. 355, f. 267; Prop. to Cullen, 30 July 1864: ACPF, *LDB*, vol. 355, f. 351.

121. *IER*, vol. 1, pp. 38–9.

122. Cullen to Prop., 23 Dec. 1864: ACPF, *SC, Irlanda*, vol. 34, f. 1382 *(v)*; P. Murray, 'The Right of Resistance to the Supreme Power': *Theological Essays*, Dublin, 1853, pp. 379–407.

123. Cullen to Prop., 23 Dec. 1864: ACPF, *SC, Irlanda*, vol. 34, f. 1382; See *IP*, 24, 31 Dec. 1864, 7, 28 Jan., 11, 18 Mar., 1 Apr. 1865.

124. Cullen to Prop., 23 Dec. 1864: ACPF, *SC, Irlanda*, vol. 34 ff. 1382–3.

125. Cullen to Prop., 23 Dec. 1864: ACPF, *SC, Irlanda*, vol. 34, ff. 1382–3; Verdon (*Pres. Clonliffe Coll.,*) to Moran, 26 Dec. 1864: DDA, 320\5, *(i)*, no. 144.

Chapter Eleven

1. *Nation,* 30 Jan. 1864; *IP,* 7 Jan. 1865.

2. *FJ*, 3 Oct. 1864.

3. *FJ*, 21 Dec. 1864; O'Neill Daunt (*lay corr.*) to MacHale (*Abp., Tuam*), 6 Jan. 1865 in B. O'Reilly, John MacHale, Archbishop of Tuam, vol. 2, New York & Cincinnati, 1890, pp. 539–40; MacHale to O'Neill Daunt, 13 January 1865 in O'Reilly, ibid. , pp. 540–1; O'Neill Daunt to MacHale, 13 Jan. 1865 in O'Reilly, ibid., p. 542; MacHale to O'Neill Daunt, 14 Jan. 1865 in O'Reilly, ibid., p. 543; Dillon to Moore (*MP, Mayo co.*), 15 Feb. 1865: NLI, MS. 894, *Moore Papers.*

4. MacHale to Dillon, 6 Dec. 1864: *FJ*, 22 Dec. 1864; Redmond (*PP, Arklow*) to Murray (*Sec. Cullen*), 22 Dec. 1864: DDA, 320\5, *(ii)*, no. 47; O'Reilly, op. cit., vol. 2, pp. 536–9; *IP*, 24 Dec. 1864.

5. Duffy, op. cit., vol. 2, pp. 267–8; *IP*, 3 Dec. 1864.

6. Moore to Dillon, 13 Feb. 1865: DDA, 327\3, no. 30.

7. Redmond to Cullen, 15 Jan. 1865: DDA, 327\2, *(iii)*, no. 4.

8. *DEM*, 10 Jan. 1865.

9. *IP*, 26 Nov., 24 Dec. 1864; 7 Jan. 14 Jan. 4 Feb., 18 Mar. 1865.

10. *FJ*, 30 Dec. 1864.

11. *FJ*, 30 Dec. 1864; see also Redmond to Cullen, 5 Jan. 1865: DDA, 327\2, *(iii)*, no. 1; Cullen to Prop., 6 Jan. 1865: ACPF, *SC, Irlanda*, vol. 35, f. 173 *(v)*; Duffy, op. cit., vol. 2, p. 266; Moran, op. cit., vol. 2, pp. 283.

12. *FJ*, 30 Dec. 1864.

13. *FJ*, 30 Dec. 1864.

14. Burke (*Journ., WR*) to Cullen, 6 Jan. 1865: DDA, 327\3, no. 5; Redmond to Cullen, 1 Mar. 1865: DDA, 327\2, *(iii)*, no. 9; Fairen (*PP, Ballygawley*) to Cullen, 23 Mar. 1865: DDA, 327\2, *(i)*, no. 25; Sullivan, op. cit., p. 301.

15. Cullen to Kirby (*Rec. Irish Coll., Rome*) n.d. *(Jan. 1865)*: ICAR, *Kirby Papers*, 1865, no. 20.

16. Fairen to Cullen, 23 Mar. 1865: DDA, 327\2, *(i)*, no. 25.

17. Burke to Cullen, 6 Jan. 1865: DDA, 327\3, no. 5; Redmond to Cullen, 15 Jan. 1865: DDA, 327\2, *(iii)*, no. 4; Clinch (*Sec. Cath. Elec. Reg. Assoc. Manchester*) to Cullen, 19 Jan. 1865: DDA, 327\3, no. 11.

18. Moran, op. cit., vol. 2, pp. 320–7.

19. Cullen to Kirby, 10 Mar. 1865: ICAR, *Kirby Papers*, 1865, no. 52; MacEvilly (*Bp., Galway*) to Kirby, 10 Mar. 1865: ICAR, *Kirby Papers*, 1865, no. 53; Gillooly (*Bp., Elphin*) to Kirby, 12 Apr. 1865: ICAR, *Kirby Papers*, 1865, no. 80; *FJ*, 1, 3 Mar. 1865.

20. 'Circular to the Clergy', 20 March 1865: DDA, 327\3, no. 44; 'Circular of the National Assoc. of Ire.', 11 Apr. 1865: DDA, 327\3, no. 57.

21. Cullen to Prop., 11 Apr. 1865: ACPF, *SC, Irlanda*, vol. 35, f. 231 *(v)*.

22. Cullen to Kirby, 10 Mar. 1865: ICAR, *Kirby Papers*, 1865, no. 52.

23. ibid.

24. Whyte (*Sec. Nat. Assoc. Ire.*) to Cullen, 25 Apr. 1865: DDA, 327\3, no. 62; *FJ*, 20 June 1865; Dorrian (*Coadj. Bp., Down & Connor*) to Kirby, 2 May 1865: ICAR, *Kirby Papers*, 1865, no. 93.

25. *FJ*, 20 June 1865; see also Dorrian to Kirby, 2 May 1865: ICAR, *Kirby Papers*, 1865, no. 93.

26. ibid.

27. Whyte to Cullen, 6 May 1865: DDA, 327\3, no. 64.

28. ibid.

29. Cullen to Prop, 6 Jan. 1865: ACPF, *SC, Irlanda*, vol. 35, f. 173 *(v)*; Spalding *(Abp., Baltimore)* to Cullen, 4 Jan. 1865: DDA, 327\2, *(ii)*, no. 1; Redmond to Cullen, 27 Feb. 1865: DDA, 327\2, *(iii)*, no. 8.

30. Cullen to Prop., 6 Jan. 1865: ACPF, *SC, Irlanda*, vol. 35 f. 173 *(v)*.

31. Cullen to Kirby, 24 Feb. 1865: ICAR, *Kirby Papers*, 1865, no. 42; *Conn. Pat.*, 18 Feb. 1865; Spalding to Cullen, 4 Jan. 1865: DDA, 327\2, *(ii)*, no. 1.

32. 'Feniani non sunt inquietandi', *Conn. Pat.*, 18 Feb. 1865.

33. Cullen to Kirby, 24 Feb. 1865: ICAR, *Kirby Papers*, 1865, no. 42; Cullen to Prop., 24 Feb. 1865: ACPF, *SC, Irlanda*, vol. 35, f. 206.

34. Moran to Prop., n.d. *(Apr. 1865)*: ACPF, *SC, Irlanda*, vol. 35, f. 220; Prop. to Villavecchia *(Rec. Coll., Brignole, Genoa)*, 26 April 1865: ACPF, *LDB*, vol. 356, ff. 173 *(v)* −4; Villavecchia to Prop., 29 May 1865: ACPF, *SC, Irlanda*, vol. 35, f. 304; *IP*, 8 Apr. 1865.

35. *IP*, 6 May 1865

36. Moran *(Vice Rec. Irish Coll., Rome, Rel. Cullen)* to Prop., n.d. *(Mar. 1865)*: ACPF, *SC, Irlanda*, vol. 35, f. 9; *Conn. Pat.*, 20 Mar., 22 Apr. 1865.

37. *FJ*, 20 June 1865.

38. Dorrian to Kirby, 27 June 1865: ICAR, *Kirby Papers*, 1865, no. 141; *FJ*, 24 June 1865.

39. *FJ*, 28 June 1865.

40. *Nation*, 1 July 1865; *IP*, 8 July 1865; *CT*, 8 July 1865; *FJ*, 10 July 1865.

41. Cullen to Kirby, 16 July 1865: ICAR, *Kirby Papers* , 1865, no. 157.

42. Redmond to Cullen, 29 Sept. 1865: DDA, 327\2, *(iii)*, no. 20.

43. *FJ*, 26 July 1865.

44. Anon. *(Carrell, Bp., Covington)* to Prop., 13 July 1864: ACPF, SOCG, *(1865)*, vol. 992, f. 509 *(v)*; Kenrick *(Abp., St. Louis)* to Prop., 19 Aug. 1864: ACPF, SOCG, *(1865)*, vol. 992, f. 524; Spalding to Prop., 17 Oct. 1864: ACPF, SOCG, *(1865)*, vol. 992, f. 519; Spalding to Prop., 31 Oct. 1864: ACPF, SOCG, *(1865)*, vol. 992, f. 521; Domenec *(Bp., Pittsburgh)* to Prop., 9 Nov. 1864: ACPF, SC, America Centrale, vol. 20, f. 1118 *(v)*; Alemany *(Abp., San Francisco)* to Prop., 26 Dec. 1864: ACPF, SC, America Centrale, vol. 20, ff. 1194–5.

45. Domenec to Prop., 9 Nov. 1864: ACPF, SC, America Centrale, vol. 20, f. 1118 *(v)*; Alemany to Prop., 26 Dec. 1864: ACPF, SC, America Centrale, MDBU vol. 20, ff. 1194–95.

46. Prop. to Domenec, 23 Jan. 1865: ACPF, *LDB*, *(1865)*, vol. 356, f. 31; Prop. to Alemany, 29 Mar. 1865: ACPF, *LDB*, *(1865)*, vol. 356, f. 152.

47. Prop. to Monaco La Valletta *(Assess., Holy Office)*, 16 Mar. 1865: ACPF, *LDB*, *(1865)*, vol. 356, f. 719.

48. Prop. to Cullen, MacHale, Duggan *(Abp., Chicago)* and Wood *(Bp., Philadelphia)*, 13 July 1865: ACPF, *LDB*, *(1865)*, vol. 356, f. 292 *(v)*; Prop., to Spalding, Purcell *(Abp., Cincinnati)*, McCloskey *(Abp. New York)*, Conroy *(Bp., Elect Albany)*, Fitzpatrick *(Bp., Boston)*, Loughlin *(Bp., Brooklyn)*, Timon *(Bp., Buffalo)*, de Goesbriand *(Bp., Burlington)*, McFarland *(Bp., Hartford)*, Bayley *(Bp., Newark)*, Bacon *(Bp., Portland)*, 13 July 1865: ACPF, *LDB*, *(1865)*, vol. 356, ff. 293–4.

49. Prop., to Spalding, Purcell, McCloskey, Conroy, Fitzpatrick, Loughlin, Timon, de Goesbriand, McFarland, Bailey, Bacon, 13 July 1865: ACPF, *LDB*, *(1865)*, vol. 356, ff. 293–4.

50. Dixon *(Abp., Armagh)* to Prop., 31 July 1865: ACPF, *SC, Irlanda*, vol. 35, ff. 368–9; Leahy *(Abp., Cashel)* to Prop., 10 Aug. 1865: ACPF, *SC, Irlanda*, vol. 35, ff. 388–90; Anon. *(Kirby)* to Prop., n.d. *(Dec. 1865)*: ACPF, *SC, Irlanda*, vol. 35, f. 437.

51. Prop. to Monaco La Valletta, 22 Nov. 1865: ACPF, *LDB*, vol. 356, f. 610.

52. Curley *(PP, Whelling)* to Prop., 8 Dec. 1866: ACPF, SC, America Centrale, vol. 21, ff. 849–50; Barker *(ex Student Prop.)* to Prop., 1 Jan. 1867: ACPF, SC, America Centrale, vol. 21, f. 706; Prop. to Barker, 19 Feb. 1867: ACPF, *LDB*, vol. 358, f. 182 *(v)*; Prop. to Whelan *(Bp., Wheeling)*, 22 March 1867: ACPF, *LDB*, vol. 358, f. 280; Prop. to Whelan, 20 May 1867: ACPF, *LDB*, vol. 358, f. 464; Curley to Prop., 2 July 1867: ACPF, SC, America Cetrale, vol. 21, ff. 923–4.

53. 'Io m'era risoluto di non pensare più all'affare, e di lasciare le cose andare di male in peggio', Cullen to Prop., 17 Sept. 1865: ACPF, *SC, Irlanda*, vol. 35 f. 414; see also

Cullen to Prop., 29 Sept. 1865: ACPF, SC, Irlanda, vol. 35, f. 401 (v).

54. Cullen to Prop., 17 Sept. 1865: ACPF, SC, Irlanda, vol. 35, f. 414; Cullen to Prop., 29 Sept. 1865: ACPF, SC, Irlanda, vol. 35, f. 401; Cullen to Kirby, 1 Oct. 1865: ICAR, NC, III, 3, 1, no. 120; Cullen to Prop., 9 Oct. 1865: ACPF, SC, Irlanda, vol. 35, f. 405; Cullen to Prop., 10 Dec. 1865: ACPF, SC, Irlanda, vol. 35, ff. 452 (v) −3; Cullen to Prop., 18 Dec. 1865: ACPF, SC, Irlanda, vol. 35, f. 451 (v).

55. Cullen to Prop., 17 Sept. 1865: ACPF, SC, Irlanda, vol. 35, f. 414.

56. Cullen to Prop., 17 Sept. 1865: ACPF, SC, Irlanda, vol. 35, f. 414; Cullen to Prop., 29 Sept. 1865: ACPF, SC, Irlanda, vol. 35, f. 401; Cullen to Prop., 9 Oct. 1865: ACPF, SC, Irlanda, vol. 35, f. 405; Cullen to Prop., 10 Dec. 1865: ACPF, SC, Irlanda, vol. 35, ff. 452−3; Cullen to Prop., 18 Dec. 1865: ACPF, SC, Irlanda, vol. 35, f. 451.

57. Cullen to Kirby., 1 Oct. 1865: ICAR, NC, III, 3, 1, no. 120; Cullen to Prop., 9 Oct. 1865: ACPF, SC, Irlanda, vol. 35, f. 405 (v).

58. Cullen to Prop., 17 Sept. 1865: ACPF, SC, Irlanda, vol. 35, f. 415.

59. 'Tutta Dublino è contentissima di ciò che fece il governo, e non si e mosso alcun cittadino a difendere i poveri Feniani che pochi giorni sono, si vantavano d'avere centinaia di migliaia d'associati', Cullen to Prop., 17 Sept. 1865: ACPF, SC, Irlanda, vol. 35, f. 414 (v); see also Cullen to Prop., 29 Sept. 1865: ACPF, SC, Irlanda, vol. 35, f. 401 (v); Cullen to Prop., 9 Oct. 1865: ACPF, SC, Irlanda, vol. 35, f. 405 (v); Cullen to Prop., 18 Dec. 1865: ACPF, SC, Irlanda, vol. 35, f. 451.

60. Cullen to Kirby, 1 Oct. 1865: ICAR, NC, III, 3, 1, no. 120; Cullen to Prop., 10 Dec. 1865: ACPF, SC, Irlanda, vol. 35, ff. 452−3; Cullen to Prop., 18 Dec. 1865: ACPF, SC, Irlanda, vol. 35, f. 454.

61. 'Questo povero paese … sarebbe totalmente rovinato da una rivoluzione Mazziniana quale ci preparavano i Signori Feniani', Cullen to Prop., 17 Sept. 1865: ACPF, SC, Irlanda, vol. 35, f. 415 (v); see also Cullen to Prop., 29 Sept. 1865: ACPF, SC, Irlanda, vol. 35, f. 401 (v).

62. 'Grazie a Dio ci siamo liberati da un gran pericolo che ci minacciava', Cullen to

Prop., 17 Sept. 1865: ACPF, SC, Irlanda, vol. 35, f. 415; see also Cullen to Kirby, 1 Oct. 1865: ICAR, NC, III, 3, 1, no. 120; Cullen to Prop., 9 Oct. 1865: ACPF, SC, Irlanda, vol. 35, f. 405; Cullen to Prop., 10 Dec. 1865: ACPF, SC, Irlanda, vol. 35, f. 453.

63. Cullen to Prop., 17 Sept. 1865: ACPF, SC, Irlanda, vol. 35, f. 415 (v); Cullen to Prop., 29 Sept. 1865: ACPF, SC, Irlanda, vol. 35, f. 401.

64. 'Siamo liberati dalle insidie dei Feniani', Cullen to Prop., 13 Oct. 1865: ACPF, SC, Irlanda, vol. 35, f. 408; see also Cullen to Prop., 10 Dec. 1865: ACPF, SC, Irlanda, vol. 35, f. 453.

65. 'sciocchi cospiratori', Cullen to Prop., 13 Oct. 1865: ACPF, SC, Irlanda, vol. 35, f. 408.

66. 'Io temo che il nostro governo farà impiccare molti di questi disgraziati', Cullen to Prop., 9 Oct. 1865: ACPF, SC, Irlanda, vol. 35, f. 405 (v); see also Cullen to Kirby, 1 Oct. 1865: ICAR, NC, III, 3, 1, no. 120; Cullen to Prop., 13 Oct. 1865: ACPF, SC, Irlanda, vol. 35, f. 408.

67. Cullen to Prop., 10 Dec. 1865: ACPF, SC, Irlanda, vol. 35, f. 452 (v); Cullen to Prop., 18 Dec. 1865: ACPF, SC, Irlanda, vol. 35, ff. 451 (v), 454; Cullen to Prop., 29 Dec. 1865: ACPF, SC, Irlanda, vol. 35, f. 470.

68. 'Erano sul punto di provocare una rivoluzione, che non poteva terminare altrimenti che nella rovina totale e nel massacro dei poveri nostri cattolici', Cullen to Prop., 29 Dec. 1865: ACPF, SC, Irlanda, vol. 35, f. 470.

69. Cullen to Kirby., 1 Oct. 1865: ICAR, NC, III, 3, 1, no. 120.

70. Cullen to Kirby, 1 Oct. 1865: ICAR, NC, III, 3, 1, no. 120; FJ, 2 Oct. 1865; Cullen to Prop., 9 Oct. 1865: ACPF, SC, Irlanda, vol. 35, f. 405; Cullen to Prop., 18 Dec. 1865: ACPF, SC, Irlanda, vol. 35, f. 454.

71. Cullen to Prop., 10 Dec. 1865: ACPF, SC, Irlanda, vol. 35, f. 452 (v); Cullen to Prop., 18 Dec. 1865: ACPF, SC, Irlanda, vol. 35, f. 454.

72. Cullen to Prop., 9 Oct. 1865: ACPF, SC, Irlanda, vol. 35, f. 405 (v); see also Redmond to Cullen, 13 Dec. 1865: DDA, 327\2, (iii), no. 26.

73. Cullen to Prop., 17 Sept. 1865: ACPF, SC, Irlanda, vol. 35, f. 415 (v); Cullen to Prop.,

29 Sept. 1865: ACPF, *SC, Irlanda*, vol. 35, f. 401; Cullen to Kirby, 1 Oct. 1865: ICAR, *NC, III*, 3, 1, no. 120; Cullen to Prop., 9 Oct. 1865: ACPF, *SC, Irlanda*, vol. 35, f. 405 *(v)*.

74. Cullen to Kirby, 1 Oct. 1865: ICAR, *NC, III*, 3, 1, no. 120; Carroll *(lay corr.)* to Cullen, 13 Nov. 1865: DDA, 327\4, no. 81; Kirby to Prop., n.d. *(Dec. 1865)*: ACPF, *SC, Irlanda*, vol. 35, f. 437.

75. Lavelle *(PP, Partry)* to Prop., 26 April 1865: ACPF, *SC, Irlanda*, vol. 35, ff. 250–3; Lavelle to Pius IX, 27 May 1865: ACPF, *SC, Irlanda*, vol. 35, f. 302; Lavelle to Prop., 27 May 1865: ACPF, *SC, Irlanda*, vol. 35, f. 303; Lavelle to Pius IX, 28 June 1865: ACPF, *SC, Irlanda*, vol. 35, f. 330; Lavelle to Prop., 28 June 1865: ACPF, *SC, Irlanda*, vol. 35, f. 329; MacHale to Prop., 30 June 1865: ACPF, *SC, Irlanda*, vol. 35, f. 343; Lavelle to Prop., 5 Aug. 1865: ACPF, *SC, Irlanda*, vol. 35, f. 374; Cullen to Kirby, 1 Oct. 1865: ICAR, *NC, III*, 3, 1, no. 120; Cullen to Prop., 10 Dec. 1865: ACPF, *SC, Irlanda*, vol. 35, f. 453 *(v)*; Cullen to Prop., 18 Dec. 1865: ACPF, *SC, Irlanda*, vol. 35, f. 451; *FJ*, 30 Sept. 1865.

76. Moran, op. cit., vol. 2, p. 388; see also Collins *(lay corr.)* to Cullen, 28 Oct. 1865: DDA, 327\4, no. 68; Carroll to Cullen, 3 Nov. 1865: DDA, 327\4, no. 73.

77. Moran, op. cit., vol. 2, pp. 388–404.

78. J.C. Beckett, 'Gladstone, Queen Victoria, and the disestablishment of the Irish Church, 1868–9', in *IHS*, vol. 13, p. 41, *(Mar. 1962)*.

79. Carroll to Cullen, 13 Nov. 1865: DDA, 327\4, no. 81; Walker, op. cit., p. 104.

80. Dillon *(MP, Tipperary co.)* to Cullen, 24 Nov. 1865: DDA, 327\4, no. 90; 'Address of the Committee of the National Association of Ireland to the people of Ireland', n.d.: DDA, 327\4, no. 119; O'Reilly *(MP, Longford)* to Cullen, n.d. *(1865)*: DDA, 327\4, no. 121; *FJ*, 8, 11 Dec. 1865.

81. Forde *(PP, Booterstown)* to Cullen, 14 *(Nov.)* 1865: DDA, 327\1, *(iii)*, no. 14; *FJ*, 4 Dec. 1865.

82. Cullen to Prop., 13 Oct. 1865: ACPF, *SC, Irlanda*, vol. 35, f. 408; Cullen to Prop., 10 Dec. 1865: ACPF, *SC, Irlanda*, vol. 35, f. 453; Cullen to Prop., 29 Dec. 1865: ACPF, *SC, Irlanda*, vol. 35, f. 470; Grant *(Bp., Southwark)* to Cullen, 25 Dec. 1865: DDA, 327\1, *(ii)*, no. 28.

83. Cullen to Prop., 10 Dec. 1865: ACPF, *SC, Irlanda*, vol. 35, f. 453; Wood to Cullen, 11 Dec. 1865: DDA, 327\1, *(ii)*, no. 24; Purcell to Cullen, 17 Dec. 1865: DDA, 327\1, no. 25.

84. 'Dublino è piena di truppe', Cullen to Prop., 10 Dec. 1865: ACPF, *SC, Irlanda*, vol. 35, f. 453; see also Cullen to Prop., 17 Sept. 1865: ACPF, *SC, Irlanda*, vol. 35, f. 414; Cullen to Prop., 29 Dec. 1865: ACPF, *SC, Irlanda*, vol. 35, f. 470; Grant to Cullen, 25 Dec. 1865: DDA, 327\1, *(ii)*, no. 28.

85. Cullen to Prop., 10 Dec. 1865: ACPF, *SC, Irlanda*, vol. 35, f. 453; Cullen to Prop., 29 Dec. 1865: ACPF, *SC, Irlanda*, vol. 35, f. 470; see also Grant to Cullen, 25 Dec. 1865: DDA, 327\1, *(ii)*, no. 28.

86. 'Pare che il Fenianismo andrà ora a terminare in fumo ... Io sono persuaso che non v'è il più remoto pericolo di turbolenze', Cullen to Prop., 10 Dec. 1865: ACPF, *SC, Irlanda*, vol. 35, f. 453; see also Wood to Cullen, 11 Dec. 1865: DDA, 327\1, *(ii)*, no. 24; Purcell to Cullen, 17 Dec. 1865: DDA, 327\1, no. 25; Grant to Cullen, 25 Dec. 1865: DDA, 327\1, *(ii)*, no. 28; Cullen to Prop., 29 Dec. 1865: ACPF, *SC, Irlanda*, vol. 35, f. 470.

87. 'Tutto il clero è impegnato a tener il popolo tranquillo ed ubbidiente, e coll'aiuto di Dio riusciremo', Cullen to Prop., 29 Dec. 1865: ACPF, *SC, Irlanda*, vol. 35, f. 470; see also Redmond to Cullen, 17 Dec. 1865: DDA, 327\2, *(iii)*, no. 27.

88. 'i loro scritti rivoluzionari e antireligiosi', Cullen to Prop., 18 Dec. 1865: ACPF, *SC, Irlanda*, vol. 35, f. 454.

89. 'I Protestanti prendono occasione dalla congiura per escludere i cattolici da ogni carica di fiducia o d'emolumento sotto pretesto che i Feniani e i loro fautori erano cattolici', Cullen to Prop., 18 Dec. 1865: ACPF, *SC, Irlanda*, vol. 35, f. 454.

90. 'Questi mali si devono attribuire in gran parte al celebre Lavelle ed i suoi aderenti', Cullen to Prop., 10 Dec. 1865: ACPF, *SC, Irlanda*, vol. 35, f. 453 *(v)*; see also Wood to Cullen, 11 Dec. 1865: DDA, 327\1, *(ii)*, no. 24; Purcell to Cullen, 17 Dec. 1865: DDA, 327\1, no. 25; Cullen to Prop., 18 Dec. 1865: ACPF, *SC, Irlanda*, vol. 35, f. 451.

91. Cullen to Prop., 12 Jan. 1866: ACPF, *SC, Irlanda,* vol. 35, f. 630; Sullivan *(lay corr.)* to Monsell *(MP, Limerick),* 12 Jan. 1866: NLI, MS. 8318, (5), *Monsell Papers;* Gillooly to Cullen, 12 Jan. 1866: DDA, 327\5, *(i),* no. 35; Redmond to Cullen, 14 Jan. 1866: DDA, 327\6, *(iii),* no. 3; Galvin *(PP, Rathdrum)* to Cullen, 25 Jan. 1866: DDA, 327\6, *(iv),* no. 2; Cuffe *(PP, Rochester)* to Cullen, 30 Jan. 1866: DDA, 327\6, no. 11; Gillooly to Cullen, 2 Feb. 1866: DDA, 327\5, *(i),* no. 47; Gillooly to Cullen, 15 Feb. 1866: DDA, 327\5, *(i),* no. 75; Redmond to Cullen, 25 Feb. 1866: DDA, 327\6, *(iii),* no. 9; Redmond to Cullen, 5 Mar. 1866: DDA, 327\6, *(iii),* no. 12; Redmond to Cullen, 20 Mar. 1866: DDA, 327\6, *(iii),* no. 13; Redmond to Cullen, 25 Mar. 1866: DDA, 327\6, *(iii),* no. 14.

92. Collins to Cullen, 5 Jan. 1867: DDA, 327\7, no. 7; Cullen to Kirby, n.d. *(Apr. 1866):* ICAR, *NC, III,* 3, 1, no. 133; Redmond to Cullen, 19 Jan. 1866: DDA, 327\6, *(iii),* no. 4; Redmond to Cullen, 4 Feb. 1866: DDA, 327\6, *(iii),* no. 5; Redmond to Cullen, 15 Feb. 1866: DDA, 327\6, *(iii),* no. 6; Redmond to Cullen, 16 Feb. 1866: DDA, 327\6, *(iii),* no. 7; Redmond to Cullen, 25 Feb. 1866: DDA, 327\6, *(iii),* no. 9.

93. Smithwick *(PP, Baldoyle)* to Cullen, 7 Feb. 1866: DDA, 327\6, *(i),* no. 14; Redmond to Cullen, 16 Feb. 1866: DDA, 327\6, *(iii),* no. 7; Cullen to Kirby, n.d. (Apr. 1866): ICAR, *NC, III,* 3, 1, no. 133; O'Connor *(Relg., Baltimore)* to Cullen, 21 Feb. 1866: DDA, 327\6, *(v),* no. 6; O'Connor to Cullen, 24 Apr. 1866: DDA, 327\6, *(v),* no. 9.

94. Cullen to Kirby, n.d. *(Apr. 1866):* ICAR, *NC, III,* 3, 1, no. 133.

95. *FJ,* 24 Jan. 1866; *Times,* 25 Jan. 1866; Manning *(Abp., Westminster)* to Cullen, 5 Feb. 1866: DDA, 327\5, *(ii),* no. 2; Conaty *(Bp., Kilmore)* to Cullen, 2 Mar. 1866: DDA, 327\5, *(i),* no. 97; Gillooly to Cullen, 11 May 1866: DDA, 327\5, *(i),* no. 145.

96. Keane *(Bp., Cloyne)* to Cullen, 1 Jan. 1866: DDA, 327\5, *(i),* no. 2; Dixon to Cullen, 2 Jan. 1866: DDA, 327\5, *(i),* no. 3; MacHale to Cullen, 2 Jan. 1866: DDA, 327\5, *(i),* no. 4; Gillooly to Cullen, 2 Jan. 1866: DDA, 327\5, *(i),* no. 5; Moriarty *(Bp., Kerry)* to Cullen, 2 Jan. 1866: DDA, 327\5, *(i),* no. 7; Moriarty to Cullen, 3 Jan. 1866: DDA, 327\5, *(i),* no. 8; Butler *(Bp., Limerick)* to Cullen, 3 Jan. 1866: DDA, 327\5, *(i),* no. 9; Derry *(Bp., Clonfert)* to Cullen, 3 Jan. 1866: DDA, 327\5, *(i),* no. 10; Dixon to Cullen, 3 Jan. 1866: DDA, 327\5, *(i),* no. 11; Dillon to Cullen, 5 Feb. 1866: DDA, 327\7, no. 22; Collins to Cullen, 5 Jan. 1867: DDA, 327\7, no. 7; McGee *(CC, Dundalk)* to Cullen, 16 Jan. 1867: DDA, 327\6, *(i),* no. 4; Dillon to Cullen, 21 Apr. 1866: DDA, 327\7, no. 69; *FJ,* 1, 19, 21 Mar., 19 Apr. 16 May 1866.

97. Cullen to Prop., 18 Feb. 1866: ACPF, *SC, Irlanda,* vol. 35, f. 609; Cullen to Prop., 6 Mar. 1866: ACPF, *SC, Irlanda,* vol. 35, f. 612 *(v);* Redmond to Cullen, 26 Mar. 1866: DDA, 327\6, *(iii),* no. 15; *FJ,* 1, 19, 21 Mar., 19 Apr., 16, 26 May, 14 June 1866; *Parl. Deb.* ser. 3, 183: 994–1010, 1029.

98. Cullen to Prop., 18 Feb. 1866: ACPF, *SC, Irlanda,* vol. 35, f. 609; Cullen to Prop., 6 Mar. 1866: ACPF, *SC, Irlanda,* vol. 35, f. 612.

99. Redmond to Cullen, 2 Mar. 1866: DDA, 327\6, *(iii),* no. 11; Redmond to Cullen, 5 Mar. 1866: DDA, 327\6, *(iii),* no. 12; Redmond to Cullen, 20 Mar. 1866: DDA, 327\6, *(iii),* no. 13; Lynch *(Bp., Toronto)* to Cullen, 24 Mar. 1866: DDA, 327\5, *(iii),* no. 6; Redmond to Cullen, 25 Mar. 1866: DDA, 327\6, *(iii),* no. 14; Cullen to Kirby, n.d. *(Apr. 1866):* ICAR, *NC, III,* 3, 1, no. 133; Keane *(Bp., Ross)* to Kirby, 6 Feb. 1866: ICAR, *Kirby Papers,* 1866, no. 24.

100. Cullen to Prop., 18 Feb. 1866: ACPF, *SC, Irlanda,* vol. 35, f. 609.

101. ibid.

102. Cullen to Prop., 12 Jan. 1866: ACPF, *SC, Irlanda,* vol. 35, f. 630.

103. ibid.

104. Cullen to Prop., 12 Jan. 1866: ACPF, *SC, Irlanda,* vol. 35, f. 629; Cullen to Prop., 6 Mar. 1866: ACPF, *SC, Irlanda,* vol. 35, f. 612 *(v);* Cullen to Prop., 23 Mar. 1866: ACPF, *SC, Irlanda,* vol. 35, f. 624 *(v);* Moran to Cullen, 3 Aug. 1866: DDA, 327\5, *(v),* no. 12; Redmond to Cullen, 14 Sept. 1866: DDA, 327\6, *(iii),* no. 40; Redmond to Cullen, 16 Sept. 1866: DDA, 327\6, *(iii),* no. 41; Redmond to Cullen, 17 Sept. 1866:

DDA, 327\6, *(iii)*, no. 42; Redmond to Cullen, 18 Sept. 1866: DDA, 327\6, *(iii)*, no. 43; Redmond to Cullen, 22 Sept. 1866: DDA, 327\6, *(iii)*, no. 45; Redmond to Cullen, 23 Sept. 1866: DDA, 327\6, *(iii)*, no. 46; Galvin to Cullen, 25 Sept. 1866: DDA, 327\6, *(iv)*, no. 17; Redmond to Cullen, 30 Sept. 1866: DDA, 327\6, *(iii)*, no. 47; Redmond to Cullen, 16 Oct. 1866: DDA, 327\6, *(iii)*, no. 49; Herbert *(lay corr.)* to Cullen, 25 Oct. 1866: DDA, 327\8, no. 46; Redmond to Cullen, 26 Oct. 1866: DDA, 327\6, *(iii)*, no. 50; Redmond to Cullen, 1 Nov. 1866: DDA, 327\6, *(iii)*, no. 52; Redmond to Cullen, |4 Nov. 1866: DDA, 327\6, *(iii)*, no. 53; Redmond to Cullen, 29 Nov. 1866: DDA, 327\6, *(iii)*, no. 57; Redmond to Cullen, 4 Dec. 1866: DDA, 327\6, *(iii)*, no. 60; Cullen to Prop., 6 Dec. 1866: ACPF, *SC, Irlanda*, vol. 35, f. 864; Redmond to Cullen, 11 Dec. 1866: DDA, 327\6, *(iii)*, no. 61; Cullen to Prop., 23 Dec. 1866: ACPF, *SC, Irlanda*, vol. 35, f. 902 *(v)*.

105. Cullen to Prop., 12 Jan. 1866: ACPF, *SC, Irlanda*, vol. 35, f. 629.

106. Cullen to Prop., 12 Jan. 1866: ACPF, *SC, Irlanda*, vol. 35, f. 630; Cullen to Prop., 18 Feb. 1866: ACPF, *SC, Irlanda*, vol. 35, f. 609; Cullen to Prop., 6 Mar. 1866: ACPF, *SC, Irlanda*, vol. 35, f. 612; Moran to Prop., 29 Mar. 1866: ACPF, *SC, Irlanda*, vol. 35, f. 647.

107. Cullen to Prop., 12 Jan. 1866: ACPF, *SC, Irlanda*, vol. 35, f. 630; Cullen to Prop., 18 Feb. 1866: ACPF, *SC, Irlanda*, vol. 35, f. 609; Cullen to Prop., 23 Mar. 1866: ACPF, *SC, Irlanda*, vol. 35, f. 624 *(v)*.

108. Cullen to Prop., 12 Jan. 1866: ACPF, *SC, Irlanda*, vol. 35, f. 630; Cullen to Prop., 6 Mar. 1866: ACPF, *SC, Irlanda*, vol. 35, f. 612; Redmond to Cullen, 26 Mar. 1866: DDA, 327\6, *(iii)*, no. 15; Cullen to Prop., 6 Dec. 1866: ACPF, *SC, Irlanda*, vol. 35, f. 864 *(v)*.

109. Cullen to Prop., 18 Feb. 1866: ACPF, *SC, Irlanda*, vol. 35, f. 609 *(v)*; Cullen to Prop., 6 Mar. 1866: ACPF, *SC, Irlanda*, vol. 35, f. 612.

110. Cullen to Prop., 18 Feb. 1866: ACPF, *SC, Irlanda*, vol. 35, f. 609 *(v)*; Cullen to Prop., 23 Mar. 1866: ACPF, *SC, Irlanda*, vol. 35, f. 624 *(v)*.

111. Cullen to Prop., 6 Mar. 1866: ACPF, *SC, Irlanda*, vol. 35, f. 612 *(v)*.

112. Cullen to Prop., 18 Feb. 1866: ACPF, *SC, Irlanda*, vol. 35, f. 609 *(v)*; Cullen to Prop., 6 Mar. 1866: ACPF, *SC, Irlanda*, vol. 35, f. 612.

113. Cullen to Prop., 18 Feb. 1866: ACPF, *SC, Irlanda*, vol. 35, f. 609 *(v)*; Cullen to Prop., 6 Mar. 1866: ACPF, *SC, Irlanda*, vol. 35, f. 612; Cullen to Prop., 23 Mar. 1866: ACPF, *SC, Irlanda* MDNM, vol. 35, f. 624 *(v)*; Redmond to Cullen, 14 May 1866: DDA, 327\6, *(iii)*, no. 24.

114. Cullen to Prop., 18 Feb. 1866: ACPF, *SC, Irlanda*, vol. 35, f. 609; Cullen to Prop., 6 Mar. 1866: ACPF, *SC, Irlanda*, vol. 35, f. 612.

115. 'Questi sono i benefizi che riceviamo dal patriotismo del Lavelle e d'altri che da quattro anni incorraggivano un sistema che non poteva produrre niente di buono, e che di sua natura tendeva al male', Cullen to Prop., 12 Jan. 1866: ACPF, *SC, Irlanda*, vol. 35, f. 630; see also Cullen to Prop., 6 Mar. 1866: ACPF, *SC, Irlanda*, vol. 35, f. 612 *(v)*.

116. Redmond to Cullen, 28 Feb. 1866: DDA, 327\6, *(iii)*, no. 10; Cullen to Prop., 23 Mar. 1866: ACPF, *SC, Irlanda*, vol. 35, f. 624 *(v)*.

117. Cullen to Prop., 23 Mar. 1866: ACPF, *SC, Irlanda*, vol. 35, f. 624 *(v)*; Cullen to Prop., 20 Apr. 1866: ACPF, *SC, Irlanda*, vol. 35, f. 652 *(v)*; Redmond to Cullen, 27 May 1866: DDA, 327\6, *(iii)*, no. 29; O'Connor to Cullen, 21 May 1866: DDA, 327\6, *(v)*, no. 12; O'Connor to Cullen, 21 May 1866: DDA, 327\6, *(v)*, no. 13.

118. O'Connor to Cullen, 21 May 1866: DDA, 327\6, *(v)*, no. 13; Redmond to Cullen, n.d. *(May 1866)*: DDA, 327\6, *(iii)*, no. 28.

119. *FJ*, 16, 26 May, 14 June 1866; see also *Parl. Deb.* ser. 3, 183: 152; 1097–1102.

120. *FJ*, 19 June 1866; *Parl. Deb.* ser. 3, 184: 693–743.

121. Grey *(Ed., FJ; MP, Kilkenny)* to Cullen, 4 May 1866: DDA, 327\7, no. 79; Dillon to Cullen, 8 May 1866: DDA, 327\7, no. 85; O'Reilly to Cullen, 8 May 1866: DDA, 327\7, no. 86; Redmond to Cullen, 8 May 1866: DDA, 327\6, *(iii)*, no. 22; Dillon to Cullen, 9 May 1866: DDA, 327\7, no. 88; Redmond to Cullen, 16 May 1866: DDA, 327\6, *(iii)*, no. 25; Jones *(Relg., Dublin)*

to Cullen, 19 May 1866: DDA, 327\6, *(v)*, no. 11; Kavanagh *(lay corr.)* to Cullen, n.d. *(1866)*: DDA, 327\7, no. 106.

122. Russell *(Brit. unofficial agent,Vatican, Rel. PM)* to Clarendon *(Foreign Sec.)*, 5 Mar. 1866: FO, 43\96 a, f. 92; Clarendon to Russell, 6 Mar. 1866: FO, 43\96 a, f. 92; Russell to Clarendon, 6 Apr. 1866: FO, 43\96 a, f. 136; Manning to Cullen, 29 May 1866: DDA, 327\5, *(i)*, no. 10; Galvin to Cullen, 31 May 1866: DDA, 327\6, *(iv)*, no. 11; Strain *(Bp., Abila, Vic. Apost. Eastern dist., Scotland)* to Cullen, 31 May 1866: DDA, 327\5, *(iii)*, no. 12; Thompson *(lay corr.)*, 13 June 1866: DDA, 327\7, no. 102; Redmond to Cullen, 15 June 1866: DDA, 327\6, *(iii)*, no. 31; Brown *(Bp., Newport & Menevia)* to Cullen, 28 June 1866: DDA, 327\5, *(iii)*, no. 14; Moran to Cullen, 2 July 1866: DDA, 327\5, *(v)*, no. 7; Grimley *(Bp., Antigonia and Cape of Good Hope, Western Province, Vic. Ap.)* to Cullen, 13 July 1866: DDA, 327\5, *(iii)*, no. 17; Barron *(lay corr., Waterford)* to Cullen, 19 Aug. 1866: DDA, 327\8, no. 4; Ennis *(MP, Athlone)* to Cullen, 19 Aug. 1866: DDA, 327\8, no. 6; McCloskey to Cullen, 20 Aug. 1866: DDA, 327\5, *(iii)*, no. 20; MacCarthy *(lay corr.)* to Cullen, Aug. 1866: DDA, 327\8, no. 9; Bowyer *(MP, Dundalk)* to Cullen, 23 Aug. 1866: DDA, 327\8, no. 10; Collins to Cullen, 6 Sept. 1866: DDA, 327\8, no. 14; Derry to Cullen, 15 Aug. 1866: DDA, 327\5, *(i)*, no. 160; Walshe *(Bp., Kildare & Leighlin)* to Cullen, 18 Aug. 1866: DDA, 327\5, *(i)*, no. 162; Cantwell *(Bp., Meath)* to Cullen, 23 Aug. 1866: DDA, 327\5, *(i)*, no. 164; Durcan *(Bp., Clonfert)* to Cullen, 24 Aug. 1866: DDA, 327\5, *(i)*, no. 168; Whittle *(PP, Dunlavin)* to Cullen, 30 Aug. 1866: DDA, 327\6, *(i)* no. 74; Cuffe to Cullen, 26 Oct. 1866: DDA, 327\6, *(i)*, no. 86; Lynch to Cullen, 2 Nov. 1866: DDA, 327\5, *(iii)*, no. 26.

123. Moran to Cullen, 14 June 1866: DDA, 327\5, *(v)*, no. 4.

124. Moran to Cullen, 20 July 1866: DDA, 327\5, *(v)*, no. 10

125. MacEvilly to Cullen, 19 July 1866: DDA, 327\5, *(i)*, no. 158.

126. Whittle to Cullen, 30 Aug. 1866: DDA, 327\6, *(i)*, no. 74; Redmond to Cullen, 27 Oct. 1866: DDA, 327\6, *(iii)*, no. 51;

Redmond to Cullen, 1 Nov. 1866: DDA, 327\6, *(iii)*, no. 52; Redmond to Cullen, 4 Dec. 1866: DDA, 327\6, *(iii)*, no. 60; Redmond to Cullen, 21 Dec. 1866: DDA, 327\6, *(iii)*, no. 64.

127. Sanfee *(lay corr.)* to Cullen, 17 Sept. 1866: DDA, 327\8, no. 24; Collins to Cullen, 18 Sept. 1866: DDA, 327\8, no. 26; Grey to Cullen, 29 Sept. 1866: DDA, 327\8, no. 29; Herbert to Cullen, 25 Oct. 1866: DDA, 327\8, no. 46; Grey to Cullen, 17 Nov. 1866: DDA, 327\8, no. 51; Grey to Cullen, 29 Nov. 1866: DDA, 327\8, no. 54; Grey to Cullen, n.d. (1866): DDA, 327\8, no. 69; *FJ*, 17 Sept. 1866.

128. Parker *(CC, SS. Peter & Paul, Cork)* to Cullen, 5 Oct. 1866: DDA, 327\6, no. 81; Redmond to Cullen, 1 Dec. 1866: DDA, 327\6, *(iii)*, no. 59; Connolly *(Abp., Halifax)* to Cullen, n.d. *(Dec. 1866)*: DDA, 327\5, *(iii)*, no. 35; *Irishman*, 13 Oct. 1866. MacEvilly to Cullen, 4 Dec. 1866: DDA, 327\5, *(i)*, no. 204; MacEvilly to Cullen, 13 Dec. 1866: DDA, 327\5, *(i)*, no. 210.

129. *FJ*, 31 Oct. 1866.

130. 'un … flagello che minaccia d'esser peggio del cholera', Cullen to Prop., 6 Dec. 1866: ACPF, *SC, Irlanda*, vol. 35, f. 864 *(v)*; see also Cullen to Prop., 17 Oct. 1866: ACPF, *SC, Irlanda*, vol. 35, f. 841.

131. Cullen to Prop., 6 Dec. 1866: ACPF, *SC, Irlanda*, vol. 35, f. 864 *(v)*.

132. ibid.

133. Lavelle, *Patriotism*, 1867, p. 11.

134. Cullen to Kirby, 27 Nov. 1866: ICAR, *Kirby Papers*, 1866, no. 323, Cullen to Kirby, 2 Dec. 1866: ICAR, *Kirby Papers*, 1866, no. 329; Cullen to Kirby, 7 Dec. 1866: ICAR, *Kirby Papers*, no. 339; Cullen to Manning 7 Feb. 1867 in S. Leslie, 'Irish Pages from the Postbags …', *Dublin Review*, vol. 165, no. 331, 1919, pp. 165–66; Cullen to Manning 13 Feb. 1867 in Leslie, op. cit., p. 167.

135. *FJ*, 11, 12, 15, 22, 23 Oct., 31 Dec. 1866; Cullen to Kirby, 2 Jan. 1867: ICAR, *Kirby Papers*, 1867, no. 3.

136. Moran, op. cit., vol. 3, pp. 15–25.

137. 'Io sono persuaso che non v'è alcun pericolo affatto di sommosse o turbolenze', Cullen to Prop., 23 Dec. 1866: ACPF, *SC, Irlanda*, vol. 35, f. 902 *(v)*; see also MacCarthy *(Relg., Dublin)* to Cullen, 31 Dec. 1866: DDA, 327\6, *(vi)*, no. 39.

Chapter Twelve

1. *FJ*, 9 Jan. 1867.

2. *FJ*, 7 Feb. 1867

3. *FJ*, 20 Feb., 28 Mar. 1867.

4. *FJ*, 21 June 1867

5. 'Questa povera gente ha sofferto una prigionia assai crudele per le sue pazzie, e spero che sarà più savia per l'avvenire', Cullen to Prop., 8 Feb. 1867: ACPF, *SC, Irlanda*, vol. 35, f. 971 *(v)*.

6. 'Pare che il Fenianismo sia ora pienamente defunto in Irlanda. Almeno non se ne parla più', Cullen to Prop., 8 Feb. 1867: ACPF, *SC, Irlanda*, vol. 35, f. 971 *(v)*; see also Cullen to Prop 5 Mar. 1867: ACPF, *SC, Irlanda*, vol. 35, f. 985.

7. Manning (*Abp., Westminster*) to Cullen, 28 Jan. 1867: DDA, 344\4, *(ii)*, no. 1; Manning to Cullen, 10 Feb. 1867: DDA, 344\4, *(ii)*, no. 2.

8. Curley (*PP, Wheeling*) to Prop., 8 Dec. 1866: ACPF, SC, *America Centrale*, vol. 21, ff. 849–50; Barker (*ex Student Prop.*) to Prop., 1 Jan. 1867: ACPF, SC, *America Centrale*, vol. 21, f. 706; Prop. to Barker, 19 Feb. 1867: ACPF, *LDB*, vol. 358, f. 182 *(v)*; Prop. to Whelan (*Bp., Wheeling*), 22 Mar. 1867: ACPF, *LDB*, vol. 358, f. 280; Prop. to Whelan, 20 May 1867: ACPF, *LDB*, vol. 358, f. 464; Curley to Prop., 2 July 1867: ACPF, SC, *America Centrale*, vol. 21, ff. 923–4.

9. Cullen to Prop., 5 Mar. 1867: ACPF, *SC, Irlanda*, vol. 35, ff. 984 *(v)* –5.

10. Cullen to Prop., 8 Feb. 1867: ACPF, *SC, Irlanda*, vol. 35, f. 971 *(v)*.

11. Cullen to Prop., 8 Feb. 1867: ACPF, *SC, Irlanda*, vol. 35, f. 971 *(v)*; Cullen to Prop., 5 Mar. 1867: ACPF, *SC, Irlanda*, vol. 35, f. 984 *(v)*.

12. Cullen to Kirby (*Rec. Irish Coll., Rome*), 22 Feb. 1867: ICAR, *NC, III*, 3, 2, no. 59; Kirby to Prop. n.d. (*Feb. 1867*): ACPF, *SC, Irlanda*, vol. 35, f. 980; Moran (*Vice Rec. Irish Coll., Rome, Rel. Cullen*) to Kirby, 5 Mar. 1867: ICAR, *Kirby Papers*, 1867, no. 73; Cullen to Kirby, 18 Mar. 1867: ICAR, *Kirby Papers*, no. 100; *FJ*, 20 Feb. 1867.

13. Kirby to Prop. n.d. (*Feb. 1867*): ACPF, *SC, Irlanda*, vol. 35, f. 980.

14. *FJ*, 20 Feb. 1867; see also Kirby to Prop., n.d. (*Feb. 1867*): ACPF, *SC, Irlanda*, vol. 35, ff. 979–80.

15. ibid.

16. Cullen to Prop., 5 Mar. 1867: ACPF, *SC, Irlanda*, vol. 35, f. 985.

17. *Tralee Chronicle*, 19, 22 Feb. 1867; S. O'Luing, 'Aspects of the Fenian Rising in Kerry, 1867' in *Kerry Archeological and Historical Society Journal*, no. 3, (1970), pp. 131–53; ibid, 4, (1971), pp. 139–64.

18. 'I telegrafi portarono la notizia da principio che v'erano otto mila uomini armati preparati d'assalire il governo, ma in due o tre giorni si seppe che il loro preciso numero era trentasette, il qual corpo formidabile era risolto di rovesciare la potenza dell'Inghilterra. Una rivoluzione di questa natura è troppo ridicola da parlarne seriamente', Cullen to Prop., 5 Mar. 1867: ACPF, *SC, Irlanda*, vol. 35, f. 985; see also Kieran (*Abp., Armagh*) to Cullen, 17 Feb. 1867: DDA, 334\4, *(i)*, no. 15; O'Donoghue (*MP, Tipperary*) to Cullen, 16 Feb. 1866: DDA, 334\6, no. 16.

19. Dairy of David Moriarty (*Bp., Kerry*), 17 Feb. 1867: KDA, *Moriarty Papers*; see also Cullen to Kirby, 22 Feb. 1867: ICAR, *Kirby Papers*, 1867, no. 59; Cullen to Kirby, 18 Mar. 1867: ICAR, *Kirby Papers*, 1867, no. 100; TC, 19 Feb. 1867.

20. Cullen to Kirby, 22 Feb. 1867: ICAR, *Kirby Papers*, 1867, no. 59; see also Redmond (*PP, Arklow*) to Cullen, 21 Feb. 1867: DDA, 334\5, *(iii)*, no. 11; Cullen to Kirby, 18 Mar. 1867: ICAR, *Kirby Papers*, 1867, no. 100.

21. 'Le cose qui stanno assai quiete e credo che non vi sia pericolo d'alcun movimento serio', Cullen to Prop., 5 Mar. 1867: ACPF, *SC, Irlanda*, vol. 35, f. 985; see also Cullen to Prop., 15 Mar. 1867: ACPF, *SC, Irlanda*, vol. 35, f. 992.

22. Kavanagh (*Pres. Carlow Coll.*) to Cullen, 21 Mar. 1867: DDA, 334\5, *(i)*, no. 33; Galvin (*PP, Rathdrum*) to Cullen, 27 Mar. 1867: DDA, 334\5, *(iv)*, no. 9; Leahy (*Abp., Cashel*) to Cullen, 5 Apr. 1867: DDA, 334\4, *(i)*, no. 30.

23. Furlong (*Bp., Ferns*) to Cullen, 9 Mar. 1867: DDA, 334\4, *(i)*, no. 26; Furlong to Cullen, 13 Mar. 1867: DDA, 334\4, *(i)*, no. 27.

24. Cullen to Prop., 15 Mar. 1867: ACPF, *SC, Irlanda*, vol. 35, f. 992.

25. Redmond to Cullen, 8 Mar. 1867: DDA, 334\5, *(iii)*, no. 13; Cullen to Prop.,

15 Mar. 1867: ACPF, *SC, Irlanda*, vol. 35, f. 992; Leahy to Cullen, 15 Mar. 1867: DDA, 334\4, *(i)*, no. 28; Manning to Cullen, 17 Mar. 1867: DDA, 344\4, *(ii)*, no. 4; Manning to Cullen, 30 Mar. 1867: DDA, 344\4, *(ii)*, no. 5; Redmond to Cullen, 16 Apr. 1867: DDA, 334\5, *(iii)*, no. 19; *FJ*, 15 Mar. 1867

26. Cullen to Prop., 15 Mar. 1867: ACPF, *SC, Irlanda*, vol. 35, f. 992.

27. *FJ*, 15 Mar. 1867.

28. 'Si vede che il governo ha ragione d'esser grato a tutti i cattolici tanto ecclesiastici che laici per la fedeltà che hanno mostrato in questa occasione. Ciò nonostante io non spero che si adotterà alcuna misura per metter fine ai mali di questo paese, che sono la vera causa del Fenianismo', Cullen to Prop., 15 Mar. 1867: ACPF, *SC, Irlanda*, vol. 35, f. 992.

29. 'E cosa singolare in relazione alle turbolenze che un gran numero dei maestri delle scuole nazionali vi presero parte eppure il governo sempre è determinato di mantenere il sistema misto nell'Irlanda è d'escludere la religione dalle scuole benchè vede che una tal maniera d'agire produce frutti così cattivi', Cullen to Prop., 15 Mar. 1867: ACPF, *SC, Irlanda*, vol. 35, f 992 *(v)*; see also Cullen to Prop., 16 Dec. 1867: ACPF, *SC, Irlanda*, vol. 35, f. 1332.

30. Leahy to Cullen, 15 Mar. 1867: DDA, 334\4, *(i)*, no. 28; Greene (*CC, Kilcommon & Robeen*) to Cullen, 14 May 1867: DDA, 334\5, *(i)*, no. 53; Redmond to Cullen, 16 May 1867: DDA, 334\5, *(iii)*, no. 26.

31. SPO, CSO, RP, 1867\3780, 4314, 8399.

32. Lynch (*Bp., Toronto*) to Cullen, 7 Feb. 1867: DDA, 334\4, *(iii)*, no. 1; Manning to Cullen, 10 Feb. 1867: DDA, 344\4, *(ii)*, no. 2; Cullen to Prop., 5 Mar. 1867: ACPF, *SC, Irlanda*, vol. 35, f. 985; MacEvilly (*Bp., Galway*) to Cullen, 6 Mar. 1867: DDA, 334\4, *(i)*, no. 25; Fitzpatrick (*Bp., Boston*) to Cullen, 12 Mar. 1867: DDA, 334\5, *(v)*, no. 5; Cullen to Kirby, 18 Mar. 1867: ICAR, *Kirby Papers*, 1867, no. 100; Cullen to Prop., 7 May 1867: ACPF, S C, Irlanda, vol. 35, f. 1096 *(v)*; Kirby to Prop., n.d. (*1867*): ACPF, *SC, Irlanda*, vol. 35, f. 919; *Conn. Pat.*, 20 Apr. 1867.

33. 'E cosa assai cattiva di pubblicare dottrine rivoluzionarie e d'istigare alla resistenza

alcuni poveri artigiani o contadini che vengono così esposti a certa distruzione', Cullen to Prop., 5 Mar. 1867: ACPF, *SC, Irlanda*, vol. 35, f. 985; see also Cullen to Kirby, 18 Mar. 1867: ICAR, *Kirby Papers*, 1867, no. 100; Lynch to Cullen, 21 Mar. 1867: DDA, 334\4, *(iii)*, no. 13; 'A Scotch Priest' to Cullen, 23 May 1867: DDA, 334\5, *(i)*, no. 57; Cullen to Prop., 7 May 1867: ACPF, *SC, Irlanda*, vol. 35, f. 1096 *(v)*; Kirby to Prop., n.d. (*1867*): ACPF, *SC, Irlanda*, vol. 35, f. 919; *Conn. Pat.*, 20 Apr. 1867.

34. *FJ*, 15 Mar. 1867; Cullen to Kirby 5 Apr. 1867: ICAR, *Kirby Papers*, 1867, no. 128.

35. O'Dwyer (*PP, Doon*) to Cullen, 11 Mar. 1867: DDA, 334\5, *(i)*, no. 30.

36. *FJ*, 2 May 1867; Anon. (*Kirby*) to Prop., n.d. (*June 1867*): ACPF, *SC, Irlanda*, vol. 35, f. 1106.

37. See Cullen to Kirby, 10 May 1867: ICAR, *Kirby Papers*, 1867, no. 170.

38. *FJ*, 15 May 1867; Anon. (*Kirby*) to Prop., n.d. (*June 1867*): ACPF, *SC, Irlanda*, vol. 35, f. 1106; Redmond to Cullen, 16 May 1867: DDA, 334\5, *(iii)*, no. 26.

39. *FJ*, 24 May 1867; Anon (*Kirby*) to Prop., n.d. (*June 1867*): ACPF, *SC, Irlanda*, vol. 35, f. 1106.

40. *FJ*, 25 May 1867; see also Anon. (*Kirby*) to Prop., n.d. (*June 1867*): ACPF, *SC, Irlanda*, vol. 35, f. 1106.

41. Cullen to Kirby, 6 June 1867: ICAR, *Kirby Papers*, 1867, no. 219; Anon. (*Kirby*) to Prop., n.d. (*June 1867*): ACPF, *SC, Irlanda*, vol. 35, f. 1106; Kennedy (*PP, James St.*) to Cullen, 26 May 1867: DDA, 334\5, *(i)*, no. 59.

42. *FJ*, 27 May 1867; Anon. (*Kirby*) to Prop., n.d. (*June 1867*): ACPF, *SC, Irlanda*, vol. 35, f. 1106.

43. ibid.

44. *FJ*, 28 May 1867; Redmond to Cullen, 28 May 1867: DDA, 334\5, *(iii)*, no. 30; Anon. (*Kirby*) to Prop., n.d. (*June 1867*): ACPF, *SC, Irlanda*, vol. 35, f. 1106 *(v)*.

45. Conroy (*Sec. Cullen*) to Cullen, 8 July 1867: DDA, 334\4, *(vi)*, no. 4; Cullen to Prop., 23 Sept. 1867: ACPF, *SC, Irlanda*, vol. 35, f. 1232 *(v)*; Manning to Cullen, 7 Oct. 1867: DDA, 334\4, *(ii)*, no. 12.

46. Cullen to Prop., 23 Sept. 1867: ACPF, *SC, Irlanda*, vol. 35, f. 1232 *(v)*.

47. Anon. (*Kirby*) to Prop., n.d. (*June 1867*): ACPF, *SC, Irlanda*, vol. 35, f. 1106; Forde (*CC, Booterstown, Blackrock, Dundrum*) to Cullen, 13 July 1867: DDA, 334\4, *(v)*, no. 18; Butler (*Coadj. Bp., Limerick*) to Moran, 3 Aug. 1867: DDA, 334\4, *(i)*, no. 49; Cullen to Prop., 23 Sept. 1867: ACPF, *SC, Irlanda*, vol. 35, f. 1232 *(v)*.

48. Moran, op. cit., vol. 3, p. 89.

49. ibid., pp. 85–9.

50. Cullen to Prop., 16 Dec. 1867: ACPF, *SC, Irlanda*, vol. 35, f. 1331.

51. ibid.

52. *FJ*, 19 Nov. 1867; see also Petre (*Brit. Dip.*) to Redmond, 3 Nov. 1867: DDA, 334\5, *(iii)*, no. 58.

53. Cullen to Prop., 16 Dec. 1867: ACPF, *SC, Irlanda*, vol. 35, f. 1331 *(v)*.

54. Cullen to Kirby, 22 Nov. 1867: ICAR, *Kirby Papers*, 1867, no. 423; Cullen to Prop., 24 Nov. 1867: ACPF, *SC, Irlanda*, vol. 35, f. 1285; Cullen to Prop., 11 Dec. 1867: ACPF, *SC, Irlanda*, vol. 35, f. 1322*(v)*.

55. *FJ*, 20 Nov. 1867.

56. 'Il governo ha fatto impiccare tre Feniani ieri, allo stresso tempo si lodano i Garibaldini che hanno fatto mille volte più male che i disgraziati Feniani', Cullen to Prop., 24 Nov. 1867: ACPF, *SC, Irlanda*, vol. 35, f. 1285; see also Cullen to Kirby, 22 Nov. 1867: ICAR, *Kirby Papers*, 1867, no. 423; Cullen to Prop., 11 Dec. 1867: ACPF, *SC, Irlanda*, vol. 35, f. 1322 *(v)*.

57. Cullen to Prop., 16 Dec. 1867: ACPF, *SC, Irlanda*, vol. 35, f. 1331 *(v)*.

58. MacEvilly to Cullen, 23 Nov. 1867: DDA, 334\4, *(i)*, no. 87; Nulty (*Bp., Meath*) to Cullen, 25 Nov. 1867: DDA, 334\4, *(i)*, no. 88.

59. Cullen to Prop., 16 Dec. 1867: ACPF, *Irlanda*, vol. 35, ff. 1331 *(v)* –2.

60. Cullen to Prop., 16 Dec. 1867: ACPF, *SC, Irlanda*, vol. 35, f. 1332; Redmond to Moran, 6 Jan. 1868: DDA, 341\1, *(ii)*, no. 2.

61. Doud (*lay corr.*) to Cullen, 13 Dec. 1867: DDA, 334\7, *(i)*, no. 82; Cullen to Prop., 16 Dec. 1867: ACPF, *SC, Irlanda*, vol. 35, f. 1332; Furlong to Cullen, 26 Dec. 1867: DDA, 334\4, *(i)*, no. 96; MacEvilly to Cullen, 27 Dec. 1867: DDA, 334\4, *(i)*, no. 98; TC, 31 Dec. 1867, 10 Jan. 1868; *Times*, 6 Jan. 1868.

62. Cullen to Prop., 24 Nov. 1867: ACPF, *SC, Irlanda*, vol. 35, f. 1285; see also MacEvilly to Cullen, 23 Nov. 1867: DDA, 334\4, *(i)*, no. 87; Cullen to Prop., 11 Dec. 1867: ACPF, *SC, Irlanda*, vol. 35, f. 1322 *(v)*; Cullen to Prop., 16 Dec. 1867: ACPF, *SC, Irlanda*, vol. 35, f. 1331 *(v)*; Lynch to Cullen, 16 Dec. 1867: DDA, 334\4, *(iii)*, no. 29; Cullen to Prop., 10 Jan. 1868: ACPF, *SC, Irlanda*, vol. 36, f. 76; McGinty (*lay corr.*) to Prop., Apr. 1869: ACPF, *SC, Irlanda*, vol. 36, f. 442 *(v)*.

63. Cullen to Prop., 10 Jan. 1868: ACPF, *SC, Irlanda*, vol. 36, f. 76.

64. Sullivan (*lay corr.*) to Monsell (*MP, Limerick co.*), 10 Dec. 1867: NLI, MS. 8318 *(5)*, *Monsell Papers*; Cullen to Prop., 11 Dec. 1867: ACPF, *SC, Irlanda*, vol. 35, f. 1322 *(v)*; Cullen to Prop., 16 Dec. 1867: ACPF, *SC, Irlanda*, vol. 35, f. 1331 *(v)*.

65. Cullen to Prop., 16 Dec. 1867: ACPF, *SC, Irlanda*, vol. 35, f. 1331 *(v)*.

66. Russell (*Brit. Dip., Rel. PM*) to Stanley (*Foreign Sec.*), 7 Jan. 1868: FO, 43\101, f. 89; see also McAuliffe (*lay corr.*) to Severn (*Brit. Dip*), 8 Jan. 1868: FO, 43\102; Stanley to Russell, 17 Jan. 1868: FO, 43\101, f. 101; Russell to Stanley, 20 Jan. 1868: FO, 43\101, f. 114; Russell to Stanley, 21 Jan. 1868: FO, 43\101, f. 116–8; Severn to Stanley, 22 Jan. 1868: FO, 43\102; Severn to Stanley, 29 Jan. 1868: FO, 43\102; Severn to Stanley, 19 Feb. 1868: FO, 43\102.

67. Cullen to Prop., 16 Dec. 1867: ACPF, *SC, Irlanda*, vol. 35, f. 1332; Manning to Cullen, 30 Dec. 1867: DDA, 334\4, *(ii)*, no. 20; Cullen to Prop., 10 Jan. 1868: ACPF, *SC, Irlanda*, vol. 36, f. 76.

68. Martin (*lay corr.*) to Cullen, 6 Dec. 1867: DDA, 334\7, *(i)*, no. 75.

69. Petre to Redmond, 30 Mar. 1868: DDA, 341\1, *(ii)*, no. 12.

70. MacEvilly to Cullen, 1 Jan. 1868: DDA, 334\8, *(i)*, no. 1; Langdale (*lay corr.*) to Cullen, 2 Jan. 1868: DDA 341\2, no. 1; Lynch to Cullen, 2 Jan. 1868: DDA, 334\8, *(iii)*, no. 1; MacEvilly to Cullen, 4 Jan. 1868: DDA, 334\8, *(i)*, no. 2; Cullen to Prop., 10 Jan. 1868: ACPF, *SC, Irlanda*, vol. 36, f. 76; Duggan (*Abp., Chicago*) to Cullen, 2 Feb. 1868: DDA, 334\8, *(iv)*, no. 4; Redmond to Cullen, 2 Feb. 1868: DDA,

341\1, *(ii)*, no. 4; Waterworth (PP, St Georges', Worcester) to Cullen, 29 Feb. 1868: DDA, 341\1, *(i)*, no. 23; Moran to Cullen, 18 Oct. 1868: DDA, 334\8, *(vi)*, no. 5; Crane *(lay corr.)* to Cullen, 9 Nov. 1868: DDA, 341\1, *(iii)*, no. 33; Cullen to Prop., 10 Dec. 1868:ACPF, *SC, Irlanda*, vol. 36, f. 327.

71. Redmond to Cullen, 21 Feb. 1868: DDA, 341\1, *(ii)*, no. 8.

72. *Times*, 23 Jan. 1868; see also *FJ*, 3, 21 Jan. 1868.

73. ibid.

74. Scandella *(Bp.,Antinoe,Vic.Apost. Gibraltar)* to Cullen, 3 Jan. 1868: DDA, 334\8, *(iv)*, no. 1.

75. *Times*, 29 Jan. 1868.

76. ibid.

77. *IP*, 28 Dec. 1867.

78. 'Il celebre Lavelle scrive lettere terribili contro il governo ben calcolato a promuovere uno spirito di rivoluzione nel paese', Cullen to Prop., 10 Jan. 1868: ACPF, *SC, Irlanda*, vol. 36, f. 76.

79. 'Senza dubbio si possono dire molte cose vere e forti contro il governo ma è una vera pazzia e una grandissima scelleraggine [sic] di spingere un popolo povero, diviso e senza armi e disciplina ad assalire un governo potentissimo, e che ha alla sua disposizione flotte ed armate preparate per qualunque scopo', Cullen to Prop., 10 Jan. 1868: ACPF, *SC, Irlanda*, vol. 36, f. 76.

80. Carvell Williams *(lay corr.)* to Cullen, 22 July 1867: DDA, 334\7, *(i)*, no. 6; Whyte *(Sec. Nat. Assoc. Ire.)* to Cullen, 26 Oct. 1867: DDA, 334\7, *(i)*, no. 40.

81. Conroy *(Sec. Cullen)* to Cullen, 8 July 1867: DDA, 334\4, *(vi)*, no. 4; Whyte to Cullen, 26 Oct. 1867: DDA, 334\7, *(i)*, no. 40.

82. *FJ*, 21 Mar. 1868; Collins *(lay corr.)* to Cullen, 8 Apr. 1868: DDA 341\2, no. 55; Redmond to Cullen, 16 Apr. 1868: DDA, 341\1, *(ii)*, no. 14; O'Malley *(lay corr.)* to Cullen, 16 Apr. 1868: DDA, 341\1, *(i)*, no. 37.

83. *FJ*, 27 Jan. 1868.

84. *Times*, 30 Jan. 1868, MH, 30 Jan. 1868.

Chapter Thirteen

1. *Parl. Deb.*, ser. 3, 190: 1765–71; 191: 32–3; *FJ*, 23, 24 Mar. 1868; J. Morley, *The Life of William Ewart Gladstone*, London, 1903, vol. 1, pp. 569, 574.

2. *Parl. Deb.*, ser. 3, 191: 469–70, 495, 575, 790, 837; *FJ*, 4 Apr. 1868.

3. Cullen to Kirby *(Rec. Irish Coll., Rome)*, 2 Jan. 1867: ICAR, *Kirby Papers*, 1867, no. 3; Cullen to Kirby, 22 Mar. 1867: ICAR, *Kirby Papers*, 1867, no. 108: Cullen to Kirby, 5 Apr. 1867: ICAR, *Kirby Papers*, 1867, no. 128; Cullen to Manning *(Abp., Westminster)*, 8 Apr. 1867 in Leslie, op. cit., p. 167; Cullen to Manning, 17 Aug. 1867 in Leslie, ibid., p. 168; Cullen to Kirby, 15 Apr. 1868: ICAR, *Kirby Papers*, 1868, no 126; Cullen to Kirby, 10 May 1868: ICAR, *Kirby Papers*, 1868, no. 154; *Parl. Deb.*, ser. 3, 191: 1338, 1466, 1583, 1675, 1949; 192: 314; *FJ*, 9 Jan., 20 Mar., 24, 29 Apr. 1867; 1, 8, May 1868.

4. 'Per la prima volta cercarono a trattare i Cattolici nella stessa maniera che trattarono i Protestanti ... Se agissero sempre così sono persuaso che i cattolici tutti, ricchi e poveri, sempre sarebbero fedelissimi sudditi – ma la superbia Inglese generalmente è malcontenta se non puo maltrattare e calpestare gli altri', Cullen to Prop., 15 May 1868: ACPF, *SC, Irlanda*, vol. 36, f. 168.

5. Moran *(Sec. & Rel. Cullen)* to Prop., 29 Mar. 1866: ACPF, *SC, Irlanda*, vol. 35, f. 647; Petre *(Brit. Dip., Tuscany, Resident in Rome)* to Redmond *(PP,Arklow)*, 30 Mar. 1868: DDA, 341\1, *(ii)*, no. 12.

6. 'le Fenianisme est bon pour quelque chose', Keane *(Bp., Cloyne)* to Kirby, 24 Apr. 1868: ICAR, *Kirby Papers*, 1868, no. 137.

7. Kirby to Prop., 1 July 1868: ACPF, *SC, Irlanda*, vol. 36, f. 227; Redmond *(PP, Arklow)* to Cullen, 15 July (*1868*): DDA, 341\1, *(ii)*, no. 30; Moran to Prop., 19 July 1868: ACPF, *SC, Irlanda*, vol. 36, f. 225; Antonelli *(Papal Sec. State)* to Kirby, 25 July 1868: ICAR, *NC, III*, 3, 2, no. 34; *FJ*, 17 July 1868.

8. Kirby to Prop., 26 July 1868: ACPF, *SC, Irlanda*, vol. 36 f. 242; MacEvilly *(Bp., Galway)* to Cullen, 15 Aug. 1868: DDA, 334\8, *(i)*, no. 57; McCabe *(PP, Dun Laoghaire, Monkstown & Glasthule)* to Cullen, 19 Aug. 1868: DDA, 334\8, *(i)*, no. 58; Pie *(Bp., Poitiers)* to Cullen, 23 Aug. 1868: DDA, 334\8, *(iv)*, no. 16; Moran to Prop., 23 Aug. 1868: ACPF, *SC, Irlanda*, vol. 36, f. 246; Cullen to Prop., 11 Sept. 1868: ACPF, *SC, Irlanda*, vol. 36, f. 268; Derry *(Bp., Clonfert)*

to Cullen, 15 Sept. 1868: DDA, 334\8, *(i)*, no. 60; Manning to Cullen, 15 Sept. 1868: DDA, 334\8, *(ii)*, no. 20; Grimley *(Bp., Capetown)* to Cullen, 15 Sept. 1868: DDA, 334\8, *(iv)*, no. 19; Grant *(Bp., Southwark)* to Cullen, 18 Sept. 1868: DDA, 334\8, *(iv)*, no. 20; Kenrick *(Bp., Elect. Arathia & Coadj. Bp., Philadelphia)* to Cullen, 30 Sept. 1868: DDA, 334\8, *(iv)*, no. 21; Donnelly *(Bp., Clogher)* to Cullen, 29 Oct. 1868: DDA, 334\8, *(i)*, no. 65; Cullen to Prop., 29 Dec. 1868: ACPF, *SC, Irlanda*, vol. 36, f. 352 *(v)*; Wood *(Bp., Philadelphia)* to Cullen, 29 Dec. 1868: DDA, 334\8, *(iv)*, no. 37; Cullen to Kirby, 31 Dec. 1868: ICAR, *NC, III*, 3, 2, no. 43; 'A Religious' to Cullen, 2 Jan. 1869: DDA, 321\1, *(iv)*, no. 2; Cullen to Kirby, 13 Jan. 1869: ICAR, *NC, III*, 3, 2, no. 47; Cullen to Kirby, 20 Jan. 1869: ICAR, *NC, III*, 3, 2, no. 48; Leahy *(Abp., Cashel)* to Cullen, 23 Jan. 1869: DDA, 341\8, *(i)*, no. 3; Manning to Cullen, 27 Mar. 1869: DDA, 341\8, *(ii)*, no. 1.

9. *FJ*, 3, 16 Nov. 1868.

10. Cullen to Monsell *(MP, Limerick co.)* n.d. *(1868)*: NLI, MS., 8317 *(3)*, *Monsell Papers*; Bowyer *(MP, Dundalk)* to Prop., 17 Feb. 1869: ACPF, *SC, Irlanda*, vol. 36, ff. 419–22; Cullen to Prop., 23 Mar. 1869: ACPF, *SC, Irlanda*, vol. 36, f. 434 *(v)*; DEP, 5 Aug. 1868; *FJ*, 10, 11, 30 Sept., 2, 7, 8, 13 Oct., 6, 16, 26 Nov. 1868; CE, 16 Nov. 1868.

11. *FJ*, 13 Nov. 1868; Thornley, op. cit., pp. 53–5.

12. *FJ*, 13 Nov. 1868, 23 Dec. 1868; 6, 14, 20, 26 Jan. 1869.

13. *FJ*, 23 Dec. 1868.

14. Corish, 'Cardinal Cullen and the Nat. Assoc. of Ire', *Rep. Novum*, 3, no. 1, pp. 56–9.

15. *Parl. Deb.*, ser. 3, 194: 159–60.

16. *FJ*, 23 Feb. 1869.

17. Cullen to Kirby, 24 Mar. 1869: ICAR, *NC, III*, 3, 2, no. 57.

18. *Parl. Deb.*, ser. 3, 194: 1349–51, 1997–9; *FJ*, 8, 18, 19 Mar. 1869.

19. Cullen to Kirby, 3 Jan. 1869: ICAR, *NC, III*, 3, 2, no. 45.

20. Cullen to Kirby, 3 Jan. 1869: ICAR, *NC, III*, 3, 2, no. 45; Nolan *(Hon. Sec. Central Amnesty Committ.)* to Cullen, 27 Feb. 1869: DDA, 321\2, no. 35.

21. Cullen to Kirby, 3 Jan. 1869: ICAR, *NC, III*,

3, 2, no. 45; Glynn *(Relg., Dungarvan)* to Cullen, 20 Mar. 1869: DDA, 321\1, *(iv)*, no. 16; Cullen to Prop., 23 Mar. 1869: ACPF, *SC, Irlanda*, vol. 36, f. 435 *(v)* –6; Cullen to Kirby, 24 Mar. 1869: ICAR, *NC, III*, 3, 2, no. 57; *DEM*, 19 Mar. 1869.

22. Cullen to Kirby, 3 Jan. 1869: ICAR, *NC, III*, 3, 2, no. 45; Cullen to Prop., 23 Mar. 1869: ACPF, *SC, Irlanda*, vol. 36, f. 435 *(v)*; Cullen to Kirby, 24 Mar. 1869: ICAR, *NC, III*, 3, 2, no. 57; Nulty *(Bp., Meath)* to Cullen, 3 Apr. 1869: DDA, 341\8, *(i)*, no. 26; O'Connor *(Relg. Baltimore)* to Cullen, 25 June 1869: DDA, 321\1, *(iv)*, no. 26.

23. Cullen to Kirby, 3 Jan. 1869: ICAR, *NC, III*, 3, 2, no. 45

24. *Irishman*, 6, 13 Mar. 1869.

25. Cullen to Prop., 23 Mar. 1869: ACPF, *SC, Irlanda*, vol. 36, f. 435 *(v)* –6; Cullen to Kirby, 24 Mar. 1869: ICAR, *NC, III*, 3, 2, no. 57.

26. Cullen to Kirby, 24 Mar. 1869: ICAR, *NC, III*, 3, 2, no. 57; Cullen to Prop., 23 Mar. 1869: ACPF, *SC, Irlanda*, vol. 36, ff. 435 *(v)* –6; MacEvilly to Cullen, 20 Mar. 1869: DDA, 341\4, no. 3; Leahy to Cullen, 4 Apr. 1869: DDA, 341\8, *(i)*, no. 28; Cullen to Kirby, 2 Nov. 1869: ICAR, *NC, III*, 3, 2, no. 89.

27. *FJ*, 13 Mar. 1869; see also McCabe to Cullen, 20 Mar. 1869: DDA, 341\8, *(i)*, no. 20; Cullen to Prop., 23 Mar. 1869: ACPF, *SC, Irlanda*, vol. 36, ff. 435*(v)*–6; Cullen to Kirby, 24 Mar. 1869: ICAR, *NC, III*, 3, 2, no. 57.

28. *FJ*, 13 Mar. 1869.

29. O'Hagan *(lay corr.)* to Cullen, 15 Mar. 1869: DDA, 321\2, no. 58; Cullen to Prop., 23 Mar. 1869: ACPF, *SC, Irlanda*, vol. 36, f. 436.

30. Taylor *(PP, Maryborough)* to Cullen, 13 Mar. 1869: DDA, 321\1, *(ii)*, no. 38; Shanahan *(PP, St Michaels, Limerick)* to Cullen, 23 Mar. 1869: DDA, 321\1, *(ii)*, no. 40; 'A Catholic who loves justice and hates scandal' to Prop., n.d *(Mar. 1869)*: ACPF, *SC, Irlanda*, vol. 36, f. 417.

31. Cullen to Prop., 23 Mar. 1869: ACPF, *SC, Irlanda*, vol. 36, f. 436; Nulty to Cullen, 8 June 1869: DDA, 341\8, *(i)*, no. 47; Conroy *(Sec. Cullen)* to Cullen, 10 Dec. 1869: DDA, 341\8, *(vii)*, no. 7; Conroy to Cullen, 16 Dec. 1869: DDA, 341\8, *(vii)*, no. 9.

32. *Irishman*, 29 May 1869; *FJ*, 31 May 1, 2, 9 June 1869.

33. Cullen to Prop., 23 Mar. 1869: ACPF, *SC, Irlanda*, vol. 36, f. 435(v).

34. *DEM*, 19 Mar. 1869; Cullen to Prop., 23 Mar. 1869: ACPF, *SC, Irlanda*, vol. 36, f. 435 (v).

35. O'Donoghue (*MP, Tipperary*) to Gladstone (*PM*), 9 Aug. 1869: BM.Add. MS. 44421, ff. 258–9, Maguire (*MP, Dungarvan*) to Gladstone, 17 Sept. 1869: BM.Add. MS. 44422, ff. 40–3; *FJ*, 8 Sept., 18, 19 Oct. 1869.

36. Vaughan (*PP, Barefield, Ennis*) to Cullen, 7 Aug. 1869: DDA, 321\1, *(i)*, no. 108; O'Dwyer (*PP, Doon*) to Cullen, 17 Oct. 1869: DDA, 321\1, *(i)*, no. 101; White (*PP, Carrigaholt*) to Cullen, 27 Oct. 1869: DDA, 321\1, *(i)*, no. 105; O'Donoghue (*PP, Tubbercurry*) to Cullen, 30 Oct. 1869: DDA, 321\1, *(i)*, no. 106; Quaid (*PP, Callaghans Mills*) to Crowley (*lay corr.*), 13 Nov. 1869: DDA, 321\1, *(i)*, no. 112; *Irishman*, 28 Aug., 10 Oct., 9 Nov. 1869; *Flag of Ireland*, 7 Aug., 18 Sept., 16 Oct., 6, 13, 27 Nov. 1869; *FJ*, 2 Nov. 1869;

37. Lavelle (*PP, Partry*) to Cullen, 9 Nov. 1869: DDA, 321\1, *(i)*, no. 109; see also Redmond to Cullen, 21 Nov. 1869: DDA, 321\1, *(ii)*, no. 25.

38. *FJ*, 22, 29 Oct. 1869.

39. Cullen to Kirby, 12 Feb. 1869: ICAR, *NC, III*, 3, 2, no. 49.

40. Cullen to Prop., 24 Mar. 1869: ACPF, *SC, Irlanda*, vol. 36, f. 475; Cullen to Kirby, 7 May 1869: ICAR, *NC, III*, 3, 2, no. 65.; Cullen to Kirby, 20 Oct. 1869: ICAR, *NC, III*, 3, 2, no. 88; Cullen to Kirby, 2 Nov. 1869: ICAR, *NC, III*, 3, 2, no. 89; Dunne (*Pres. Carlow Coll.*) to Anon. (*Moran Sec. & Rel. Cullen*), 6 Dec. 1869: ICAR, *NC, III*, 3, 2, no. 94; *Irishman*, 13 Mar., 20 Mar., 19 Nov. 1869.

41. Cullen to Kirby, 2 Nov. 1869: ICAR, *NC, III*, 3, 2, no. 89; Dunne to Anon. (Moran), 6 Dec. 1869: ICAR, *NC, III*, 3, 2, no. 94.

42. Nulty to Cullen, 8 June 1869: DDA, 341\8, *(i)*, no. 47.

43. Cullen to Kirby, 26 Apr. 1869: ICAR, *NC, III*, 3, 2, no. 63.

44. Russell to Clarendon (*ex Lord Lieut., Ire*), 5 May 1869, in Blakeston, *The Roman Question*, London, 1962, pp. 363–4.

45. Cullen to Kirby, 16 May 1869: ICAR, *NC, III*, 3, 2, no. 67; Cullen to Conroy, 1 Nov. 1869: DDA, AB4\42\8; Cullen to Kirby, 2 Nov. 1869: ICAR, *NC, III*, 3, 2, no. 89; Cullen to Conroy, 11 Nov. 1869: DDA, AB4\42\8; Cullen to Conroy, 17 Nov. 1869: DDA, AB4\42\8; Cullen to Conroy, 28 Nov. 1869: DDA, AB4\42\8; Cullen to McCabe, 11 Dec. 1869: DDA, AB4\40\4; Cullen to McCabe, 20 Dec. 1869: DDA, AB4\40\4; Cullen to McCabe, 22 Dec. 1869: DDA, AB4\40\4; Cullen to Conroy, 30 Dec. 1869: DDA, AB4\42\8.

46. Cullen to Kirby, 13 Nov. 1869: ICAR, *NC, III*, 3, 2, no. 91.

47. Moran, op. cit., vol. 3, pp. 260–9.

48. *Irishman*, 20 Nov. 1869.

49. Cullen to Kirby, 2 Nov. 1869: ICAR, *NC, III*, 3, 2, no. 89; Redmond to Cullen, 13 Nov. 1869: DDA, 321\1, *(ii)*, no. 24; Conroy to Cullen, 20 Dec. 1869: DDA, 341\8, *(vii)*, no. 10; *FJ*, 2, 29, 30 Nov. 1869, *Irishman*, 13 Nov. 1869.

50. Cullen to Kirby, 2 Nov. 1869: ICAR, *NC, III*, 3, 2, no. 89.

51. *FJ*, 10 Nov. 1869, *Irishman*, 13 Nov. 1869.

52. *Irishman*, 27 Nov. 1869.

53. Cullen to Kirby, 2 Nov. 1869: ICAR, *NC, III*, 3, 2, no. 89.

54. See Shanahan to Russell, 12 Mar. 1869: DDA, 321\1, *(ii)*, no. 36; MacEvilly to Cullen, 1 Apr. 1869: DDA, 341\8, *(i)*, no. 24; MacEvilly to Cullen, 5 May 1869: DDA, 341\8, *(i)*, no. 38.

55. Conroy to Cullen, 3 Dec. 1869: DDA, 341\8, *(vii)*, no. 5; Conroy to Cullen, 10 Dec. 1869: DDA, 341\8, *(vii)*, no. 7; McCabe to Cullen, 16 Dec. 1869: DDA, 341\8, *(vi)*, no. 14; Conroy to Cullen, 20 Dec. 1869: DDA, 341\8, *(vii)*, no. 10; Reynolds (*St Mel's Coll., Longford*) to Cullen, 24 Dec. 1869: DDA, 321\1, *(i)*, no. 119; Smyth (*PP, Ballymahon*) to Cullen, 24 Dec. 1869: DDA, 321\1, *(i)*, no. 120; Conroy to Cullen, 31 Dec. 1869: DDA, 341\8, *(vii)*, no. 14; *FJ*, 23, 26, 29, Nov. 1869, *Times*, 26 Nov. 1869; *CE*, 26 Nov. 1869, *Irishman*, 4 Dec. 1869.

56. Moran, op. cit., vol. 3, p. 277–81; Conroy to Cullen, 10 Dec. 1869: DDA, 341\8, *(vii)*, no. 7; Conroy to Cullen, 24 Dec. 1869: DDA, 341\8, *(vii)*, no. 11; Earl of Granard to Cullen, 25 Dec. 1869: DDA, 321\3, no. 78.

57. Forde (*PP, Booterstown*) to McCabe, 13 December 1869: DDA, 341\8, *(vi)*, no. 13;

McCabe to Cullen, 16 Dec. 1869: DDA, 341\8, *(vi)*, no. 14.

58. Maher (*PP, Carlow–Graigue, Rel. Cullen*) to Cullen, 9 Dec. 1869: DDA, 321\1, *(i)*, no. 118; Conroy to Cullen, 13 Dec. 1869: DDA, 341\8, *(vii)*, no. 8; Conroy to Cullen, 16 Dec. 1869: DDA, 341\8, *(vii)*, no. 9; Conroy to Cullen, 20 Dec. 1869: DDA, 341\8, *(vii)*, no. 10; McCabe to Cullen, 23 Dec. 1869: DDA, 341\8, *(vi)*, no. 15; Conroy to Cullen, 24 Dec. 1869: DDA, 341\8, *(vii)*, no. 11; Earl of Granard to Cullen, 25 Dec. 1869: DDA, 321\3, no. 78; Conroy to Cullen, 26 Dec. 1869: DDA, 341\8, *(vii)*, no. 12; Conroy to Cullen, 27 Dec. 1869: DDA, 341\8, *(vii)*, no. 13; McCabe to Cullen, 31 Dec. 1869: DDA, 341\8, *(vi)*, no. 17; *FJ*, 16 Dec. 1869.

59. Conroy to Cullen, 13 Dec. 1869: DDA, 341\8, *(vii)*, no. 8; McCabe to Cullen, 16 Dec. 1869: DDA, 341\8, *(vi)*, no. 14; Conroy to Cullen, 16 Dec. 1869: DDA, 341\8, *(vii)*, no. 9; Cullen to Conroy, 17 Dec. 1869: DDA, AB4\42\8; Conroy to Cullen, 20 Dec. 1869: DDA, 341\8, *(vii)*, no. 10; Cullen to McCabe, 20 Dec. 1869: DDA, AB4\40\4; Cullen to McCabe, 22 Dec. 1869: DDA, AB4\40\4; McCabe to Cullen, 23 Dec. 1869: DDA, 341\8, *(vi)*, no. 15; Conroy to Cullen, 24 Dec. 1869: DDA, 341\8, *(vii)*, no. 11; Conroy to Cullen, 26 Dec. 1869: DDA, 341\8, *(vii)*, no. 12; McCabe to Cullen, 26 Dec. 1869: DDA, 341\8, *(vi)*, no. 16; Conroy to Cullen, 27 Dec. 1869: DDA, 341\8, *(vii)*, no. 13; McCabe to Cullen, 31 Dec. 1869: DDA, 341\8, *(vi)*, no. 17; Cullen to McCabe, 8 Jan. 1870: DDA, AB4\40\4; *FJ*, 11, 16, 20, 24 Dec. 1869, 14 Jan. 1870; *Irishman*, 18 Dec. 1869, 8 Jan. 1870.

60. McCabe to Cullen, 16 Dec. 1869: DDA, 341\8, *(vi)*, no. 14; Conroy to Cullen, 20 Dec. 1869: DDA, 341\8, *(vii)*, no. 10; McCabe to Cullen, 23 Dec. 1869: DDA, 341\8, *(vi)*, no. 15; Conroy to Cullen, 24 Dec. 1869: DDA, 341\8, *(vii)*, no. 11; Conroy to Cullen, 26 Dec. 1869: DDA, 341\8, *(vii)*, no. 12; Conroy to Cullen, 27 Dec. 1869: DDA, 341\8, *(vii)*, no. 13; McCabe to Cullen, 31 Dec. 1869: DDA, 341\8, *(vi)*, no. 17; *FJ*, 24 Dec. 1869.

61. 'The Irish Bishops meeting in Rome have disapproved of Dean O'Brien's canvassing the signatures of priests throughtout Ireland to a document emanating from him', n.d. (*1869*): DDA, 341\8, *(i)*, no. 87.

62. Forde to McCabe, 13 Dec. 1869: DDA, 341\8, *(vi)*, no. 13; Cullen to McCabe, 20 Dec. 1869: DDA, AB4\40\4; Cullen to McCabe, 22 Dec. 1869: DDA, AB4\40\4; Cullen to Conroy, 23 Dec. 1869: DDA, AB4\42\8; McCabe to Cullen, 26 Dec. 1869: DDA, 341\8, *(vi)*, no. 16; Conroy to Cullen, 26 Dec. 1869: DDA, 341\8, *(vii)*, no. 12; Conroy to Cullen, 27 Dec. 1869: DDA, 341\8, *(vii)*, no. 13; Cullen to Conroy, 28 Dec. 1869: DDA, AB4\42\8; Cullen to Conroy, 30 Dec. 1869: DDA, AB4\42\8; Conroy to Cullen, 31 Dec. 1869: DDA, 341\8, *(vii)*, no. 14; Cullen to Conroy, 7 Jan. 1870: DDA, AB4\42\8; Cullen to McCabe, 8 Jan. 1870: DDA, AB4\40\4.

63. Conroy to Cullen, 10 Dec. 1869: DDA, 341\8, *(vii)*, no. 7.

64. 'Resolution of the Irish Bishops present in Rome to lay before the Cardinal Prefect of Propaganda Fide a letter of Rev. Patrick Lavelle ... claiming that Fenians do not incur the censures on Secret Societies', 22 December 1869: DDA, 341\8, *(i)*, no. 85; Cullen to McCabe, 22 Dec. 1869: DDA, AB4\40\4; Cullen to Conroy, 23 Dec. 1869: DDA, AB4\42\8; Conroy to Cullen, 27 Dec. 1869: DDA, 341\8, *(vii)*, no. 13; Cullen to Conroy, 28 Dec. 1869: DDA, AB4\42\8; Cullen to Conroy, 30 Dec. 1869: DDA, AB4\42\8; Cullen to Conroy, 7 Jan. 1870: DDA, AB4\42\8; Cullen to McCabe, 8 Jan. 1870: DDA, AB4\40\4.

65. 'Resolution of the Irish Bishops present in Rome to lay before the Cardinal Prefect of Propaganda Fide a letter of Rev. Patrick Lavelle ... claiming that Fenians do not incur the censures on Secret Societies', 22 Dec. 1869: DDA, 341\8, *(i)*, no. 85; Conroy to Cullen, 27 Dec. 1869: DDA, 341\8, *(vii)*, no. 13.

66. Conroy to Cullen, 31 Dec. 1869: DDA, 341\8, *(vii)*, no. 14.

67. Forde to McCabe, 13 Dec. 1869: DDA, 341\8, *(vi)*, no. 13; Conroy to Cullen, 16 Dec. 1869: DDA, 341\8, *(vii)*, no. 9; McCabe to Cullen, 23 Dec. 1869: DDA, 341\8, *(vi)*, no. 15; McCabe to Cullen, 26 Dec. 1869: DDA, 341\8, *(vi)*, no. 16;

McCabe to Cullen, 31 Dec. 1869: DDA, 341\8, *(vi)*, no. 17.

68. Conroy to Cullen, 16 Dec. 1869: DDA, 341\8, *(vii)*, no. 9; Conroy to Cullen, 24 Dec. 1869: DDA, 341\8, *(vii)*, no. 11; Conroy to Cullen, 31 Dec. 1869: DDA, 341\8, *(vii)*, no. 14.

69. Conroy to Cullen, 16 Dec. 1869: DDA, 341\8, *(vii)*, no. 9; Conroy to Cullen, 20 Dec. 1869: DDA, 341\8, *(vii)*, no. 10; McCabe to Cullen, 23 Dec. 1869: DDA, 341\8, *(vi)*, no. 15; McCabe to Cullen, 31 Dec. 1869: DDA, 341\8, *(vi)*, no. 17; Conroy to Cullen, 26 Dec. 1869: DDA, 341\8, *(vii)*, no. 12.

70. Conroy to Cullen, 16 Dec. 1869: DDA, 341\8, *(vii)*, no. 9; Conroy to Cullen, 24 Dec. 1869: DDA, 341\8, *(vii)*, no. 11.

71. 'Societatem Americanam seu Hibernicam Fenianorum appellatam comprehendi inter societates vetitas ac damnatas in Constitutionibus Summorum Pontificum et praesertim in nuperrima Ejusdem Sanctitatis Suae edita quarto Idus Octobris 1869: Incip.: "Apostolicae Sedis" quae sub num. 4 Excommunicationi latae Sententiae Romano Pontifici reservatae obnoxii declarantur "Nomen dantes sectae Massonicae aut Carbonariae aut aliis ejusdem generis sectis quae contra Ecclesiam vel legitimas potestates seu palam seu clandestine machinantur; necnon iisdem sectis favorem qualencumque praestantes; eorumve occultos coriphaeos ac duces non denunciantes, donec non denunciaverint"': ACPF, *SC, Irlanda*, vol. 36, f. 877; ibid. ASS, 5, 369–70; ibid. *IER*, 6, p. 240; 'Lettera del S.V. ad un prelato sulla condanna dei Feniani', 12 Jan. 1870: VECAR, Talbot Papers, no. 1591.

72. Russell to Clarendon, 23, 24 Jan. 1870; Blakeston, op. cit., pp. 382, 385; Russell to Clarendon, 31 Jan. 1870: PRO, FO, 43\106, No. 31; Gladstone to Clarendon, 1 Feb. 1870: PRO, FO, 361\1, 437–8; Clarendon to Russell, 1 Mar. 1870: PRO, FO, 361\1, 335; Cullen to Conroy, 20 Jan. 1870: DDA, AB4\42\8; Cullen to Conroy, 24 Jan. 1870: DDA, AB4\42\8; Cullen to Conroy, 28 Jan. 1870: DDA, AB4\42\8; Cullen to Conroy, 2 Feb. 1870: DDA, AB4\42\8; Cullen to Conroy, 10 Feb. 1870: DDA, AB4\42\8.

73. O'Connell to Prop., n.d., *(1870)*: ACPF,

SC, America Centrale, vol. 23, ff. 437–8; Prop. to Borgess *(Coadj. Bp., Adm. Detroit)*, 23 Aug. 1870: ACPF, *LDB*, vol. 364, f. 717 *(v)*; Prop. to Purcell *(Abp., Cincinnati)*, 24 Aug. 1870: ACPF, *LDB*, *(1870)*, ff. 725 *(v)* –6; Purcell to Prop., 16 Sept. 1870: ACPF, SC, America Centrale, vol. 23, f. 499; Prop. to Assess. of Holy Office, 15 Nov. 1870: ACPF, *LDB*, *(1870)*, f. 944.

74. *Irishman*, 5, 12 Feb. 1870.

75. *Irishman*, 5, 12, 19, 26 Feb.; 5, 12, 19, 26, Mar.; 2, 9, 23, 30 Apr. 1870.

76. Moran, op. cit., vol. 3, p. 286.

77. ibid

78. Cullen to McCabe, 11 Dec. 1869: DDA, AB4\40\4; Cullen to McCabe, 22 Dec. 1869: DDA, AB4\40\4; Cullen to Conroy, 30 Dec. 1869: DDA, AB4\42\8; Gladstone to Cullen, 6 Mar. 1870: BM.Add. MS. 44425, 192–8; Cullen to Gladstone, 12 Mar. 1870: BM.Add. MS. 44425, 243–4; Clarendon to Russell, 7 Mar. 1870: PRO, FO, 361\1, 341; Clarendon to Russell, 28 Mar. 1870: PRO, FO, 361\1, 344; Norman, op. cit., pp. 133–4.

79. *Parl. Deb.*, ser. 3, 200: 81; *FJ*, 18, 21, 23, 25, 26 Mar. 1870.

80. Moran to Kirby, 13 Apr. 1870: ICAR, *Kirby Papers*, 1870, no. 83a; *FJ*, 12 Apr. 1870.

81. Moran, op. cit., vol. 3, pp. 290–304; *FJ*, 2 May 1870.

82. ibid. p. 295.

83. ibid. p. 299.

84. See Oliver P. Rafferty, *The Church, the State and the Fenian Threat 1861–75* (London, 1999).

85. Galvin *(PP, Rathdrum)* to Cullen, 20 July 1870: ICAR, *NC, III*, no. 3, 3, no. 19; see also Moran to Prop., 5 July *(1870)*: ACPF, SC, Irlanda, vol. 36, f. 745.

86. Cullen to Kirby, 10 Aug. 1870: ICAR, *NC, III*, no. 3, 3, no. 25: Cullen to Kirby, n.d., *(Aug. 1870)*: ICAR, *NC, III*, 3, 3, no. 27

87. Cullen to Kirby, n.d., *(Aug. 1870)*: ICAR, *NC, III*, 3, 3, no. 27.

88. Cullen to Kirby, 9 Oct. 1870: ICAR, *NC, III*, 3, 3, no. 36.

89. Cullen to Kirby, 7 Nov. 1870: ICAR, *NC, III*, 3, 3, no. 42.

90. Moran, op. cit., vol. 3, pp. 313–21.

91. *FJ*, 20 Dec. 1870; Cullen to Kirby, 18 Dec. 1870: ICAR, *NC, III*, 3, 3, no. 51.

92. Cullen to Kirby, 8 Dec. 1870: ICAR, *NC, III*, 3, 3, no. 49.

INDEX

5